Italy's Witches and Medicine Women
Volume 1

Karyn Crisis

Credits:

Edited by Ben Larson and Karyn Crisis
Book cover (front and back) design and layout: Daniel Hamilton Jones
Interior layout: Christine Parsons

Translators in Italy: Fabiano Rizzi, Domenico Garofano, Simone Scuri
Translators of Italian interviews, documents and books:
Christian Dellavedova, Davide Tiso, Domenico Garofano, Fabiano Rizzi, Karyn Crisis

ISBN: 978-0-692-96138-4

Dedicated to Aradia

Table of Contents

Preface

The interesting thing about this book is that it could have been plucked wholly from my own journaled experiences of my encounters with the spirits of Italy: both the women accused as witches and Spirit guides called Goddesses. They wanted me to feel the history beyond just words. Through the visions I received, the ecstatic trances I was drawn into, the dreams and mediumistic communications I had with the spirits of Italy, I was guided through this learning process. This was not just about giving me information, but about brining to life memories, emotions, sensations, and the dynamics of their challenges. Had I only written about these things, it would have been my story.

I also could have told this story just using the 23 interviews that were given to me and the cures I took from the people I met and stayed with in Italy both times, who took me on all-day walking tours of their lands deep into wild forests and high onto mountain peaks, educated me on the history, the facts, the reality behind the superstitions and imaginary ideas. However I didn't understand the concepts behind many of the words they were using and because of this many things would have been lost or remained mysteries and their story might not have been told.

What's most exciting is that all of my visions met up with reality in Italy, in both modern days and in the very ancient past: in the lives and traditions of people I met, in the historical records, in the cures and in the nature and in the structures themselves. What began as my personal passion and spiritual journey ended up shining as a light of truth.

In this way I'd encourage everyone who is on an inner path to trust your heart and trust your intuition. The evidence to validate your experiences will come later, but when it does, you'll realize it was the journey itself that was the biggest treasure; the mysterious Universe's unfoldment of your path, the sometimes painful, sometimes glorious bit-by-bit breadcrumb trail that is much more expansive and magical than the encapsulation of these wondrous experiences into mere words.

Enzo Gravina, a researcher and author from Benevento, told me, "There's a very old Napolitano poet who says: 'before telling me who you are, tell me what you did in your life,' because anyone can say they are anything even if they have no qualifications to say so."

So, to tell you what I have done...

I'm a natural born Medium who didn't have the chance to decide if ghosts or angels were real or not because they've always been a part of my life since my earliest days in childhood.

I came out out "hiding" several years ago when my Guardian Guide, Aradia, strongly suggested I train as a Medium. I found myself doing so at a Spiritualist Center in San Francisco under the guidance of a minister certified with the National Spiritualist Association of Churches in a chartered community. In a very short amount of time I became a platform Medium there, testing my skills in public, and then advanced to a Mediumistic healer, a speaker and then a teacher of Mediumship.

Before this, in 2009, I packed up everything I owned and flew to Tuscany, Italy where I'd meet my future husband and my Guardian Guide in a little guest house in the middle of olive fields in Castagneto Carducci. This Guide was not just an Italian witch spirit, she'd tell me, but a teacher, a healer, an encyclopedia of history...a Madonna Oriente of the modern age, but not from the Orient. She was very proud of Tuscany. She would teach me how to read the signs from the nature around me. She'd teach me technical aspects of healing that I'd later find out are true. She'd tell me historical information about Italy's cultural melting pot that I'd later find out actually occurred. She'd teach me how to use the nature around me in that place: the olive trees, the rosemary bushes, the pomegranate tree. She'd guide me to make protection spells that would literally shake the earth I buried them in. She taught me how to recognize, through deeply moving emotional sensations, the people and places of the "witch" story in Italy.

Several years after returning to the Bay Area of California, I would return to Italy. This second time I would stay among locals in Italy's Ligurian region, Lazio region, Campania region, and Friuli-Venezia Giulia region.

I interviewed 23 people, such as: streghe, nonna healers, authors, historians, museum directors, ancient folk story experts, Inquisition researchers, local women from healer Lineage families, Longobardi historical re-enactors, and the secretive group Benandanti.

I walked on remains of 2,000 year old Goddess temples and left prayers buried in their remains, I climbed down to the Sabato river, I received cures from Italian witches and "nonnas," walked for 9 hours a day in fog-filled mountain forests, spent June's full moon at a haunted apotropaic pagan landmark along with hundreds of spirits at midnight, learned about Europe's 500 year long Inquisition, translated a dozen books into English from Italian, and crawled along the cobblestones where women were burned...to delve deep into the heart of what truly is an "Italian Witch."

I don't know if that makes me a "writer" but that's what I've done.

I didn't do it alone, and I have many people to whom I say THANK YOU:

Davide Tiso, Jacquelyn Smith, Ben Larson, Carlo Napolitano, Domenico Garofano, Christian Dellavedova, Federico, Alecia Caine, Jenny Capozzi, Fabiano Rizzi, Simone Scuri, Giorgia Maspes, Irene Barbina, Mara Devincenti, Alex Barnaba, Gabriele Zorzi, Manuela Saccone, Paolo Portone, Rosanna Scocca, Enzo Gravina, Antonietta Ghetta, Doriana Fraschiroli and Aziende Agricole Castellarone, Filomena Foschini, Francesco, Tana delle Volpi a Triora, Fabrizio Giannese and Tanya Keller, Luciano Lamanna, Mauro Spadoni and Diana Coccia, Lilia, Silvio Falato, Silvia Pigna, Lilia, Silvio Falato, Silvia Pigna, Fabrizio Sodaro, Sandro Oddo, Rito Martignetti, Patrizia Costanzo, Germanna Stella, Antonio Spike Onze, Orso Tosco and Sergia, Sirio Novello, Sonia Gershwin, Sheri Toczko, Clara Lunato, Kathryn Lloyd, Alex Braboy, Daniel Hamilton Jones, Maria Gimbutas, Merilee Bigelow, Karen Hager, Jessica Hoch Reilly, Bernadette Montana at Brid's Closet, Ammo O'Day, Melissa at Catland, Laura and Napa at Scarlet Sage Herb Co., Missy and Rory at Ritual Cravt, the Sacred Well, Borderlands Cafe, Ritual Coffee, Paxton Gate, Dandelion Chocolate, Crimson Horticultural Rarities, Tart-To-Tart Cafe, Caffe Trieste, Lorraine Nacamulli, Franchetta Borelli, Francesca Bezzone, Angela Among Strangers.

CONTRIBUTORS to my Research Trip:

Richard Hartshorn, Jan Lavespere, Jennifer Sacheli, Nova Calise, Paul DeBlassie, Arlene Giudice, Lindsay Arnold, Lauren Zapien, Christopher Robertson, Kevin Pope, Leanne Ridgeway, Eric Smith, Valerie Beattie, Bobby Popolla, Amanda Maynard, Flynn Sauer Pauly, Jerry Adams, Kim Gill, Sarah Walter, Marilyn Hammer, John Essex, Neal Busby, Fraser Martin, Elsa Alfonso, Benjamin Rivera, Shawn Moyle, Andrea Centrella, Joaquim Allen Rocha, Maranda Lussky

Aradia Diana Iside Inanna Ellegua White Eagle Cibele Grande Madre Grande Dea

Village List

This is a list of the places in Italy (villages, areas, sacred sites) that I stayed in and visited.

1. LIGURIA Region:

   Genova
   Finale
   Castellarone
   Triora
   Molini di Triora
   SanRemo
   Badalucco
   Dolceaqua
   Castelvecchio
   Ospedaletti
   Bussana Vecchia
   Glori
   Finalborgo
   Albenga
   Savona
   Bajardo

2. VENETO Region:

   Padova
   Venezia

3. FRIULI-VENEZIA GIULIA Region:

   Udine
   Cividale del Friuli
   Tricesimo
   Piano delle Streghe

4. TOSCANA Region:

   Castagento Carducci
   Livorno
   Cecina
   Bibbona
   Populonia
   Siena
   Firenze
   Pisa

5. EMILIA-ROMAGNA Region:

   Ravenna

6. LAZIO Region:

   Roma
   Sutri
   Lago di Nemi, Tempio di Diana
   Tempio di Mitra

7. CAMPANIA Region:

   Guardia Sanframondi
   Benevento
   Ceppaloni
   Avellino
   Petruro Irpino
   San Lupo
   Stretto di Barba
   fiume Sabato
   Ponte Leproso
   Ponte delle Janare

"If you're really listening,

if you're awake to the poignant

beauty of the world,

your heart breaks regularly.

In fact, your heart is made to break;

its purpose is to burst open

again and again

so that it can hold ever more wonders"

– Andrew Harvey,
"The Return of the Mother"

First Secrets

I have prepared my altar and my room for the full moon ceremony I hope to perform and partake in.

These past many months I have become like a nun, meditating first thing in the morning with the Goddess spirit teachers who have taken time to introduce themselves to me, each one having a very specific energy, a way of teaching, distinctly different dispositions, and offering various types of knowledge.

I also meditate with them each night, devoting my sleep to learning through my dreams, and connecting my creative time to the direction of my Goddess teachers.

On this night, I kneel in front of my simple altar and prepare to begin my ritual, casting my circle, when suddenly all my Spirit guides and Goddess teachers appear to me looking impatient. My Guardian Guide Aradia throws my altar tools aside, conveying a message to me that they are "sweet, but not necessary," and tells me it's time to "do real work." The circle of white light I have cast becomes an almost blinding, blazing tangible band that begins to undulate and move in a clockwise direction and I am thrown off my knees and onto my back where I see, at the north end of my circle, an enormous and bright white "form" enter my room.

She is the one whose energy has blown me onto my back where I will remain for two hours, watching these Divine Feminine teachers show me many things, in what I can call an ecstatic trance-like experience. Her shape is like that of a white cross. The energy is so strong I cannot move, nor do I want to.

I am alive and electric and so amazed at what is taking place before me. I experience the "oneness" people sometimes describe when they die and go to the light..before they are sent back to live on earth. I am in love…the feeling is so strong I am not so aware of my body anymore. When I first saw the entrance of the White Lady, all the cells in my body felt like they were opening and little lights were turning on..much in the way we feel when we say we "fall in love," that electric tingle…only this is not from another flesh and blood person…this is energy and it is so much stronger. This is Cibele…whom I have met before, briefly, but she has brought someone older, more powerful, more ancient and formless…

Cibele's energy has been misconstrued in writings left behind, but I can understand why: it is the unimaginable joy of oneness. It feels like receiving a Reiki attunement but more…also of being in love with the universe but more. There is a sexual component but it is not earthly: it is the feeling of being suspended in an orgasm…but no human being is causing it..it is simply the result of being in love with being. There is no climb, no release…just climax. It is healing and empowering. It it purely feminine energy and I have a new understanding of the power of this inner, secret world of women. This Divine feminine energy is much bigger and more whole than anything that can be achieved by flesh alone. I was not expecting this.

The next day, my husband calls me. We haven't spoken in a week. I feel like telling him about my experience but I'm not sure where to begin. So, I ask him if he enjoyed the full moon. He tells me he went to see a band play live, a band he's always wanted to see. During a particular song, right around midnight, he suddenly saw onstage an immense white light in the form of a woman. He'd seen the same White Lady of my circle.

Chapter 1:

"A Sweeping Herstory; the Hidden Womb of Witchery"

"History is a set of lies agreed upon."
- Napoleon Bonaparte (1769 - 1821)

Witch... The mere mention of the word for some people makes them fall into an uneasy silence, fearfully imagining a lonely, spiteful old woman casting a spell to harm another over a bubbling cauldron against a raging fire. In more modern times, a witch has become a stylish vamp, reclaiming her power by defeating enemies with magic. For some she is a healer or a midwife, for some, she is a practitioner of magic, and yet for others she's evil. Looking past these fanciful stereotypical descriptions, which witch is the witch? And more to the point, what is an Italian witch?

Many questions can be asked regarding this subject, and often, in the answers, more questions will be raised: Where does the practice of an Italian witch come from, and is it limited only to women? Has there ever been a unified witch cult in Italy? What do Italians call "witches"? What does a modern witch in Italy look like? Is there a difference between Italian witchery and paganism?

These are just some of the important questions I'll answer in this book, along with many more. All of them have complex answers. To answer them we must look back to the ancient past, one that's been buried under waves of patriarchal invasions. We must examine the heritage of words and symbols; languages that have been usurped. We will acknowledge the theft of spiritual practices, healing methods and magic, and we'll come to understand that we've been looking at life through a masculine lens whose aim, at times, has been to destroy the feminine connection to nature.

History has ignored the validity of feminine lineages who channel advanced knowledge from the Spirit World and history has tried to hide evidence of how this knowledge has improved the quality of life in the most vital ways for many indigenous peoples in remote communities. We should not forget the historical turning points which brought into our earthly lives this legacy originating in the Spirit World, even as these lineages are dying out. These lineages are the key to understanding Italian witchery, but there are likewise similar feminine practices around the world. Italy's witches are the living legacy which points back to our pre-pagan Divine Feminine hidden history. And they are, in fact, quite hidden.

Italian Witches as Healers

Globally, societies have, at some point, inflated a social and moral fear of women who are psychic, mediumistic, and naturopathic. These inflated fears have served as a deterrent, a divide-and-conquer effort, keeping many people from asking and answering their own questions about life, death, and the Universe, for fear of being labeled "crazy" from a cultural position or "evil" from a religious one. This fear of "stepping out of the governing pack" and instead remaining globally subservient to masculine control over societies and religious practices has sealed our fate as enemies of this natural earth, rather than as her caretakers, and has kept us all in a perpetual battle of divisiveness: of men from women, of binary genders from other genders, of people from their psychic senses, of the physical world from the Spirit World, and of human beings from nature. Ironically, it's the patriarchy who has traditionally tried to control nature and people, places, and things in the natural world, all the while accusing "witches" of doing this, even though witchery's many practices all work in harmony with the cycles of nature.

In Italy, this far-reaching social stigma inflamed by the church, has kept women in hiding, as Benevento author and researcher Enzo Gravina told me, *"Many grandmas (nonnas) knew and still know how to heal, but because women were hunted in Italy, and because life here is quiet, people kept this quiet. We didn't go outside on the street and advertise 'my grandma is a healer.' We didn't spread those things. But we grew up with it, it's something very imbedded in our roots. For people who haven't grown up with this, it's something different and new, and when something is new, people can get excited and change some things or spread ideas in a wrong way."*

So most importantly, I will be offering information from insider experiences, opening ever slightly the doorway into these secret lives of women, and some men. This should finally serve a different perspective than has been offered by religions, historians, archaeologists, anthropologist and other non-practicing outsiders, who fall prey to this "delegitimizing," as author Fabio Garuti has named this process, of naturally intuitive people who are sensitive to ways of living outside the acceptable norms of societal pressure.

To truly understand what is an Italian Witch and where Italian witchery came from and how it is expressed in Italy, you first need to let go of what you may think the world "witch" is all about. After all, "'Streghe' (witches) are women judged by men," states Doriana, an herbalist who lives on a mountaintop. "Strega, Bajiue, Maschera, Maschiare, Masca, Striis, Lamia, Janara, Majare, Zobiane, Brusas, Maga, Magara"…these names come from OUTSIDERS. While they were created in the past, they still remain in modern times.

These are all modern names for witches that come from the patriarchy's invasion of and attempt to eradicate a feminine-based community way of living in harmony with nature's cycles. These names all have derogatory meanings attached to them. "Bajiue," for example, in Ligurian dialect means "bitch" as well as "witch." I've found that people have different understandings of these names depending on which Italian region they come from and what their personal experiences are, and this indeed is a land rich in stories of personal "supernatural" experiences.

These are names that are generally agreed upon to mean "witch" or "strega" as a unified concept of a particular type of woman. This conceptual name is always in reference to a woman's sexuality being associated with evil. Particularly, these names attack women from the viewpoint of male obsession over her mysteries, and in direct competition with her knowledge of nature's secrets, of birth, death, and life. For example, these names don't just mean "witch as a magical woman who makes spells," as we see depicted in modern times. In Italy they rather they depict a type of woman who lives away from society, a solitary, non-married one who allegedly steals newborn babies' lives away and doles out death. She was the midwife, and the church turned her into the vampire. During Italy's Inquisition, she was also connected with the perverse fantasy of the woman who had sex with "Satana," or Satan. She was also credited by the church with cursing people with illness and disease, and she was the scapegoat for any bad thing happening in the village.

These names largely began to appear during Medieval times, a sort-of "kick off" propaganda for the Inquisition. But truly, this attempt to turn natural nurturing women and their Goddess symbols into "evil agents of death and "Satana" began in the Neolithic period of patriarchal invasions into Old Europe, when peaceful, abundant matrilineal and gylanic societies (ones in which genders lived in harmony without hierarchy) were invaded by warring, destructive masculine tribes and in which Goddesses were either demoted to wives and supporters of "Gods" or were given bad reputations to turn peoples' spiritual adoration towards a new and synthetic influx of Gods, artificial living, and societal control.

It's most important to note that in daily reality, these names were used to incite the public into fearing often poor and uneducated women who, despite socio-economic limitations, successfully and miraculously cured disease with a vast knowledge of indigenous plants and herbs and who had an intimate connection with nature's healing powers. And there are lineage healers who still do. In some regions, however, these healer women were even rewarded lucratively for their cures. In fact, the church first targeted the financially successful healers because they had clients who could pay for treatments, and this was the clientele the new male doctors (who were supervised by the church) of course needed, rather than the peasant community who went to the peasants healers for free.

You may see a pattern here: women's healing powers discredited, her sexuality demeaned, her clientele deterred as men attempted to become doctors, and any income she had, challenged.

Women have been healers since our founding days: natural doctors using nature as their pharmacy, developing an intimate knowledge of their own anatomy through giving to birth their own children and assisting other women to do so, knowing how to naturally end pregnancies with herbs, caring for life, nurturing all forms of it, and educating others. As stated in "Witches, Midwives, and Nurses: A History of Women Healers:"

"For centuries women were doctors without degrees, barred from books and lectures, learning from each other, and passing on experience from neighbor to neighbor and mother to daughter. They were called "wise women" by the people, witches or charlatans by the authorities. Medicine is part of our heritage as women, our history, our birthright[...], often the only healers for women and the poor. [...]. If anything, it was the male professionals who clung to untested doctrines and ritualistic practices – and it was the women healers who represented a more humane, empirical approach to healing."[1]

Regarding this "humane approach to healing," I learned from several authors, historians and researchers in Italy, that women cured diseases and they had a higher success rate than did educated doctors and monks. They didn't invade the bodies of their patients to cure them as does the more modern medical establishment. Gerry Delfino, an editor from the Ligurian region, told me his grandmother would gather indigenous herbs to cure the people with. *"In the past, in my grandma's time, men who were surgeons were also barbers."* Men at this time were trying to deliver babies, which in itself was an aberration of a natural female practice. After barring women from doing so as male doctors began to study in Italy in the early 1200s, these barber-doctors replaced natural birthing techniques with cold metal instruments and other unnatural procedures in their synthetic form of midwifery. Again,the synthetic patriarchy replacing the natural matriarchy. Gerry found a bag of surgery instruments from the 1800s that men used to deliver babies, and in the bag was a large stake used to kill the baby as a means of brutal abortion and likely death of the mother as well. In contrast, women healers used herbs to induce abortion during that same time period.

"Before there was the modern study of herbalists and homeopathy, there were the women who knew all the secrets about that," Enzo tells me, *"because while the men were completely dedicated to their jobs and their work, the women had to work at home taking care of domestic tasks. So they had to be able to feed their families from the herbs and things they found at that time in the countryside, in poor times. They had no education, but they were able to heal with herbs."* And they still do in Italy. Enzo's fellow researcher from Benevento, Rosanna Scocca told me, *"These women had a very important power: they had the power between life and death, because they knew the plants, they were able to let you live or die, all with no education."*

In fact, people I spoke with in every region I visited told me that despite what the political atmosphere appeared to show, that Italy was indeed a matriarchy, and every family has its own history with a "nonna" grandma who has healed them before doctors came around. *"The 'nonna' type healer has always been in families, and not even really considered magic, nor witches, just accepted,"* Sivio Falato, a published folk lore expert and etymologist from Guardia Sanframondi told me, *"Our grandfathers didn't go to the doctor, because the medicine, as we know, nowadays, didn't start until the beginning of this century. These women we are talking about are much more ancient."*

These inner-family healers, these women (and some men) still today use very specific and fast-acting cures. They quickly cure issues of blood, bone, and nerves with common items such as oil and water as well as a palpable, channeled, larger-than-life energy. Their abilities to cure are much more specific and fast acting than a general "energy" healing of modern times. Healing coincides with the disappearance of pain first [...] and the defeat of the disease at the conclusion of the secret signatures and marks for three consecutive days.[2] This I would experience personally with cures I received from Antonietta in Triora in the "City of Witches of North" and from Filomena in Guardia Sanframondi, near Benevento, the "City of Witches of the South."

When Universities came into existence in Italy in the 1200s for the purpose of training physicians as an organized practice, only men were allowed to study this form of medicine. In fact, the medical art was forbidden to clerics, Jews and women.[3] In the century that preceded the beginning of the "witch-craze"– the thirteenth century– European medicine became firmly established as a secular science and a profession. The medical profession was actively competitive with female healers, forbidding them to be part of the medical universities, and requiring all doctors to have university training. The church imposed strict controls on the new profession, and allowed it to develop only within the terms set by Catholic doctrine. University-trained physicians were not permitted to practice without calling in a priest to aid and advise them, or to treat a patient who refused confession.[4] This would be a relationship designed by the church for its benefit.

"By the fourteenth century their [medical doctors] practice was in demand among the wealthy, as long as they continued to take pains to show that their attentions to the body did not jeopardize the soul. In fact, accounts of their medical training make it seem more likely that they jeopardized the body."[5]

Even with women barred from Universities, the schooled doctors were baffled that women already had knowledge of the body and its systems and had been putting it into practice saving lives. "Herbariere" (herbalists) were not just taking care of the medical cure, they were able to deal also with clinical cases without any prefix knowledge and superstition.[6] We don't have anything written about this [from the viewpoint of the healer].The official historians did their very best to cancel any trace that these women had in society, but fortunately, and ironically, we have information of this right from the trials that claim more often than not, that these women were herbalists, were taking care of birth deliveries, and of all the medicine that was not just Roman but also Druid derivations.[7] Outside of these female practices, official medicine was largely unsuccessful.

In fact, doctor practices consisted of a variety of odds and ends that can be accused of looking "magical," such as writing prayers on the jaw of a toothache patient, or making a broth of black snake flesh to cure leprosy. Such was the state of medical "science" at the time when witch-healers were persecuted for being practitioners of "magic."[8] It was witches who developed an extensive understanding of bones and muscles, herbs and drugs, while physicians were still deriving their prognoses from astrology and alchemists were trying to turn lead into gold.[9] So great was the witches' knowledge that in 1527, Paracelsus, considered the "father of modern medicine," burned his text on pharmaceuticals, confessing that he "had learned from the Sorceress all he knew."[10] But even today, in modern times, there are women Lineage healers who can trace back their healing secrets in their family lines 500 years prior, and whose cures truly heal ailments such as sciatica, intestinal worms, psoriasis and more.

Author Fabio Garuti, in his book "Le Streghe di Benenvento, La Grande Bugia" (The Witches of Benevento, the Big Lie), describes the important role women had on a daily basis was in direct competition with the monks, but not because the women created the competition. They were natural midwives "levatrici" and herbalists. The doctors competed to be midwives over the women. The Monks, claims Garuti, wanted to have female herbalists disappear so they could gain a popular role in society. The monks' knowledge was mostly known around the monastery, while the herbalists were many and we well-known in the territory.[11] Garuti describes how the monks wanted to get attention around the monastery for cataloging the typology of plants and their characteristics (a very male need, to document and then to own) in books they called "Hortuli."[12] Herbalist descendants of the Druids didn't have any need to write down or share their knowledge because their memory was extremely ancient and orally transmitted for thousands of years.[13] While Garuti laments the loss of this knowledge, I can offer a different view as a professional Medium: this knowledge was given to people from the Spirit World to begin with, and it can be given again. This is perhaps the most mysterious part of Italian Witchery as it survives today, this "advanced knowledge" in the hands of uneducated women.

Enzo explains, *"While the medical officials of these times were all men who studied, they couldn't admit that women who were not educated could exercise the alternative medicine. That's why women were deemed 'bad.'"* Natural practice was how women for over 20,000 delivered their own babies or terminated their pregnancies, and cared for their nutrition and bodies. These educated, so-called men of medicine, who had to study in a school in order to learn properties of plants, couldn't understand how these uneducated and often single, elderly women were able to cure disease non-invasively, nor how they came into possession of this vast knowledge and understanding of plants and other methods of curing specific diseases. But also, the women used oral tradition (as did many other groups such as the Druids) so their practice was impenetrable by school, doctors, the church...no one could get to their secrets.

So, as has happened in history before, men went about creating synthetic substitutions for the natural practices. This competition would be the beginning of yet another wave of attacks on women that would bleed into the 500 year Inquisition period in Europe. If in the Middle Ages the practice of woman using herbal cures had a minimum of social recognition and was felt as an integral part of popular culture, in the '500s and especially after the Counter-Reformation the combination of medicine and magic was the object of persecution.[14]

Authors Barbara Ehrenreich and Deidre English call our attention to the elitism of economics involved with healing and the medical arts:*[...] "The suppression of women health workers and the rise to dominance of male professionals was not a "natural" process, resulting automatically from changes in medical science[...] It was an active takeover by male professionals[...]Political and economic monopolization of medicine meant control over its institutional organizations, its theory and practice, its profits and prestige[...]when total control of medicine means potential power to determine who will live and will die, who is fertile and who is sterile, who is 'mad' and who is sane.The suppression of female healers by the medical establishment was a political struggle; first, in that it is part of the history of sex struggle in general [and] second, in that it was part of a class struggle. Women healers were people's doctors, and their medicine was part of a people's subculture[...] . Male professionals, on the other hand, served the ruling class – both medically and politically."*[15]

And yet, with all the efforts to forbid women to cure and to "evil-ize" them during the Inquisition, there was nothing tangible the church nor the doctors could take away nor study from the women healers except for some traditional herbal knowledge and magical practices stolen when the patriarchy first invaded Italy in Neolithic times. After all, while women were gifted the invention of writing in ancient times, men learned the art from them, then forbade them to use it once they'd convened into warring tribes. As far as the secret marks and signatures that made their cures actually cure, women kept these secret and still haven't documented their techniques in written form. Even today this tradition is perpetuated.

The Italian "witch" Lineages consist in part of specific actions, specific ingredients, and specific secrets that have been inherited from someone, who, down the line into the long ago past, originally received these actions and secrets and knowledge from the Spirit World. This Divine Feminine energy watches over and channels through these healing practices, and I experienced this on more than one occasion, and this channeled energy is unlike any other I've experienced through a healing modality.

Italian Witches as Channelers

A most interesting trail between Italian witches and the ancient, pre-pagan Goddesses remains present in Italian witchery that exists in Lineage traditions today, and this trail is also left in Italian documentation, often in response to the most ugly challenges men have brought against women, and often incidentally. Often the most negative attacks against women were documented by men who, in trying to cover up women's spiritual symbolic language and practices (which show the Lineage connection between the Divine Feminine energy and human earthly women…in other words, feminine shamanism) unwittingly captured evidence of Old European shamanism in female lineages and how it has been passed down from generation to generation. The men weren't meaning to do this: they were trying to usurp these practices and erase all traces of the pre-Christian, pre-Pagan, and peaceful founding unified vision that the Universe's energy is Divinely Feminine at the start. Later, during Europe's 500 year plus Inquisition, and its path through Italy, they tried to find something evil in this female magical curing power, but instead they found more evidence of female shamanism, channeling, and the Spirit World assisting women with gifts of advanced knowledge.

The divide of the matrilineal society is one of the factors that brought about Goddesses appearing in spiritual practices once again in new forms to repair the "interrupted" female practices of curing and caring for life. Women learned by oral tradition, receiving the master teachings along "energy lines" we would nowadays call "channeling" when lineages and home/family/community structures were broken by invaders. Women transmitted these healing actions and energy secrets within family lines (grandmother to daughter, sometimes mother-in-law to new bride), as is still done today. Kept within the family, passed onto members who will remain in the community, the lineages are intact and knowledge is unbroken.

Christina, an Italian American midwife living on a mountaintop in Appalachia said during one of our conversations, *"You and I can have these wonderful talks about the technical descriptions of these things, having learned them at this point in our lives, but we know that it happens much more naturally, and you don't have to know what to call it to receive the knowledge."* Keeping this in mind, this "outsider versus insider" categorizing of intangible things is important: you won't be able to go to Italy asking for the women who channel Divine Feminine energy and find them answering your call. These healers are quietly living the life; they are in no need to describe their process to anyone. This is the key to understanding why women don't write their practices down: they are not using their healing abilities in Italy to make business, nor do they market themselves, and they consider their power borrowed. As my translator and guide in Guardia Sanframondi told me while explaining that people know where the healers are, but why it may be difficult to meet some: *"They're there, on the mountain, but they only take visitors who need a cure."* It's been historically the male practitioners of magic or men attempting herbalism who do seek to capture this information in documented form, and then to ban others from using it while claiming ownership of knowledge that they got from someone else to begin with. While there are Italian women who write down their secrets, they don't share the details, and their books, the inherited ones I've seen, often look like a simple lists of herbs but no instructions on how to combine them or use them: all that is in her memory; having been orally passed down.

From the Grande Madre to the Buona Dea and the Signora di Gioco, these are Italy's "supernatural teachers" who we can simply call Spirit Guides. Whether taking the form of Goddesses or the greater and more formless and ancient "Grande Dea," Great Goddess of all the Goddesses, this specifically Divine Feminine Infinite Intelligence is the provider of this magical healing system of Witchery in Italy.

The initiatory process that comes from the Spirit World is given to the chosen ones: often "contadini"- uneducated peasant women who wouldn't even know what to call "channeling". Women who are living normal lives in their communities or in remote countryside areas, devoted to remain in those very same communities who need their cures.

However, there is also the passage of this knowledge to women who were outcast from communities during the Inquisition, to single women living outside society, to family-less women, and in our modern days more organized, educated women. There is a tradition in Italy of the healer woman being a single, older woman who lives alone, like modern Mediums who often serve the larger community as a family rather than their personal families.

This direct channel (a flow of information from the Spirit World to earthly women means that nothing need be written down...whenever knowledge is needed, it is "listened to" or"received" as inner thoughts. The "phone line to the Spirit World" when it's working properly, isalways open, so this advice from a higher source is always available and its energetic component means the information travels fast.

Additionally, I learned these curing women of Lineages don't alter or change the curing methods they are taught. There are no "Do-It-Yourself" efforts here; the practices of secret actions and secret prayers and invocations are considered to be a "borrowed responsibility" and are honored and fully trusted in their inherited forms. This is one of the aspects modern world healing modalities misses: transmission from the Spirit World along with honored practice of the original form. A quick look around the internet shows that these days many people boast their own self-created healing methods that are derivatives of something else. This doesn't mean the practices don't offer a cure. However, as the modalities become watered-down and custom-made, so too the cures become more drawn-out and less potent.

That the Universe' wisdom is associated with Goddess as Mother of All is further evidenced in the ancient customs of honoring "omphalos" stones, symbolizing the center of the Great Mother's body; the "navel of the Universe" from which all life comes. The "omphalos" stones are associated with places where Pythia, and before them Sibyls channeled advice from the Spirit World in a more isolated format than the Italian Witchery Lineage, but nevertheless another form of channeling connected to women and the Divine Feminine.

Italy's Witches as "Mediums" of the Great Mother

As we look back through the Neolithic period of Italy, and further back to the Paleolithic periods of matrilinear and gylanic communities, before the patriarchy began a divide-and-conquer of these peaceful communities and introduced war, slavery, animal husbandry, and assumed control over people, societies and nature, we have our founding spiritual (meaning "energetic, psychic, mediumistic") language and incidences of Goddess Spirit teachers appearing to women (in visionary form and intuitively) to assist their lifestyle of nurturing and caring for life. All the spiritual language left in Old European, Italian, Maltese and Sardinian statuary, symbols and graves express this. And, in the later Neolithic period, when again women are cut off from each other and the natural world and their lineages interrupted, we have in Italy more documentation about Goddesses as Divine Feminine consciousness reconnecting with earthly women to give this knowledge to them once again. But before we designate the dates these invasions began, thus creating a first rift in society which dramatically changed lifestyles of all peoples, let's look back at those 20,000 years of Goddess worship to understand what life was like before the patriarchy....since this history has been buried so deeply since then.

In Old Europe, the persistence of Goddess worship for more than 20,000 years, from the Paleolithic to the Neolithic and beyond, is shown by the continuity of a variety of a series of conventionalized images: her specific aspects of power such as life-giving, fertility-giving, and birth-giving are extremely long lasting.[16] The main theme of the Goddess symbolism is the mystery of birth and death and the renewal of life, not only human life but all life on earth and indeed the whole cosmos.[17] The earliest religious works of art are figures of the solitary Great Goddess-the Paleolithic images of Mother, before there was any Father either on earth or in heaven.[18] The Goddess-centered religion existed for a very long time, much longer than the Indo-European and the Christian (which represents a relatively short period of human history).[19] These systematic associations in the Near East, southeastern Europe, the Mediterranean area, and in central, western, and northern Europe indicate the extension of the same Goddess religion to all of these regions as a cohesive and persistent ideological system.[20]

In Europe, the Great Goddess was thought the sole omnipotent deity.[21] Fatherhood was not incorporated into religious thinking, because in clan life it was a very frail bond, even if recognized.[22] Scholars knew that, "In the beginning the Goddess everywhere antedated, or at least was predominant over, the God. It has been affirmed that in all countries from the Euphrates to the Adriatic, the Chief Divinity was at first in woman form."[23] Modern male scholars often tried to conceal or dent the evidence of the ancient matriarchate.[24] Whenever possible, some automatically converted references to the Great Mother into the word "God," as was done in translating the Bible.[25] In this usurpation, we also see the traditional patriarchal assume of "control," and thereby a synthetic relationship with nature. In contrast, the Goddess always embodied natural cycles of nature, and Paleolithic spiritual statuary used symbols to represent these aspects of nature. Women, having been taught by the Goddess intuitively learned the cycles of nature and how to work with them, in harmony and in "attunement," or in greater understanding.

The relationship between the Goddess and earthly women is like the Macrocosm to its microcosm, where the microcosm of earthly woman (the part) reflects the whole (macrocosm) of the Goddess and vice versa. And in the pre-Indo-European culture of Italy, matrilinear life was based on caring for life, and while paternity was not know, so men were not as sedentary. Life was peaceful, without hierarchy, and looked to nature, and women's connection with nature, for care. Genders were also equal, even while believing the Universal life force to be

Divinely Feminine. It contrasted sharply with the ensuing proto-Indo-European culture which was patriarchal, stratified, pastoral, mobile, and war-oriented.[26] Before the patriarchy organized itself, and during the early evolution of the human race, motherhood was the only recognized bond of relationship[27] in parallel to the spiritual bond of people to the Goddess as the Great Mother. Neolithic village cultures with their matriarchal family-based governments were cooperative, unwarlike, and nonviolent.[28] Their lack of destructiveness has been attributed to the life-loving spirit of affirmation that scholars find at the core of the most matriarchal societies.[29]

This connection to nature (on earth) and connection to the Great Goddess Mother (in the Spirit World) is the cornerstone of Italy's legacy of witchery. While witchery is predominantly passed alone female lines, the male lineage healers have this same connection to both nature and the Spirit World. In Italian Witchery, the "Grande Dea" (Great Goddess) is not a figure reserved for rituals as in Paganism: in Italian Witchery the Grande Dea is omnipresent, and her service work (healing) is given as needed, and human needs of the healer are also provided for, as needed. There are no rituals in Italian Witchery, and there is no male "Great Father" equivalent. This is an invention of Paganism that did not exist in earlier spiritual practices. It is an artificial structure often attributed to but not part of Italy's Lineage Witchery. Italy's Lineage Witchery is based in nature, and its practices reflect nature and the feminine energy in nature, and the Italian family reflects this female-centric dynamic. The Grande Dea is the provider of abundance in whatever form it is needed. Italy's Witchery is often confused with paganism, wicca, and magic. But those three categories are another thing.

Italy's Witchery as a living Legacy of our foundation on earth; gifts from Divine Feminine Consciousness

The root of civilization was the kinship bond that kept groups together to evolve mutual cooperation.[30] The bond was maternal because no paternal relationships were perceived, or even guessed, by such early groups with their shifting, temporary sexual attachments.[31] The connection between sexuality and childbearing was unknown to primitive men.[32] Women were the keepers of calendrical records, another traditionally female skill that most men thought beyond their comprehension and the secret of Fatherhood can only have been revealed to men by the women themselves, because women were keepers of calendrical records,[33] a result of being pregnant and observing the passing of time, and of working with growth cycles of edible plants. But also, being provided with information from the Spirit World. There is a reason Goddesses who appear throughout Italy's history are often connected with health and childbirth and that is because they were known to assist women in this way.

Before the founding of Rome, Italy was governed by the Sabine matriarchate, when not even kings knew their fathers.[34] Romulus, Ancus Marcus and Servius Tullis had only mothers.[35] When the myth of Romulus and his men was written down, it was said Romulus made his followers marry Sabine women because, as men, they lacked "sanguie ac genus," or the blood of the race.[36] This could only come from the female owners of the land.[37]

As may be found still in many groups of people, motherhood alone was the foundation of clan loyalties. Nearly everywhere, kinship bonds only passed through the female line, as in the ancient system deliberately reversed by the Bible's "begats" which recognized only male ancestors.[38] Several years ago, when I was staying near St. Petersburg, Florida and standing among some trees, I was visited by the spirits of Seminole Indians and they guided me to research their history, which was also matrilineal. The clans all have a specific animals and the clan bears the woman's name. A man marrying her becomes part of her clan, under her name and the animal spirit. But also, these Seminole were scattered by invaders and their name means also "orphan" and "runaway". Globally, this pattern can be found: in Assma the social unit of tribes was maharis "motherhoods." The Malay family was a sa-mandei, "motherhood."[39] Among the Garis and Khasis, mothes headed the family groups and bequeathed all property in the female line; men could inherit nothing…[40] Pharaohs ruled by matrilineal succession and styled themselves "Rulers from the Womb,"[41] Egyptians traced their descent through their mothers, calling themselves X born of the Lady Y, omitting their father's name.[42] On Egyptian funerary stelae, the mother's name was given but the father's was omitted.[43]

Another enduringly important albeit mysterious cultural group of Italy's past, the Etruscans, also disregarded fathers on their tomb inscriptions.[44] The Etruscans are respected in Italian history for being a peaceful,loving, and advanced culture. As Silvio Falato, a folklorist and etymologist from Guardia Sanframondi told me, in 1500 BC, the Indo-European (Latin, Greeks, Minoan) patriarchal invaders came into Italy, but the locals who were already there, the Etruscans, were a matriarchal culture.The Etruscans called themselves "Rasenna". When married [Estruscan] couples were buried together, only the wife's name was written.[45] Late Roman texts reversed this usage, writing the name of the husband and omitting that of the wife.[46] Leaving few written records, however, we know little about them. I visited their "Bosco Sacro" in Sutri, the sacred forest where they wrote their prayers and then buried them in the soil at the foot of trees. Learning about this practice startled me because I'd been guided to do the same thing by my Spirit Goddess Guides in my daily life.

"Home and Mother" are written over every phase of neolithic agriculture.[47] It was the woman who wielded the iggins stick and the hoe; she who tended the garden crops and accomplished the masterpieces of selection and cross-fertilization which turned raw wild species into the prolific and richly nutritious domestic varieties; it was woman who made the first containers, weaving baskets and coiling the first clay pots.[48]

I would find this tradition of clay associated with women and the Goddess had perpetuated into Roman times (more than 2000 years ago), during the active phase Diana's Temple period at Lago di Nemi near Rome.Though at this time Diana had been given a "makeover" by men; her temple was designed as a square, her image a warrior goddess and hunter (anti-life) people still came to temple for healing requests, which they left at the temple in the form of clay effigies. They asked Diana for healing and for protection during childbirth and other motherly assistance. Diana, after all, presided over childbirth and was called "opener of the womb."[49] Clay, clay pots, and clay figurines are one of the skills the Goddess transmitted to earthly women and are commonly made votive offerings left at Goddess temples and healing sites.

Neighboring Italy, in Niederbronn, Alsace, where in Celtic times Diana was worshipped as the Goddess of sacred wells [made of stone], to this day women carry water from the mineral spring to nearby mountains. There, they pour it over stones with circular depressions to ensure pregnancy.[50]

Clay pots for holding water and clay effigies holding the vibrations of prayers are just the beginning of the creative inspirations (and production know-how) given to women in Italy from the Spirit World. This is, however, a global phenomenon that took place in the ancient past:

Among the Hittites, priestesses known as Elderly Women taught the art of writing, kept records, advised kings, and practiced medicine.[51] In Babylonian times, the noble art of tablet-writing [...] belonged to the special scribes called "matyanu".[52] A similar Egyptian word for scribe was "Maryen" or "Mahir": "great one" or "mother".[53] The triple Goddess of Fate was incarnate in three "Gulses" or writers corresponding to the Germanic Fates called "Die Schreiberinnen," the Writing-Women, and the Roman mother of destiny Fata Scribunda, the "Fate who Writes."[54] In pre-Hellenic Greece, the original alphabet was attributed to the original three Muses, who were identical with the Fates of Graea, eponymous mothers of Greek tribes.[55] Rehtia, a Goddess of Italy's northeastern region near Padua is considered to have gifted writing to the people.[56]

The latin alphabet was created by the archaic Goddess Carmenta, mother of "carmens" or charms.[57] Egyptians revered the Goddess as measurer or time, mistress of the house of books, mistress of the house of architects.[58] As foundress of the science of architecture she was named Seshat, "Lady of the Builder's Measure,"and she built the "abode of a king in the next world," a pyramid.[59] In the middle east also, numbers and letters were the invention of the Goddess and the special concerns of her priestesses.[60] In Inanna's story, written by her female priestess, we see a rarely documented glimpse inside this female tradition written by a female scribe. We see her priestess writing poems to her..which are early traces in writing, one of the very few, of an inner female priestess circle...elevating the female form. Sanskrit "matra", like the Greek "meter" meant both "mother" and "measurement"... mathematics is, but derivation, "mother-wisdom."[61] Root words for motherhood produced many words for calculation: metric, menstruation, mete, mens, mark, mentality, geo-metry, tri-gono-metry, hydro-metry, etc.[62] Women did temporal and spatial calculations for so long that, according to the Vayu Purabna, men once thought women were able to give birth because they had superior skill in measuring and figuring.[63]

Besides creating the world and everything in it, the Goddess created the civilized arts: agriculture, weaving, potting, writing, poetry, music, the graphic arts, calendars, and mathematics.[64] Stories of menhirs turning in circles and dancing at night in parallel to the stories about women dancing around wells; suggestions that henges marked vortexes of energy helpful to childbirth who also point to nearby water sources; Italy's "streghe," or witches, using water to "read" a disease and to cast it out; engravings on stones of owls who symbolize the Goddess with her connection to the afterlife and regeneration of life; caves as womb-like places of initiation from various Goddesses; the ability to cure disease with knowledge of thousands of indigenous plants; knowing how to plant and harvest these plants, understanding the calendrical movements of the sun and moon and planets; how to pass on knowledge through lineage traditions; writing and building...all skills attributed to not only the Goddess, a higher consciousness who birthed the Universe, the true "god", but also skills attributed to women.

These seemed to have developed mostly in the hands of women as outgrowths of the maternal nest-building, communication, and play behavior,[65] or so archaeologists and historians will tell you. Technically, these systems of highly developed skills are received from the psychic ability to receive thoughts, images, and energetic communication from higher consciousness, through channeling and Mediumship, rather than from a slower process of human trial-and-error development.

So while the Goddess created these advancement tools, she gifted them to earthly women for the purpose of bettering practical life. This co-creative relationships improved the quality of life. Ritual art and offerings represent an understanding of the Universe's workings and in the past it came from the cornerstone of the Spirit World-to-women relationship: the Mediumistic process of channeling, just as it does in modern times. Also established in the ancient past is the reality of "spiritual service" being an invitation, or an "initiation" from the Spirit World to earthly women. The consciousness with greater perspective and knowledge (the Spirit Teacher Goddess) finds her students and adepts (regular women with needs and responsibilities and willingness) and the lineage process of "handing down knowledge" begins. The spiritual knowledge represents an understanding of how energy moves in the Universe. The knowledge of basic life needs is represented in woman's ability to help each other give birth, feed each other, and teach.

We see documented social responses, in organized communities, to these advanced skills women were gifted. For example, among Barbarian tribes of northern Europe, women were property owners, clan heads, and religious leaders.[66] Roman writers called the northern nations "lands of women" governed by "kvaens" (queens).[67] As child bearers and nurturers, naturally women became closely in tune with planting and harvesting. They became producers, storers, and distributors of vegetable foodstuffs, hence the owners of the land they used for cultivation their economic and social power thus evolved the early village communities in matriarchal form.[68]

Symbols in Nature Which Point to the Goddess "come down to earth"

Italian Witchery and all the tools of life-living associated with her are traced back to this time, even if many of those traces have been erased, usurped or burned. All the great symbols of nature, which point to the Great Goddess and her Universal energy flow are also associated with and connected to Italian witches...some by others and some because they "put themselves in these places," as Domenico, my translator from Guardia Sanframondi would tell me regarding the Janara who used a specific river in that area. He was one of many people to tell me of associations.

Months after returning from this second stay in Italy, I discovered in June I had indeed walked among specific caves and cliffs where clay Goddess figures were found from the Neolithic period in the Ligurian region, but that would be the tip of the buried historical iceberg. I would find that anyplace in Italy that had a marker associated with a Goddess, could be found a cave nearby that was used for initiations, or water sources in the forms of rivers and fountains. Mountains are now mostly honored with processions dedicated to Saints (male ones), but they are hiding original Goddess temple remains and sacred sites.

Maneula Saccone, responsible for the didactic activities at the Archaeological Museum of Finale Ligure in Finalborgo, Italy helped direct my research towards Paleolithic and Neolithic discoveries in Italy, such as clay figurines. She also suggested a book which documents the practice pregnant women leaving clay offerings and sacrifices to the Goddesses Enodia and Artemis, asking for her support during childbirth. Among the offerings to these Goddesses were clay figurines of the Goddess in a seated position which is the symbol of the Goddess as life-giver.

The Goddess' connection to stone, and therefore woman's intimacy with stone is ancient and yet another example of parallelism between macro (Goddess) and micro (earthly woman); higher intelligence channeled as wisdom and taken into earthly actions. Trees are also associated with ancient Goddesses, and sacred sites around Italy contain sacred tree groves, and the most famous walnut tree of all, the Benevento Walnut.

If we connect the dots of the feminine language buried underneath the masculine one, the Universe and all of life in it begins to make much more sense. While mathematics, metallurgy, writing, curing, and other advanced practices have been attributed to men in modern times, in our founding times they were considered to be talents that women received from the Goddess intelligence. Spiritual language represented the way energy moves in the universe, and points to animals and shapes that refer back to feminine anatomy in relation to the life cycles. Simple and yet complex: women are our founding mothers, and as such they needed assistance to care for the lives coming out of their bodies. All the knowledge and its layers of usefulness in bettering life conditions came to women from the Spirit World in a natural, intuitive way. This ease is at the root of the patriarchal jealousy, this natural connection of women to the Universe's womb, and the direct connection women have to the Spirit World of Goddesses and spirit helpers.

Hidden Feminine Provider Antecedents

This relationship of regular people communicating with, or "being visited by" the Spirit World is not unique to Italy. This way of life exists, and has, globally since ancient times. These incidents of societies existing where knowledge is handed down to earthly people fully developed as tools or systems for living is a world-wide phenomenon and exists everywhere we see "legacies."

In "Fingerprints of the Gods" a book by Graham Hancock largely about legacies in Egypt and South America, he says of legacies, "rather than developing slowly and painfully, as is normal with human societies, the civilization of Ancient Egypt [...](which he believes is a legacy), emerged *all at once and fully formed*."[69] Where technological skills that should have taken hundreds or even thousands of years to evolve were brought into use almost overnight."[70] In other words, the monuments and ancient technologies we can't seem to replicate nor completely understand are not simply human made, but rather made with human hands who've been given superior knowledge from the Spirit World teachers.

It is the same with indigenous plant cures, which are an integral part but just one aspect of Italy's witchery. Systems of herbs, they should rather be called, consist of enormous amounts of plants and uses women carried (and still carry in Italy) in their minds. Rather than the suggested idea that humans, through "trial and error" discovered thousands of curing herbs simply can't explain healing arts like Italian Witchery. Trial and error takes too long and has too many casualties to have resulted in such a precise and life-saving art at the hands of uneducated women living in remote areas that aren't connected to one another through technology. These cures are fast-acting and complete, and cure actual diseases and ailments (in muscles, nerves, blood, and bones). Some of the cures use simply oil and water and, the main ingredient, channeled Divinely Feminine energy.

Italian witchery is also unchanged from healer who passes the transmission to the healer who receives it. The "streghe" I met learned from their family lines not only the cures but also how to identify the herbs and plants and what do do with them, how to harvest them, and more. These are not "do-it-yourself" practices that we find in modern times, in which it's a common practice for modern healers to vaguely learn healing modalities and then add their own flair. These indigenous traditions are also transmitted orally. In this way, Italian Witchery and the witcheries of Old Europe are more like Shamanism practices around the world than to the covens of the patriarchy's Paganism. In fact, they are completely unlike Paganism.

The uniqueness of Italy is in its female lineage, which has been documented throughout Italy's history in rather confusing, superstitious language enfolded into folk tales to sound, in the end, irrational and absurd. The other examples I will share have not been discredited in the same way, and rather documented with honor. Our founding connection with wisdom was through the female lines of communication: from Spirit World Goddess to earthly women, and down the family lines, and yet the more popular and longest -lasting tales are ones of male shaman and male gods assuming the roles of their antecedents: the Goddess and the women.

In his book, Hancock shares many legends of a tall, bearded man who has a very different appearance from the people he visits in South America, for example, such as the people of the Andes. He is "known by many different names in many different places" [...] always recognizably the same figure: Viracocha, [coming from the] Foam of the Sea, a master of science and magic who[...]came in a time of chaos to se the world to rights.[71] He was a scientist, an architect of surpassing skills, a sculptor and engineer[...] this gentle, civilizing 'superhuman' who healed the sick and was a teacher.[72] Viracocha brought to Peru such varied skills as medicine, metallurgy, farming, animal husbandry, the art of writing, and more.[73] One legend describes Viracocha as being accompanied by "messengers" called "shining ones"[74] who traveled the world spreading his message.

Hancock's research goes on to describe the mysterious Olmec civilization having emerged "all at once and fully formed" like that of Ancient Egypt, including their complex written language that was structured at the outset".[75] Although women are completely cut out from these stories, a pattern can be seen in the idea of a higher-conscious being with advanced knowledge assisting humanity by sharing that knowledge.

The female versions of these stories I found in Italian books and they share many consistencies. They are true treasures which are evidence of the Spirit World presence and its purpose in Italy when expressed through feminine Spirit helpers. Even Italy's Inquisition, with all its horrors, accidentally did women a favor by documenting their "night meetings" with "The

Good Lady." In In post- Inquisition times, there has been documentation of practices that have been received from the Spirit World, handed down as legacies from higher-consciousness, which have then been passed onto human beings to benefit life on the planet. Shamanism around the world is one example (I am referring to the indigenous practices, not the modern-day weekend-intensive Shaman courses who conceptualize the lifestyle of a shaman and appropriating it into modern living), Spiritualism and Reiki being others.

In the early 1800s on the east coast of the United States, the Spirit World began to create such a large amount of psychic phemonena of the Spirit World reaching out to regular people in the earthly one (sounds, levitating objects and people, evidential communications, curing of diseases) in naked-eye observable ways, that a religion developed as a result. Spiritualism is the Science, Philosophy, and Religion of continuous life, based upon the demonstrated fact of communication, by means of mediumship, with those who live in the Spirit World.[76]

Interestingly, these events occurred during the Victorian period, which was rife with sexism, racism, and repression. So while the societal culture was retracting, the Spirit World was helping people expand. (Importantly, this also occurred in Italy each time women were oppressed). The Victorian era was marked by an explosion of innovation and genius, per capita rates of which appear to have declined subsequently.[77] The Victorian era has been highly touted by historians as one of the most productive in human history: inventions, observations and highly acclaimed art and music from that time still resonate today.[78] Researchers suggest Victorian-era people more intelligent than modern-day counterparts[79] and The Victorians achieved so much because they were cleverer than us, a new study suggests.[80] Perhaps those clever achievements were aided by all the Spirit World interventions. While the studies don't mention the Spiritualism boom occurring simultaneously as the discoveries and achievements touted, the following quote sums up the spiritual sentiments quite well from an insider perspective (while the historical ones focus on outsider aspects) The Spiritualist Gerald Massey claimed that Darwin's theory of evolution was incomplete:

"The theory contains only one half the explanation of man's origins and needs spiritualism to carry it through and complete it. For while this ascent on the physical side has been progressing through myriads of ages, the Divine descent has also been going on – man being spiritually an incarnation from the Divine as well as a human development from the animal creation. The cause of the development is spiritual. Mr. Darwin's theory does not in the least militate against ours – we think it necessitates it; he simply does not deal with our side of the subject. He can not go lower than the dust of the earth for the matter of life; and for us, the main interest of our origin must lie in the spiritual domain." [81]

In other words, the Spirit World helps the earthly world advance in jumps and leaps rather than in slow developments. Old Europe's Paleolithic and Neolithic women were aided by these same jumps and leaps.

In the early the 1920s, a Japanese man named Mikao Gyoho, known later as "Dr. Usui," received the Reiki healing practice transmission during a vision quest on a mountaintop. He went there seeking a way to help people after his business failed and he no longer wanted to seek a material-based life.[82] This healing practice was given to him fully-formed and was used to cure diseases of the body. Westerners have created their own versions of the healing practice, which is passed orally, teacher to student, after an initiatory "transmission" process called "attunement." This practice is watched over and assisted by Spirit World guides connected to it.

Many prominent Spiritualists were women, in the 1800s, and as Spiritualists they supported causes such as the abolition of slavery and women's suffrage. Reiki is also largely known as a woman's healing practice, even though many men are Reiki healers as well. Once, someone tried to insult me after learning I was a Reiki Master Teacher by declaring that it was a practice that "all modern housewives can do," as though, in his eyes, that meant it was not worth anything compared to someone with degrees. It was interesting to note this seems to be the very old competition between male healers against female ones since the patriarchy reared its separatist head.

Despite social stigmas, healing arts are still associated with women in modern times, and spiritual and religious practices also used to be as well. In fact, the people's religion had been largely in the hands of women since Caesar's day, and so it remained up to the 12th and 13th centuries when active persecution of "witches" began.[83] So what happened? Where was the divide? The Inquisition in Europe that lasted over 500 years, has ingrained in us the belief that women were just "evil beings" who needed to be taken out of society through torture and death.

Not just in Italy but globally, the most primitive hunting cultures have legends of still earlier ages, when women possessed all magical arts and men had none.[84] West African tribesmen testified that "women were more powerful than men, for to them alone the mysteries of the gods and of secret things were known".[85] In Tierra de Fuenab men said women used to rule the world by witchcraft, and all religious mysteries belonged to their Goddess, the moon.[86] Women founded the magical Egbo society, but after men learned their secret rites, they kept women from participating anymore.[87] In Queensland, once men learned magic, they forbade women to practice, on the ground that women had too much natural aptitude for it.[88] A transparently mendacious Iatmul legend said women invented sacred objects and secrets of magic, then "gave " these things to me and asked the men to murder them so no woman would have the secrets anymore.[89] In Cologne in 1332, Petrarch saw "women conjuring in the Rhine" in what was described as a "rite of the people".[90] Female elders once had political power among the clans, but patriarchal religion and law gradually took it away from them and called them "witches" in order to dispose of them.[91]

In Italy, the church accomplished such a fearsome Inquisitorial invasion among its people, leaving folk stories mixed with pagan anti-woman propaganda in its wake, along with missing Inquisition records, thus quite successfully leaving only remnants of stories of a forbidden nature and the truth having crawled deep into nature's sanctuaries of the mountains, the rivers, forests, and in the private hearths and homes of the few remaining women and men who keep the lineages alive. Who, not seeking public attention, but rather keep busy honoring the "work" and their service to it.

At what point did our association become dislocated from the great creative progress of the Goddess teachers? And how did a "witch" become a miscellaneous hodgepodge person, at once folk-filled with evil and with powers amorphous when she was previously a source of such concrete and functional tools? Witchery was a gift from the Great Mother to earthly mothers; and then passed on to mothers of their own children and from mothers to communities.

This is what lineages are, traditional oral teachings and actions which hand-down knowledge: the priestess traditionally gets initiated from the Spirit World, her dedication and devotion being on a soul level. Her duty finds her and she can't escape it. It's a solitary path that requires the ability to move, change, uproot, to have her home within her, and to share her knowledge to the ones the Goddess points out to her. The mother lineage is to those with the same dedication and devotion who have also made an earthly dedication to be grounded and sedentary; a fixed point in a community, with the purpose of passing her knowledge to flesh-and-blood relatives to maintain a continuance of services, or to adopt those family-less ones into the "ways."

There are markers in time that show a change from matrilinear, equality-based communities to patriarchal synthetic replacements where women are demoted and written out of history and spirituality altogether. These historical changes being times of turmoil are therefore also injected with new waves of Goddess teachers who appeared to assist women separated from their earthly female support systems and communities once again, to keep them from forgetting the "ways". We can see the morphing of pre-patriarchal order of communal life into post-patriarchal changes in structure of the family unit and of religious practices as illustrated in the development of the Longobard foundation stories.

The Mix-Up: Italy's Witchery Devolved By Paganism, Nature Devoured by Synthesis

Also called the Lombards, they descended from a small tribe called the Winnili,[92] who lived in Scandan, (southern Scandinavia) before migrating to seek new lands in the 1st century AD. Scandan is hypothesized by modern scholars to have been "the region of southern Sweden called Scania."[93] The Winnili claim that their ancestors descended from a primal, virgin mother, Gambara, who had no spouse.[94] The story says that the Winnili tribe, governed by two brothers, Ibor and Aio, along with their mother Gambara, was challenged by another tribe, who demanded them to pay tribute.[95] The Winnili refused, and this set the two tribes into a battle, but the night before the battle was to occur, both tribes appealed to the God Wotan for victory. It was the Winnili, however, and Gambara specifically, who also appealed to the Goddess Frigg (Freya) for help, and she gave them the upper hand in a rather "supernatural" way. They won the battle and changed their name from Winnili to Longobards, [...] and they also changed their old agricultural fertility cult to a cult of Odin, thus creating a conscious tribal tradition.[96]

Here we have illustrated a very important transformation of spiritual traditions: one in a series of transitions that has been mixed into the cauldron of witchery and has covered it with a thick layer of muddle, somehow replacing it with paganism, a creation of the patriarchy, but nevertheless remaining tied to witchery's name. Once it's understood that Paganism is from the Patriarchy, it's not so difficult to see the common pattern of women-centric practices being usurped by invasive male-created ones. But before that funeral procession is brought to light, let's first examine the Longobard story.

The first mention of the Lombards occurred around AD 9 (they were still known as a post-Winnili tribe called Suebi in AD 1). Most traditions of this tribe were handed down orally and undocumented until invaded peoples of other countries began writing down their personal observations of and experiences with the Longobards as they were invaded. As it unfolds in documentation, the Longobard story shows us the transformations that took place socially, which are reflected in the religious "spiritual" stories. Here we have a tribe whose creation story is like that of the matrilinear and matriarchal communities in the pre-historic and Paleolithic times: families consisting of Mothers and their children (as the fathers, not knowing paternity wandered; women and families were sedentary).

This tribe consists of a founding Mother and her two sons. Mother as teacher, nurturer, wise woman, natural leader. As I mentioned earlier, even Roman emperors didn't know their fathers, and these matrilinear family lines were a worldwide phenomenon into time periods considered "modern" and "advanced." Matrilinear means: following the female line, so for example, people born unto a woman or being married to her become part of her tribe bearing her name. The lineage is female. Matriarchal means to denote power, so for example, a community or society where a woman is at the head. In-between each of these specific ways of life there is also considered to have been a social order called "gylany." Old Europe and Anatolia, as well as Minoan Crete, were a gylany: a social structure where both sexes were equal, where a balanced non-patriarchal and non-matriarchal social system is reflected [...]by studies of the social structure of Old European and Minoan cultures, and is supported by the continuity of the elements of a matrilineal system in ancient Greece, Etruria, Rome, the Basque, and other countries of Europe.[97] So this means there was in fact a time in history, much longer than our time now, where men of a patriarchy (meaning male power)were not "in charge" of everyone else, and life was not looked at through a masculine lens of perspective. We have simply forgotten this, and have taken on a confusing, synthetic view of life which makes little sense, and buried a more natural, holistic one.

The first recognition of such a matristic order of thought and life antecedent to and underlying the historical forms of both Europe and the Near East appeared in 1861 in Bachofen's "Das Mutterrecht," where it was shown that in the codes of Roman Law vestigal features can be recognized of a matrilinear order of inheritance.[98] Ten years earlier, [..] Lewis H. Morgan had published in "the league of the Ho-de-no-sau-nee, or Iroquois," a two volume report of a society in which such a principle of "Mother Right" was still recognized and in a systemic review, subsequently, [...] he had demonstrated an all but worldwide distribution of such a pre-patriarchal order of communal life.[99]

So while the beginning of the Longobard story harkens back to this time of matrilinear female communities, the story also continues to tell us: this tribe is led by a mother, into battle, with help from the Spirit World; a Goddess.

PAUSE HERE FOR A MOMENT.

Because here, at this point, already we see an incorporation of the patriarchy's invasion into matrilinear community life that is reflected in the socially dominant spiritual practice. It's important to see this as a turning point from where witchery came to where witchery was covered over and turned into a patriarchal structure of hierarchy. If you're one of the many people who deeply loves witchery but feels that your practice just isn't reaching deep enough into some intangible connection to the past, this is why: Patriarchal invasions reflect patrilineal philosophies, gods, hierarchies, and other synthetic substitutes based upon matrilineal ones. Patriarchy's paganism, and its earlier forms, as will be discussed in depth later, also committed the same crimes as did patriarchy's "church" religion and Inquisition's strategists: usurp female symbols of holistic achievement and benevolence with stories of "evil women," and seal these propagandas with convincing deterrents of: weapons-filled invasion, enslavement, and war.

The Goddess-centered art with its striking absence of images of warfare and male domination, reflects a social order in which women, as heads of clans or queen-priestesses, played a central part [100]. [...] In Europe, some nine to eight thousand years ago[...]the Neolithic farmers evolved their own cultural patterns in the course of several millennia: food gathering gave way to food producing and hunting to a settled way of life, but there was no corresponding major change in the structure of symbolism, only a gradual incorporation of new forms and the elaboration of a transformation of the old. [101] [...] *What is striking is the [...]symbols of the aspects of the Goddess [...] can all be traced back to the period when the first sculptures of bone, ivory, and stone appeared, around 25,000 BC. Their symbols of vulvas, triangles, breasts, chevrons, zig-zags, meanders, cup marks -to an even earlier time.*[102]

The battles, in the Longobard story, are already a characteristic of post-patriarchal invasion re-structuring, even though their founding myth is aligned with matrilinear and gylanic lifestyles. Women joining their husbands in battle is also part of the Longobard story, and it is also a post-patriarchal twist. Beyond the language of "matriarchy and patriarchy" the core of what this means should be seen: a first order of holistic, natural way of living in harmony with nature and, through Spirit World teachings, an understanding of how to use the tools nature offers with which to have a balanced life (herbs to cure, plants to feed, weather cycles to plant and harvest, water to cleanse, and more, which developed into natural communities as women were left with birthing and child-rearing needs...versus an invading lifestyle (meaning a separatist type of living that actively attacked already established communities) that used weapons, control, torture, rape, confinement, forced life-animal husbandry rather than natural mating-to impose a forced lifestyle upon another). Interestingly enough, I've been told by Friulian Longobardian re-enactors who actively study their history and their gravesite finding, that as the Longobards invaded, they took on practices and lifestyles of those they invaded, rather than stamping out the local culture.

When they first entered Italy in 566, in the far north-eastern region, some Lombards retained their native form of paganism, while some were Arian Christians.[103] Practicing paganism, they related to Wotan and Freya, both male and female symbols of the Divine Creative Force, even though the Goddess in paganism had been demoted to "wife" and "symbol of "fertility," having lost all her other representational aspects. [Still...] they did not enjoy good relations with the Catholic Church.[104]

In Cividale del Friuli, the first city to fall to the Longobards in the spring of 568, there was already a long-standing tradition of "striis" or "witches," from lineages harkening back to matrilineal times, as well as widespread folk-beliefs in faeries, among other "Spirit World" beings. Additionally, when the Longobards established themselves in the south of Italy, they would have found groups of "streghe" and "janare" already there practicing matrilineal witchery. They had an unusual arrangement with "streghe" of allowing women into their tribes to learn magical practices in return for protection.

In Benevento, "City of Witches of the South" of the Sanniti region, the Longobards in fact became woven into the "witch" legends, having their own rituals around sacred trees, which was a practice already connected to the "streghe" in local folklore. In historical stories of the southern Sanniti region, Longobards even became an "advocate" of sorts for the Magic Walnut Tree of Benevento (an alleged gathering place for witches in Benevento), preventing it from being chopped down by San Barbatus of Benevento, for a while, until they finally caved in and converted. Unlike the "streghe" around Italy who were burned (in the north, north of Umbria), and beaten (in the south), the Longobards were not tortured and imprisoned, neither before or after conversion, but rather were able to establish their own churches; an important distinction showing that they had a power and a social structure that was not entirely a threat to the church.

The "streghe," "janare," and "striis", in contrast, had no political power. In contrast, early medieval England had female clan-leaders who exercised matriarchal rights in lawgiving and law-enforcement; the Magna Carta of Chester called them "iudices de wich"- judges who were witches.[105] Italy's witches were not woven into Italian political positions of power, neither the poor, remotely located ones nor the richer, studied women, and were therefore sidelined as the church sought to establish more social control in Italy. This is in important contrast to practices with male leaders who had political power and public structures, as the Longobards did after converting to Christianity, and schools, such as the Mitra Temple.

Paganism's Bond with War, Patriarchy's Directive of Divide and Conquer

There are enduring archaeological records of these "trumped" establishments, remnants left for us by the Roman practice of conquering older Emperors for new ones, even though this was a much older patriarchal practice. The "new" being subsumed from the old was celebrated through various propaganda tools such as: presenting the new Emperor in an awe-inducing "grand entry" parade, and placing the new Emperor's visage on coins, creating stone reliefs and statues of the new Emperors to replace the older stone reliefs and statues in public areas.

In the workings of this publicity machine, the new Emperor's personality traits are also glorified by connecting him in partnership to a god with similar personality traits, while the older Emperor is criticized and morally decimated to turn people away from his traits and teachings and leadership. Promoting the new Emperor's "god" of this new alliance and "killing off" the God of the former Emperor in epic battles, in which the "new Emperor and his chosen Deity always are victorious, blur a line between humanity and "heaven's helpers" who are supposed to be of a higher nature. This patriarchal practice is a social set-up for humans to create "gods" in their image, and vice versa, giving human males a seeming "natural order" and right in being in control through a means of violence. During this Roman time period we also see that the church, inspired by this successful propaganda machine, copied Roman efforts by employing Priests as "live journalists" to verbally "spread the news of change" and also using the public speech platform to verbally "kill off" former gods as well as people they wanted the public to turn away from such as homosexuals and witches.

We see no records of Goddesses killing off each other in mythological tales. We see no records of Goddesses being violent or war-like in nature until after patriarchy's waves of invasions and enslavement, after the patriarchy re-modeled spirituality to fit male directives of divide, conquer, and control. Goddesses have always shown a natural connection to death in our founding spirituality, but it was always in connection with "regeneration." Our founding spirituality was spiritualist: Death was not seen as a failure until the patriarchy began its invasions and created their own warring spiritual practices.

In fact, in the patriarchy's records written against women and their Goddesses, they fabricated stories focusing on earthly women as witches "killing newborn babies" and causing illness upon community members (as a way to make people fear these traditional midwives and healers and to rely, instead, on male doctors), but not even in these stories do they try to show women killing off one-another for "new" Goddesses to emerge. In reality, Goddesses do come in new waves, and many exist simultaneously, not needing to "kill one to make room for another," all equally valid and all expressing knowledge and abilities that are above human limitations, extending their reach into the earthly human world by way of gifting humans knowledge of life.

In the story of Inanna, a Mesopotamian Goddess whose influence has touched down in Italy as well, we see both Inanna and her sister as agents of the Divine Feminine: their services having to do with earthly healing of men and keeping the "underworld" Spirit World in order. Inanna's story was written during the patriarchal takeover, but still retain many original feminine practices. But paganism and the patriarchy, in contrast, have directives of control in common: Social control and control of genders, versus acceptance of nature. Interestingly though, paganism is a slight aberration from the church, one step removed from the total synthetic replacement the church offered because paganism does acknowledge the cycles of nature, albeit in a synthetic way with "man" as "head" of the creative life force and "woman" as his supporter in creation and in war.

In Northern Europe, the Vanir or Elder Goddess, led by Mother Earth and the Goddess Freya , were overthrown by the new patriarchal deities from Asia, the Aesir led by Father Odin; In the Aegea, followers of Father Zeus fought the pre-Hellenic worshippers of Mother Rhea or Hera.[106] In Babylon; worshippers of Marduk rebelled against the primal mother Tiamat, in Mexico the legendary leader of the Aztecs overthrew his sister Malinalxochitl [..]afterwords described as a "bad witch".[107] "Many [...] examples show that the defeat of the matriarchate was mythologized as a violent attack of men upon women.[108] Such mythos of leadership forcibly wrested from women occur throughout the world and cannot be overlooked.[109] As Engels noted, "The overthrow of mother-right was the world-historical downfall of the female sex."[110] In some ways, it may have meant the downfall of all humanity from a basically peaceful social order to a hierarchical structure established and maintained by aggression.[111] Patriarchal societies insisted on pecking orders; matriarchal ones tended to be more egalitarian.[112]

Invasions by the Patriarchy and Continued Breakup of Feminine Shamanism in Old Europe

While European cultures continued a peaceful existence and reached a true fluorescence and sophistication of art and architecture in the 5th millennia BC, a very different Neolithic culture with the domesticated horse and lethal weapons emerged in the Volga basin of Russia after the middle of the 5th millenium.[113] This new force inevitably changed the course of European history.[114] This early militarized attempt to control nature rather than live in harmony with it, and his was the beginning of the industrialization of life. Innovations like weaponry patriarchy, and the coming of small-scale agriculture, we see a new synthesized dominance over nature, All can be traced back to the the middle of the 5th millenium BC in the middle and lower Volga basin.[115] These characteristics match what have been reconstructed as proto-Indo-European [...] and they stand in opposition to the Old European gylanic, peaceful, sedentary culture with highly developed agriculture and with great architectural, sculptural, and ceramic traditions.[116]

It was during these times of invasions in Italy, however, that we see new Goddesses manifesting themselves, coming to help women reconnect with the Old Ways that had been given to their ancestors for the purpose of having an abundant life. The concept of Abundance, and therefore the Law of Attraction, began with matrilinear practices of channeling wisdom from the Divine Feminine. While we hardly hear the concept of the Divine Feminine connected with modern day popular spiritual traditions of manifesting, for example, this ancient practice of "the Secret," of "The Law of Attraction" and "the Law of Abundance" began in the most ancient of times and was what the original Goddess shamanism is all about: the Universe providing for all our needs even when we are "without" money, social status, etc. No wars were needed, and no wars can attain this magic anyway because it is received from Spirit World communication and not from math-like formulas. This "magical" practice was given to those without the means to create weapons of war in the first place. Shamanism was the advantage of the disadvantaged; magic was the currency of the poor.

In contrast to the mythologies of the cattle-herding Indo-European tribes that, wave upon wave, from the 4th millennium B.C., overran the territories of Old Europe and while male-dominated pantheons reflected the social ideals, laws, and political aims of the ethnic units to which they appertained, the iconography of the Great Goddess arose in reflection and veneration of the laws of Nature."[117] In other words, during time of destruction towards nature and the abundance of living a spiritual life (spiritual meaning connected to the Spirit World and nature's energy as a means of being provided for and living in harmony with one's environment), the Sprit World would intervene time and time again to appear to those willing to receive assistance, passing down the same age old information about plants that cure, seasonal cycles of nature, systems of counting and other means of magic (getting tangible results from the intangible) in the face of limitations and challenges. Humanity's part to understand and live in harmony with the beauty and wonder of Creation [...] is in every aspect contrary to the manipulated systems that in the West have prevailed in historic times.[118]

Neolithic village cultures with their matriarchal family-based governments were cooperative, unwarlike, and nonviolent[119] until the invasions began to change this. This magic of abundance is also STOLEN MAGIC. The roots of healing and magic, because of the invasions and usurping and destruction of our founding spiritual practices (which explain the mysteries of the Universe) can only be found by traveling far back into time before the invasions occurred to the remaining archaeological evidence of the timeless symbols of Divine Feminine abundance, cures, and magic. A must-do and worthy travel would be to the Italian island of Malta: the temples found here with their spirals, triangles, circles, and sound technology, pre-date the Egyptian pyramids. Shaped like the female body, these structures and their spiritual sculpture are the connection to our very roots. The same symbols found here, along with representational sculptures, burial objects, and more can be seen all over Old Europe. This even extends its reach to many other areas around the world: Ireland, Scotland, South America, Italy; so many more. It is an ancient code that is still used today by spiritual practitioners of many modalities in every land on Earth.

"For a long time men feared to oppose women because they were convinced women were more closely aligned with the forces of nature",[120] and perhaps this is why the patriarchal divide occurred in the first place.

Waves of invasion from separatist male patriarchal groups from the Russian steppe occurred roughly between 4300 BC and 2800 BC.[121] With this, the founding natural psychic and mediumistic lifestyle where the Spirit World provided for the needs of people of the earthly world was overrun by a new masculine way of life which introduced a synthetic way of living against and controlling of nature : animal husbandry, weaponry and forced submissions, control of food, subsuming of founding Divine feminine spiritual symbolic language and myth. This is where paganism comes from:

"The repeated disturbances and invasions by "Kurgan" people put an end to the Old European culture, changing it from gylanic and andocratic, from matrilineal to patrilineal. The aegean and Mediterranean regions and western Europe escaped the process the longest; especially in the islands of Thera, Crete, Malta [Italy], and Sardinia[Italy]. Old European culture flourished [...]until 1500 BC, a thousand to 1500 years after central Europe had been thoroughly transformed."[122]

In addition to all this historical talk about changes in community lifestyles, visual language, and spiritual practices, written language "was tampered with in late Minoan times when invaders from Central Asia began to substitute patrilinear for matrilinear institutions and remodel or falsify the myths to justify the social changes.[123] Robert Graves, in his book "The White Goddess" (in reference to the light of the moon), recounts this as he explains the origins of the purpose of poetry: "that the language of poetic myth anciently current in the Mediterranean and Northern Europe was a magical language bound up with popular religious ceremonies in honor of the Moon-goddess, or Muse, some of them dating from the Old Stone Age, and that this remains the language of true poetry- "true" in the nostalgic modern sense of the 'unimprovable original, not a synthetic substitute."[124]

The language was further changed when the early Greek philosophers strongly opposed magical poetry as "threatening to their new religion of logic."[125] These important poetic tales told by a guild of Welsh minstrels, among others, who were "popularly credited with divinatory and prophetic gifts," another demonstration of psychic channeling for disseminating magical information through common language. Like witchery and early Goddess Religion, Graves says of poetry, "European poetic lore is, indeed, based on magical principles, the rudiments of which formed a close religious secret for centuries but which were at last garbled, discredited, and forgotten,[126] the function and use "once a warning to man that he must keep in harmony with the family of living creatures among which he was born." From this very brief historical examination we can still see that witchery was originally given to women, psychically and Mediumistically from the Spirit World, for the purpose of improving life and understanding the human relationship to nature's ever-circular movement.

The Purpose of an Italian Witch

The purpose of an Italian witch is the same as it was in our founding, ancient times: to improve life. It's a shamanic legacy, not a human-made system; its healing practices having been created made by higher consciousness for human usage, passed down after original transmissions along mostly female family lines, for the purpose of improving life (animals, plants, and people).Why is this knowledge secret? Because coming to know it, as the Spirit World teaches it, unfolding each mystery one-by-one, the answers to the mysteries point back to the Spirit World: so earthly human beings can learn what lies beneath the surface of physical matter, so as to understand themselves and their place in the Universe. We can't know the unknown, the Spirit World, from down here on earth unless it reaches out to us in glimpses and sensations.

Although Italian witchery has been often confused with magic practices like spells and sorcery and even rituals including figures of High Priests and Priestesses, these are not the same thing. Spell work does have a place in Italian witchery, but not in the way you might think. The more "crafty" the magical spell, the more likely it was created once poverty settled into new communities who experienced this poverty due to patriarchal invasion and control of resources. The "never enough to go around" experience came from the separation of women from each other during these invasion periods, and lineages were broken and darker, lower desperation set in. The secret Lineages are about more than "moving energy," as in magic. They are about Mediumship. Not only knowing the Spirit World exists, but working in partnership with it, not just during isolated rituals, but on a daily basis, naturally.

Ritualistic practices are from a masculine-created pagan and patriarchal structure who based their rites on the natural version between women and the Spirit World but warp their original design to support male directives of male-based creation, war, taking things through force and control. Patriarchal living parallels their spiritual practices, as does the early peaceful, abundant feminine-based community parallels the founding Divine Feminine Spiritual practices.

The original Divine Feminine Shamanism was about practical application of "miraculous magic" for improving life with indigenous plants and available natural resources in the immediate environment, and most importantly, waiting on the Spirit World to provide the knowledge and instruction to do so; whereas paganism created synthetic "training grounds" for magical schools and forced pairing of binary gender shared-God and Goddess roles and man-made magical recipes. While some of these schools such as at the Temple of Mitra in Rome, channeling was utilized, most pagan practices were based on getting what one needs through war, and using magic to get what one needs when one needs it.

Second Secrets

Everything from Nothing

After pining away since 2009 to return to Italy again, I had some unexpected money appear in my mailbox in 2016 from a job I recently left. I immediately bought a plane ticket to Italy.

My plan was to go to the south of Italy to visit author Carlo Napolitano, and to then just remain there for a few months, getting to know the locals and then, hopefully, to be led to what and whom I was looking for.

I didn't speak the language and had been relying on my husband to be the translator and guide, but he wasn't able to go due to prior commitments. I didn't know how I would travel within the country, but I determined to go anyway. I made this resolution while walking to work, when my ipod suddenly began playing a song that had a connection to the city of Benevento, the "city of Witches of the south." I took it as a sign, which only strengthened my resolve.

Upon my husband's suggestion, I contacted an acquaintance who lived in Liguria, asking him if he and his wife would mind picking me up from the airport in Genova and helping me to rent a car there.

"Of course you have to begin your trip here," Simone wrote me, "because the Inquisition started here!"

So already, my trip began to take on another shape: a journey I hadn't even realized my Spirit guides and had been preparing me for all along.

I also quickly put together a short film about my quest to raise money for this research through a crowdfunding campaign that was interactive: people would be able to help financially support my research there, and in return I'd leave their prayers buried in Italy's soil and place gemstones at sacred sites connected to witches and Goddesses.

But much more than just money came in...email after email came to me through facebook, as a result of my promotional campaign, and before I knew it I had people offering to introduce me to "streghe healers" in medieval villages, herbalists on mountaintops, professors, authors, museum directors, Goddess experts, folk experts, and even secret shamanic groups. I had people offer to be my drivers and translators, and everyone would say the same thing: "it's like these people are waiting for you, Karyn. They don't normally take visitors."

I had created a "control" list of questions to ask everyone, wondering how "insiders" (the witches themselves and magical practitioners and locals living the "legends") and "outsiders" (historians, authors, researchers) would respond to the same questions.

However, each person had at minimum a two hour talk or demonstration prepared for me which answered all of my questions without me having to ask, as if they had already anticipated my questions: whether Antonietta with her herb harvests and cures, Doriana with her mountaintop herbalism tour, Manuela explaining to me historically what I'd experienced ecstatically, Paolo with his historical information about the Inquisition, Carlo taking me to the place I consider to be the most important and charged area in south of Italy: the Sabato Rivers' Stretto di Barba. Domenico, my translator and driver from Guardia Sanframondi took me to his grandmother who performed "occhi" for me to release my past-life curse, we filmed it. I got to crawl over the 2000 year old stones of Diana's Temple remains at Nemi because of Fabrizio's tenacity, and even Alecia, an American I'd connected with online emailed me before I left for Italy because she felt the need to tell me, "If you're ever in Italy I just bought a place there…" and her place was exactly 30 minutes from where I originally planned to stay: Benevento.

I would travel this time between 5 regions. This journey was planned by invisible helpers, and I was lovingly looked after by everyone I'd meet. This journey was about connections: connections between men and women, between the Spirit World and the earthly one, and connections which honor the women in Italy called "witches."

Chapter 2:

"Reclaiming Italy's Witchery from Patriarchy's Paganism"

Lineages, the Living Legacies from our Founding Days in Italy

This is it. The giant swirling cauldron of "herstory" you just read through, in its brief and sweeping capsule, is where Italian witchery comes from: those earliest days of women being left alone to give birth and care for life, often without the men who took part. These were women naturally formed female communities, being assisted by the Divine Feminine Spirit World who "reached down to earth" to guide them in this great responsibility. This is the origin. Now, let the untangling begin…

So what is an Italian Witch? As this book's content demonstrates, there is not a singular, simple answer, because there is no singular unified Witch Cult in Italy, nor has there ever been. There is not even one name that means the same thing to all Italian people. What some women do is considered witchery by others but not by the "practitioners" themselves. I met and received cures from women who practice techniques that modern outsiders would likely identify as "magic" or as "witchcraft," but the women themselves who practice these curing techniques told me "streghe" (witches) are other types of women, mainly "bad ones," but not them. The exception being Antonietta, a healer from Puglia who I met in Triora, who made distinctions to me between "streghe cattive" (bad witches) and "streghe buone" (good witches). Some of the women I met who call themselves "strega"(witch) as Antonietta does, do things that Americans would not understand as "witchcraft" at all. There has been so much freedom, since the Italian witches are very hidden, for modern imaginations to run wild and "dream up" versions of who they are: their magic is real and powerful and unlike anything I've ever experienced, but it's not really "magic" at all, and it is nothing like paganism nor modern witchcraft nor wicca. It is not glamorous, and its practitioners don't go to the "store" to buy supplies for their cures. Are you feeling a bit confused yet? More questions than answers? Perfect!

If you're looking for a book that gives you twelve steps towards becoming an Italian Strega, you're not going to find anything authentic in that vein. There is no such singular thing. As for magic in Italy, that's another story and that's another thing.

Perhaps still the best way to describe an Italian witch is: a channel of higher knowledge with which to care for life around her, assisted by the Spirit World, in whatever form that needs to take place. The "witch" as the channel, the Medium between worlds, helps other people by offering services which overcome the limitations of earthly life so as to balance, elevate, cure, and improve the quality of life. Her purpose is not to teach the knowledge itself but to offer its benefits.

Looking back to the historical origins of the practices of Italian witchery and Italian Paganism helps us get a much clearer picture by taking stock of what was inherited and why.

Firstly, Italian Witchery is Indigenous. The Lineage practices were handed down to women who, often uneducated and poor, had little resources other than the nature at their feet, the water in the river, and the moon above. Their only temples were the forests, the caves, the mountaintops. The Divine Feminine, through channeling, taught the women how to use what was around them in their immediate environment. The Great Goddess taught them how the female biology is connected to the secrets of the Universe. This is what Italian Lineage Witchery inherited and this is how it continues today: The women who cure with herbs today harvest their own plants from the wild near where they live. The women are dug deep, "planted" in communities and families. In some traditions which don't utilize herbs, nature is still the conduit: water and oil are used in inherited pots and pans vessels; matches or grasses tied together create diagnostic tools in the shape of "croci" (crosses) in some Lineages as well.

Italy's paganisms, or more appropriately we should say: all the cultural pagan practices that found their way into Italy, come from other lands, or were remodeled by the Romans into something "Italian." They are man-made and they follow a masculine system that synthetically puts the man and the God as the source of all life even though they have no wombs and therefore no parallel in nature. They are synthetic "mothers." Their systems of practice are based on this. Having no natural ability to birth life, war is the the way they take lives, animal husbandry is the way they industrialize life, and usurping the founding Divine Feminine from symbols that point to parallels of her energy in nature to the way her energy works in the Universe into man as source of all. Even temples men built for Goddesses are built in the shapes of squares and rectangles: whereas the original Divine Feminine temples were build in connected circle shapes that represented the female body. These pre-Egyptian pyramid temples are filled with statuary and symbols expressing the Divine Feminine in all of life, even in death. The pagan temples, though honoring Goddesses, only allow men into their most sacred areas; women are delegated to the outskirts of the temple grounds.

In ancient times, "witchery" was born out of necessity and given to women who were left with the challenge of not only giving birth to new life, but of also caring for this new life, on their own. They needed to know, urgently, how to care for their own bodies during and after birth, how to care for their babies, to feed, to restore health when illness occurred, to care for plants and planting and harvesting at the right times, to care for animals. There was no time for "trial and error." The knowledge they received enabled them to improve life by: understanding anatomy, keeping calendars, teaching, writing and communicating with each other and with their ancestors. They needed to know nature's cycles, their bodies' cycles (because the female body does in fact keep time) and how to work with the passages of time. They needed vessels to cook with and hold water and they needed instruction on caring for lifeless, decomposing bodies. This came first, and the advent of paganisms came with the masculine participation in agriculture in Italy and Old Europe and with the invasions of male separatist warring tribes which repeatedly took place from 4300 BC- 2800 BC.

Women received this secret knowledge first because it supported all the life that was in their care. Because it took a very long time for paternity to be understood, and fathers weren't needed for life to exist after the brief male part in what could become a life, naturally women were sedentary, men were not. Relationships were naturally not like our modern day partnerships. There were no "moral contracts" holding couples who copulated together. But mothers were mothers to ALL life forms around them: plants, animals, people.

As communities of women were naturally formed, this knowledge was passed around. Then, as nuclear families formed, and a certain amount of delineation or separation occurred, this knowledge continued its life by being passed through the family lineage. As family dynamics were broken apart and women's roles changed by invading warring patriarchal tribes, documentations show recurring appearances of a variety Goddesses in Italy to reconnect women with vital knowledge such as the secrets of curing herbs and instructions on how to use them. These Goddesses or Spirit Teachers or Guides are named in documentation as: "Signora di Gioco," "Bona Dea," "Bonae Res," "Abundia," "Madonna Oriente" to name a few. They continued to visit women in more modern times such as we find documented in the 1500s: single women, outcasts, women not from family lineages, and old widowed women. These Spirit Teachers appeared to Italian women in visionary experiences documented in detail, surprisingly, by Inquisitors who were trying to find "confessions" meant to catch women in evil acts. Instead, they found this female-to-female, Spirit World-to-earthly world lineage whose accounts contain the same type of descriptive language found in accounts of shamanism and ecstatic trance. However, while shaman historically have been considered "wise in their ways" or even feared with respect from outsiders, the Italian women who've given these accounts have been described as crazy and diabolical.

What is most exciting about Indigenous practices, and specifically Italy's "witcheries" is that they are a wonderful example of the "supernatural" world affecting the physical material world: as there were human needs, the Spirit World provided the means. No currency was needed to get this information, as it's not for sale. No education was needed, no social status, but something deeper, something more loving and selfless. Channeling information through the psychic senses is how the Spirit World reaches through to the physical world. Mediumship is the practice that earthly humans can employ to reach into the Spirit World.

The means for needs were provided to regular, everyday women through what was readily available around them in Italy: water, plants, oil, stones, fire, and the knowledge was transmitted through the psychic senses as channeled conscious energy. This partnership with the Spirit World provided for specific needs then, and continues to provide for specific needs now. Lineage healers cure muscle twisting issues and other body issues experienced by farm field-workers such as"storte"(twisted muscles) and "colpo delle streghe" (the blow of the witch, a back issue), stomach infections in babies, instructions for when to harvest crops, cures for sports injuries, headaches, colds and flu, heart ailments, how to help birth babies and provide aftercare, for sciatica and eczema, psoriasis, and onward. As the times changed and became more modern, we see the response from the Spirit World to provide cures through Lineages which heal specific ailments in specific environments. In Italy, it's amazing to see these Lineage women in action and be able to see the connection to our founding days on earth. In contrast, magical practices such as found within Paganism respond to needs with spell work and ritual where the focus is on the intention of the person in need, the person doing the spell.

The "witches" I received cures from have a surprising ability to heal specific diseases and ailments, and they do so quickly. They used natural elements along with channeled energy to cure me within and without: one fruits and herbs and other edible ingredients, another with oil and water, another with just energy. Consider that Antonietta, the 89 year old "strega" in Triora, had only been to the doctor once in her life, during her 89th year of life. Previously she had always been cured, when needed, by her "nonna" and herself. Filomena used oil and water and a secret prayer. But much more happened when they made their actions than just what can be seen with the physical eyes.

Their methods felt magical, psychical, mediumistic, energetic, and among other things, unbelievably beautiful in their simplicity. At no point did these women touch me, although they do have curing techniques that involve specific touch to cure specific ailments. Their power was unlike anything I've felt before, and it was humbling. The presence of "someone" not in a physical body moving around me while the women performed their actions to cure me is undeniable. They are absolutely channeling a very high vibrational consciousness that expresses itself as also feminine…very ancient and all powerful and universally loving…but beyond that, remains formless. The cures I experienced from these women and this channeled "partner" continue to change my life in positive ways, even though they immediately took effect on the physical level.

However, try to talk to these women about the "otherworldly" part of the cure experience, as I did, and you will get a serious and "knowing" look, but also chuckle that politely waves away a discussion on the matter. These women are powerful but humble and yet some won't encourage any talk about the more "supernatural" element of what they do. This is the mark of someone who has come in contact with the great energetic Divine Feminine power but clearly knows it is separate from who they are. They know and honor the power to cure comes from someone else; they do not own it, nor want to market it, nor take any credit for it. This humility is a rare thing in our modern days.

In many cases they don't have a name for this Spirit consciousness, but some call her the Great Mother (Grande Madre) or Great Goddess (Grande Dea) among other general terms, if they use a term at all. There is a resistance in Italy to attach specific form or name to this Divine Feminine energy.

Nearby one of the villages where I met a lineage healer are the remains of temples to ancient Goddess. These remains of the newer (still very old) structures mark sites where the Goddess is alleged to have manifested herself in physical form. I visited these sites and the energy in these places is undeniably palpable. So, I decided to ask these healers about them. One particular 83 year old lineage healer laughed at me when I asked her if she had any connection to the Goddess Diana. I've come to find out that Italians don't consider Diana to be an Italian Goddess and they consider her modern persona to be a remodeled creation of the Romans, based on the ancient Grande Dea. This same Lineage healer, however, did tell me about knowing a "lupomannaro" (wolf man, or werewolf) as did many other Italians who believe they are real and born on the same night witches are born: December 24th. So while we outsiders consider one folk tale absurd and other myths the truth in relation to what we may think is Italy witchery, in Italy we just might find the opposite.

Even among young Italian witches is a common reaction feigning the notion of attaching a specific Goddess or God names to this higher conscious energy, and they also feel the Greek and Roman Gods and Goddesses to be "made-over" in ways that don't properly express the power of the Spirit energies themselves. I find this so refreshing. Deciding who or what someone is before experiencing it/them cuts off an opportunity to learn. In Italy, witches old and young are adept in communicating with the Spirit World. They are very engaged in the process. The younger ones are more apt to discuss this and while using modern terms, but they acknowledge the danger in trying to "own" what you think you know or "claim" you have the answers before you let spirit show you what it actually is. After all, this is what Big Religion as done: deciding who God is without ever having met God. Even more than this, there is a reluctance by people to "name" themselves too. The ones who are living life "as a witch," in the way outsiders would consider witchery do not call themselves witch or anything…they are just busy living. I was told that the Inquisition left its mark in this way because the church literally reached into homes and took people away. But I found this wasn't the reason for everyone: the younger people also don't "name" themselves for many reasons, one of the most common ones was: the sense of duty towards their own personal learning on this path, and the honor towards the traditions.

Italy's "witchery" in all its forms and "categories" in is true essence has no human founder. This remains true in the modern world: people in Lineages consider themselves to be part of something they did not create. And young witches also honor the ancient age of their traditions and seek to reconnect with the origins. The practice is a legacy, handed down in fully developed, ready-to-use knowledge to whomever needed it in part or parcel during whatever time period it was needed *from the Spirit World.* As earthly women had needs, Divine Feminine Infinite Intelligence provided the means.

And in Italy, there are Lineage practices descended from ancient times, still alive, having survived the many patriarchal changes of the land. The "witches" I received cures from don't call what they do by a "magical" name at all. They don't have a technical name for most procedures, rather the names explain what they do: "occhi" removes "il Malocchio" or the evil eye. "Strofinare" is simply a finger massage that cures muscles, tendons and even bones. "Segnatori" (marks) which are kept secret, are what the "guariotri (healers) draw on the bodies of patients seeking cures. Simple.

Because Italy's witcheries were not created by a human person and then developed over time and through experimentation but were rather received as fully-developed "legacies," their actions and secret energetic invocations have not been amended or changed by the users. They are honored in the exact form in which they were received from ancestor to ancestor who practiced and then passed on the secret energy transmissions and the knowledge. My husband's mother's mother, from Caserta, healed people with a special song she would whisper which she said came from God. She did not create the song herself and she refused to tell anyone the song's melody or words because she said it didn't belong to her. She took that song to the other side, remaining a secret, when she recently passed.

Paganisms and Patriarchy, Devolving the Goddess

Paganism, in contrast, created practices devoted to Gods and Goddesses. The temples, rituals, magical recipes, structure of a coven with a High Priest and High Priestess, even the myths of their Gods and Goddesses are man-made, collages of much older practices combined with new man-as-Source of life and war as means to "get what we need" of patriarchy (versus the Abundance of the Goddess in earlier Divine Feminine spirituality). This does not mean they have no real value: they do, and Italy's fervent followers of pagan cults prove this without a doubt. But the many paganisms, while connected to nature, did not arise in natural ways.

Paganisms have usurped the feminine part of the practices with masculine ones, or have eliminated women from them entirely, with the exception of fertility, which the Goddesses, and as a social result, the women were relegated to. Paganism is studious: offering schools to learn in and temples in which to worship and arrange ritual. These spiritual arrangements also colored social life: where into the early Inquisition period in Italy we see paganism and the church remarkably similar and social life consisting of arranged marriages (forced binary coupling) and we see people resisting this even though they couldn't escape it . As Paolo Portone writes, "The power of love, so dear to the poets, was in the reality of time denied, and viewed with suspicion in a society where marriage was a contract, often contracted against the intimate wishes of its contractors." In his essay "Erotic Obsession and Sexual Spell in the Processes [Trials] of the Holy Office" describing the atmosphere of Italian life in 1542 he describes how unhappily wedded couples went to sorcerers for spells to attract the attention of those they loved instead of the ones they were married to. "From the end of the sixteenth century to the early decades of the eighteenth century, emerges a sorrowful female humanity, enclosed in the rigid roles assigned to them by Catholic morality and a society centered on patriarchal authority."[127]

The Tempio di Mitra (Temple of Mithra) in Rome is an important example: In the underground temple, we have a place of learning that is not in nature, therefore it is not natural. It is a synthetic structure, made of stone: not a cave, but a man-made structure. There is a purpose to this: like an isolation chamber, this underground stone enclosure and its school rooms block out all earthly distractions. This is a parallel that exists in meditation: to meditate, we close our physical eyes to shut off from the physical realm so that we can peer into the darkness of our inner world, to find the light.

There is a room in the Temple of Mithra where a bull is slaughtered in front of the group of spiritual adepts. The bull, in our founding Divine Feminine symbolic spiritual language, represents the Goddess Mother's regenerative energies: the bucranium, or bull skull, is shaped like the earthly woman's uterus, ovaries, and fallopian tubes from which life-giving blood emanates. In the oldest megalithic temples, on Malta, they are both both wombs and tombs, and the bucranium was found placed facing the bones of the dead to symbolize: after death, life comes again.

Women have used, and still use, their catamenial (menstrual) blood in ritual, but men don't have this biological occurrence. So in the Mithraic cult, the bull is slaughtered to use her blood as the "life force." In the temple of Mithra are also school rooms I am convinced were used to train students not only psychcically but also as Mediums. This is an honorable "copy cat" of early Divine Feminine practices, created for use by men. Mitra is represented as a male, however, taking control of the bull…usurping the natural …

Our earliest spiritual practice was "spiritualist" after all: the belief that life comes after death includes the belief that post-death life can be communicated with, since it is still living. Spiritualist traditions are oral: channeling eliminates the need to write things down…and we see this with the Druids and Etruscans and many other cultural groups who didn't write down their spiritual teachings but rather created symbolic art.

Of course there is valid science in the paganisms found in Italy: examining a list of trees deemed "magical" I found that almost every one was "monoecious," meaning it had both female and male parts; monoecious plants have both male flowers and female flowers in separate structures on the same plant: so a co-existence of both masculine and feminine "energy" that is the foundation of paganism. In biodynamic farming in Italy, both the sun and the moon have important roles in the development of plants and are considered to have masculine energy (the sun) and feminine energy (the moon), and each has attributes similar to the gender personalities to which they are associated. But in paganism we also have the focus on binary gender and often, criticisms of homosexuality and an eradication of other genders in myths.

What occurred with the advent of paganisms in Italy was the creation of synthetic structures (temples) for worship and spiritual practices. Women were often barred from these temples, or from the important inner sanctums of them. An ironic example is the (no longer standing) Temple of Isis in Campania's city of Benevento, Italy. This temple was built by a male Emperor, Domeziano, who was enamored with the Goddess Isis. The aberration here is that Isis is a Divine Feminine Mother whose purpose is to care for women and their autonomous sexuality…She is a healer and a teacher of Mediumship. Yet here, in this temple, as with many others, women are forbidden from entering the "heart " of her temple: the inner sanctum: they must worship her from outside, while only men are allowed in.

It will again be helpful think of Italy's witchery as having more in common with "Sciamani," or Shaman than with modern depictions of witches or with paganism. Merriam-Webster offers this definition of a shaman: "a priest or priestess who uses magic for the purpose of curing the sick, divining the hidden, and controlling events." And Dictionary.com offers "a person who acts as intermediary between the natural and supernatural worlds, using magic to cure illness, foretell the future, control spiritual forces, etc." This Spirit World partnership is one that naturally exists on a daily basis, and the Lineage woman follows the path the Divine Feminine carries her along.

In Italy's paganism, channeling is often reserved for ritual and other special events, planned moments when the human participants decide that this event shall have a channeling experience or an ecstatic trance occurrence. It is done with a man and a woman representing the God and Goddess, or a marriage of masculine and feminine energies.

Witchery is a natural relationship with the Spirit World that has practical applications; paganism is ceremonial. Italian witchery takes place in the home and in nature, paganism utilizes temples and ritual and arranged celebrations as means to have spiritual experience.

This is why temples to Goddesses in Italy are not associated with Italy's witches: because they were created not by male Lineage witches or by male healers, but by pagan Emperors and war leaders, as well as other men who remodeled the Goddess to support his needs.

Additionally, Paganism involves magical practices, rituals, and the learning of procedures (taught by other human beings) in places that synthetically reproduce natural surroundings (such as bringing the outdoors inside, and "creating" a ritual moment that is not already naturally occurring on its own). Paganism is a structured practice. This is what school is like essentially: working with a condition that is in a vacuum or a sterile environment (with no outside interference), so that it, and peoples' interactions with it, can be studied in a controlled environment. By using synthetic replicas of natural experiences and rewards based on performance and other (masculine) forms of hierarchy, we have an environment that offers constancy and repeatable experiences to learn from (and also the goal to reach of becoming a teacher who, in turn, can teach this structured practice to others). The magic practiced here strives to work in harmony with the flow of energy and its laws. Mystery Schools of Italy's past, such as the Tempio di Mitra, are exactly this: interior schools for learning, which take place in subterranean stone structures and who incorporate channeling of higher wisdom as part of their practice.

In contrast, ancient Italian witchery is a practice learned in private; "witches" are solitary practitioners who cure disease or battle the spirits or work with the Spirit World. They also cure in private: there is generally no audience allowed in during the curing session. Learning and training occurs one-on-one in some cases: for example, a lineage-receiver learns from her Lineage-giver relative for a period of time until she must practice on her own. And remember, these Lineage provide cures for specific diseases: they are not like our modern modalities of healing and magic where we feel "something" occurring, but usually not an immediate and miraculous absence of pain and disease that occurs immediately. While our modern healing methods do work, they work largely as a process that takes time; Italian Lineage cures, the ones I tried, change the illness imbalance immediately. When we do magical work we feel changes but as to exactly when the change occurs (as a result of our ritual) we can't always be exactly sure: in Lineages, there is no disconnect of time between the invocations, secret marks traced on the body, the prayers and actions: it is clear the energy is changing things in those very moments, coming through those Lineage women.

Italy's witchery is made up of practices whose actions, like those of shamanism, largely take place in an unseen, intangible world, while all the physical "tools of the trade" are merely representational of what cannot be seen with the naked eye nor uttered with the audible voice: for example, the secret prayers and invocations that are part of some of the curing practices. Those of us who attempt to document and write about these practices, who try to "name" and categorize the methods have to do the antithesis of what the practitioners do: name things with specific titles. In this way, so much disservice has been done to this secret world with the written word, and so much misinformation has been offered up as "evidence." These are psychic and Mediumistic practices, which take place in the intangible and infinite "energy" or Spirit World, and therefore language, which is part of our finite world, causes limitations and misunderstandings. Italy's witchery takes place in the practical, mundane world. The more mystical Lineage witches in Italy, the ones given transmission from the Spirit World of Goddesses, also take place in the natural world: caves, rivers, mountains, trees…these are her places of education.

Another example is an "orphan" being "adopted" as an "adept" to a Goddess who learns directly from the Spirit World. In the modern community "circles," women are taught by a community "mother," but much of the learning is done on private time, and there is no "hierarchy" within the circle.

Paganism is ceremonial. Paganism is hierarchical. There are levels of authority. The ability for a spiritual practitioner to "rise up" in position in the pagan path is dependent upon judgement from other human participants. Paganism is a choice.

The women I met who have been called to this lifestyle take their work seriously: not in the way they present themselves to others, but in the way they "serve the work." They are humble. This is a first important distinction: women are "called" to this work: they are chosen, they don't do the choosing for themselves. They agree to the "call," and the "call" is a contract, and the process of being given the transmissions and secrets and actions and knowledge is a very secret and private affair. There are very specific actions to take, specific things to learn. These women are deeply imbedded in the land, in their quiet communities, on mountaintops, in the peasant countrysides, not in the modern stylish cities. One cannot seek this path out in modern schools or classes. This is part of its inherent mystery.

Who Italy's witches are will ultimately be established in their own words and stories throughout the duration of this book, including interviews with young modern Italian witches. Before the Italian insiders speak for themselves, we must do a little more digging, past all the outsider archaeological and anthropological ideas, under the historical claims based on previously documented findings of non-spiritual practitioners and folklore, and even then we will have to keep digging to uncover more of the truth: under modern church structures built on top of earlier matrilinear history, under the melting pot of paganism and its patriarchal devaluation of women, under the weight of the Inquisition and its negative propaganda and burned corpses, beneath modern DIY cultural interpretations.

Italy: separate but together

Witches in Italy are, and have been, a country-wide phenomenon (even if we won't be able to use this "unifying" term to name all of them). Every village and region has witch stories and also living witches (some modern witches and some of the true remaining lineage holders, and some solely "fantasized" creations of the patriarchal popular folklore). The interesting thing of note is that Italy hasn't ever been a truly unified country. That is, until fairly recently, in 1861 when Italian became the official language of the nation. Italian people had been speaking their own dialects for centuries before standard Italian language was "born," and Italians themselves will tell you it still isn't really a unified country. There is the regional Italian language emanating from the Tuscany region, but also other languages (such as Albanian, Catalan, French, Sardo) and many regional indigenous dialects, but also in the south Greek dialects, for example can be found. However, the dialects are not linguistically true, meaning that they are not varieties of the standard Italian, but rather languages that evolved locally and rose independently of what would become the standardized Italian language long before that occurred. What this means is that people in one region can't understand the dialect of the region next to them and vice versa. My husband, for example, speaks a dialect from the Veneto region (north eastern Italy) , and he can't understand the dialect of his relatives in Caserta (south western Italy, in the Campania region). He can speak with his younger cousins, but not with his older relatives who only speak dialect. Unified Italian is spoken in many places but not all. There are parts of Italy that are even considered "like another country" to most Italians.

In Italy I found that while there are differences in languages and dialects from one region to another, there are also cultural differences: many imprints and melting-pots have settled and become part of the fabric of certain regions and not others. Other cultures left their marks on Italy long ago such as Phrygians, Celtic Druids, Gaulish Druids, Scandinavians, the Scottish, Greeks, and more, having brought over their oral spiritual traditions and leaving them to flourish, often simultaneously, in parts of Italy.

People in one region may not know anything about the history of another region, even if there is a common link. For example, even though the Longobards occupied most of Italy for a time, the folk legends about them in the south's Campania region are completely different to the northeast's Friulian region (the area where Longobards took their first Italian city) where grave sites and archaeological remnants are on display in a museum and re-enactors, like La Fara, give educational presentations on historical findings and their educational re-creations of these findings. But talk to people in each region, and you'll find the Longobards, in the regional histories and knowledge, seem like two completely different tribes of people with very different traditions.

In the Benevento province, local tales are full of stories about Longobards and "streghe," or Italian witches, being both confused with one another, and also with having similar practices and even having formed alliances. Also found are churches and temples (attributed to the Longobards) in each region that bear no similarities to each other. The Longobards, unlike Italian "witches," factor into historical records and archaeological documentations, and even so, here we have a lack of connection between regions. Consider also, the Longobards, after agreeing to "convert" to the church's religion, were taken into "the club;" they had their own churches and business.

In great contrast, the only documentations about Italy's "witches" come from the church's Inquisitors, looking for confessions to fit their specific propaganda agenda (mostly regarding women having sex with "Satana" and causing problems for the community) or folkloric fear-inducing stories that were part of the patriarchy's propaganda to turn people away from the "evil witch." Witches were a concept created by the church in the first place, as a "divide and conquer" tactic. Witches were accused of fake "evilness" created by the church, and even if they confessed they were not spared torture and death. There was no opportunity for rehabilitation nor joining "the club" for these women.

Italy's "witches" had no political power as a group nor as a tribe (like the Longobards, an actual tribe); there were no monuments nor churches built by them, they had no interactions as a group nor as a tribe with the church or military. Their many traditions are from an oral tradition. Historically, except for propaganda against them, they have been invisible. Not being a tribe or a cohesive social group, they didn't invade other communities, as social groups had a proclivity to do, nor did they establish codes of living in societies, nor were there "towns and communities of witches." There were, however, towns of Greek settlers, or Etruscan strongholds, for example. Paganism is marked by temples and churches in Italy, which take financing to build. They also require attendees and groups of people working for the temples. They require leaders and teachers to maintain the experiences for the attendees and to maintain their schooling and attention. This is business. Spiritual business, but business nonetheless.

It's important to note that pagan cults received passionate followings in Italy, and they were difficult for the church to stamp out because they were not small nor remote: they had power, they were engaged with the public in a groups setting, and they had propaganda: like the church. Unlike the church, people were having ecstatic experiences. There were simultaneously pagan cults to various Gods and Goddesses: we know as humans we believe what we experience, so the fact that these cults had such fervent followings means something significant was happening here. Still, the "happenings," the "experiences" were in the hands of the ones in charge, external people. This is the same model as the church: that God can only be talked to by the Priests.

Italy's witches, in contrast, are directly connected with the Grande Dea.

In the past, as is now, the connecting "tissue" among all these women living in remote areas, separated by terrain and different dialects is the living Spirit World and its knowledge and capabilities to assist earthly people. There are no limitations for energy, in contrast to physical limitations. So while there has not ever been one unified witch "cult," the unifying factor is there in the way these humble, uneducated women received advanced knowledge that was the envy of the church: their Spirit World connection. And, as was documented in Milan, the most average of women would receive visionary visitations from the Great Goddess, who taught them the secrets of nature and offered other information that was always true. These women were not priestesses, just average women being visited by the supernatural.

Why is this information about regions and separations important? Because while there is currently one unified language in Italy, there are many factors that make Italy, in the words of native Italians, not a unified country at all. While the folklore speaks of a "Cult of Witches," no one really knows who they are. This is why one singular system or practice of witchery in Italy cannot be traced back to a single origin except for the original transmissions in pre-historical times. Calling witchery in Italy "Italian Witchcraft" is the act of naming something that doesn't exist as a single, unified practice with a set of tools and rules you can read in a book and learn and call yourself a practitioner of. "Stregoneria" is an historical name which brings up more questions and more mystery.

There is a whole other world of poverty- driven magic, male-based ceremonial magic, folk magic and more, and none of it is the same as the Lineage practices. Even trying to entitle one specific path as "Italian Magic" would be erroneous, because… which type of magic? Italian Lineages are the only consistent "ways" that have existed in Italy because the Lineages are not created by earthly human beings and are therefore not limited by economics, nor talents, nor ego, nor will. Magic is craft whose successes depend upon many factors, mostly on the abilities of the user.

Dedication to promoting the truth, honoring the path of women

Italy is a place heavily laden with folklore and fantasy, and I found much of the fantasy-side of witchery to be perpetuated by male writers: both writers from the past and modern authors who are mesmerized by the secret world of these women. In translating the dozens of books I was gifted while in Italy from all my gracious hosts, I found that male writers were difficult to translate, their writings being full of these imaginary and fantastical ideas or very dry facts about life during the time period of these women. Male Italian writers have a wonderful gift of listing and categorizing facts and figures previously reported, so their writings are often resources of names of Goddesses and Gods and old folklore stories and mythical legends and reports of lifestyles and collections of magical recipes. Thankfully, they are reiterated in their books and not forgotten, but as to the true core of witchery's apple, you probably won't find it in the many male-published writings, but you would rather important documentation about the atmosphere around them. And their documentation gave me other perspectives and ideas that helped me understand myself and my context in all of this in new ways.

In fact, stories about witches that entered the popular tradition, as it is called in Italy, are always negative and unruly and ugly sounding; whereas pagan myths represent power, structure and order. Both sets of stories are written by men in power. Italy's witches have never had their own "public propaganda" machine.

There are however, Italian men who've devoted their lives and their writings to reclaiming Inquisition documents as well as historical information as they are, so that some truth shines out there. Author and professor Paolo Portone is one of these men and has been a constant source of assistance for me during my research as well. Another author who is the main reason I returned to Italy this second time is Carlo Napolitano, a sincere writer whose work walks a fine line between the Great Mysteries and actual places where they occurred, and myth; Fabio Garuti, whose earnest research delves deep into the underbelly of what women endured during the Inquisition but also shares their vast amount of knowledge; Enzo Gravina is an author and researcher from Benevento's who's documented magical history, curing herbs, spells and recipes from Campania; Silvio Falato, a folk lore expert on the Janara and etymologist, Sandro Oddo whose books document curing traditions of the Valle Argentina as well as Triora's Inquisition. Two female authors of note: Luisa Muraro whose work focuses on the feminine shamanism as documented in Italy's Inquisition, and the most exciting book I've read that gives the most precise outsider look inside the Lineage healers of Emilia Romagna is by author and anthropologist Antonella Bartolucci. Additionally, I was guided towards this ancient Divine Feminine spirituality threaded through Italian Witchery and the historical moments when the spirit- world-to-earthly women happenings occurred by Manuela Saccone, of Finalborgo's Museum, and I was guided to Carlo Ginzburg's books by the Benandanti themselves.

Miraculously enough, or perhaps I should say "magically enough," the people I met, was cured by, given lessons by, whom I interviewed and lived with are the ones who told me all the truths in this book. In their recorded interviews I literally have everything from the inside to the outside. However, all the authors, researchers, museum directors and professors gave me another way to understand what the women had showed me and told me, because while I knew I was witnessing incredible things, I didn't realize always at the start how profound all these meetings and experiences and interviews would be: it was all so natural…and humbling and deeply healing, and my Spirit Guides offered me an understanding that went even deeper, as a Medium. That's the magic of Italy truly; that magic and miracles are everywhere, right under your nose (at least outside of the cities where I spent my time), but if you decide what Italy's witchery is before you open yourself to experience it…you might just walk right on by it.

All of these Italian native authors contribute to the explanation of what are Italian Witches, along with Marija Gimbutas' decades of work compiled in her book "Language of the Goddess" to show that this Italian tradition has more in common with Shamanism and its solitary practitioners who remain connected to the Spirit World's guidance, whether naturally or in very aware and educated ways. It is a far cry from modern forms of witchery, paganism, Goddess churches, and ritualistic groups. These are completely unrelated to Italian witchery traditions. It is not possible nor correct to list here a handful of spells and call these "Italian Witchcraft," in fairness to all of Italy which has a very long history, cultural melting-pot influences that are different per region, many diverse expressions, and all the other interwoven modern practices that have been attached to the name "Italian witchery" but are not.

In our current times, establishments like modern ones serve an important purpose, however, and are necessary for those of us still seeking and who feel cut-off from our own traditions. It's a common feeling for many spiritual seekers to feel disconnected from their communities as they begin to "remember" who they are. In this way, these public organizations and public personas act like lighthouses in a rough sea for the rest of us who are still coming out of the "broom closet," as a point of light we can search for and find, to help us reflect ourselves upon someone else's path as we search for our own. But that's what they all are: someone else's path with often no roots in history.

Clarifications need to be made as much as they can be, as I've been encouraged to do by many of the people I met in Italy, since so much damage has been done to the reputations of "Italian Witches" for hundreds of our modern years and many more before that, through lies and strategic misinformation by people in positions of power. So to clarify, the only unifying factor among Italian witches of all regions is: the Spirit World helpers who pass on the knowledge: the Signora di Gioco, the Buona Raes, Madonna Oriente, or, if you prefer to call it: the energy from which we all come: the Grande Dea.

The Differing Characteristics Between Italy's Witchery and Pagan Practices

The women I met (and a few men), of various Lineages all had these things in common:

- Italian witchery is solitary practice: the Italian witch operates on her own after being taught specific techniques that remain as they are handed down to her, unaltered.

- At a certain point in their lives they went through a specific transition.

- The transition occurred at a specific age: 15 or 16

- Their relative (grandmother or mother) gave them a transmission (a touch through the hands most often), then

- Their relative shared with them secret actions, prayers, marks to make, invocations to use during a curing session

- They were taught procedures (like using oil and water to make "occhi" and then they had to learn on their own).

- They do not share the secrets of her powers, and often doesn't get paid in any form for a cure.

- They are allowed to teach what they can, in discretion, but some things must remain secret.

- They learned, for a period of time, how to cure (especially with finger massage and other anatomical procedures) alongside their relative until they were then set out on their own.

- There's a sense that they are embedded where they are: they are in service, and as women in service they need to be available, so these are not women who are traveling around, exploring. This is also why the Lineages are dying out, with the last remaining ones of the lines now in their late 80s and 90s.

- The training is one-on-one

- Lineage cures are mostly about other people: they have the ability to cure her own physical, mental, and spiritual imbalances, but their work is for the service of others.

- The power to cure is considered "borrowed" because it is channeled: it is not inherently the power of the earthly Lineage healer.

- There are no covens.

- There are no group rituals.

- Italian witches are initiated: either by a direct family member who is of a Lineage, or of an inherited family member (such as an In-Law) who is of a Lineage, or directly from the Spirit World, through "transmission." The Spirit World Lineage is also very specific, and the teachings occur during an unfoldment path that clearly shows the Initiate the consequences of properly or improperly using the Lineage secrets.

- In some cases, when a person was meant to be given the transmission but their relative passed to the Spirit World before completing the process, the relative, from the Spirit World, completes the transmission of energy through an earthly living relative. Then the Spirit relative continues to teach the new earthly Lineage healer from the Spirit World just as they would had they been on earth.

- In some Lineages, women pass their secrets when it is time for them to pass out of this earthly life and into the Spirit World: upon their death transition. Once they pass the transmission, the power disconnects from them and connects to the new Lineage healer. The older Lineage woman has now completed her purpose, and her life force also leaves her physical body.

- The Lineage secrets and energy transmissions do not always get passed down. I met many women from families with Lineages who did not get passed the transmission. Being born into a family with Lineage healers does not mean you are meant to become one. It is not your choice.

- Among the ones who use herbs, because not all do, they harvest their own plants from the nature near them, they don't buy herbs at the store.

- The path is a contract: one does not begin and then abandon the path. There is only one Initiation: it is not a reward but rather signals the beginning of the path, which is continually guided by the Great Mother Goddess and also aided by ancestors.

- There is no male god counterpart to the Great Mother Goddess teacher nor the earthly Lineage Mother. There are male Lineage healers, and while they mostly receive the Lineage secrets through their male family lines, the process is still feminine and receptive, both a service and a channeled energy. A male "mago" (magician) or "stregone" (wizard) is another thing.

With the herbalists, these commonalities expressed in similar ways:

- They learned what they know orally, through an older relative

- The more "modern" ones went to school also briefly, and learned from a solitary teacher

- They were then on their own, to learn in nature from nature, how to become planters and harvesters

- There's a sense that they are embedded where they are: they are in service, and as women in service they need to be available, so these are not women who are traveling around, exploring. They live on the nature, to tend to it. They don't buy their medicinal herbs from a store, but gather them in the seasons from the wild. (The exception being the modern herbalists who may teach occasional classes in the villages and cities or on their land).

Italian lineage healers feel it is a duty to keep the secrets because they are a great responsibility; not because the women who have them consider them a material possession that they own. Similarly, with the herbalists I met, they follow the ephemeris for planting and harvesting cycles, and use only sunlight and moonlight to infuse medicinal plants into oil and water: no artificial lighting nor heating is used, only nature. They care for the nature so the nature can do what it already knows how to do.

Myths: the Patriarchal Cover-up of the Great Goddess as Source of All Life

To untangle the web that Italian witchery has been mistakenly woven into with modern witchcraft and paganisms and wicca, ceremonial magic and folk magic, it's necessary to look at this historical roots of these practices to understand where the come from, what is their inheritance, and what was their original purpose.

The significant difference between Paganism and Italy's Witcheries is most easily seen when we look to the Pagan Gods and Goddesses and their stories: here we see the changing of feminine and matrilinear nature into a synthetic masculine "creative force" that makes absolutely no sense in a Macrocosm/Microcosm parallel.

For example, in the creation story of Roman Mithras, he was born from a rock (not from a mother). According to the Roman poet Ovidius, Jupiter had previously given birth to his daughter, Minerva, through his forehead using only his mind. This is a pattern, and these are just a few examples of men giving birth from parts of a body which can't scientifically give birth. There are no examples on earth of animals or people giving birth in these ways. And yet, in Italian folklore and in current religious beliefs, "miracles" coming from the men, such as the saints, are seen as truth, no matter how strange their claims are Miracles coming from women have a negative and "devilish" taint to them, thanks to strong propaganda (followed up with convincing tortures) by the church.

The Pagan Goddesses (not the original ancient ones) have equally unnatural creation stories: Minerva was the Roman goddess of wisdom, and she was born with weapons from the head of Jupiter. Hesiod's story is that she sprung from the sea foam that formed around the severed genitals of Uranus. Bellona was an Ancient Roman goddess of war. In the historical times preceding the Roman times, there was no evidence of women leading wars nor needing to protect themselves with weapons, and yet we see in Paganism all the Goddesses "reborn" as warriors: not as conceptual warriors, but as battling warriors. While they are associated with gifting metallurgy and other arts and crafts, the purpose of this gifted knowledge was to better the quality of life (for women) and not to end it through death nor worsen it through subjugation, which are things that do happen to life in the presence of people wielding weapons.

The roles here have been reversed, and the gods have powers that have been taken from the Goddess through "overthrows" of her natural abilities. Of course, no "Goddess" was overthrown or "killed;" she was simply "written" out of power and usurped in folk tales with "stronger gods." The stronger "God" overthrowing the Goddess stories supported earthly men in their overthrow of other people; showing by example "hey, the gods do it, so it's ok for us to do it;" a form of propaganda that we see over time being used again and again to usurp "perceived" enemies and to affirm the male might. This is a technique utilized in Roman times: when a new Emperor took the throne, his image and his patron God were advertised through coinage and sculptures and murals: the former Emperor was depicted as being "defeated," along with his God patron.

Matrilinear communities were not based on war, and yet in Paganism suddenly we see Goddesses as hunters, weapons-wielding war-participants. The historical records show that it was the patriarchal invading tribes who created weapons and wars and enslavement of animals and people; unnatural ways of living that were against nature. Even in Italy today, there are magical battles between women, and some of them are quite ugly in poorer areas, but they use magic and not weapons. The exceptional strength of women has always been in using our minds; our secret inner worlds, our inner reserves of strength, our inner magic and our emotions to protect ourselves and process our experiences.

So this strange evidence of usurpation is there for all to see, documented by the men in power themselves, and these stories of gods as creators are part of paganism. In these myths, men have been re-modeled into gods who, like the Universe, give birth to all, when in truth he cannot by any natural means. The macrocosm-microcosm parallel doesn't work, even though the world has accepted that "God" is a man and the "Father" of all based on religious myths. Simply, the unnatural creation myths support the unnatural patriarchal order.

Men can't give birth to any life form without the female because they have no wombs. Men have a physically different relationship with the process of birthing life; not being able to receive "seeds" into their bodies to be nurtured and then harvested/birthed as new, independent life. Their relationship with life is outside of that process, it is different. There's no need to fight this. There are also women who can't have babies or choose not to, there are people of other genders who don't give birth either: it's not only about the physical process of birth but more so the inner world of feminine energy and its receptiveness to all other energies. The feminine energy inherent gives a positive connection to life. Every human's body is a vessel for their spirit.

The male creation of war and weapons doesn't improve life; they damage it. In order for the male gods (and socially influential myths) to claim a leadership position over Goddesses and their omphalos-like womb, men re-created stories, which largely have to do with invasions, wars, and destruction of Goddesses and women, in order to support their tactical lifestyle. They synthetically re-created and re-versed the natural and "supernatural" creation stories to support man as being like the male god, including the power to give birth, and supporting all their other synthetic ways of of producing life (animal husbandry, rape, food distribution, medicine, the industrialization of life).

The macrocosm-microcosm parallel makes natural sense with the Great Mother/ Goddess/earthly mother parallel, being that mothers on earth do give birth through their bodies, they do nurture babies-to-be in their bodies until they become independent life forms, they feed (from their bodies and later with external nourishment), they teach and care for children throughout life, they trade tips with other mothers, and in this way they are natural community leaders (or can be).

The feminine community is about being present in the moment: answering the call to who needs care and how can they be cared for. In this way, it's an inclusive community that came about naturally: no other lifestyle needed to be "overthrown" or targeted as an enemy. This natural community is about life and offering opportunities for balance when brings challenges into the mix. In contrast, men are seen as being active outside the home doing their things in the greater world, on the terms of the world's societies (or making new ones). Pairs of Gods and Goddesses have been "remodeled" by the Minoans, then Greeks and Romans to represent the patriarchy's directives: war, social dominance, control of women, and more.

That in these pagan myths gods had to "overthrow" Goddesses, they kill their powerful mothers and sisters, is another important reveal: there was a power and a system already in place BEFORE the "heavenly god overthrows" and earthly invasions: the Matrilinear and Matriarchal ones. Therefore, in historical, spiritual and and global truths, the mediumistic power and connection between women and their Goddess teachers and femi-centric life came first: both in the physical world and as reflected in spiritual stories and artifacts. Then, men took over, and we have the result: our broken, rotting, disconnected, poison and war-filled unnatural world as a result.

Even if you don't want to believe the founders of the earthly world were "witches," and even if you don't want to believe historically there was a universal agreement among earthly peoples that the Divinity was believed to be Female; a great mother, that all came from her and her parallel on earth is the earthly woman, even if historians and archaeologists don't want to acknowledge this: the people of the times who created the myths did: they believed in that Divine Feminine power, which is why they usurped the original and turned is masculine using the symbolic language that pointed to her and re-directed it in unnatural ways to eradicate her or sublimate her under the new masculine power.

While paganism is a much more natural religion than Big Religion, and science does support the symbols and practices (which is why is was and is still a threat to the Church), nevertheless it expresses synthetic and male-organized systems that unnaturally put "man" at the center of the Universe, center of family, center of society and all creation; where previously was the Divine Feminine Creatrix who offered purposeful knowledge to bettering life for all.

Paganism embraced both Gods and Goddesses in some of the branches' practices, but women were in fact demoted to being wives, fertility symbols, and partners to men and always connected to them and also always disconnected from the anything to do with life and life-production other than in a smaller, more earthly way: the Universe in Paganism is dominated by the gods. Even the "underworld" realm, in myths the place where our relatives and friends pass over to after death of the physical body, has become the domain of men.

In the more ancient Goddess religion, "she" was the Medium, the communicator with both higher consciousness a as well as with the ancestors. Death was not seen as a failure. Her womb is also the tomb: death and regeneration work together and are inseparable. But in Paganism, we see the "gods" having stolen this place and as dangling the keys for example, in the myth of Proserpina. In this myth, she is kidnapped and forced to submit to his will in the underworld. Facing her death by his force, surrendering to his will, she is instead given the "keys to the knowledge of the Universe," which she didn't need having already been gifted it by the Goddess long, long ago. Pagan myth tries to paint this story as one of romantic "love and the heart" opening the doors to knowledge; but really it's the story of man enslaving woman, or a woman being rewarded for submitting to male violence. After all, there are Italian sculptures depicting what they call "The Rape of Proserpina."

We can see how these stories and myths this can impact society: where even in Paganism there is room for woman alongside man as long as she supports him: a good wife is like a good

Goddess: she supports war, killing, his needs, is jealous and petty and will attack other women. There are the Goddesses in their pagan make-overs: being like average, everyday, petty earthly women...disconnected form all her natural power and magic, where her wildness is looked at negatively, as something that needs to be controlled by man.

And where does this leave people of other genders? In the quiet worlds of shamanism around the world, there is an acceptance of many genders: not just the binary and standard "man and woman." Just as naturally as there are energies seen as "masculine and feminine" which are different from what is a societally created man and woman, there are blends of energies and people who are born with these different blends of energy. Only the more structured and socially-controlling religions practice "divide and conquer," "right and wrong."

The patriarchy has damaged men as well; with its role-models of invaders seeking to "kill" the feminine, to "hunt" after life, to control and takeover nature, leaving no inspiration to receive, to surrender to anything other than a weapon, thus closing off the subtle psychic realm. It's no coincidence that I know quite a few young Italian men who grew up with macho fathers or no fathers at all, and have had to work through this masculine damage through meditation and other receptive practices that connect them with healing feminine energy, and in several cases, through Goddesses themselves. These are examples of men I know being reached out to by the Divine Feminine as she works with them in meditation to heal. The Goddesses are not reserved for only women.

Italian witches, like Antonietta, have survived war and are still traumatized by it. She has never been a supporter of war. The town center of Triora, which she now calls home, had been hit by the war. In fact, the new Ethnohistorical Museum of Witchcraft, which had its official inauguration in December 2016, and whose Science Director is author Paolo Portone, is housed in a building that was ravaged by the war but reconstructed and preserved as a landmark. In this town is Antonietta's home, in an old medieval building, and it's full plants; living plants and dried ones, all of which she cares for and has harvested by herself.

An Italian woman's place of power is her home and its surroundings. This is where her practical magic takes place. The Hearth has long been considered to hold fire, the "brilliant guest," a gift of the Goddess, providing a living center of the family and community.[128] It's in the Italian woman's kitchen that she works with the herbs and plants and the knowledge to use them for nourishment and curing.

Paganisms in Italy created special buildings for magical ceremonies and ritual.

Society has tried to turn this into something negative: " a woman's place is in the home," with a derogatory meaning, a patriarchal value of the home being something "lesser than" out in the world, a place to keep women segregated and tucked away from the world's offerings and power. But in this secret inner world is her power. This is her the earthly omphalos where the nurturing comes from, the cures, the illumination of magic in daily life.

Whether an Italian witch who channels the Goddess knowingly as her practice, or a humble healer using magic in her secret inner world: this Magic is from the Mother.

Second Secrets

Before I met my husband in person, we were introduced online, and we came to know each other as energy, rather than as flesh-and-blood people. I lived in the Bay Area of California, and he lived in Italy. Being 9 hours apart, I would inevitably be asleep when he would reply to my emails. Yet each night, I would suddenly awake at 2 am or so, often feeling an enormous, expanding sensation of energy coming out of my heart. On occasion, this energy was strong enough to lift my head and torso off my pillow and bed. Upon each awakening, I'd run to my computer and see an email from him, having been sent one or two minutes ago at the most.

During this time I was training as a healer using Reiki energy to cure physical symptoms of people and animals in person, and I was also experimenting with healing people "at a distance," by sending it, for example, to someone who lived 3,000 miles away.

At a certain point, as we got to know each other, I felt the need to ask him if I could send him some healing energy. He said yes, and we arranged a time where he could be cognizant of my efforts, so we could share our experiences with each other after-the-fact. He wrote me after our arranged time, reporting that he did feel the energy moving to a spot on his body where he'd been having pain in his intestines (which he hadn't told me previously). Also, he told me his own hands heated up (apparently he'd learned pranotherapy from someone before). I urgently convinced him to go to the doctor. He emailed after his visit to tell me he would in fact be going to the hospital to stay for a a few days because now that his secret illness had been "outed," the pain became too great to hide. The doctor told him he was too inflamed to have a little camera search inside of him. First, they'd need to care for him and reduce the inflammation before they could even examine him completely.

I sent him healing energy for those 3 days, and we eventually shared our experiences of that time. The doctor sent him home with medicine and a suggested diet.

But I sensed something was wrong and asked him how he felt. "Still in pain," was his answer. I asked him his diet. He told me what he'd been eating, and my response was that his medications were too strong and his diet was dehydrating him. I urged him to return to the doctor, so he went to see a different doctor in France who told him: his medications were too strong and his diet was dehydrating him.

I asked him if I could continue to send him energy to heal his intestines and he agreed. When he returned to his original doctor to get the internal exam, the doctor could find no trace of him having any intestinal illness whatsoever.

Chapter 3:

"Categories of Italian Witches"

"My Truest Life is unrecognizable, extremely interior
and not a single word can describe it"

- Clarice Lispector, tr. by Benjamin Moser, from "the Hour of the Star"

Italy's witchery is a female Lineage shamanism, given to earthly people from the Spirit World. This Lineage is how earthly human beings survived all the limitations of life on earth, and learned the mysteries of consciousness, beginning in our founding days. The Spirit World's purpose has been to assist human beings to improve life through communication with the Spirit World (called channeling). This communication has put earthly women, who may be limited by poverty and socio-economics, in touch with the exact knowledge to cure, to teach, to know whatever they need whenever they need to know it. This access to unlimited knowledge is the true magic.

The 3 categories of Italy's Witches I will share with you here follow a pattern: whenever communities and societies went through harsh changes and women were subjugated under men yet again and forbidden to cure, to read, write, communicate with each other, etc, the Spirit World's Divine Feminine Guides appeared in visionary form to reconnect women with advanced knowledge of the Universe, to be used in practical, down-to-earth ways. The categories themselves are a response to societal changes. This is "service work," after all, and just as needs of early Mothers changed over time and the Spirit World continued to provide the means, the Spirit World also acknowledges the needs of those who seek the help of the Witches and provides through these channels as well.

We have three main time periods for women in Italy: foundational matrilineal and gylanic, post-patriarchal invasions, post-Inquisition. These post-gylanic periods witnessed women abused, subjugated, and forbidden to use their secret knowledge, even murdered for it. The division between men and women deepened and criticisms of other genders began.

It is important to know that one category does not have all the knowledge, neither in their own category nor across categories. Each category serves and important purpose for specific environments. This is the basis of Spirit World relationships-the earthly channel must trust their Spirit Helpers, even when they can't see the entire picture. In fact, this is how, in Mediumship training, students learn to communicate with the Spirit World in the first steps: bit by bit…asking a question and receiving a portion of an answer..and building in trust, from there.

CATEGORY ONE: Earthly Mothers as LINEAGE healers

Earthly mother Lineage healers are humble, everyday women who embody something "otherworldly"- The Divine Feminine brought down to earth. These women would never take this credit. They aren't connected to modern culture. They are entrenched in their communities, and they've lived a life of service : to their families, to their communities, and to their borrowed knowledge.

Lineage healers follow a specific set of actions to cure ailments (in-person and at-a-distance) that have been handed down to them from a direct-line family member (mother "madre," grandmother "nonna," or grandfather "nonno," or in some regions to a daughter-in-law. In rare cases, a Lineage healer will pass their Lineage to someone who is not blood family.

These actions and secret processes and are not amended, they are respected and honored just as they are received. They are accompanied by the use of secret prayers, invocations, or songs that always remain secret. A lineage is passed partly through energy transmission and partly through oral teaching. It is not uncommon for the Lineage healer to not understand how the cures really work. They have received the "gift" but cannot explain it.[129]

HOW IT STARTED:

In the earliest days, earthly women shared their knowledge with each other, as freely as it was given to them. They were all "community," and the community took care of each other. As tribes and families developed, "Lineages" for these "legacies" (of knowledge and its application, such as cures), were created through a process of "passing it down." Earthly women were guided in these secret procedures to pass them onto younger women in their family line or tribe (if someone was chosen, and if someone was in need.)

This system began with the earliest mothers in time, who were left to care for babies without their fathers. These women were gifted knowledge from Spirit World of Goddess teachers about all the necessary female support they would need to care for life around them: the secrets of midwifery, planting and harvesting, curing with plants, teaching, nurturing, calculating, building shelter and containers, and more. Instead of partnerships with men, in these days the partnership bond women had was with Spirit Women.

HOW IT WAS ADAPTED BY SPIRIT:

In response to the patriarchal invasions of female and gylanic communities, when women became cut off from each other and the men established themselves as head of the household" and partnerships became binary in gender (and women were also held captive as slaves and for sex) this historical divide-and-conquer was met with assistance once again from the Spirit World reaching into the earthly one to provide a consistent system of "passing it down" through new types of family lines (our more modern version of families: small nuclear groups).

This category was originally provided to remain within family lines so it could be preserved and perpetuated. As time passed, and this ancient practice is still utilized in Italy, Corsica, Sardinia, and Sicily, the "passing it down" tradition expressed consistencies (which are now changing once again due to changes in the family structure).

The traditional coming-of-age for a healer to receive the secret knowledge and energy transmission is at 15 or 16 years. This could be called the "Initiation," but it is the "one and only" the Lineage healer will go through. It is not a reward, as is in some pagan practices, but rather marks a change in life, one that will endure for the remaining years of the Lineage healer's life, and one that marks their partnership with the Spirit World who will now heal through them, using them as the channel.

For the Lineage healer who is "passing it down," the tradition is for her to orally pass the secret knowledge as well as the energy when she is nearing the end of her life on earth. After she passes her Lineage, the energy withdraws from her, and her purpose is completed. Her cures depend on her being alive to give them, to be the physical channel for the Divine Feminine energy to channel-through.

Not all Lineage healers pass down their Lineage. The Lineages are dying out because their children are disinterested, with the age of new medicine, new careers, and the ability to explore the world, they don't want to remain in their villages. So the Lineage healers are guided to not "pass down" the Lineages. The purpose of the Lineage healer is to be available to cure who needs the cure, so the Lineage healer must also remain "constant;"to able to be found by the people who need her cures. Traditionally she remains where she is planted, so-to-speak.

I met several Lineage healers who have not passed down their Lineages, and I met several adult women whose mothers and grandmothers are Lineage healers but they have not received the Lineage from them.

Because the modern family structure is also changing, and people are choosing more "synthetic, city-living" over natural, living-in-nature and village-living, the Lineages are dying out. However, the Lineages are also trying to adapt. Antonella Bartolucci, in her spectacular book "Le Streghe Buone" (The Good Witches) explains that healers are trading information with each other over the internet these days, to keep Lineages going.

The new occurrence is that Lineage healers, without interested relatives to pass the Lineage, are passing down their knowledge outside the lines, and to other people who are adults, long past the 15, 16 years of traditional age. However, it seems the "constant" that has been retained, whether the knowledge is passed through the internet or in person, is that the Initiation Transmission occurs still on Christmas eve, December 24th.

LINEAGE METHODS:

The secret actions and marks or ingredients of the various healing Lineages are often mixed with religious prayers which have a Christian construct to them, largely due to the syncretism with Catholic religion. The prayer is simply the "medium," the channel through which energy flows from the Spirit World to the earthly one. The prayer itself does not cure, otherwise the person needing the cure could use the prayer to do so, and the belief behind the prayer is larger than the social construct of Catholicism.

In some Lineages there are specific prayers used connected to specific to saints who preside over specific areas of the body.

Some Lineages use only prayers to cure, such as in prayers songs that are whispered over the client who needs curing.

Other Lineages use common household objects given as a talisman of sorts through which to transmit the cure along with prayers.

Some Lineages just use water to cure, running the water over the affected body part, "washing away" the evil.

Some lineages just use herbs to cure disease. They create hot steam baths and facial steams and poultices. Herbs are also infused into oil, naturally, aided by heat from the sun and a cooling down from the moon, or they are drunk as teas.

Some Lineages cure with just a prayer and a person's name (at-a-distance) over the telephone or even with no connection, using the light of the moon in specific phases.

Some Lineages employ the cupping method.

Others use pots and pans with heated water to which they add crosses made of straw to diagnose the illness. Then the water, once cooled, is used to wash over the body part to cure it, to "wash away the evil." In the past, some healers, mostly men, used a lamb's heart and pins pushed into it to remove the evil causing the illness or as an exorcism. Others use teacups and straw crosses.

They don't take payment for their cures.

There are male Lineage healers called "sciatica cutters" and ones called "firemen" and "magnetizers" who use the application of heat through two pieces of metal (a household spoon with a hole in its center and a pointed tube) along with prayers to relieve the pain of sciatica.[130] Incidentally, "magnetism" was a name given to a Mediumistic healing modality discovered by a physicist named Franz Mesmer who is considered to be an important part of the foundational days of early Spiritualism. This technique reportedly cured people with the help of Spirits and was put into use during 1780 and 1850.

Filomena, a Lineage healer from Guardia Sanframondi, used "occhi" with oil and water to diagnose and cure "Il Malocchio." She also uses a pointy-finger massage called simply "zfrca," which is the dialect form of "strofinare," meaning to rub.

There are many methods, and a commonality among all the channeled energy that is not talked about. If you ask many Lineage healers how their methods work, they will tell you they don't exactly know and they don't question it, because it works, and they leave the mystery to remain the mystery.

With the exception of Antonietta, who credited the Madonna for saving her life, but she didn't particularly like that "title" most remaining Lineage healers are in their 80s and 90s and don't like to put a name to the Divine energy they channel.

The younger ones are more able to express what they do and how they do it with more modern language: *"We have kept a connection with the world of spirits,"* says a healer from Corsica in a must-read article called "Les guerisseurs, au-dela de la Science" (The Healers, Beyond Science) [131] Being that this is a type of shamanism, where many things occur "unseen to the naked eye," and not fully understood by the healer the energies that pass through them, it is difficult for them to explain their processes. The Spirit healers who channel through the Lineage healers know so much more than we earthly people do: Some healers do learn about these technical aspects, from the Spirit World, but most just "do the work, the service," and let the mysteries be the mysteries.

And this, this Mediumistic connection, is indeed the true secret. The Spirit Healers do the actual healing through the human healer and the human patient. The earthly people are willing conduits for this miraculous process.

I believe the mysteries should remain secret and hidden. These mysteries are different from the ones available through magic. They are more expansive than what is available through magic. The acts of magic (and the always not entirely knowable results) are dependent upon the skills of the magician..but they are also symptomatic of the magician's benevolence or malignancy. Magic can be forced, and it can be forced upon someone as well, breaking the free will of another.

The miracles available through Lineage Mediumship are not in the command of the earthly person. They are given to the earthly person temporarily, for the duration of the service. They remain unknowable. Therefore, the Mediumistic relationship, in its most positive and expansive version, is based on the concept of "to love is to let go." After meeting Lineage healers I believe this is why they refuse payment, why they don't want any lingering debts or ties to their patients, why they operate "under-the-radar," and why they blend into the environment around them. There is no ego nor stardom here, no potential for Big Business.

This does not mean these miracles are unattainable. The attainment is the result of a surrender, trust, service and devotion to a higher consciousness. In our modern social terms we would also consider this to be a type of "sacrifice," because we tend to want to be free to "do what we want." While Lineages certainly are not gloomy prisons, for sure thoughts have passed among their minds of other types of dreams and hopes, or of personal desires to do other things, even with all the gratitude they have for their "borrowed gifts." Because you won't find a Lineage healer who complains, but it is natural, when one is put "on a path," to recognize, through comparison, how differently the "rest of the world" lives their lives. The Lineage healer is the constant: the train station through which all the trains and people pass. The train station cannot disdain its purpose, because then its purpose would dissolve. Its purpose is to be of service, "to love and to let go."

"Pranoterapia: (pranic healing) is used in Italy as well. Like Reiki, it is not naturally uses as a Mediumistic healing modality (not used with the help of Spirit healers) but it can be. Someone who learns pranic healing can learn to channel higher Spirit energy along with the Universal energy of the pranic healing, but it is truly up to the Spirit healers to decide if they will "adopt" the earthly healer or not. Pranic healing is therefore not the same thing as Lineage healing, but it can become one of the Lineage healer's methods.

Technical Names for Lineage Practices

- healers (guaritori)

- meridian healers (medgona)

- midwives (levatrice)

- sciatica cutters (sciatica tagliatori)

- fire breaker/cutters (taglia fuoco)

- magnetizers (magnetizzatori)

- healers-scorers (guiaritori-segnatori)

The Number 3:

- The number 3 is significant in Lineage healing.

- Marks, when used, are traced on the body three times.

- A full cure is performed three times.

- When making "occhi" for "Il Malocchio,"(the Evil Eye) putting the oil in the plate of water must be done three times.

- Prayers are often said 3 times.

Both Diagnostic and Curative:

- With Lineage cures, there is both a diagnosis and a cure.

Specific Ailments Cured:

- "Colpo delle streghe," the "blow of the Witch" for example, which consists of a slight slip of the cartilage disks that lie between the vertebrae. The most common symptom is acute and widespread pain in the lower back which is resistant to medications.[132]

- "Bad blood," or stagnant blood that causes illness.

- Intestinal worms (people and animals)

- Nerve disorders

- Eczema

- St Anthony's Fire (a painful skin issue that feels like fire)

- Herpes

- Muscle and tendon sprains and twists

- Burns

- Inflammation

- Sore throat

- Lumbago (low back pain)

- The Evil Eye "Il Malocchio"

- Warts

- Sty

- Heart Conditions

- Liver disease

- and more...

CATEGORY TWO: Community Mothers and Adopted Witch Daughters

This category refers to the type of "Teaching Mother" who works often with groups of trainees, still in a relative amount of secrecy, whereas Lineage healers give their Transmission to only one person, or one person at-a-time.

This form of spiritual "adoption" developed naturally and historically: This natural community type of service is also from early historical times of invasions and disruptions to the harmonious feminine way of living and expressing an abundant and Divine Feminine spirituality. As communities and feminine groups were split apart by men (Minoan invaders, various Italian Emperors, the church and its Inquisition), many women chose to not be in families, considering the "nuclear family" structure is a result of male invasions and wars. In more modern times, because of this ability and desire to live alone or among women, they were often a target of Inquisition and church as being "abnormal." This period in Italy, after all, is marked by the church arranging marriages as a form of social control, while they were also deterring people from going to women healers (so as to push clients towards the church's "healers," who incidentally, were unsuccessful in healing anyone…that is, until the men "died" and became saints. Allegedly then they, after being "sainted," sent their healing powers back to earth through statues. But while on earth they were quite successful in instigating hatred towards their competition, so ferociously that attention was detracted from their lack of cures).

Often young women who were not married, in particular in the Triora, Albenga, Badalucco, among other villages in the northwest, were were kicked out of their families and communities in these early 1500s due to social fears of being targeted as witches and potential nervous-neighbor finger-pointing. These young and sometimes single or widowed old women had to live out under the oak and walnut trees, thus becoming outcasts and orphans. Others still, as the Inquisition rolled forward, escaped to the city of Benevento in the south, a city which became a safe haven from the Inquisition due to strange political circumstances.

These women were visited by the Spirit World's "Bona Dea" and "Signora di Gioco" to be given the knowledge yet again. Being no longer part of their own family Lineage, they became "new Lineages but not quite the same." Their services were not for the nuclear family but, as was adapted to their circumstances by the Spirit World, theirs were services for the community. This Community Medium, we could say, is for healing townspeople, offering a variety of curative and often magical services, and as a teacher to other young women, and sometimes men.

In fact, author Enzo Gravina told me that there was indeed an "official witch school" in San Bartolomeo in Galdo until the 1940s. The "boss" of the school was called "Mary of The Red Hair."

Several young witches I met in the eastern part of Italy, in the region of Udine, learned from a Community Mother, which was someone they found online and met with, physically, in a group, to learn magical spells and practices. There was not an emphasis on healing in their "circle," but rather learning more about about the Spirit World and their duties within it, herbs, and magical workings, and dreamwork.

This is not the same as Lineage healers and it is not taught as a Mediumistic method, even though this is how it began originally, with the Mother Teachers receiving their knowledge through channeling from the Spirit World. The students are not taught to be mediumistic healers, though students are taught to work with the Spirit World. The focus is on "ghostly" passed-on earthly people, as in learning to discern who they are and help them cross over, if necessary.

They do have initiations, the details of which they are not able to fully disclose to the public. While they did share more with me, this is the version of what I can share with you:

"It's quite hard to draw a line between what can be said and what cannot. I think it's safe

to describe the rite as a strongly symbolical one, involving the image of the soul traveling in the otherworld in a path that leads it to be born again. Our initiation had a more "ceremonial" allure with a strong symbolic structure. It had traditional elements but it wasn't in itself 'traditional.'

Our mother didn't die after passing us our "marks" although our initiation marked the beginning of the decline of her power and consciousness" Historically speaking, a witch was bound to give her/his own power to an heir just before he or she died. The power was transmitted by touch, holding hands. In some cases this seems to be happened in modern times too but we had a specific initiation rite."

In training with a "community mother," all "students" are considered to be "on the same level." Growth is not determined by the Mother Teacher, but is rather supported by her. The Mother Teacher does impart the Initiation, but Initiation is the invitation "in," rather than the reward. This is what connects Italian witchery in every form to our most ancient history: Initiation being a symbolic "death" of one's relationship to the physical world in a conceptual sense. Initiation marks the beginning of a new way of living, both intimately and forever changed by the mark of the Initiation. The Initiation is the mark of this new way of living in service; it is not an honor nor a reward bestowed up-on a person "from the votes of her peers," nor as something "earned" due to accumulation of hard work.

The community Mothers-student relationship is one that I probed further about, curious about "do-it-yourself" magic versus learning magic in a training environment in Italy.

I asked: Are rituals/actions of a witchcraft nature able to "work properly" without the initiation? In other words, is it the special power that makes the witchery work, or the recipe/ritual/actions?

"We are not entirely sure about other people's experience under a statistical point of view but we can say that there is a solid difference in consciousness, ability to feel and manage spiritual energy and to see patterns in magic and reality. It literally gives you more access to power (your own) and more tools to work with it, although it's important to remember that access to initiation is gained through a long process of learning and evolving. The process itself, though, doesn't give you the same "benefits" of a proper initiation and, actually, as far as we know, stopping before the initiation leads to a quick decline of ability and consciousness. This, of course, doesn't mean that somebody can't be powerful and effective without an initiation: it just means that this is the way our path goes. It's a bit of a "everything or nothing" kind of arrangement, we don't know why."

There is no male teacher parallel partnered with the Community Mother Teacher in the learning circle. This way of learning still retains the ancient Divine Feminine form. We still do not find the system nor structure of a "coven" with a male high priest and female high priestess emulating the "masculine and feminine" aspects of energies in an earthly representative. Among the people I asked about this, they all told me this concept was from wicca or somewhere else, but not Italy.

"In traditional witchcraft there are no actual "priests," not meant as in a wiccan coven. But you can learn different skills from male and female teachers.

We believe that the special "something" runs in families but the transmission itself can be done outside the family, when needed. (i.e. if the 'mother' witch doesn't have children on her own, or the 'daughter' witch doesn't have magic practitioners alive in her family). I, for one, have a male lineage but in my generation most cousins are female. I also came from a big family and both my grandparents had the same family name. In both branches of the family there was a certain 'something.' My great-grandfather was a Medium."

These groups who learn with Community Mothers don't really have a name except, as I was told by young witches in the east, "a circle."

The only hierarchy is related to experience and age. *"Basing on what we have been taught and historical evidence, groups of witches seems to have acted as equals once they reached the same initiation level." And they told me this is the way it is in their circle also."*

These witches performed for me a very special fire ritual that took place very late at night and lasted at least 5 hours, perhaps going even longer. We all sat outside, around a large iron cauldron for which they created a fire using plants and woods from their own land. They created a special circle formation with invocations to the Spirit people they work with in a very symbolic procedure. I can't share those details, but I asked them to describe the inside of the ritual for you:

"I think that we can say that the fire acts as transformation element. We put inside it a series of symbolical 'ingredients' the fire transforms in something that is both the sum of everything and something different. There is a purification meaning, and we are purified by the fire that burns the DNA - carrying parts we burn (it's usually hair and nails but it can be lady pads too, for example) that symbolize ourselves and that is also useful because is not safe to leave them around since they can be used to perform magic against us. But there is also a transformation-transubstantiation meaning since everything is burned and 'cooked' together and is born again in form of spiritually charged ashes that have both our 'identity' transformed, and the power of the fire (spiritually charged in itself so it's like the archetype of fire, the meaning of fire and not just the fire itself."

Also put into the fire was old wax and a variety of specific indigenous herbs that were part of a family recipe. They repeatedly stoked the fire with addition of these items until the fire burned everything down into a black powder. Only then the ritual was completed. The energy of this ritual was so high-vibrational that I had difficulty in maintaining consciousness and "nodded out" frequently. I had only experienced energy at this high a frequency several times before, due to special circumstances in the presence of incredible trance channelers.

The result was this special powder to be used at a later time for a protection ritual that had its own invocations and actions to be performed while using it. I was most generously gifted some of this powder along with the instructions to use it during a significantly challenging time I had while working on this book. At the time, I was translating Inquisition documents about Franchetta Borelli, and the spirits of Inquisitors who had been trying to keep me from doing this began to amp up their influence the best ways they could: often through influencing people around me to induce angry outbursts as a way to "bully" me. I lived, at this time, in a typical haunted San Francisco house, so the spirits in the house as well as the other earthly people were being affected and directing their aggression towards me even though I had done nothing thought nor action-wise that had offended them. They were unconsciously accepting negative influence. And equally, on my side, while I was protected by my Spirit Guides and under nor true danger, the experience offered me, for the sake of learning, the sensations and feelings of being in very alarming danger. I was It was an isolating feeling, and these witches came to my aid and this powder brought all this secret "bullying" as negative spirits can be prone to do, to a head.

And in this way, women training under a Community Mother also are in the position to "pass down" knowledge as they see fit. So the circle of learning, in part, continues outside the localized "circle."

Community Mothers teachers have variety of knowledge and are more aware of what to "call" this knowledge, coming from less remote farmland areas and having more education and experience with modern lifestyles. Many Lineage healers are uneducated and can't even write. These are more generalized practices, similar to what we consider "magic witchery" in our modern communities today; practices that do a variety of work which focus more on magic than curing. Italians take their practices very seriously, honoring the long process it takes to master techniques.

CATEGORY THREE: The Wandering Witch, the Daughter of the Goddess, The One Who Knows the Secrets

While Lineage healers of Category 1 are often naturally intuitive, they are not always entirely aware of their Spirit partnerships, at least not having the language or technical understanding to truly express this idea. Consider that these women (and some men) are mostly in their late 80s and 90s now, and remain haunted by the idea that "witches" are evil and any aberration from normality would be punished by death. So that is a strong deterrent from "making too much noise," and it is also a deterrent from too much personal exploration of the Spirit World. It is common to find among these Lineage healers the belief that "evil" causes illness: evil thoughts and also evil spirits, so that healing often includes some type of exorcism. But, don't expect anyone to want to talk more about the Spirit World than this due to social misunderstandings that are so easily caused. Take also the fact that people tend to not want to attach humanity to the idea of the Infinite, so there is the resistance to create form around this Higher Consciousness.

In Category Three we have very "aware" Mediums.

These are Mediums who are "adopted Daughters" the Great Mother Goddess, and have "met" one or many incarnations of specific Goddesses (all of whom are traced back in their own lineage to the Grande Dea; the Divine Feminine energy from which all comes. These Mediums serve as an intermediate "mother" for seekers to whom she is directed by the Great Mother Goddess. And in some ways, these women are also "married to the moon," to the Goddess herself." Their communications with Goddess teachers is ongoing. This is an "all or nothing" path, and interestingly, this path presents itself to the Medium: it's not something she has planned for, but as her path unfolds, she discovers her entire life has been orchestrated to prepare her for the "aware" relationship with the Goddess. This is a path that gradually becomes more demanding, and the Medium finds herself, over time, living in the Spirit World much more than the earthly one, inevitably "unplugging" from the illusions of material life.

As mentioned before, channeling can occur naturally. Channeling is expressed in a variety of ways, In this Category, channeling is almost unnoticeable: the Goddesses' words come through the Wandering Witch as if they were her own. The earthly Witch is aware of everything that is happening. There is no loss of consciousness. The Goddess or whichever Spirit Guide and teacher is using the earthly Witch like a radio. This is a highly functional way for both parties to work together. These Mediums are aware of and communicates with Guides, Angels, and Spirits of all sorts. She is guided by the Spirit World to learn the Laws of Energy as the Spirit World knows them to be (and not the often misconceived notions of earthly humans) so that she can: navigate Spirit World experiences of all sorts, and recognize spiritual seekers on all paths.

In the past, this occurred among solitary women living in nature, as opposed to living in the villages and family configurations. This includes the "outcasts" who fled the northern regions during the Inquisition and came to Benevento and surrounding areas for safety under the strange political agreement that protected the city. These women, like the ones in the north excommunicated from their communities, lived under the shelter of nature. They were forced out of the material life of the rest of society. As part of this "runaway, outcast" condition, the Goddess offers them sexual healing and autonomy.

In this category, at a certain point her channeling becomes focused on Mediumship: the practiced art of regularly communicating with Spirit, and in this case, with Divine Feminine Spirit Guides. She will come to know more than one Goddess, and she will become aware that they have a Lineage just as human beings do. She then becomes a willing participant in this "teaching" service, and she moves where the Goddess Teacher Guides ask her to move. She can be like a lighthouse: shining the way for ships venturing into new waters, not directing their path specifically but helping the ship understand its own navigational abilities.

Several learning and teaching characteristics of this Category are:

- Using menstrual blood

- Understanding the passage of time beyond months and years and into a much more Universal perspective

- She recognizes as mother, as community mother..paths people are on..

- Using fire

- Learning a practice similar to tantra

- Reclaiming sexual power

- Natural teaching

- Healing

- Reclaiming historical secrets

- Understanding the technicalities of Mediumship

- Recognizing common threads in all spiritual practices

- Solitary, inner practice

- Daily channeling, communication

- Dreamwork- meeting people in dreams to teach or heal

- Recognizing other "adoptees" of the Goddess

- As a "teacher of a secret path," she cannot directly "name" herself to her "students:" the seekers must recognize her.

This last point is an interesting oddity: people living close to her in daily life can be completely unaware of who she is, whereas when the "aware" person comes along and this "teacher and student" are meant to learn from each other, 'school begins," and there is an understanding that occurs that doesn't need to be expressed.

In Paganism there is the persona of the High Priestess, who is a public figure expressing devotion to or a connection with a specific Goddess and performing a variety of services in private and in public, often part of the public temples, or as part of modern wiccan and magical circles, leading organized rituals. They teach and sometimes channel wisdom of their Goddess. They are paired with a male High Priest. While there is a history of women being Priestess and in charge of religious "institutions," this is a different role than the wandering witch.

The trouble with naming these women as "priestesses" here is that the most common usage of this term has been in Paganism and due to usage within this system (which is from the patriarchy) it denotes one half of a whole; the other half being the male version of her: the priest. In Paganism, these masculine and feminine roles serve a group of people, often called a "coven" (but not limited to this name because some "schools" are segregated by gender, such as the practitioners of Tempio di Mitra). Then purpose of these pagan systems is to gather as a group to practice and honor sacred spiritual practices and rituals for spiritual growth and learning. The group is led by other human beings, and there is a hierarchy in place (and opportunities to rise up in the hierarchy based on judgements of other people in the group so there is an external "leadership" relied upon: human beings obeying human authority.

Additionally, Paganism involves magical practices, rituals, and the learning of procedures (taught by other human beings) in places that synthetically reproduce natural surroundings (such as bringing the outdoors inside, and "creating" a ritual moment that is not already naturally occurring on its own). Paganism is a structured practice . This is what school is like essentially: working with a condition that is in a vacuum or a sterile environment (with no outside interference), so that it, and peoples' interactions with it, can be studied in a controlled environment. By using synthetic replicas of natural experiences and rewards based on performance and other (masculine) forms of hierarchy, we have an environment that offers constancy and repeatable experiences to learn from (and also the goal to reach of becoming a teacher who, in turn, can teach this structured practice to others). The magic practiced here strives to work in harmony with the flow of energy and its laws.

In Italian witchery, this path is very private and one-on-one. Men are not involved in this practice in any sort of partnership as teacher nor a lighthouse figure; there is no male counterpart to this "wandering witch" or secret "priestess" of Italian witchery. The Goddess brings men into the Medium's path to protect her on her journeys of discovery and for the men to learn the presence of feminine energy: this can bring them pain and this can bring them joy. It usually requires men to experience a great deal of struggle. The Medium attracts men who need healing, and she falls when she forgets this. "Standard" relationships do not work well for her. The "magic" the Wandering Witch will use is taught by the Goddess to her "in the moment," this expressing the concept of abundance. Additionally, magical "acts" such as spells fall away because of the lower nature of them and the consequences they often incur. The work of the Wandering Witch is about raising vibrations up, creating positive energetic changes for other people to experience.

Mystery Schools in Italy's past, such as the Tempio di Mitra, are exactly this: interior schools for learning, which take place in subterranean stone structures and who incorporate channeling of higher wisdom as part of their practice.

In contrast, the Wandering Witch's teachings are not reserved for only elevated studies within groups of people already "aware" of their own spiritual abilities, but rather among the everyday person, to help them remember their own magic. The Goddess' purpose as "provider of abundance" cannot be abundantly experienced in a "members only" environment.

The REASON

In these ancient spiritual practices perpetuated in modern times, the energy from which all people, places, and things come is "expressed" as being birthed from a Divinely Feminine Universe. Masculine energy is important and has a purpose, but it is naturally limited and temporary. The eternal flow of life is feminine energy.

This is naturally reflected in nature itself, seen more clearly in human pregnancy: while the male sperm is introduced into the womb of the female, this is the extent of his participation in co-creating a new life. He has no conscious participation after this, and even this act may not result in pregnancy. If the woman's body decides to have her eggs fertilized, it's the life force of the woman who incubates the process, it has nothing to do with male "will."

If the woman does become fertilized, for the next 9 months her body will be the source of nutrition and supply life for what will eventually become an independent baby human. Throughout the 9 months however, it is the mother's body who regulates itself as well as nurtures a developing new life which is wholly and completely dependent upon her. The coming baby will have no contact with the father until it becomes an external and independent form of human being which only occurs after it transitions out of the womb.

Likewise in nature the soil is like the fertile womb, the potential of the constant feminine flow. Once a seed is planted, the earth and all of her natural elements (water, sun, air, soil) care for the seed until it sprouts a new form of life. Masculine energy is stimulatory and can help to focus the stream of feminine energy into a manifested form. While nature takes its course regardless of human interference, for example, the act of fertilizing planted seeds helps to grow crops, both literally and conceptually. That moment of stimulation into a specific direction is the masculine energy: the flow, the constancy, the evolution is female.

John Randolph Price, a teacher and author of the Abundance Principles and author writes, *"The Law [of Abundance] is Presence, a Creative Mind possessing the absolute certainties of universal decrees […] The Divine Feminine within as the Law, Force, and Power of all manifest form and experience. This aspect of the Whole spirit known as the Divine Mother is the source of all visible effects. She is creative energy, substance, light, the agent of Divine Will. She is universal and individual, eternally flowing through the state of consciousness that we are holding before her."*[133]

Some examples of the way this Abundance is expressed coming from the Spirit World and passed down to the earthly one in this category as I've experienced them:

DREAMS

I have regularly been told by people, for most of my life, that I appear in their dreams and protect them or help them in some way. Sometimes I receive emails from people I haven't ever met. These people have seen my art or heard my music. Sometimes I receive emails or text messages from work acquaintances. Sometimes these admissions come from friends or people I have met in the past through musical performances.

The admissions fall into the same categories:

People have reported dreams where they have found themselves in danger and suddenly I appear and protect them from this danger. This danger can is sometimes related to a real experience they had in their life: for example, a work acquaintance shared with me that she's had a recurring dream for years where a male teacher from her past is trying to find and capture her. After we met, she reported having that same dream, but I appeared in the dream and shielded her from this man when he was searching for her, and this broke her dream pattern. Sometimes the danger is in the form of stress, where people have reported that I appeared in their dream and gave them a feeling of calm, and I protected them from whatever danger was about to happen.

I've also had men report to me that I appeared in their dreams and ignited a sense of hope and helped to repair something in them that was broken (mentally, emotionally).

A common admission from women is that I appear to teach them: sometimes I give them verbal solutions and advice to troubling situations, sometimes I offer encouragement. For example, a friend (who lives 3,000 miles away) told me she was dreaming that I was teaching her how to decipher ancient hieroglyphs and codes. Her sister came into the dream and knew exactly wha the codes were, expressed this, and walked away. My friend became frustrated, so I advised her to pay attention to the details and to not rush through things (which she admits she usually does).

EMBODYING GODDESS ENERGY FOR OTHERS TO EXPERIENCE

When I was regularly teaching Mediumship, both to beginners and to advanced students, I was also becoming more deeply acquainted with not only my Guardian Guide, but also the other Goddesses she was introducing me to. This is not something I shared with my students. However, during class exercises, students repeatedly reported seeing bright white Divine Feminine figures "behind and around" me, and would also report the energy feeling "very calm and peaceful, but also powerful enough to make them wobble on their feet."

THE GODDESS WATCHING OVER CREATIVE PROJECTS

During this time, I was also involved in a musical project, and had similar reports from the musicians:

I was meditating next to the room where my husband was checking files of the songs he'd written for our project. He is a prolific composer and is very adept at using technology to record. We had agreed that the songs were perfect, but for some reason he tried to change some parts. To his astonishment, both his computer and the protools program would not let him: each time he tried it would freeze or revert to the original, or in some way prevent him from making changes by doing something he'd never seen before. When I came out of my meditation he asked, bewildered, *"What were you doing in there?!"*

A session drummer I hired to record, 3,000 miles away, was writing sketches of the songs to send for us to listen to, for our approval. One of the songs bears the name of my Guardian Guide. He reported that he doesn't remember writing his parts for that song, nor the recording of them. He said that he just remembers pressing the recording button, but that his parts just wrote themselves.

Another drummer who recorded parts remotely reported, when he was done, he felt surrounded by Spirits who had been watching him.

APPEARING AS AN APPARITION

When I spent several years regularly giving Reiki healing energy to people, something began to happen when I'd sent it at "a distance;" sent healing energy to someone who was hours or thousands of miles away. They would all report, no matter in which country, seeing me appear with the energy, as a winged angel. This alarmed me because I was told that the Reiki energy comes from the Universe and not from individual people.

THE FEMALE BODY AS THE ECSTATIC TRANCE ITSELF

One of the ways my Guides continually teach me about this subject matter is to use my ability to sense, see, and experience people, places, and things as a Medium. If we think about the timing of this, my own abilities expanded after becoming a healer right before I went to Tuscany for the first time and was "re-introduced" to my Guardian Guide. This Guide led me on a trail that would have me train as a Spiritualist Medium. In this training I would test my ability to gather information from passed-on relatives, friends, and loved ones to discover if the communications I was having could be substantiated. This occurred for a couple of years and prepared me for my next trip to Italy. Before I went to Italy, I also spent almost a year seeing a naturopath who was trying to repaid my health conditions. One of those conditions was that, due to the American Medical Association destroying my immune system by pushing large amounts of prednisone into my body from a very young age, is that I didn't have regular menstruation periods. Many years I would only have one. Or none at all. My life was one without periods and without PMS…until this year before I went to Italy, I suddenly found myself, at 43 years of age, having regular periods…each month, the week of the full moon, following this exact same time schedule. This allowed me to be able to practice the use of catamenial blood in ritual, as was taught to me by Franchetta Borelli from the Spirit World before I went to Italy. Franchetta would pull me into her memories to show me how she used the blood, and to have me sense how the experience would feel.

When I returned from Italy, these Goddess teachers wanted me to understand the process of Hieros Gamos from an inside experience. They also wanted me to understand this feminine Tantric practice from the inside out and how this is connected to the old woodcut prints of women dancing in a circle around a singular male horned figure of the Devil. In fact, there was never a central male figure nor a Devil in "charge" of the tantric experience nor the Hieros Gamos. The central figure in these depicted rituals is the Goddess, and the rituals are "inner rituals" that come from ecstatic trance.

A consistency in the older language and reported Italian experiences by women of interactions with the Spirit World make little distinction between the "physical world" and the "Spirit World," except for tell-tale signs of humans combined with animal parts and "processions" of other dead people. Part of this is due to cultural expression but part of this, they explained to me, is the experience itself: as my own Goddess teachers pulled me into trance, they did so not when I was sleeping nor meditating nor listening to anything hypnotic: they created the trance and pulled me in. In this way, my experience was also that the physical world and the Spirit World were melded into one.

The trance always begins with the presence of one Goddess teacher who unmistakeable sensations upon the Medium's body who then knows it's time to begin. The trance is heightened and maintained by a large group of Spirit women wearing deep red robes. There are images present of fire, caves, and initiatory elements. A more formless and ancient form of the Great Goddess appears at a specific point of the tantric passage, teaching through imagery and clairaudience. The entire length and sensations of this tantric experience are regulated by the Goddess. This is a recharge, repair, renewal and empowerment of specifically feminine energy.

ANIMAL COMMUNICATION

While I have always loved animals, my ability to communicate with them would become much more specific and clear after Goddess teachers and I began communicating regularly. For example, my own cat would help me find missing items, he would take me to my bed to lie down for quick "vision naps" when I would be too busy to meditate but my Guides were trying to get my attention in earlier days, and he told me when he would die so I could take the week off from work to spend time with him. He passed on the exact day he told me he would, in the exact way.

I make agreements with animals. For example, I had been feeding a stray cat for a few months before a friend moved into the 3rd bedroom in our house. He brought his cat who became territorial of our yard area which many cats used to visit. I asked my housemate's cat to tell me when my stray cat was waiting to be fed. As an appreciation, I told my housemate's cat that I would also give him some food. So, every morning and every night, sometimes several occasions each, no matter where I am: in my room, in the bathroom, in the middle of a conversation, etc, my housemate's cat will come yell and me and tell me the stray cat is waiting to be fed…and he always is.

There have also been periods of my life where every dog I would come in contact with would roll over and give me his belly, which of course, warranted confused looks by the pet owners.

This is the path of the Female Mysteries. This lifestyle is not a "choice" in the traditional sense, nor is it an "initiation" "determined to be awarded" by another human being: this is a soul agreement and a service-filled life.

These are individual women chosen by the Spirit World to receive not only transmissions of knowledge, but also an invitation (through one or more initiations) to live a life in deep partnership with a spirit Goddess guide (or several or many); in constant connection to and for the purpose of expressing and of and teaching the Abundance of the Divine Feminine. Her connection with the Divine Feminine is daily, not reserved just for ritual.

Her life may look strange in comparison to the lives of others around her at any given time period: he life will be dictated by this soul agreement, and she may find herself moving in and out of solitary practice and public expression in many ways, rather than following one career path.

This path takes place over a lifetime of "quest-like" series of events. This path offers autonomy to women of a social and sexual nature and is subtly guided by the Spirit World from the earliest moments in a woman's lifetime. For some, the growth can be rapid and the path clearly realized; for others, it's a much longer process that makes more sense as time passes.

At times, these Mediums also serve the public, secretly, in a variety of ways: from unsuspecting jobs that put them in connection with people of different lifestyles and belief systems, to actual teaching jobs, traveling, being a mother, engaging in community, being an artist or musician. Just as the Goddess can channel her energy through anything: a pot, oil, water, a person, so too can the Wandering Witch offer opportunities of growth and expansion in daily, mundane interactions.

The Wandering Witch has perhaps a more surprising expression: because part of her path is to demonstrate, through example, the abundance of the Divine Feminine, it will be very easy for her to "take on a new practice, job, or artistic expression," without studying like others need to. She may also excel and become popular in the culture. She will channel the Divine Feminine through her work and seem larger-than-life when she is doing this, but then seem much "smaller" when she is not. She may move around often, almost having "no home" and yet always someplace will welcome her. This can be confusing for people who enter into "friendships" and "relationships" with her who don't understand the channeling process. They will wonder, at times, where her power has gone, not realizing the power isn't hers to begin with.

These Mediums will be found hiding "in plain sight," and it's up to the seekers to recognize her. Like the "Little Mermaid" story, she will not be able to say things she'd like to share, it's as if the words come out...and what unlocks these words and this dissemination of knowledge are the questions of the seeker.

Fourth Secrets

Just 4 hours after landing in Genova at midnight, I'd awaken and drive with Simone for 1.5 hours towards Molini di Triora, and then ascend the mountain for what would be a full day of meeting with an herbalist on another mountaintop, and a soggy 6 hour trek through winding mountainous trails with medieval remains.

But first, we would meet my Ligurian translator and driver who would take me there. He suggested I first visit the Ca'Botina, the place where witches were burned, having seen glimpses of my past life there.

So the two men let me walk there alone, in the early waking hours, to feel the stones and sense the ghosts and do what needed to be done:

I walked slowly down the cobblestone road, letting my hands drag along the brick walls. I turned into the sheltered and gasped out loud: I recognized this place.

I fell to the ground in front of a mock-prison scene and found myself scraping my fingers against the cobblestones and dirt…heaving up the sobs of despair coming from centuries before me…images of women standing around me, placing their hands upon my torso…all of us in a funerary wail, releasing the cavernous moans of a seemingly endless sound wave of the deepest sadness cracking open thousands of hearts imprisoned by hatred…we sobbed, our bodies trembled…we shook the airwaves until the grief released into the misty, fog-filled air clinging to the stones as our collective breathing moved out the heavy weight of the feminine pain lived for centuries in private agony as the the mists dissolved their imprisonment.

Our cries were carried out to the walnut grove and into the deeply glowing greens of mosses and grasses old.

Then, crawling onto the platform on the mountain's edge I stood among their vespers, feeling my body free of the weighted chains of drowning in waters of sadness…as fire began to rise, rise, rise…I saw the burned ones, the tortured ones, but we no longer felt sad…we were clarified now and we knew this didn't belong to us, nor our bodies, these evil acts of abuse…and as they screamed like banshees I found my hands grasping the cobblestones, my fingers curled into their well-worn fissures like scorpions about to strike, my body arched like a wild cat, a focused wold…and I heard myself screaming their screams… but these were no longer screams of terror…for now we are together, RECLAIMING out right to be who we are, RECLAIMING our power, RECLAIMING the fires they used against us…like phoenix birds we burn our own suffering down and rise, rise, rise from our ashes…deep from within the mother earth we are restored and we shine brightly with love and power from our Grande Madre…illuminated within.

Chapter 4:

"Women of the Mountains of the North West"

"The figure of the healer has its ancient roots in the peasant society,
and bears all the signs and values"

-Antonella Bartolucci, "Le Streghe Buone"

"Le Streghe Buone"
The Good Witches of the NorthWest

"There's an old 'strega' who lives at the top of a mountain. She cures people with herbs. No one's sure if she's still alive, but I'm trying to see if she'll meet with you." This was how I first heard of Antonietta from a young man who grew up near the medieval mountaintop village of Triora, Italy. He would be my translator and guide in the Ligurian region, an area of small villages both in the mountains and along the sea that was a hard target of the European Inquisition. *"She would like to see you,"* was his next message, *"and it's odd, it's like she's waiting for you."*

This is something I would be told again and again: people who didn't normally take visitors were "waiting for me" and ready to share, to be interviewed, and to educate me, even though most of these people don't take visitors. It was as if a magical message had crawled around Italy through a veritable grapevine, connecting me with people, places, and things who knew I was coming and agreed to help me. Though perhaps "tree roots" are a better comparison, being that trees communicate under the soil, and because the people I met were all taking me to the roots of Italy's Witcheries. Now I was here, in the "City of Witches of the north," walking down medieval cobblestone streets whose narrow corridors swirled with mists of morning fog, through the dreamy old stone walls that were sprouting lush mosses and maidenhair ferns. Doriana, an herbalist from the top of another nearby mountain, and my translator felt our every move was being watched by stray cats, and for some reason they all hissed as I passed by.

Outside Antonietta's well-hidden two-level house, behind piles of flourishing philodendrons and ferns and pothos and coleus plants all full and healthy and filling the steps leading to her her front door in this peaceful yet mysterious medieval village, there was a gruff old man demanding to know who we were and why we were there: Antonietta had cured him so he was now a believer and, like the rest of the town, keeps her well-protected. The entryway to Antonietta's home looks like what your imagination might expect from a witch: there's little light filtering in, the doorway is painted a burnt umber color and to the right side of the door are small corner wooden shelves holding candles, gourds, and dried plant bundles. Above the doorway are more dried plants.

She welcomes us in with the softness and love of an old woman who's happy to have guests. She is 89 years old, but her voice defies her age: it is youthful and bright, even if she looks a little tired. She has returned from the hospital recently, while I was waiting to hear if I'd get to meet her. It was the only time she's ever been to the doctor. Ever. She has always been able to cure herself, but this time she had a collapse due to a heart issue. She showed us the medicine the hospital gave her. Scrawled across the box she has written: "VELENO" which means POISON. She has never trusted chemical medicines and she tells us these pills are harming her.

In her kitchen are hanging strips of orange skins and other dried plants. She tells us, *"When you eat an orange, don't throw away the peel. You can use it for pies and cakes."* There are old iron pots bubbling and steaming with slow-cooking remedies. She takes us to the wall of all her little keepsakes and begins to show me all of them. She only speaks Italian, and she doesn't stop talking for another 2.5 hours, with a smooth voice that sounds like it belongs to a teenager. I give her a small black box that has inside of it some moss holding a large earthly colored jasper gemstone egg. She asks me, *"What's this?"* I tell her, *"for the Grande Madre."* She looks at me with an intense, knowing eye, and calls me a "good girl."

Born in 1928 in Puglia, she moved to Triora in 1947 after visiting a friend who lived there. She remained and married her husband one year later. *"I've seen many things,"* she tells us, *"war included. I went through 42 attacks where bombs were dropped. I used to live in Arma di Taggia, and that's when we survived the bomb attacks. We were hiding ourselves in a tunnel that now is connected to Sanremo. They are just memories,"* she says, but she still seems quite haunted by World War ll. Likely the town center of Triora doesn't help, as it may serve as a reminder of the war: the Palazzo Stella and the historic buildings there have been recovered and restored after being damaged during World War II. In fact, December 10, 2016 celebrated the inaugural opening of the new "MES: Museo Etnostorico della Stregoneria di Triora" which means the Enthohistorical Museum of Witchcraft of Triora." It is located inside one of the historical buildings that has been remodeled, and outside its doors is the threeheaded Cerberus mosaic (on the ground in front of a church that is alleged to be built upon an older pagan temple), that also gives Triora's name "Tre Bocche" or "three mouths," which is a reference to its importance as a crossroads of Medieval and earlier times.

Anotnietta invites to the second floor, and we climb a steep set of darkly painted medieval stairs that lead to a bright, sun-filled room bursting with plants , both alive and also dried. There are baskets everywhere full of curing herbs, such as one filled with 6 different types of chamomile ("chamomilla romana" roman chamomile, "chamomilla san giovanni" Saint Giovanni chamomile, and more). She has decorative vases filled with dried Lunaria Selvatica and other beautiful dried plants with unique shapes and also and bushy tropical-looking living ferns, next to be most perfect escargot begonia I've ever seen. The centerpiece of this room is a large dining room table filled with bowls of dozens of herbs in baskets and in clear bags, little bottles of oil infusions , with such a variety of colors and shapes they seem like "art supplies" from nature. Antonietta calls her herbs "spontaneous," meaning that they grow wild, rather than farmed or mass-produced herbs. Healers with plant knowledge like Antonietta know how to identify them, when to harvest them and how to pluck them from their natural growing patches in forests, on mountains, and growing from walls, like the maidenhair ferns and "strigonella," the herb of the Madonna, in the fields, and from fountains.

Antonietta is a CATEGORY 1 "Strega," a Lineage healer. She is one who works almost exclusively with herbs and plants and edibles: all things that can be plucked from the land around her. She also uses spider webs to close wounds, like a natural "band aid."

She uses herbs in various forms to cure. Her applications of herbs are:

1) As "FUMENTI," which are steaming treatments where herbs are added to boiling water and then a person puts a towel over their head while their face is over the steaming water, to inhale the heated water and herbs. The steam comes from heat either from the stove top or on a log fire where the flame has gone down and is retained in the charcoal of the wood.

2) BAGNO or BATHS: herbs are added to boiling water on the stove, and then the hot water is put into the bath. The patient sits in the water, absorbing the herbs through the skin and breathing the steam.

3) OIL INFUSIONS: high-quality olive oil infused with wild grown herbs which can be used on the skin.

4) As "TISANE" or TEAS from dried herbs, flowers and leaves. Sometimes these teas don't look like the typical herbal teas: they look more like fermented parts who are then added to hot water as needed. These fermented drinks can contain cherry stems, orange peels, onions and other natural ingredients that have been boiled down.

5) AS FOOD/ IN UNCHANGED FORM: Antonietta says juice from a raw potato cures an acid stomach. She also recommends eating the large snails from the graveyard because they are very beneficial for the liver, but only the large ones. She uses herbs in her cooking as well. Every edible thing has a purpose.

Her cures work on specific ailments like flu and colds, but also heart issues, sciatica, psoriasis, and liver issues, lymphatic disease, muscle twists and bone issues. Additionally, she cures with a "distance healing" technique: she is famous in Triora for curing the "colpo delle streghe" which is know as the "blow of the witch," a particular issue with the back where the spine becomes hunched over. *"I say a "pregheria" (a prayer), to cure this, I don't even need to meet the person, I just need to know the name. I can do it by telephone. The moon is important for this,"* she says. *"I also cured a man with St. Anthony's Flames (also known as "erysipelas" or the shingles, an acute infection with a fiery hot skin rash) by using a ring."*

"I'm a contadina, my father was a contadino," she says (contadina is the feminine word for "peasant, someone who lives in the countryside on the land. "contadino" is the masculine version of this word). *"I learned everything I know from older farmers, and particularly my father was important for me. He wasn't able to read or write but he had an extremely high knowledge of herbs."* Antonietta is quick to let us know she didn't go to school when Doriana mentions her own schooling. *"I'm a farmer, so I don't know the formal names of things."*

All of Antonietta's herbs here have been gathered by herself in the forest, in pathways, in the fields, and as she tells me, some from the walls and fountains (codi de cavallo and cavellina). There is no store where she can buy the herbs she uses: they grow in nature, wild, according to their natural cycles, she harvests them when they are in season. *"I harvested 'biancospino,' 'erbe la madonna,' 'strigonella', right before I got sick in April."* In the winters, there is snow and there are no herbs, so she uses what she harvests before the snow. Though we met in May and June, I spoke with her by phone in December and she was worried about her herb stores being very low, and she mentioned she doesn't have anyone helping her with daily tasks or harvesting of plants. She says all the young people leave the village for more adventurous lives than the village offers.

That's the thing that's perhaps most interesting to me: she's a harvester. She knows the natural cycles of plants and she knows when and where she can go out in the land to find them. The large snails she gathers from the graveyard is at highest point of Triora, a mountain peak that was even difficult for me to climb, but they are so good for the liver, she must. Her philosophy is that everything you ingest has a purpose, an intention.

Some of the curing plants (and their uses) she shows me for the months of April, May and early June in Triora, Italy are: *"Sambuco'* with *'il biancospino' (hawthorn) is good to manage the stomach and cystitis. 'La camomilla' (Chamomile) and 'la passiflora' (Passionflower) is good for headache. 'Calimedro' (Calimero) as a tea is necessary to cure the liver and you find it in the walls. 'L'iperico'(St. John's Wort) for insect bites, sunburn, and as natural antibiotic, you can make it as tea or oil infusion. Calendula can be used to wash your hands, your face, your eyes, and use it for cosmetics. 'La corteccia di melograno' (pomegranate bark) for dysentery. Hawthorn is for the heart. 'L'ortica' (Stinging nettle) tea is good for your kidneys, it cleanses you. 'Gambie di ciliege' (the stems of cherries) are good for kidneys. An apple and dry stinging nettle together are good to clean the kidneys. 'Folgia di oliva' (olive leaves) are for blood pressure and heart . 'Coda cavallina' (horse tail), you can use for your kidneys too. 'La Callega' is a plant grows everywhere in the countryside fields, that's good for diabetes. 'Malva' and 'tarassaco' (dandelion)...those plants saved my life on the 23rd: you can it eat both boiled or raw, the roots are even more charged than the leaves and extremely good to clean up your body. Lime ("tiglio") you can find everywhere...soon it's time to harvest it. The 'erbe della Madonna' also known as 'strigonella,' has 7 virtues...considering how the body is made, anything that you might need this herb will fix and it's a very strong diuretic."*

"I use 7 different qualities of herbs for the kitchen for the 'aromi' (aromatic smell): 'salvia' (sage), 'timo' (thyme), 'rosmarino' (rosemary), 'dragoncello' (tarragon), 'alloro' (laurel) cooked with meat, fish, potatoes, whatever you want. 'Dried ortica' (stinging nettle: you touch it and they sting you)." She says, *"you dry it up and mash it and can do an awesome tagliatelle. 'Origano' (oregano) for pizza and fish and sauce, it has a nice perfume. 'Finocchio selvatico' (wild fennel) can be used in cakes and herb tea. Ubumego/assenzio (artemisia absinthum), as tea or liquore."* She shows us 'ginepro' (juniper) and tells us she loves 'lavanda' (lavender). She has gathered all these plants by herself. She harvests these herbs in the forest and other areas she knows when they are in season. There is no store where she can buy the herbs she uses: they grow in nature, wild, according to their natural cycles. She is in a working partnership with nature. In the winters, there is snow and there are no herbs...she uses what she harvests before the snow, and then uses any honey, lemons, and oranges that are available. Being in her presence, inside her home, one really gets the sense of the solitary.

Being in her presence, inside her home, one really gets the sense of the solitary nature of her work. She lives in the house alone, she harvests alone. Her knowledge is within her. She hasn't passed on her lineage knowledge to anyone. Her family doesn't live in her village. Her social life, in a way, is in the curing. This is the plight that faces all healers: the practice is to learn the knowledge and to be available for people who need its practical application.

This comes from an internal drive, a calling, a personal duty to serve her practice, which is a combination of sacred knowledge and actions and duties to recipes and client needs. Without clients, is someone still a healer? And how long does a healer have to wait on others and be of service? And when her time of healing is done, and she has no one to pass down her knowledge, then what?

I found myself asking these questions of myself when I was deeply involved in healing arts, and they have a heavy weight and finality to them. I chose to leave the healing practice, but first I "backed away," if you will. I learned, however, if you are a healer, people will sense that whether or not you are advertising it. I was uncomfortable with the pull of clients to "meet them where they are," I was hungry to learn a lot more, to find to new experiences and to keep learning. But women like Antonietta, they don't choose to leave. They stay true to their duty, so they can be ready to offer this great body of knowledge. I'd find this to be true in other areas of Italy as well: women don't pass another the lineage if they don't sense someone else will keep using it.

I notice Antonietta is very powerful; she has great knowledge, but there's something more filling the room from somewhere else besides just knowledge. She keeps humble and hidden. It's just out of focus, but it comes out the more she teaches us. As a practicing Medium, it's normal for me to notice the presence of "ghosts" (earthly spirits like friends who have passed over, or relatives) and other spirit people who are helpers such as angels, spirit guides, figures like the Buddha and other "higher-wisdom" beings who are known around the globe by similar or various names. I notice that there is a presence of a spirit person in the room, but it's not a ghost, it's something higher and brighter and it reminds me of a Divine Feminine figure like the Mother Mary, but I can't understand her name. She's definitely got a feminine energy but she defies my efforts to give her a specific form and a specific name in my imagination. She feels enormous and very old, ancient. I welcome this mystery; it means I have more to learn.

The experience reminds me of shaman healers who have spirit people working through them to cure their patients. A woman I know who is a shaman healer reports sensations of her healer spirit guide "putting their energy into her arms and guiding them." She feels this as a tingling sensation along her neck, upper back, and through her arms. Often people who receive healing from a shaman report the shaman giving them some warning that their voice or appearance might change as their spirit healer helper's energy comes into their body. In shamanism practice, the healer can experience a sort of temporary "jump," where a spirit person seemingly "jumps into their body" by blending their energy with that of the healer's, or "sharing the space," inside an earthly person's body. This is what some people call (when it's a negative experience) possession. In the positive experience, where the earthly human being has awareness and shared control, it's often called "trance channeling."

This would be the first time I'd experience this sensation with Italian healers, but not the last. And it's different, because I sense the spirit of this Divine Feminine figure walking around Antonietta, or moving around me, but not "plugging into," nor "jumping in" nor "possessing" her (nor any of the other women nor men I'd meet who also were healers). I see a giant glowing white figure in the room following Antonietta around, sending energy through her, while she's still herself.

While the only mention of anything "supernatural" Antonietta speaks of is that she can sense earthquakes before they happen, I kept feeling a Divine Feminine presence in the room, following her around, unlike any other I'd experienced in my profession as a Medium. I asked my translator to mention this to her. "I feel the Madonna with you, a presence in the room like the Mother Mary, or the Grande Madre," I ask him to say, struggling for the appropriate "name." When he told her this she looked right into my eyes as she sat down, with a very intense look, and the entire room changed with that stare: the air became brighter, as if this presence spread out its molecules to fill the room with lightness. This presence feels enormous, loving, beautiful, powerful, so bright and full of wisdom that I feel tiny and in the presence of someone truly "Great" and we all three begin to cry. *"Belissima,"* is all I can utter. *"Ci Credo (I believe),"* she said, *"I believe the Great Mother saved me and my daughter,"* she said, *"Ci credo."* She asks me *"Sensitiva?"* (if I am a psychic senstive). *"Si,"* I reply. She says, *"Brava"(good)* to me, and holds her fist in the air, *"Brava, Dai forza"* (we are strong). Then she went back to being a regular old lady.

After we leave Antonietta's, Doriana, who had been very scientific and unemotional, was visibly changed. When we parted ways and I hugged her, she wouldn't let go. We just stood there in the embrace of each other. It was captured in a photo and it can be seen a great, deep love having touched us, as our faces radiate something similar. We are glowing. These are "the mysterious, untouchable, indescribable...Secrets."

I return to see Antonietta once again, for another long visit, in June. She has dozens of entirely different herbs on her table upstairs; a completely new harvest. She agrees to give me a cure for my digestion. She asks me how it feels and she says, *"It must be something you ate,"* revealing her simple philosophy that is very correct: a healthy diet should not produce any bad effects on the body. My digestion has been twisted and burning during a lot of my trip. I know some of it is practical: I'm eating foods I am mildly allergic to every day. But since I am also experiencing a lot of spirit people as a Medium, and sensing their emotions as though they were in my own body, I also believe this is the cause of some of my indigestion.

She takes something out of her refrigerator, a dark amber liquid, and heats some water to add to it. I drink it, and immediately feel an immense and smooth sensation of warmth spreading throughout my entire internal body. My intestines make a few gurgles, as if they are re-adjusting themselves, and I feel the warmth spread through my entire body, and within a minute I feel perfect relief. As the warmth spreads through my body, in a way that seems physically impossible and more like air expanding within me, I feel completely released of uncomfortableness, and my body feels happy again. I also feel a sensation AROUND my outer body, a very quiet but immense warmth and power, someone who is fully in charge. Antonietta is not standing near me right now, she's on the other side of the wooden kitchen table. But it feels like a giant person is standing around me. It feels like there is someone, much larger than I, wrapping me in a gently warm blanket (but the warmth also penetrates my body and every cell) simultaneously pulling things out of my body. It's a feeling of comfort and I feel safe and loved and somehow I don't feel like I even have a body; I just feel warmth and energy and a glowing sensation, as though I am radiating like the sun. And just like that, I am cured and for the duration of my visit, and although I continue to have to eat foods I'm allergic to, I have no more stomach issues.

I try to pay Antonietta, but she refuses. *"I'm poor but rich inside,"* she says, *"But when we were doing good we had the goats, rabbits and a little farm, a small piece of land where you grow vegetables."* In fact, after our first lengthy time together, she refuses to take any money from me as well, reminding me that I already gave her a gift (the egg). I insist this time again, but she refuses again. (When I return to the U.S. I send her another gift) and we speak again in the winter.

Antonietta is also someone who calls herself, or allows herself to be called a "strega," who is the first Italian woman to make a distinction between "good witches" and "bad ones" to me. She told me that if she'd been alive during the Inquisition, that surely the "bad witches" would have turned her in. The reason I found this significant, is because all over Italy, some women who do the exact same practice do not call themselves "strega," (witch in the singular) and they consider "streghe" (witches) to be very bad: ones who give illness. Some women proudly call themselves "strega"- and I'm referring to the older ladies of lineage lines, and not the younger women.

Below are some RECIPES rom Antonietta's "Grimoire: translated as "To Cure with Medicinal Plants:"

- FUMENTI For Flu and "Raffredore" (a cold when your nose gets blocked): Lime (Tiglio), Rosemary (Rosmarino), Thyme (Timo), Honey (Miele), Orange (Arancia), Onion with milk (Cipolla com latte).

- FUMENTI for Cystitis : sambuco, Lime (Tiglio) , golden herb (Erba d'oro) , Chief of the Venus (Capo venere)

- FUMENTI: for Sore Throat: Lemon (Citronella), Lavender (Lavanda), Sage (Salvia), hot water.

- FUMENTI: for Sore Throat: hot water, salt, eucalyptus, sodium bicarbonate

- BAGNO/ BATH: For the Heart: Hawthorn(Biancopsino), leaf of Laurel (foglie di alloro) Boil them, add a handful of herbs in two liters of water, then pour the water in the bath so you can soak in it.

- TISANE/ TEA: to cure cystitis: Elderberry (Sambuco) , Golden Herb (herba d'oro)

- TISANE/ TEA: to cure Cough: hot water, Lemon (Citronella) , Honey (Miele)

- TISANE/ TEA: to Sleep: Lime (Tiglio) ,Passionflower (Passiflora), Orange peel

- INFUSIONE di OLIO/ OIL INFUSION: for Insect stings, burns, sprained ankle, warts: St. John's Wort (L'Iperico)

- As FOOD/ UNCHANGED FORM:

- to take INFLAMMATION) out of a body part: Mallow (malva), Apple (Mela), Plums (susine), Red Leg/Partridge Leg (gamba rossa).

- when you have TOOTHACHE where the /gums/ jaw swells: take the bark of sambuco tree, then scrape and grind it and put on the skin outside the jaw

- for SCIATICA: boil leaves of Cabbage (Cavolo), when the leaves are warm, place them on the skin over the spine (can also put on the knees when they have pain)

- STRIGONELLA, the "herb of the Madonna" can be used for many things that go wrong

Antonietta is a "strega" who cures with plants/edibles, oil and water, sometimes a ring, and she can cure someone with prayer who is in a different location from her, perhaps with a mysterious Divine Feminine energy we will refer to as the Gande Dea (Great Goddess) or Grande Madre (Great Mother) as women do here in this region. This is one of the longstanding curing traditions found in Triora and the surrounding lands, and some healers can trace their lineage back 500 years.

Continuing with the importance of herbs and plants and nature as a source of healing, there is the biodynamic "erborista" (erbalist) named Doriana, who owns a mountaintop property called A. Z. Agriculture Castellarone, just a few mountain peaks away from Triora in Montalto Ligure. Her property is literally up so high the clouds bumble by your shoulders like ghostly trains while the sun simultaneously warms the land. It was quite a lengthy process of driving up the mountain to meet her. After our first car ride, we had to park and let her husband drive my interpreter and I up the rest of the way, up rocky, narrow mountainside dirt roads with beyond-hairpin turns.

Doriana is a caretaker of the earth who believes nature is a conduit of knowledge. She believes in protecting the earth so the earth to take care of itself, which it already knows how to do. She lets plants grow wild on her property, and she harvests them. She sells them as dried herbs ("erbe") and "powders," she makes them into TISANE (teas), and also UNGUENTI (ointments) and OLIO D'INFUSIONE (oil infusions). The science behind what she does, according to how she plants and harvests and listens to the earth, would be considered a living "paganism," as you will see in her interview. Biodynamic famers and pagan ways of caring for the earth are common in Italy.

DORIANA, Herbalist at Aziende Agricole in Castellarone, Montalto Ligure (in far western Italy):

Doriana: *25 or 30 years ago I worked with an herbalist for 5 years, and she taught me to prepare some products, and to know the herbs and and use the properties of the herbs.*

Karyn: How did she teach you the properties of each plant?

D: *She showed me the recipes of how to use herbs. She used to cure people with the herbs.*

K: Did she have certain plants she considered to be Master Plants, or ones that had more ability to heal manycailments, or favorite plants?

D: *Yes, She used some "l'Iperico"(St John's Wort), "Helicriso"(Helichrysum). I used these, these two plants are very important and very strong to cure the people.*

K: And your teacher, do you know how she learned about plants and how to heal? Did she learn from family or another teacher?

D: *She went to school, an herbalist school. Not from family. She's an herbalist and a Medium, she cures with the hands.*

K: Since she's a Medium, does she feel she learns more about the plants from the Spirit World than just school?

D: *Yes.*

K: So when she heals with her hands,…because when I saw a vey old photograph from Sardinia recently of an old woman in Italy healing with her hands, the polarity they created due to their positioning reminded me of the way I learned to heal with Spirit versus psychic healing. In Mediumistic healing, a Medium acts as a conduit for healing energy to come from a Spirit Healer through the Medium into the patient. The hand positions are usually in such a way that one hand (the right hand) is on the front of the forehead or chest, and the other hand (the left hand) is on the back of the head and/or chest at the same point. The Medium's hands do not have to touch the patient's body for the energy to go into the patient. The hands create what is called "a polarity" in this way. The photograph of the Italian old lady with a babushka on her head had her left hand on the back of a young woman's skull and her right hand was on the forehead of the young woman, creating a polarity.

K: So, does your teacher, is she guided by her Spirit Teacher Guide to heal with her hands or did she learn a technique?

D: *Si, yes, she has a Guide also.*

K: Fantastic, I thought so, that's what I was looking for.

D: *I think that only Mediums have this Spirit Guide.*

K: Well, Mediums are aware of Spirit Guides, but everyone has Spirit Guides, that is the belief. Where you put your focus you know, it comes.

D: *But the Mediums know the Spirit Guides, the normal people don't know.*

K: Of course

D: *We have the knowledge of the medicinal plants, normal people, in our DNA. We have the knowledge of our medicinal plants, it's not just learning, it's ancient. And when you live in Nature, you remember the use of medicinal plants. It's a natural process.*

K: I believe that.

D: *It comes by itself, like being an animal, living in the nature, just understanding what is surrounding you. The animals know the plants, and we, in the past we knew the plants.*

K: We were discussing this on the way up, in modern times people don't live in nature, well, I live in a city.. so there's a connection that has been lost to this natural information. So there are artificial means to get it. Like being in nature, as you say, you feel the plants talk to you, or…

D: *People that live in the city today search for this connection with nature, and some people come to me to learn. And when I speak with these people, they are so surprised and excited…but for me, it's just daily life. And these people aren't in contact with nature, and so they are unhappy, because…*

T: There's like a missing link, it's a natural thing for human beings to be connected to nature.

K: You were speaking of people being disconnected from nature in the city, but also I find that they are disconnected from their own bodies speaking to them as well, so this whole connection of communication and trust is broken, and in modern times people are trying to connect but in a very non-holistic way; little piece by little piece, they don't quite understand the big picture. For me, I was born with a lot of health issues as a baby, and my mother took me to a doctor who treated me with chemical medicine…

T: You had anaphylactic shocks, that time you almost died, it was from the chemical medicines?

K: Yes, and many time when my mother would take me to these doctors for chemicals [prednisone injections], I would hear a voice telling me "do not take these chemicals." So when I became older, I stopped taking those medicines, and then this voice would tell me to go buy a plant supplement or [an herbal ointment] to heal myself, and this was during a time when I had no knowledge of plants or herbs, but they were very specific plants [suggested to me by this voice]. And years later, when I went to see a naturopath, the doctor put me on the same herbs and plants for my regimen (originally suggested to me by this voice). So for me, my knowledge is not great of plants, but as a Medium, I listen sometimes for the guidance. Its' not complete for me, but it made me think that body of knowledge of the plants comes from some other source that knows all of these things.

K: Can you speak a little of the importance of light from the sun and the moon with planting, seasons, and cycles?

D: *For St John's Wort herb ("l'iperico"), it's most important that on the 24th of June you have to pick this plant. The only time you can pick this plant is when the sun is at its zenith, and that happens in Italy on the 24th of June. The properties of St John's Wort are augmented by the sun at this time. The plant gains the properties of the sun at this time, so you have to pick the plant when the sun is at its highest, strongest point of energy. You have one week of time to collect it, actually. For St John's Wort, this is very important.*

K: Are there similar times for planting the seeds?

D: *We plant the seeds for flowers, specifically, with the waxing moon (when the moon's light is growing). Biodynamic agriculture follows planting not only to the moon, to the sun, but also to the planets..and also to collect with the according planets.*

D: *So plants are not just attached to the sun and the moon, but also to the planets…so you have to make this connection to the planets as well..*

K: How?

D: *There's a specific calendar, every year is different.*

K: It's so exciting because these are fundamental ideas so important to everything on the planet, but these are fundamental ideas that people to think of "oh, an ancient idea" in a negative way, and not give so much credence to it. But you can see with the modern times stepping away from that fundamental care of the earth, we see destruction of seeds,growing of and synthetic plants…So I wonder how much you notice the changing of the planet from these attitudes towards nature…with your plants, or do you feel the energy of the sun, moon, and planets is unaffected by the physical world so much?

D: *VERY influenced! I noticed in the past 20 years the way plants are growing has changed because of these problems. 20 years is not a long period of time, and yet the changing is very fast.*

K: Does it change your calendar for picking and planting?

D: *Yes, it's more difficult to collect, because some flowers grow in winter. The nature is confused. We allow our plants to grow wild, just by themselves. We don't interfere. We try to keep all the external cycles the way they naturally are to to let the pants grow wild by themselves. It's not like we are working on on the plants; we are working on what's "around" the plants.*

T: If you try to let plants with medicinal properties grow in an artificial way, like the greenhouses with all those windows…like when they grow weed they use artificial light.. if you try to grow a plant in an artificial way, it won't work..especially if they are medicinal plants.

K: So you are trusting the plant's own knowledge of how to take care of itself.

D: *Yes, protecting them from external interference.*

K: Like bugs and weather?

D: *No, not really, we want to keep the nature the way it is. We protect the nature, whatever and however it is. We leave the plants to grow alone with insects, animals, with other plants. The plants communicate with each other.*

K: I heard that also about trees..that through their root system they can communicate with each other.

D: *Yes.*

K: It's the same with medicinal plants?

D: *Yes. The plants adjust, even if they are different form each other, as far as they can communicate with each other they keep growing, they don't have any problems.*

D: *Usually when you go to farms you see people growing plants, and they want to make the plant grow faster, or in big quantities, they use products to do this, and they cut down other plants around the ones they want to grow. We don't do that.*

K: What about the masculine and feminine energy of the plants and the process for pollination, since some are flowers? Or like trees...some trees are monoecious, meaning they can reproduce within themselves because they have both the masculine and feminine parts within them, so no cross-pollination is necessary. With your plants, what is the process? Is everything pollination?

D: *Through the bees.*

K: So it's external pollination. Do you notice a decrease in bee population?

D: *Yes, they are very confused [Note: Doriana's property is at the top of a mountain. She's not part of a village at the top of the mountain, it's just her, her family, and her herbs on the top of this mountain, with no village or city nearby] They fly in a circle and drop down, dead. The climate changes, the pesticides..but not just climate changes, also problems with wifi, chemicals, sprays...The problem is the bees can't find their way back home. They get lost and fall dead.*

K: I see that often happening at my feet, a bee will fall and die.

D: *You're not drinking your tea. [NOTE: D has a gigantic jar of oil being infused with bright colored flowers].*

K: What's in it?

D: *A mix of "Melissa" (Lemon Balm) and "Petulla."*

K: It's affecting my asthma, making my lungs tight. I can't breathe well. Often I'm allergic to helpful plants. When I was young, I had to take so much chemical medicine that destroyed my immune system before my body could develop natural relationships: prednisone, it affects the kidney and adrenal glands and their ability to make their own cortisol.

D: *Cortisone?*

K: When I was a child, doctors gave me tons of this.

D: *It's bad for immune defense.*

K: So for helping the plants to be used as medicine, is there a fluid vehicle that is more important, such as oil or water or steam, or do they all have their relevance in making a medicinal plant available for use in the body?

D: *"Le tisane" (Tea) , "l'olio" (oil), I use the medical herbs through teas or oils on skin; the skin absorbs really really fast…and "unguent" (ointment).It's so simple to make it that way, it's kind of out of date if you go to a store, it's no longer used, the simple form.. people say oils and teas are a very ancient way to absorb the plant for your body.*

K: in 1993, I was having some health issues, so I went to an herbalist in New York City where they just sold dried herbs. The woman there gave me a recipe for how to make an infusion with heat and oil and with teas. I didn't make the teas, but I made the oil infusion with calendula, and it worked so well, it calmed my skin down and healed it. I baked them in the oven then strained out the calendula flowers. It was better than anything I have bought since in a store for the skin.

D: *We don't use heat because it's artificial. We leave the oil and plant infusion in a jar in the sunlight for 40 days. The sunlight and moonlight are important.*

K: The moonlight is important even during the infusion process?

D: *Yes.*

K: Can you explain some of the technical aspects behind that or the science behind that?

D: *When the sun warms up the oil it helps the oil to take the active principles out of the flowers. And the moon, "la luna," cools it down, stabilizes it. So the properties come out with the sun, and the moon balances every thing and cools it down.*

K: So the sun is like the action and the moon is the nurturing of what has been created. That's lovely.

D: *It's very important, to have the balance. But not every type of plant needs both the sun and the moon. For growing, yes, but to turn into medicinal uses, no. For example Calendula is attached to the sun. So when making an infusion of Calendula the plant only needs the sunlight for the infusion process, it doesn't need the moon to cool it down. The INFUSIONS are a way to make the herb "usable." By allowing the plant properties to leave the plant and go into the oil, then the oil can be used on the skin, as a quick way for the body to absorb the medicinal properties of the plant. If plants are more delicate, that's when they don't need both the sun and the moon. For example: Lemon Balm ("melissa") and Verbena, Yarrow and Ahcilles ("achillea") are more delicate, so the just need to be left in moonlight during the infusion process.*

K: Are there similarities between plants only need sun?

D: *Yes, they are for men and men's issues.*

K: And plants that only need moonlight?

D: *They are for women's issues, for example, with the uterus. There are plants for men that are attached to sun, and plants attached to moon that work for women. Masculine plants produce more energy, external energies.*

K: Because of other folk stories I'm researching in the the area, I have to ask, would outsiders consider what you do to be witchery? Or would they consider you to be a witch? What world would they use to describe what you do? Or would you consider a witch to be someone who uses the plants that you care for?

D: *Yes, every woman is a witch. I always lived in big cities like Milano and Alondra, and yet I always loved the countryside. The first time I came here I felt at home, and that's why I'm still here. If the term witch means to be connected to the nature and have knowledge of the nature, then ok, probably I'm a witch as well.*

K: Well of course because that name came about not from the witch, but from people who were threatened by the power to cure and who wanted to convince other people there was a reason to NOT believe in the cure. So it was a publicity campaign in the negative.

D: *Yes, witches are women judged by men.*

K: This is the Inquisition in its most simple explanation.

D: *When the church took over, they made the women who were attached to nature into bad figures, for control. Before Catholicism was Paganism, which was a nature-based religion. The Inquisition was the church trying to force people into different state of mind. They didn't like the power to cure that women had because it was a real power, so people got scared. How it's possible that these women are curing people better than the doctors? Doctors were only just men. Women couldn't be better than a doctor, there's no way....she must be evil, we have to get her.*

T: So they cut the communication between nature and the individual. Then everyone started going to church, or being forced to, and we lost the communication between us and nature.

K: I meet a lot of different types of people and I notice that, like your story, people who feel naturally called to nature or who feel naturally connected to the Spirit World are not so concerned with what they "call" themselves. They don't really need to call themselves a witch, unless they are maybe trying to reclaim that word because they are deep inside that connection as a way of living. They are less connected to culture and society's styles and language,which seek to define things, and more connected to nature and the Spirit World. This, versus people from the OUTSIDE wanting to define people.

D: *A lot of people go to school, and they actually become very technical in what they are studying, but the best way is to be attached to the real thing, find a way on your own, but to be IN it, be IN the nature, to acknowledge things you don't know. It's wrong to go JUST to school.NO ONE Teaches YOU how to connect with NATURE. They can't teach you this in school. School teaches you the names of the plants, the use of the plants, only this. Nobody can teach you how to connect with the nature, you have to feel it, you FEEL the connection.*

K: That's beautiful. Do you know, for your teacher who is a Medium, does she…feel any connection to the personification of the Old Ways where nature, the masculine and feminine aspects/elements of nature, have been personified as the Horned God or the Goddess or things of the myths and stories?

D: *Yes she feels connected to the past and to the ancient gods who represent the nature.*

K: Any names in particular?

D: *No, not in particular, "Dea Madre" (Goddess Mother), Great Mother, she's very important… My teacher believes she comes from there.*

K: There is the idea that everything comes from the Great Mother.

D: *And the Moon ("La Luna"). I also feel very attached to the Moon as well.*

K: For you, do you feel a connection just to the Moon, the Great Mother the feminine side and not any of the masculine side?

D: *Both are important, the masculine and the feminine, to feel balanced. My teacher, the way she looks physically, really represents the Great Mother, she's big, and she doesn't have much of the masculine side, but I represent the masculine side as well.* [Doriana is tall and thin]

D: Now for a tour!

Doriana takes me for a short walk outside her house to see herbs growing wild: edible roses, lavender, helichrysum (golden sun), Artemesia, California poppy, "fiordaliso" (cornflower) , and more. She tells me she collected her wild fennel from another mountain. She collects only the wild ones, then cultivates them. *"It doesn't make any sense to plant it [in rows or from seeds] because it grows by itself."*

We walk towards her harvesting shed which houses a drying table and a wall with drying racks filled with beautiful herbs. She holds certain ones together, telling me that there is a synergy that can occur between plants. She shows me her cultivation of Sage, and also Rosemary. *"It's very rich in essential oils, I use this oil when I give classes because it supports concentration."* As we walk towards the other side of her mountain, a steep drop-off with small terraces ("terrazze") where some of her wild-grown herbs have been just cultivated, she continues to share her philosophy:

"The only way that plants can be healthy for you and cure your problems, is that they have to grow spontaneously, in the wild by themselves. This is very important. They have to be healthy and balanced, and the environment is part of that," Doriana says. *"In that way, I suppose they are a higher part of the knowledge that is uninterrupted,"* I muse. Doriana continues *"Many people say: "I tried to cure myself with the plants but it didn't work out,"* she says, *"but it's because the plants were no good. Good plants are are able to grow by themselves and live by themselves. Most of the pants that you buy in stores are dead plants, they have been cultivated with intensive methods which is not natural. They can't cure you if they are not able to live alone by themselves. If they can't take care of themselves, they can't take care of you. Better to speak with the plants."*

After spending most of the day with Doriana, I remember a book I was gifted called "Cellular Awakening" which struck me as evidence that paganism's symbolism of nature's cycles has a universal truth outside of its spiritual practices and those who embrace them, and this truth is evidence in science. In this book, which explains how both hydration and dehydration affects health of the human body, the author explains the importance of water: "Messages from the macrocosm are then transported, via water, through the cell membrane into the microcosm."[134] So here we have another example of not only humans being built in the image of the Great Mother and her Universe, but also our tiniest parts as well: our cells and the pieces that make up our cells. We also have been presented with a reinforcement of the importance of water, described, in most ancient of times, as "life-giving fluid form the great Goddess herself.

Aside from those parallels, and into the science, Dr. Wren explains that "in a fully hydrated body, there is a perfect polarity in the form of the perfect exchange of electrolytes taking place in our cells on a daily basis. She explains that our four main electrolytes: "sodium, potassium, calcium and magnesium charge up our bodies by charging the water they are holding as well as the water they can move around the body. Sodium and calcium are paired, and their natural position is outside the cell, while the potassium and magnesium are inside the cell. However during the day when the sun is dominant and we are in active mode, a significant amount of that sodium and calcium pass through the cell membrane into the cell. The sodium, as it moves in, displaces the potassium; the calcium displaces the magnesium. During the hours of darkness, this whole process is reversed.[134] The sun's pull against the cell is the stronger energetic force. The moon's pull is much gentler, which means it has to work harder to pull out the sodium and calcium. Therefore, if you eat a lot of salt at night time, you're taxing your body's efforts to get rid of sodium from the internal part of the cell in the first place, and this contributes to the feeling of tiredness.

When the body is in "dehydration alert," as Dr. Wren calls the body's response to being cut off from water, this changes the structure of the cell membrane in such a way that the movement of light in and out of the cell becomes more and more impaired.[135] Less water, less information, less function.

In the same way that Doriana described the sun's energy having a strong effect and the moon having a gentler affect on plants, Dr. Wren explains our cells feel these energies in the same way plants do.

The magical parallels don't stop here. As Doriana mentioned that plants communicate with each other. It's been proven scientifically that trees and other plants communicate with each other through the transmission capabilities inherent in fungi. Mushrooms have bodies made up of mycelium; a mass of thin threads that act as a kind of underground internet, linking the roots of different plants.[136]

When I first started researching trees, it was because I was curious about why certain woods were considered "magical". What I found as I researched was that many of the trees found in various "magical property" lists are "monoecious" trees. Scientifically, this means that these trees have both male and female reproductive parts within themselves, so they are self-reproducing. Paganism embraces the idea that a balance of masculine and feminine energies opens the doors to magical possibilities and spiritual growth, so this science seemed to indicate these specific trees were symbols of something unique indeed as a natural parallel to a spiritually balanced person.

I discovered that trees dominate the world's oldest living organisms.[137] Since the dawn of our species, they have been our silent companions, permeating our most enduring tales and never ceasing to inspire fantastical cosmogonies.[138] In fact, with all the legends and tales I discovered in Italy associated Goddess with trees, and trees as sacred gathering places for various spiritual seekers, it's no wonder that trees are associated with Goddess as conduits for Divinity...they can communicate with each other, why not with us as well?

Fifth Secrets

"Streghe," "Janare" (Witches) as Harvesters, Gatherers

It's wintertime, I returned from Italy 6 months ago. As I am getting dressed I open by wooden cabinet and notice a little potato I had left in there and forgotten about. I bought it because Antonietta had told me that the raw juice of a potato cures an acid stomach.

Holding this little potato, I immediately began to think of her in Triora right now with the snow beginning to fall. I have a friend call to check on her, and she explains she'd not feeling well and hopes to have enough herbs to last her through the winter. The snow stops growth up on the mountain, it's elevation is over 1700 feet, it would be cold and sparse. The full baskets of dried herbs I'd seen in her house, with the orange skins hanging over the stove would all be gone.

I thought again of the potato in my hand, wondering what she might have gathered: chestnuts? potatoes? I imagined her walking to her special places where she harvests her plants, marveling at the memory of her explaining she knows where to go to find her plants, and she knows when they will be at full potency to pluck. How wonderful is that way of living: in a partnership with nature, having needs provided for which change due to seasons, as does the abundant harvest. In the Bay Area, there are people who teach classes on "foraging:" how to gather edible plants and fruits from the land around San Francisco.

This also brought me to thinking about a folk belief Silvio Falato had shared with me. It's one of the many that is about "how to catch a 'Janara'" and reveal her identity (there are many of these stories):

"In this area," Silvio tells me, "there are Harvesters who specifically cut the wheat fields. The tale says that if you were a Harvester, a Janara would stop in her tracks if she sees you because they get afraid, they are frightened of the Harvesters. So, in this way their identity is revealed and you can know who they are."

"And here there is another tale," he continues. "In this tale is the story of some guys who wore costumes of Harvesters. They would go to the holy mass on Christmas eve at midnight ("mezza notte") and they hide behind the doors so no one knows they are there until the end of the ceremony. They wait for people to leave the church, revealing themselves then. At the end of the holy mass the normal women leave the church as anyone would, but the Janara stay in the church because they are afraid of the Harvesters, and the Harvesters are near the doors, so the Janare would remain…revealing who they are."

Considering what Antonietta told me about harvesting her plants, and that Doriana's life is also devoted to caring for plants and nature, these stories make little sense to me in the scope of things, until we look at the intended message: first, the fear of feminine power. These stories all want to reveal the identity of a "secretive woman," alleging that a Janara keeps her identity secret (and that she is bad). But, we also know Janare were known to have knowledge of the herb cures, so also here these tales are social deterrents from trusting female healers. Ultimately, it has been the historical powers-that-be who hoard food and medicines, and these folk tales seem to be written to distract people from that reality, instead blaming a literally unknown woman for doing these "bad" things: being connected to nature.

Chapter 5:

"Curing Traditions of the Ligurian Region's Silver Valley"

In Italy's Ligurian region there can be found a deep and ancient hum of nature's secrets whispering upon the mysterious fog that rolls through the land in the mornings and evenings, and a sense that even these mists are as old as time itself. These secrets tease, like the river Argentina that twists and turns and winds its way through the dominating mountains of the region, and whose cerulean blue waters suddenly appear, through thick wooded mountain walls, washing over jutted, enormous white rocks that seem to be prehistoric ribs of a giant serpent, an gigantic, ancient life-giving Goddess, fossilized as testament to the mighty power of the earth here. In fact, some of the neolithic Goddess carved figurines found in Italy are carved from greenstone, otherwise known as "serpentine."

Within these ancient beliefs, all life comes from water and water comes from the Goddess. Her waters restore broken bodies to wholeness, and the serpent is her messenger. and whose waters restore broken bodies to wholeness...and the serpent is her messenger.

The strange name of this area, "valle Argentina" (Argentina Valley) is in reference to the to the dominant color of the seemingly furred walls of mountains which dominate the skyline: the pale and bluish silvery color of the olive trees that are everywhere. Their roots go far back into time and into the earth. These lands are untouched, largely, by the hands of modern men. Even though it's called "the valley," it doesn't feel like one. Everything here is a mountain, so you are either on the narrowly hewn roads at the bottom, winding your way around the circular spiraling roads that are always pushing against the mountain on one side, or you are in the middle of the lush greens of the mountains and whatever they are hiding. Perhaps you may find yourself on the very top...like the village of Triora, perched on one of the "Tre Bocche di Cerbero" (three mouths of the Cerberus) which is the village's mythological mascot, emblazoned in red mosaic tiles in the village Palazzo center. There is no escaping the presence of mountains. This is their land. They are alive and they are watching.

Triora, Finalborgo, Albenga, Sanremo, Badalucco, Ospedaletti, Dolceaqua, Bussana Vecchia, Glori, Castelvenere, Castelvecchio, and even over into Bajardo...these are some of the many little villages I explored. Some were on top of mountains, in the mountains, at the bottom of mountains, and at the sea. While the ones near the sea were pretty, they were also more modern and touristy and lacking the magic of the mountain areas. In those mountains, it's not a challenge to understand why there are so many legends here about the Great Goddess speaking to witches in forests, or of the Spirit World's abandoned ghosts making processions through the trees. There is a great peace here, but also great mysteries, and great grief of women who were murdered and forgotten during the Inquisition.

Everywhere there are clues of the magical history here hidden in plain sight. Living are the legends of women gathering in the forests and Goddesses transmitting knowledge to them using trees and water as natural psychic conduits. The wild-growing plants themselves are, if you know the secrets, medicinal, and everywhere you look nature is reclaiming all attempts to modernize or build and to take back the old places. Mosses and ferns have woven themselves into walls and cobblestone streets and anywhere that there are stones, though oddly enough not on any church buildings. Somehow the nature looks polite and still from the outside, even though its immensity can seem overpowering. The most palpable feeling here is that there are secrets hiding all around, and a sense that within the nature, within the deeper forest, it is wild.

People live in harmony with nature here, and very quietly, along with modernized, artistic villages full of gentle but bustling city lifers. People of all ages live with the legends of witches; both with the folk stories that make the imagination run wild, and also with the very real testimonials of people being cured by witches who exist even today.

Perhaps ironically, and Italy is full of irony, is the fact that people here do magic (or receive it as cures) and yet they also fear witches. Almost every household has been blessed at one point with a Grandma or Uncle who can cure something with oil and water, with her hands, or with other strange-looking "crafty" methods using humble, daily household items. And yet in those same households, that magic is not seen as magic but rather "something that just always works, naturally." There is a distinct distrust of some elusive category of "bajiue" (witches/bitches) which people say are "bad" and separate from the other witches. Antonietta herself, whom the town of Triora calls their "beloved strega," told me that if she were alive during the Inquisition, the bad witches would have turned her into the Inquisitors. Apparently "dark" witches turned on "light" ones to take the heat off themselves or out of jealousy or who knows what...but there is a belief that there are "witches" and then there are "witches" and some are bad and some are good and that line of demarcation is also a mystery.

LILIA

Lilia owns a "strega shop" just inside the walls of Triora, at the end of the last part of the winding road leading up to this medieval village. Triora is built in the way medieval villages are: streets and stairways stacked on top of each other like a multi-dimensional labyrinth around a "town center" or "town square." Like a giant cave that's been carved into by Escher, with layers upon layers, it's hard to know where you'll end up by simply taking a turn or following a cobbled pathway that seems to go straight but ends up winding and winding. There are stray cats everywhere. Around this village are mountains and nature, olive trees, walnut trees, a fountain used by witches, and the Ca'botina, a place where outcast women lived...and were burned. But this little bit of road leading into the village itself is lined with a few wonderful shops (who all nod to the "strega" history of Triora) offering delicious hazelnut chocolates, as well as cheeses and pesto spreads. Just inside the village are a line of 4 witch shops filled with the iconic and ironic figure here: a scraggly old lady holding a broom ("scopa") and a black "witch" hat. Witch or old woman? Good or bad luck? I ask Lilia this and she tells me a few other stories and it becomes clear that here, in Italy, the lines between stories and truth are most interestingly blurred.

"Triora is 2000 years old," she tells me, and she's very proud to live here. *"Those houses were made with stones and abandoned, which you can still see. There were 30,000 people living like that, it's not like that now."* At first, she is quite guarded towards me (which I like, because it's clear she has a deep love and respect for the women witches and also the stories, which she

takes seriously, and is just being protective of them), so she only looks at my translator, who is from her region.

"So three animals represent the "Streghe"(Witch): "Il gufo" (owl), "il gato nero (black cat), "il lupo" (wolf) and "il bosco" (the forest)."

Karyn: Were trees important for witches because they were living out in the woods? Or is there a significance to the Walnut Tree?

Lilia: *There used to be big oaks here, but they're not big anymore. They were important because the witches could find repair in the woods under the oaks and under the walnut trees. Their tops were like big umbrellas and could block out the rain. I found repair under an oak one time when I was gathering mushrooms and a giant storm began. Also, because there was nothing to eat for the women, and that was an easier way to eat, to eat the walnuts. It's quite simple. I'm talking about the witches from the past. For example in a family with 3 or 4 or 5 girls, maybe only 1 or 2 were getting married. Your parents were pushing you to marry someone you didn't even want to get married with. The ladies who were not getting married, they were kicked out of the houses and sent out into the woods. During Inquisition times, especially, single women were target as being "bad witches" living apart from society. So women ended up taking care of each other out in nature. The church scapegoated the women, saying they were witches (the ones who cured) because they really couldn't explain why these herbs were curing in that specific way. The knew the properties and what they were good for, but they didn't know how to explain the miracle, and they couldn't explain things in terms like doctors could. The women knew the properties of plants and how to activate the healing process, but they couldn't define it.*

K: Everything I keep being told by people in the North, especially in Triora is that: Witches were primarily healers using herbs, who had a connection to nature and psychic 6th sense. Do you consider yourself a witch, a "strega", or what do you call yourself?

L: *Yes, I feel to be a witch, I have the feeling. I can understand the feelings of who I'm dealing with [like reading people] but I don't have a knowledge on herbs like Antonietta. The true witches are women like Antonietta.*

K: So I'm curious, are you familiar with this modern hierarchy of people who want to be part of a group of witches, so they join a coven? There's a High Priestess, High Priest, a hierarchy of people who have positions. It seems to be a carry-over of the old Convents which was female priests of the mystery schools and priests of the mystery schools, but to me they don't seem to have anything to do with witches.

L: *Covens came after the witches, it doesn't make sense to me. A woman and a man who came here, they were into the occult..it was very bad for the woman, like a brainwashing.*

K: Do you know of any connection between original witches and Grande Madre or some feminine guide or helper spirits, or even Diana, Iside, Cibele, or systems that had a hierarchy of people?

L: *I don't know. Stregoneria is not religion. I'm scared of connecting people with religion and gods. I love Antonietta, I go to her when I feel pain. I consider her a "guaritrici" (a healer). I don't see any religious or spiritual thing around her. She's a healer.*

K: When did your male relatives find out they could heal?

L: *50 years ago. I don't know where those gifts came from, a long time ago. They do "pranotherapy" (I am told this frequently in Italy), they are "guaritori," just healers, not witches or sorcerers. Healers…like Antonietta. The witches, they are just women. I'm "sensitiva." My uncle is "sensitivo," he used to heal people with his hands, my dad too.*

It seems, I think to myself, the only similarity is that there was some kind of female camaraderie because they were living in the woods together. I'm wondering if this is where the story started about women creating female-based communities just to survive, and the idea of a "coven."

K: In this town, I see everywhere these dolls and images of old women with brooms, cauldrons, scraggly grey hair. Why are they so embraced? Do they just represent old women who lived a hard life who are naturalistic?

L: *There is a local legend is saying the broom was keeping troubles away from your home… that's why it's represented with witch dolls.*

At a certain point in our interview Lilia suddenly demanded something from me. "You're sensitiva?" "Well, tell me how you see me!" She wanted a reading to test my "sensitivities," so I complied: I focused on her heart and the reading began to flow and so did energy and the emotions. It came out that she has her own way to be of healing assistance to people. We both felt very connected, and she understood just enough English to suddenly stand up and shout 'You know me!' Which broke the ice for the rest of the interview as she talked about her deep love of the witches there, and of the people she used to care for at a retirement home.

For an escalated moment, the language barrier was no more and we could feel each other heart-to-heart. This would not be the first nor the last time a deep, universal love would transcended language during my stay in Italy. In train stations, at another cafe in Benevento… women would lock eyes with me, older women who wear a great sadness, but also an inner strength, and we would be connected…like we were recognizing each other as very old friends reuniting to remind each other of who we are underneath all that sadness and loneliness and weariness of being a woman in a man's world.

L: *There's a spot where you can feel the spirits of the witches, a spot in particular where there are mosses on the walls under a light, on the road that goes to Antonietta's house..in the nook there…other Mediums have visited and reported hearing voices there. That was the spot where the women used to get together at night to help each other, the ones who were kicked out from their homes and families.*

K: I took pictures there! I was touching walls and felt the women.

L: *I feel it when I pass by, the heaviness of the women who were suffering.*

K: Yes there's a lot of grief here, the suffering, sadness, they weren't acknowledged and they don't want to be forgotten but don't want to be thought of as women who were "evil," they don't want to be remembered that way. (I explain to Lilia my synchronistic moment while taking photos there.

L: *It was a terrible moment back there.*

K: I love that you have a deep love for those women.

L: *I was born here, I grew up with the stories.*

K: I think you feel the women beyond the stories.

L: *It's a natural instinct for me to help others. I wish you the best. We are "two witches."*

In closing interestingly, Lilia tells me she was born in December. I would later find out that Christmas eve is when "retiring" healers pass on their secrets to healers-to-be. Also, there is a belief that babies born on Christmas eve are witches, if female, or werewolves ("lupomannaro") if male.

JERRY

I meet Jerry in Glori and find a wonderland of nature and history. He's publisher and he has an educational garden on his property that's set up like a fantastical magical forest, full of enormous trees of different types, like a "cork" tree, along with another section of herbs and plants. Next to his house is a temperature-controlled smaller building that's a precious time capsule of a library: full of very old manuscripts and other collectible books, from medieval times and some even older. His grandma was a healer. While she didn't pass her knowledge onto him, he did see her at work sometimes, and perhaps he got his deep love of plants from her. He's a researcher nonetheless. He also is knowledgeable about the Inquisition in the Albenga area. He is a mix of mystery and strangeness that is Italy...where old meets new and modern, although the old has the stronger and more open minds in some ways and not in others: open to the old witch ways and mistrustful of the new ones.

"I can tell you how the women I met used to cure people with herbs: The strangest cure is for: the "Erisipola," which affects small nerves in the face, causing swelling that makes the whole face enlarged. They used to cure this swelling with a silver coin putting it on the skin where the pain was, massaging, then with a little river bamboo (that had to have 3 knots) softly beating the painful spot for 9 times for 3 days (9 + 9 +9). So 9 is a multiplication of the 3, 3 knots, as the number 3 is a number very important through these rituals. And the coin had to be made in silver or gold. The silver coin was the best but sometimes they were using the marriage ring too. Silver is supposed to channel the energy better."

106

"This other ritual my grandma used to do: she used to send me to grab the "rovi" (rubus ulimfolius, or the elm leaf blackberry or thornless blackberry) then take 3 leaves off the stem to pass them across the mouths of the children for 3 times saying prayers to cure the "muchetto" (thrush). This is the same procedure to cure for the "candida," down the female sex of the women, again scraping against the outer skin for 3 times."

"For the kids when they had stomach ache, my grandma was asking the kids lie down and uncover their bellies while she would give them a 3 fingers massage. She would use some oil and also a formula of water that had been boiled with chamomile flower, tobacco leaves, rue, a slice of garlic, a little piece of "biscia" snakeskin ("biscia" is a snake that lives in the countryside and has no poison. It eats rats, etc.). During the spring when the snakes where changing their skin, the hunters used to pick up the shed skin to bring it back to the grandmas who were putting it into a jar for later use."

"Also, kids used to wear garlic as necklace. In fact in Liguria there are many paintings where kids used to wear red coral, which we can find all over Italy used as an amulet against the "evil eye" (malocchio). However, women could not wear any necklace throughout the entire time of the pregnancy 'cause it was told the baby could have gotten choked" (there is a lot of belief held in the symbolic nature of actions across Italy).

"During my grandma's time period there was an old woman who helped to give birth to every child in this one town called Calizzano."

"Twice a year the all my grandma's family used to go to pick up the herbs to cure the backache ("mal di schiena") on the top of the mountain (Madonna di Balestrina) I never found out what the name of the herb is. She also used to grow "papaveri" (poppy flowers), taking the opium out as painkiller for toothache. I always used to see the "papaveri" flower in grandma's garden, and opium was taken out from the white part of the flower. In every garden there was always poppy, garlic, rue and chamomile."

"These women who were accused to be witches," Jerry tells me, "were in real life women against people who had power such as doctors, so they taught themselves to learn the secrets of the herbs to stay away from doctors and cure themselves. "Stregoneria" just means "general" witchcraft, it doesn't mean "men's" witchcraft."

"Shepherds also knew how to cure themselves and their animals, because during long travels they were the only ones who could take care of themselves. Also they could not lose their beasts because it would have been like losing a huge amount of money." This is a sentiment I'd hear across Italy: health is everything in the country. A farm animal loss and loss of health meant income loss or an inability to care for ones self even, as with a solitary shepherd. I also saw a shepherd healer in Guardia Sanframondi who was herding his sheep and my translator told me he was known to be a healer. So Jerry one day unexpectedly could not move his body when his wife took him to Pierin, a shepherd, who with one touch of a finger managed to cure Jerry. "This man used to cure bone adjustments, swelling and other type of pains."

"There is also a woman I know who cures people from long distances just pronouncing *their names, using a terra cotta bowl where she puts water to boil, watching the boiling water she can tell if the (sunburn, for example) is gone or still there. There is a string that ties every single thing together, the "filo rouge,"* he says, before trailing off into a little rant of modern "charlatans" he calls them; *"women putting three strings in water and claiming to cure, or another woman he heard of passing out flyers claiming to cure sadness with a candle and salt."* He wouldn't be the first Italian person who had a negative idea about modern witches.

"My grandmother didn't leave any notes about her rituals, cures and recipes," Jerry says. I find it interesting that all her knowledge was inside her mind...where just a few feet away were thousands of rare books full of stories and facts and documentations that somehow, to me, seemed worth so much less than her secrets.

You really come to understand the solitary nature of witchery in Italy. Even Jerry's grandma didn't tell her family members her secrets. The knowledge find who needs it. "Witches" are chosen. Among those living around the witch, the most common attitude is that magic is regular part of life, because it helps with regular life problems. The stories and concept of "witches" that are held as being a separate species from people already practicing magic is one pumped up by legend.

METHODS

But this "good witches and bad witches" idea does find believers here, even among the many people I spoke with who know the church instigated all these stories, even among researchers and local authors. It's not so much an opinion that there are "good" and "bad" witches, (that seems a matter-of-fact, just as there are good and bad people in all aspects of life), but it seems to do with an attitude towards women who aren't healers, but do other sorts of magic that looks like healing magic but instead affects emotions or situations or other "things" that people want changed which aren't life-threatening.

While in Italy there are ancient traditions of magical "miracle' cures: the Lineages. They are truly for curing people and animals of physical ailments that interfere with their quality of life or literally, the bodies they use to work as physical farmers. They do work magically, and they produce results in the physical world.

The "jettatura" (throwing of the "evil eye") towards someone else and afflicting them with negativity is believed to cause illness. "Jetattura" is something accepted as real; all sorts of people believe in happens and of course, it has a bad reputation.

There are women who cure "il malocchio," or "evil eye. What causes "il malocchio" is also magic, but it's not the curing type. This is the distinction. Real witches cure and improve life. Bad ones do not. These witches who don't cure are seen as "crafty" or modern, not coming from the real practices handed down since the most ancient of times from the Great Goddess herself. the prevalent attitude towards "crafty" type of spells is seen as negative. Those types of spells are scoffed at by the people who revere the healers. And more than one person I spoke with called those types of people "bullshit" and "charlatans."

This distaste for the modern "craft," I surmise is really just people fearing or disdaining the artificial. Witches who cure carry knowledge that's been passed down from others, and it produces real and positive results. Most importantly, this is seen as "natural." The modern organized magic with "covens" and hierarchies are seen as artificial by older people who practice what you would and I would call "magic," I think because the modern is seen as "self-created" and coming from rootless derivates; in other words, synthetic. A copy of the original practices. People in Italy, despite the power of the Vatican, seem hesitant to put a "person's image" in the place of whatever "god," and they don't like authority in any form, and a hierarchy of "priest and priestess" is a hierarchy of authority, especially a man-made one.

In Italy I found many people who love the witches who cure and the mysterious culture around it, and they study the available history, and they don't try to own the secrets of the women but rather admire them from afar. I stayed with locals in villages in the far northwest, the far east, in the Tuscan west and central and Roman center, in the Campania of the south, and I found everyday people who are well-versed in stories of the witches, or who have "witches" in their families or have had "ghost" experiences that all the legends speak about. I also met professionals: professors, authors, museum directors, etymologists, published folk tale experts, and people who've spent 30 years of their life reclaiming Inquisition documents and whose passion is to dispel the weird rumors and replace them with facts and names of the forgotten. And then there are women and men who make "natural" magic that looks just like other magic, blurring that line between "good" and "bad" once again, including some magic that I find uncomfortable, such as in the taking of the lives of animals for cures.

In the Silver Valley exists a tradition of using the "pignatta," which is a type of pan (sometimes terra cotta) also used in other Ligurian areas as well as the Emilia Romagna region to diagnose illness and to implement its cure. The "pignatta" is used with water, often hot or boiling water. Sometimes a healer can simply look at the boiling bubbles to discern the problem or "who" caused the problem, in the case of "il malocchio," Sometimes the healer's tradition requires them to use some other item, placed into the boiling water, which diagnoses or shows a result. In Emilia-Romanga, that "other item" is often handmade "croce" or crosses, made of two matchsticks or other plant pieces of the same length, tied in the center across the right node.[139] In the Silver Valley, that "other thing" has often been the fresh liver of a young lamb, into which four pins are placed the curing phase, or a piece of skin of a young goat into which pins are placed.

In a story from 1941, a healer in Camporosso worked to heal a young girl by putting, at midnight, pins into the liver of a young goat to form a rough cross. "He put it in a pot of boiling water when suddenly an angry 'cry' sound came form the liver which had swollen to look like a leather bag, which was an indication she had "il malocchio," an illness that came from someone else's negativity. At that point, the healer, with special words "condemned" the person who gave the young girl the illness, banishing it from her."[140]

In local books such as "La Medicina Popolare Nell'Alta Valle Argentina," (Popular Medicine in the High Valley Argentina) can be found a list of hundreds of plants whose medicinal properties and applications are known by women in the Silver Valley, categorized by what body system the cure, such as "for nerves, for blood, etc. It appears obvious the abundance of herbs used and therefore the richness of the wealth of knowledge possessed, with interesting variations from area to area, probably due to the spontaneous emergence of certain species in land and suitable positions."[141]

There is no shortage of mythological plants of herbal medicine of yesterday and today, with curious local customs...for example, the poisonous "varegu."[142] Used in the Ligure region by fishermen who take the strychnine from it and absorb it into worms to be used as fish bait. While the poison does wear off, the river and lake eel who bite the worm die and are collected by fishermen. Our ancient ancestors could cure diseases and disorders of the body and soul wounds by means of the effects of the properties of the herbs known to priest or to the wizard.[143]

Alongside this classical tradition, officially recognized, there were farmers and shepherds who also resorted to the use of herbs to cure diseases, and knew to collect and properly use herbs, obtaining when needed infusions, decoctions, poultices, according to a family tradition that has for centuries the basis of the oral transmission of folk medicine practices, often influenced by superstition and magic, especially in the most isolated areas.[144] Almost all women, because women, from the prehistory, were given the task of gathering fruits and herbs, and then the care of the garden [...] recognize the link between the acquisition of modern scientific knowledge to popular tradition permeated with superstition, the survival of myths and ancient beliefs, the legacy of the true experiences of generations that we can not always define rational, but which often they allowed the victim to regain health.[145]

Among the popular herbs from ancient times who today persist are: wormwood, watercress, fennel, mallow, fenugreek, lily, privet, wild lunaria, melon, mint, rue, sage, tansy, and rosemary, which are not so unusual, but one of the most legendary, St. John's Wort, is one tied to both science and magic. While St. John's Wort ("San Giovanni" is the Italian name for this saint) is used to cure a variety of physical ailments successfully, it is deeply connected with superstitions that are widespread around Italy. These superstitions revolve around both the "eve" of St John's Wort (June 23rd) and the "day" of St. John's Wort. The eve is also called "The Night of the Witches," or "La Notte delle Streghe," in reference to the superstition of witches gathering together on this night as a group for the purpose of gathering this herb under the moonlight. The night was also considered the time of "bonfires of witches and wizards, the collection of herbs and poisons and preparation of magic potions and spells[146] in the North of Italy. The "day" of St John being of course when the sun reaches its zenith.

In the south of Italy's Campania region near Benevento, the belief is a bit different. While there is the standing tradition of gathering this herb on the eve of San Giovanni, there is also the folk belief that "on the 24th of June, St John's Night, the annual meeting around the Walnut tree in Benevento occurs between the "Streghe" and the "Janare", a general meeting where they had to take the most important decisions for themselves and for their community of the "Streghe" world. It's the only occasion where "Streghe" and "Janare" are together. They are there under the almighty presence of Satan, the Devil.

The science Doriana share tells us that St. John's Wort has to be harvested the week of the solstice due to the sun's zenith reaching it's highest point on June 24th (St. John's Day) thus ensuring the herb is plucked at its most potent time. The potency of this herb allows its curing abilities to be at their highest availability. These curing abilites are backed by science and proven to be true. It cures flesh wounds, digestive disorders and circulation problems. It must be harvested during full moon phases and never in the morning.

On the legendary and mystical side of this plant, there is an interesting story connected with a change that the flowers go through and the saint they are named after. While the flowers, once crinkled, actually turn red and can turn the skin red, and the oil from this herb is a red-blood translucent color, in addition to its other names it also was given the name "Blood of St. John," The leaves also have peculiar marks. The translucent holes on the leaves are also said to have been left by the sword with which the saint has defended himself from the devil, and for this reason it was commonly used in the Middle Ages as an amulet that could keep away the evil spirits, tucked under the shirt together with garlic and artemisia, hanging out of the houses according to the medieval tradition, or scattered on the floor of the houses.[147]

The magical belief is that this herb has the ability to "catch devils" and to "chase them away," both in the sense of physical cures and also spiritual ones, blurring the line between magical concept and curing reality is perhaps related to its effects on both stomach/digestive disorders and lifting depression. In Italian lineage cures, it is often believed that "evil" is the cause of illness (as in evil thoughts, people sending "evil" emotions towards someone else). As it is believed in holistic medicine, the stomach is the "second mind, or second brain, so that issues affecting the "harmony and function" of digestions affects "harmony and function " in the mind. If the digestion is unable to process nutrients, also the mind is unable to process experiences and emotional responses.

Considered a "light and heat carrier, it has proven useful in keeping the "demon" away that sometimes persecutes our lives, which is sadness and depression that can lead to losing stimulus and desire to live. In fact, the "l'iperico" is infused or in various forms to treat depression, anxiety and stress (depending on the entity it is always better to be advised by an expert in the field or doctor and never to be associated with other antidepressants), because, as St. John said, "The demon is afraid of the cheerful people."[148]

Personally, I have met Italian people who are not part of lineage curing traditions who use herbs in their magic in this way: using the concept of the plant itself (the way it grows, its attributes) and using characteristics that can be seen as "good" or "bad" of the plant as ideas that can be used as a "motion" to infuse spells with to move energy in the way that the plant moves. For example, a friend of mine found a weed that was in ample supply in her garden. This weed was abundant. Upon researching this plant we discovered its roots, if you pull them out instead of cutting them, start to entangle all other plant roots around them, in effect, strangling the plants. Therefore, this plant, if you follow its characteristics, can be used in spells that "bind" the harmful actions of someone else such as an "energy vampire" who feeds off the kindness and energy of others only to drain them of energy, literally.

Folk stories, magic, and science all enjoy blurred lines in Italy. You may find fact when you expect fiction, and the fiction is not as interesting as the truth. Most importantly, you will find all of these things alive and well here, even if hidden, but existing just as naturally as the nature itself.

Sixth Secrets

During the couple of years it took for this book to come together beyond just my own personalresearch passions, I experienced pervasive visions of Celtic Druids, Gaulish Druids and Scandinavian shaman having a presence in Italy.

I also kept being pointed towards the Scottish.

This series of visions began after a meditation I had with my Guardian Guide who gave me a golden tree branch as we ended our meditation time together. I asked her "what is this?" She said, "a golden bough." I asked her what that meant, but she was done teaching for today and told me to "research it." Over time, I would see this branch develop into a small tree-with both roots and branches, and from there, it would become a full grown tree. She presented it to me during every meditation we shared.

All could find at the time in reference to this was a book by James Fraser, and I didn't like it-he seemed to look down on spiritual practices from around the world as "primitive."

I was pushed, by my Spirit guides, to research Druids, and not just Celtic ones. I found they were another oral spiritual practice and that they were essentially Spiritualists: they believed that life continues for the spirit after the physical body "dies."

In my visions, I kept being shown these groups as different spiritual practices in Italy, having come from other lands, and yet, I'd see members of these groups sharing information with other groups. I thought this was so odd- from an unstudied American perspective, these practices are portrayed as being very separate. And I didn't know there was an actual history of these cultures living in Italy. But I'd come to know that there were alliances made, practices shared...sometimes due to poverty, sometimes for other reasons.

There are places in Italy which still have a Celtic flavor and whose cultural imprint is lasting: Bajardo, Cividale del Friuili...and more.

I'd also come to know exactly what "the Golden Bough" that my Guardian Guide gave me was all about, and it's a most exciting discovery...

Chapter 6:

"The Good Witches of Emilia-Romagna of Central-North and Northeastern Italy"

There is a belief that can be found in many regions of Italy which reveals itself through the examination of popular medicine. Popular medicine is defined in Italy as medicine "of the people: the common and often poor people, the ones living in villages and countryside. This definition is in contrast to the meaning of the term "popular" in America, which means "en vogue, enjoying a large following, or of the prevailing system-in-power." Popular medicine and its curing traditions (and all the forms of magic having to do with curing people and animals for the purpose of restoring health) revolve around this belief in many areas: that diseases and illness are caused by evil. Not some random, scapegoated idea, but the evil or "bad intentions" of someone else's (or self-inflicted) negative thoughts. The "jettatura' (the casting of il malocchio") is the act of giving someone the "evil eyes," meaning, sending someone negativity (jealousy, hatred, envy, ill-wishes) through the power of the eyes, which results in a headache, other illness.

This belief in "evil thoughts causing illness" is also revealed in the "nickname" of one of the most important indigenous herbs in Italy which is collected during the week of the sun's solstice, reaching its zenith on June 24th. In some areas, it is only collected on a particular night, the 23rd, called "la notte delle streghe," or The Night of the Witches." This healing herb, St. John's Wort or "l'iperico" in Italian, is also known by the name "Scacciadiavoli" which means "catching devils, or hunting devils." Illness is also believed to be removable using different secret methods which take out the evil from the body and restore it to health: for example, when a healer "catches" the evil in the knots of a fiber, or when a healer "washes out" the evil into water then "throws away" the water and the evil against a wall or "into the past," symbolically.

The term "scacciabagiue" means "witches who cast, or throw evil" or "casting witches" in the Ligurian dialect," and "abbagiurato" means that one has been the recipient of one of their spells. There is a legend in the Ligure region of "a woman named Nazzarena Trebaudo, who died at the age of 95. She was blamed for horrendous crimes, as a "bagiue" who with her eyes ensnared children." The word "scacciato" means "to cast out," so it can mean "getting rid of" something or "sending something out,"a double-entendre, just like the energetic action of something. When we think of "throwing something out" or "throwing something away," we are also "sending something elsewhere," or "giving another space our discarded item." And if we take this word idea further, that the Witch Hunt in Italian is called "caccia alle streghe" we see the ideas of "catching"and "casting" being two sides of the same coin.

In a local story from 1970, Raymond Bracco from Glori was a man who could cure the "malocchio" or "evil eye. " *He was staying in Sanremo for the winter when a woman came asked him for help because her three-month son was not sleeping and was crying continuously. Raymond diagnosed that "certainly the small boy had been "Abbagiurato," and made this diagnosis from only touching the boy's hat."*[149] Here we have the word "bagiue," the Ligurian dialect word for "witch" in combination with the action of several other words whose translations allude to a witch casting a spell on someone with her eyes.

"To diagnose the boy, he put a handmade cross in a white dish of water, placing 4 grains of salt to the extremes of it; then a few drops of oil on the salt, always cross-shaped and finally dipped his finger in water making a last sign of the cross. At that point the oil formed numerous snakes in the water and Raymond diagnose that the boy had indeed been affected by the 'evil eye.' He requested to see the boy in-person, but only after midnight that day. The mother agreed, and when Raymond began to cure the boy he did so by 'making signs of the cross on his forehead, heart and intestinal area, muttering incomprehensible secret formulas,' after which the boy was completely cured and began to eat."[150]

Stepping out of the folk tale side of this story (which encourages our imagination to delve into the realm of our worst fears), we come back to the reality of truth that these healers, often living in remove villages and offering cures to farmers and babies and other people in their immediate communities actually cure illness, and quickly, and often when "modern medicine" fails.[151] They have successfully done so for generations.

Evident in their humble but miraculous cures is a higher thought philosophy commonly expressed through slightly different language in modern healing modalities: that the body is "already in perfect health," and it's simply a matter of thoughts and stuck emotions which cause apparent "blockages" and illusions that keep us from our natural state of health. These indigenous healers are blaming "evil thoughts" on the disturbance in health, and believe that "evil" can be removed to restore the body to its health. The belief is not that the health is in "bad shape" or that the body "cannot be cured." Rather, the "evil" is seen as an interruption, a temporary disturbance.

In most energy-work modalities perpetuated in modern times, there is an effort to bring balance to the body, the mind, and the spirit through the release of "stuck" or "harmful" thoughts, emotions, and then close the distance between the physical body's will and the soul's higher perspective so that the illusion of disease or "lack" can be realized. The patient is considered to be responsible for their own health, and the Reiki healer, for example, is there to be a conduit for the healing energy that comes from the universe and goes into the patient. This process should also help the patient become aware of their own connection to the Universe and to their own ability to heal.

The healing practice of Reiki seeks to help the patient feel safe enough to let go of thoughts (such as limiting beliefs) and emotions that are stuck (from past trauma), releasing whatever is "in the way" and preventing the patient from their natural state of perfect health.

Also found in "Science of Mind" philosophies are an emphasis on the power of thought to create reality. These philosophies believe that health stems from the thoughts and emotions, and whose remedy (for ill health or ill-wealth) is to use the power of the mind to affirm abundance and healing. Author John Randall Price states, "ageless wisdom is emphatic in stating that the reason we do not enjoy the fullness of abundant life is because we do not personally identify with the third aspect of our divinity, the creative feminine medium, the Law of all manifestation."

The only trouble in "seeing this" has to do with language, culture, style, education's influence on expression and description of "insider" practices by non-experienced "outsiders," and also from misunderstandings of "insiders" from one practice towards practitioners of another one. Healers in villages have certain understandings of these things, and will not use the same terms at all, as I discovered. Many of them are humble and simple and wouldn't understand these concepts the way I explain them (or as others have tried), or they have simply "grown up" in their lifestyle and haven't had to "name" or "describe" their experiences to others because they are too busy simply "living it."

Nevertheless, they are receivers of this secret knowledge, and not in the definitions and words that simply describe this healing knowledge; they are "carrying this knowledge" in its working form and the living legacy of its effectiveness and truth. It's the outsiders who seek to define and compare, to categorize and own. In doing so, they remain completely outside of the experience itself; only in the experience of this curing magic *is* the magic.

While it's said that "evil" is the cause of disease, let's remember that the words referring to this transfer of thought-into-illness is described ultimately as "something given/taken from someone else" so, in effect, people are held responsible for giving and taking illness and health as well as for curing it.

And while these words and ideas about "throwing" and "catching" are ones I found connected to the Liguria region, they seem to apply more aptly to the current remaining secret lineage healers of the Emilia Romagna region that came across my research desk thanks to another friend in Italy. Emilia Romagna is a region whose furthest western border connects with Liguria's farthest eastern border. ER then stretches across Italy to the eastern sea coast. It's bordered by Lombardia and Veneto on its northern border and Toscana and Marche along its southern border.

Women (and some men) in Emilia Romagna who cure are known by a couple of important names: "reggitrice" and "mesiah," which mean "someone who carries something for someone else." So between the people "throwing" and "catching" negativity at one another, there are the "reggitrice" in the middle, whose service it is to "carry the evidence of others' negative actions" for the purpose of healing.

The healer, therefore, is a "medium." As defined by the Merriam - Webster dictionary, a medium is "the thing by which or through which something is done." Also, "an intervening agency, means, or instrument by which something is conveyed or accomplished," as defined by Dictonary.com. Then of course there is the extended spiritual shamanic meaning "a person through whom the spirits of the dead are able to contact the living." Also as defined by Spiritualism, " a spiritual healer is one who, either through one's own inherent powers or through mediumship, is able to impart vital, curative force to pathologic conditions."

These words are a clue to the significance of Italy's witches, and especially a key to understanding their mysterious world. This practice, this duty, is a service. People don't always choose to be a healer; the practice chooses them. And in a way, a healer/ "reggitrice"/ "mesiah"... these are the people who bear witness to everyone else's secrets and hold them in a safe, private space with unconditional love during the healing process. Held in this light, healing is a gift not just because of its curing solution, but because of its acceptance. Carrying something for someone else" certainly must "weigh down" the healer over time, to see all these secrets and suffering. Perhaps this is also why these women were targeted by the church: being a healer, one is witness to the ultimate confessions: the confessions of the body and it's mental and emotional trespasses, which cannot lie in their physical symptoms. The disease always reveals the inner-workings of mind and emotions and will.

In Emilia Romagna, these healers are also known by the name "Guaritori, Segnatori," meaning "healers, scorers", or rather "healers who make marks." In the plural, "guaritrici" means simply: healers. This type of healer traces secret "marks" over the body to cure it, hence the name. Scoring/Marks is a "therapeutic practice" where the mark is made by tapping the body of the patient, tracing one or more crosses, the pope acknowledged in 1989. Another name for this type of healer is "medgona" which means "meridian, " in relation to the tappings.

Interestingly, a modern modality of "tapping" has been created by the name "EFT", which stands for: Emotional Freedom Technique . According to their website, "EFT breathes fresh air into the healing process by borrowing from the Chinese meridian system." Having learned and applied this technique myself, I can tell you the EFT the procedure is: using specific fingers to tap on specific meridian points on the face and upper chest in a specific order for a specific amount of tappings while simultaneously saying specific words which bring to mind the mental dysfunction (like a fear or phobia) to be released. After applying a specific number of repetitions of tapping and speaking, the words related to the fear are replaced with positive, affirming words that bring to mind a completed cure and state of peace. I can only imagine the indigenous Italian version is in some way similar, but I haven't received that type of cure so I can't say for sure.

In a spectacular book by author Antonella Bartolucci entitled: " Le Streghe Buone: I simboli, i gesti, la parole, come muta la medicina tradizionale nell'era di Internet" (The Good Witches: symbols, gestures, words, as the Traditional Medicine Changes in the Internet Era), she documents 21 healers, (18 of 21 who were women) documented over the years between 1992 and 2016. I consider this to be the most important book I've read from Italy about "witches" who cure.

She has researched the following areas: San Martino in Rio, Correggio, and surrounding rural areas. No herbs are mentioned in her book which catalogues curing techniques by area. The average age of healers is in the late 50s, but they are as young as 29 and as old as 92.

In Emilia Romagna, there are other techniques to be found that cure disease. Bartolucci states, "Techniques of traditional healing have mostly their own origins of the belief of the hidden power of symbols, gestures, images, and words which are a a fundamental type of care and can be grouped under the terms "scoring/marks."[152]

Below is an encapsulation of her book's findings along with my own experiences:

Before the "guaritrici" cure, they diagnose.

DIAGNOSTIC TOOLS: (as designated per their specific lineage traditions) such as oil, water, heat, crosses moving upon water, and the body's own illness expressing itself as specific symptoms. "Sometimes the "pan" [ceramic, tin, a regular household one often reserved specifically for this use] is used, to "ascertain the specific ailment, to measure its severity, or to check that the signature/marks are doing well.[153]

DISEASES CURED are: herpes, worms, burns, inflammation, warts, sciatica, psoriasis, St Anthony's Flames (a burning skin condition), twisted muscles, sprains, sore throat, bad nerves, low back pain, a particular back issue called "colpo delle streghe" (meaning "the blow of the witch"), sunburn, joint pain, general muscle ailments, sty, and "il malocchio," which causes a variety of symptoms, including ones set in motion in past-lives, parasites, and some also cure domestic animals and farm animals.

OCCUPATIONS: These women (and some men) are: peasant women and men and housewives. Some of these women start working on the farmland when they are 12 years young.

COST of CURES: Across the board of areas and various healing Lineages, healers do not get paid for their services. The cost of a cure is: "Libera, non chiedere, non rifiutare"[154] meaning, free. I do not ask, I do not refuse." Healers don't want to be bound to their clients, so if someone tries to pay for their cure, often the healer will ask that they leave a candle burning in a church, or some other donation that is outside of the healer/patient connection.

TOOLS to cure: Daily objects which are often inherited such as: teacups, ceramic bowls, and tin pans. Also used are oil, water, the direction of sunlight, and the clarity of the moonlight. Handmade crosses from straw or matches are tied together in specific ways as are secret formulas of words, prayers, and invocations. Tapping marks made on the body in the area of illness experienced are made and secret signs are traced onto the body as well. Also included by some healers are secret prayers to specific saints who are associated with specific body parts, and the actions of "capturing" the health disruption in symbolic knots, water vessels, vacuum bubbles (cupping), etc, and then the actions of "throwing the evil away from the body."

METHODS of Curing are:

MARKS/SCORING: "[...] marks are made to surround evil in the part of the body affected, and by using the cross in odd numbers, often there is the use of "3" or a multiple thereof."[155] The one who marks intervenes with a sign [...] prayers, or secret words, represented by the sign of the cross and opposition of hands.[156] This opposition of hands is similar to the the polarization position I spoke with Doriana about regarding Mediumistic healing, or "healing with a spirit healer" versus using one's own psychic energy.

THE PAN: "A method placing two wooden sticks of the same length, tied together forming a cross, into the pan of water. The pan is heated, and when the hot water begins to boil, the healer makes: "3 times the sign of the cross and whispers the formula or secret prayers, often in dialect and refers to a saint or miracle worker, specific to that disease."[157]

RUNNING WATER/THROWING WATER: This method uses water in two ways: The first is to let water run over an aching limb/nerve/tendon while the healer simultaneously marks the pain with secret signs and words and tracings of the cross, using a bowl or basin to collect the water that runs over the body part that needs a cure. The second part is to take the bowl or basin holding the "used" water and to go outside the house, where the water will be "thrown away" while reciting secret prayers, facing the sun.[158]

"To practice this type of care one must be in possession of the magic formulas. With the water the evil is washed away...in an allegorical sense with the water, out of the house and behind their backs, in a place far away even, or even into the past. After a few sessions, the healer must wash their hands to let go of the evil downloaded and absorbed with their hands form the patient."[159]

MASSAGE METHOD: "through palpitation, [the healer] can locate area affected by disease upon which she can implement the treatment procedure.[160]

VERBAL and GESTURAL METHOD: Uses signs of cross with thumb over the navel area of sick person. Specific secret prayers corresponding to the ailment are used. Before speaking these secret words the healer marks with the cross herself and the patient, and then the body with smaller signs (opening and closing the index fingers and thumb) three times.[161]

CUPPING and GLASS METHOD: the use of cupping is implemented with the massage, and it's also used to resolve the inflammatory state.[162]

DURATION of TREATMENT: *"Healing coincides with the disappearance of pain, usually one of the first patient expectations. The disease is believed to be defeated at the conclusion of the signature/marks given for 3 consecutive days."* [163]

SECRECY: The "guaritrici" do not share the secrets to anyone they are not passing the lineage to. There is also a secrecy of revealing the secret methods of curing for fear of losing the energy of the cure by speaking about it. This is a belief in "keeping the energy with the spell," to ensure the energy stays with what is important: the cure itself. This is also a practical reason: because the secrets are "inherited" and later "passed to someone else," this implies they are "borrowed" and not owned by any person. There is a belief that once a healer "passes her borrowed Lineage secrets to another" that she will lose her ability to cure because also her death is approaching. It is, in a sense, a natural retirement and investment procedure. There is a need to transfer the secret at this time: so the techniques will be available to the next person who desires to be of service.

LINEAGE TRANSMISSION: Traditionally, a healer's knowledge and secret formulas are "exchanged (with a healer-to-be) at, or approaching, the time of her death."[164] There is also another type of transmission which occurs differently in this region: from a Mother-In-Law to her daughter-in-law. This takes place when the daughter-in-law comes to live with the family she married into, so that the lineage doesn't get lost even if it is broken (by the displacement of the daughter-in-law.). Women initiate women.

The special time when this Legacy of curing is handed over is on night of December

24th, Christmas Eve. According to the author, even healers who exchange secret techniques through the internet do so on this date.

It is possible, though it is much rarer to receive a cure and/or the curing techniques (and energy transmission to activate them) from the Spirit World.

Seventh Secrets

During my first couple of days in Guardia Sanframondi I note how different my experience of the Spirit World is down here. In the north I can see many spirits clearly: whether old women at the witch fountains or at the Ca'Botina, or even in the mountaintop forests nearby which are teeming with happy ghosts. But down here in Guardia, everything feels very hidden.

My dreams are also telling me this:

The first night it was revealed to me that the spirits oppressing me and trying to "scramble my thoughts" are spirits of priests and Inquisitors.

The second night I saw a little box I own in my dream: it has stars on it and it has a pendulum inside. In the dream, I was being shown that someone else had a matching box, but I was unable to see who it was, nor who was showing me this.

The third afternoon I was waiting for Domenico to pick me up and take me to another research adventure. I decided to relax on the couch next to Alecia who was working on her computer. Somehow I fell into a dream that wasn't really a dream: I was away somewhere and decided to return home to my apartment… but as I was about to go in I looked up and noticed the front door was open already…there was a gap on the right side and I could see a sliver of complete darkness behind and I sensed a wind blowing. I pushed the door open a little, cautiously, and saw a little post-it note taped to the wall on the right side. It was a note from a friend. I began reading what it said: "I just came to..—" but I didn't get to finish reading the message because someone from inside very violently tried to keep me outside my house, pushing really hard…not just against the door but also through the door. I was pushing against my door with all my strength and someone was pushing against me with great force. I was making grunting sounds from pushing all my body weight against the door….and I was aware I was also next to Alecia still at this time…and the realities blended, and I woke myself up grunting and thrashing my body trying to escape the force that was moving towards me through the door…

I asked Alecia if she heard me and she said "Yes, I just thought you were having a nightmare."

That night I dreamt an enormous German Shepherd jumped up towards my neck. It seemed he was trying to bite my necklace. He wasn't trying to hurt me and I didn't feel any bite. But my necklace, which I wear every day in "real" life, is a protection amulet. Alecia told me, after I mentioned the dream to her, that dreaming of German Shepherds means that you are being protected.

After I met Filomena, Domenico's "nonna," and she made "occhi" for both of us, I told her about my dreams.
She was unphased.

"Yes of course," she said, "because if you are not completely sleeping, and you are a bit awake, you can hear the Janare, and you feel a very big wind and you feel like someone is pushing you."

While it seems my dreams are not uncommon at all around here, and everyone I meet seems to have had encounters like these, I still don't believe the Janare are the ones to blame and I still don't believe the Janare are evil.

Chapter 7:

Il Malocchio

Campanella, the historian, writes this of "nell' occhio" (the eye) :
"The eye manifests a lot of magic things.
When a man meets with another man, pupil-to-pupil,
the light most bright of one blinds and destroys the man who cannot bear with it…
and often brings to the surface passion of the lover, anger of the irate person...
They say the Basilisk kills with the eyes,
because poisonous spirits come out from them.
Whomever likes something opens his eyes to a point where
it seems that he wants to put that thing in his own eyes...
To know it more and appreciate it more.
And while he's opening them, often escaping out of his eyes are
spirits that are eager to get that desired thing too."

[-Sud e Magia, by Ernesto De Martino]

While it's a common expression, "the eyes are the windows to the soul," this phrase has additional meanings in Italy. As I mentioned previously, there is a belief that illness comes from evil thoughts and deeds. One of the ways this evil can be transferred from one person to another as a "deed," is through the power of the eyes. With the eyes you can send energy to someone or receive it; you can curse or bless them.

This action of "transferring negative energy" from oneself to another person through the eyes is called "jettatura." "Jettatura" is often used in phrases which describe its weapon-like action, such as in "the throwing of" the evil eye" or "the casting of" the evil eye.

The result of the "jettatura" is that an intended victim receives 'il malocchio," or "the bad/ evil eye." The "evil eye" is blamed for causing illnesses which don't seem to have a diagnosable root and are therefore mysterious and troublesome; strange body issues like unending coughs, pain and fever with no source that also resist herbal cures; headaches; past life curses that are still in "effect;" illnesses which don't fit into the historical list of ailments and their corresponding lineage cures. These are the illnesses often blamed on "il malocchio," and part of that blame is often taken by malignant spirits, also known as "spirit attachments." who seemingly enter and exit through the eyes.

In previous chapters I included some very short lists of curing plants and other methods which treat illnesses that have specific causes or physiological symptoms. For example, these illnesses can be the ones that are the result of farm work, such as "storto" (twisted muscles), sciatica (spinal nerve pain), and "colpo delle streghe "(lower back pain, it's nickname is "blow of the witch"). There are also illnesses whose root is in the digestion system such as intestinal worms, "verruchi," and some in the nervous system for example. These illnesses are treated by specific lineage techniques which work the same way for each person (the "formulas" differ from lineage to lineage, but within each lineage the procedure to cure sciatica is exactly the same for a 60 year old man as it is for a 33 year old woman.

The "occhi" (the eyes) is a cure which removes the negativity received from "il malocchio." "Making the eyes" is a procedure that both diagnoses whether or not someone's illness is a result of the "evil eye" and also releases and removes the negativity, offering an immediate relief from physical discomfort. It also reveals "who has got eyes on you." As in my case, the "occhi" released a past-life curse whose cure would continue to have a dramatic change on the dynamics of my life after I'd return to the U.S.

Interestingly, many lineage healers also practice a form "occhi" in addition to their traditional "sets" of cures, but this is not consistent all across the board. For example, some women I met who cure with herbs don't use the "occhi," but they do cure ailments "at a distance" for people who can't come to visit them using the moon and the patient's name. Some women use only oil and water methods to cure, for example their "toolkit" is only: "occhi," and "massagio" (massages) with oil and fingertips. And yet, with these methods they cure everything.

Guardia Sanframondi is a southern Italian medieval village that's within the province of Benevento in the region of Campania. While living here I fell madly in love with the typical labyrinthine walkways, the equally mind-bending folk mysteries, and the warm, full-of-life personalities of the people living here. It is full of secrets and ghosts: both happy ones of the people who lived within the walls, and angry ones of the church who don't like that I'm here to research "streghe." Within an hour of arriving, the entire village knows "the girl with the pink hair from San Francisco " has arrived, and they are all very warm and friendly. Something I truly miss here is how everyone greets each other throughout the day "good morning, good early afternoon, good late afternoon, good evening, good night." The people here shared with me many stories of the Janare and the mystical San Gennaro and their own experiences with "il malocchio," they shared their food, their hearts, and more.

There's a lot of lively life in the south, and you learn to just roll with it. Sometimes the theme of the day is "pian, piano" (slowly, we'll get there), and sometimes everything and everyone feels like they are in chaos, but it's usually a joyful mess. There is a wise, if not weary, earthy-ness in the eyes of the people here. The families here all take care of a plot of land, whether for growing their own wine or tending to their own gardens in the black, nutrient-rich volcanic soil, or just because, as Domenico tells me, "we need to put our hands in the earth."

In contrast to their warmth, however, many things remain guarded and hidden, (much like the heart of the village which is protected by the medieval walls), and this can be seen in their eyes as well...if you are paying attention enough. Because everyone is watching everyone else...and the spirits are watching too.

The men tend to hang out in clumps near cafes or piazzas, and the women tend to hang out in smaller groups outside their houses. The women are most interesting to me. They look like they've worked a very hard life: they are tough as nails, though their bodies are short and soft, and many of them have razor sharp eyes. They are really sizing me up, trying to decide if they can trust me. They are very protective of their secrets, but all this is happening on a psychic level: outwardly they are very polite. I love them.

"We have a very big tradition about illness," Domenico tells me. *"My grandma, what she does is a thing called 'occhi,' the eyes. She basically prays for a while, she speaks very quietly and soft, she says something like: 'Father, Son and Holy Spirit,' and other things a few times, since the tradition is mixed with religion as well during the years, and when she puts this oil in, very soon, something happens. It depends on how the oil moves in the water. If it becomes bigger then it means that really someone put the eyes on you, so she's got to do things and we have to repeat it another time. So she starts again, until she says 'Ok, now you can go, you have not anything else on you.' I never understood, how; if it's true, if it's not true, but she used to do that for example, when I was a child and I told her "Grandma, today I have a big headache, I don't feel very well," and very soon she said 'Oh, maybe someone put the eyes on you.' So she does these things to fight 'il malocchio,' that I have to say, maybe when I was a child because I was suggested...but it works!"*

On this particular day, after having driven me to a spectacular look-out point where I was able to get a wonderful view of the vast mountains and farmland valleys of this volcanic area, Domenico mentions that he's got a headache that won't go away. Thinking the headache may be from jealousy or envy, possibly because of the attention he's getting from being connected with my presence in the village, he mentions that would like to go see if his grandma can tell if someone sent him the "evil eye." He invites me along, having already spoken to his grandma about me. Filomena has said it would be ok if I film this procedure and interview her.

Domenico and I arrive and Filomena's lovely apartment. She wears all black, except for her white cooking apron, because her husband passed away some 7 years ago, and it is religious tradition to wear this daily mourning clothing.She is outgoing, chatty and friendly, offering me candies . The two of them have a close relationship, joking with each other in dialect. In the southern way, there are a lot of activities happening at once: the tv is on in one room, Filomena is brewing espresso while we simultaneously begin the "occhi" procedures.

Filomena prepares to see if Domenico's headache is the result of "il malocchio." She has gathered plate: it's a white household soup bowl-type plate surrounded by a wide flat rim. She takes the plate and fills it with water. She takes the oil and pours it into a little espresso cup. She makes the sign of the cross with her right hand three times over the plate of water with her right hand, while quietly saying the secret prayer. She holds her right hand over the water, palm and fingers flat, as if she's sensing something. Her fingers twitch just a little bit. In her left hand is the the cup of oil, and when she is ready, she dips her pointer finger in the oil and lets a drop fall into the water. She is allowing the drops to fall off her finger in a circular pattern, as if they are numbers on a clock. She repeats this 7 times, until there are 7 drops of oil around the plate. 7 is a religious number. Then she wipes her hand on a cloth. She diagnoses: Filomena says that Domenico has the "il malocchio." She has to throw the first plate of oil and water away and she then makes the same arrangement. She has to do it three times to release it: the sign of the cross three times and secret prayer, the hand held over the water, the 7 drops into the water, the diagnosis about how the drops are moving. The release of headache pain occurs with the diagnosis.

She says the first time, if you put the oil and the oil spreads, it means that you have the "eyes." The second time, if they still spread, it means that you need a third time to release the "eyes." She said you need to watch the plate while she's doing it for you. Domenico's first time they spread, which is the indication he had the Eyes.

I ask Filomena if she'll also do it for me, she says yes!

My bowl of water and oil would behave completely differently from Domenico's: Filomena tells me to look at the plate. I sit next to her and watch the plate as she drops the oil in the water. I feel energy moving around my belly. It feels warm and comforting. I feel energy around my shoulders. It feels gentle and tingly. I feel energy around my shoulders, a strong protector, someone helping me. I feel a relief..that someone is taking good care of me. It's a huge sensation.

She says, *"You've got the Eyes, but you've got very old ones."* I say, *"That makes sense,"* because while she is working, I am seeing a vision of my past life in which I had a lot of power as a woman, magical power, and men were jealous of this...I can sense them...I can feel them...I can hear their thoughts of trying to get my power...I can see them....they are the ones who had me burned at the stake.

She says *"The drops in the plates are joining each other, that means two people put a spell on you a long long time ago...they are not fresh."* A little startled that she is confirming what I am seeing clairvoyantly, I say *"I understand, I feel that,"* and suddenly an inflow of information moves through my mind that makes sense of my life through this lens of energy dynamics between myself and men. I feel the strong sensation that someone is lifting something very heavy off of me. I feel something lifted off my shoulders, as though I've been wearing a weighted blanket. I feel something come out of my belly, and I feel the extra space, that I've been emptied of something. I feel expansiveness in my heart, a deep sense of gratefulness that seems ancient, and a deep love. She lets the oil drops fall again. She says, *"Now the second time, they are starting to spread. It means it is starting to release and be removed."*

Domenico says to me, *"The peculiarity is that the first time they joined. The second time they started to spread, they started to spread very slow."* I notice my plate looks very different from Domenico's, and my procedure is taking a lot longer too. I am feeling very deeply relaxed at this point, a warm energy within me that reminds me of the warmth I felt with Antonietta's cure, and I also feel a lightness, as layers are lifted off me, layer after layer. Again, I've experienced a cure with both inner and an outer sensations. Perhaps this one is even more dramatic considering I didn't ingest anything nor did Filomena place any hands on me nor touch my body nor even look in my eyes.

"It's done! (Fatto!)," she declares. I say, *"It's so beautiful watching you do this, it makes me emotional,"* and in fact I start to cry from the beauty. These old Italian women make me cry, they are so beautiful and I feel a deep deep love for them. The only "peculiar" thing for me is that each time I meet these older women, I feel like I am meeting old friends. I actually feel weepy, a sense of emotion that's very sentimental. How can this be? These women are strangers to me, but something or someone is connecting us. Maybe the Great Mother is showing me what these

women look like through her eyes and her heart.

She beings talking about the eyes again. Domenico tells me, *"In your case Karyn, it's interesting because when the drops start to spread, if another little little drop flows to the big one and forms, it means that who put the spell on you is women. But in your case, they didn't come out the little ones. She called them 'orecchino,' earrings, little earrings…that's the way the drops look, when little ones form attached to the big ones. But in your case they didn't come out that way so it's men who put the spell on you."* As Domenico translates this he laughs and says *"I don't know if I want to be the ambassador of this news."* But I understand this because of what I saw and sensed during this procedure and I laugh too, at the brutal and clumsy life we have.

We begin to move along with her interview, as Domenico asks her what she knows about the Janare, but she has to interrupt because she notices the oil in my plate is still moving. *"Look at that Domenico, "* she says as she looks at my plate. *"Look at how much they spread. It means they are very very very old."* I tell her I understand that very much and I think the spell is from one life before or maybe two." I decide to test the waters a little bit to see how she'll respond to my past life vision: *"I think in a life before I was burned in the fire."* She looks completely unphased and just nods her head and says, *"Si (yes), probably comes from that life."*

As we continue talking, I ask her why she uses oil, if it has a significance. Simply put, Filomena says, *"Because if you don't put oil in the water, how you can see?"*

"Oil is one of the most ancient things for humankind," Domenico explains. *"2,000 years ago oils were introduced. So they used oil because they just had oil."* Some healers let drops of water fall off their fingertips into the water, and some use spoon fulls of oil.

After meeting with Filomena, Alecia invited Siliva Pigna and her daughter to come speak with me. My first day in Guardia, Alecia was giving me a tour down the sunny cobblestone streets. As I passed under a medieval archway, I heard a female voice exclaim (in Italian) *"My daughter had hair like that!"* And I turned to see a beautiful woman with a friendly smile dressed in a '70s patterned mini dress that showed all her curves in a very stylish way, with a bit of modern tattoo showing as well. My instinct, as with all women I'd meet in Italy, was to give her a big hug and join in the joy! That was how I originally met Silvia.

"My mamma 'makes the eyes.' She cures 'il malocchio,' she told me. *"She uses oil and water and her hands. She can 'make the eyes' from a distance: On Sunday I had a headache. I took medicine but it didn't work. So I called 'mia mamma' (my mom) and she cured it. She just needed to think about me, then use the plate with water and oil and her hands, and she fixed it. She just needs someone's name to cure to them. She can cure at any distance. If from the U.S. you as ask, 'please make 'occhi' for me,' she does it."*

Silvia said something interesting about another procedure to *"kill the eyes and the bad spirits in a definitive way"* that Domenico's grandma doesn't do: *"When the 'occhi' procedure is finished, if it's winter and your fireplace is on, then you take an uneven (odd) number of* charcoals (for example, 5) and put them into the plate of oil and water. If it's not winter, she says "you can take a match and burn pieces of papers..but always in odd numbers. This is a way to kill definitively the bad spirits."

I ask her if her mamma has taught her these practices and she says *"No."* "Is there a reason she has not taught you?" I ask. *"It's her will,"* she responds. *"I haven't thought so much about 'why not' but I believe in those things. Because anytime I get a headache the medicine doesn't work, so I call my mamma and she always fixes it."* Silvia says that often she has a headache.

Domenico had joined Silvia, Alecia, Silvia's daughter Stella (a super talented photographer) and I to help translate, and now they speak in dialect for some minutes. *"Karyn,"* Domenico says, *"we are speaking about your "malocchio" being from men...women, when we hear it's from a male..."* they begin to laugh, because apparently there can be implications: (Most often the evil eye acts on the sexual sphere: this is why, according to an old custom, touching the genitals protects one from the evil eye.) *"I don't ask my mom where they come from,"* says Silvia, *"but sometimes when I call my mamma to make 'occhi' she sometimes calls me back to ask "'where you have been and with whom, because they are a lot!'."*

"Well," I respond, "you're so beautiful and confident, it's natural that many people would be jealous of you." Silvia's ebullient demeanor becomes a bit serious, *"I'm modest, but also in this period of my life, having had a daughter and been through things, I know my worth. It's important also the behavior you have with other people to keep their envy away."* Silvia has a lot of consciousness about who she is and also about how she treats other people. *"You must be very conscious of this,"* she says.

"On a less funny note," I begin, "my power is not beauty; my power is in expressing myself in the male world, so I believe in the past I was burned in the fire by men, as a 'strega', so that's the very old 'eyes' I felt with Filomena."

"For me it was the opposite, in the past I hoped to become a man, maybe to protect myself from all the bad stuff that was around me," she tells me, and I don't tell her that as a child I had the exact same hope.

This combination of oil and water is used in may other villages. Enzo Gravina, a Beneventan author tells me during a spectacular fact-filled interview which kept me on the edge of my seat. He's the author of the book, "Streghe e Magia" (Witches and Magic) which sheds much new light on a very old and repeated topic in Italy.

"Eye-fighting the Malocchio' (as he calls it) *cures headaches or other symptoms linked to envy or to the negative influences in the Sannio region and throughout Italy: Benevento in Campania, Triora in Liguria, Castelmazzano and Colobrano in Basilicata, Villacidro in Sardinia, Cavalese in Trentino, Bormio and Ribortone in Piedmont, Campolagana in Tuscany, Lezzeno in Lombardy, and the 'passage of the Tonale' (which connects the Valcamonica with the Val de Sole [...] They are the most famous names for those who 'search' to know the rites and legends about witches and their spells and where, perhaps, there are still many behaviors that go back at the time when the 'witches' were present in the life of the community, persecuted and burned at the stake by the Inquisition courts."*[165]

PLANTS

There are also plant-based methods for removing "il malocchio." In one Tuscan tradition (from "the Lungiana" specifically, an historical territory of Italy which now belongs in part to Tuscany and in part to Liguria) to cast out ("scacciato") the evil eye, a powerful amulet is needed, composed of: a blessed olive leaf, a blessed piece of wax and a piece of old stole.[166] In Villafranca (a comune within the Lunigiana), to cure "il malocchio" there is a tradition to: take three sprigs of heather (Calluna vulgaris (L.) Hull.), bathe in water and simultaneously with these three springs you must draw crosses on the sick part of yourself. This ritual is repeated three times on the first night, six times on the second using eighteen different sprigs, after which they are burned on the third night. Then while sweeping the doorstep with a broom you'd say: *"With the broom sweeping away the evil, with the fire it burns out another fire:"* (con la scopa si spazza via il male, con il fuoco si brucia l'altro fuoco).

In the Valle Argentina, the betony grass "l'erbe betonica" belongs to one of the Labiatae family of alkaloids, and is considered effective against the evil eye.[167]

AMULETS

A Sicilian-Italian male lineage healer (now living and curing in hospitals in Paris who gave me an interview) removes "il malocchio" from himself using a pendulum and a photograph.

In Sardinia, a natural amulet against the evil eye is "Santa de Santa Luxia," the eye of Santa Lucia. This is the [seashell] work of a marine mollusk, characterized by the eye (and spiral) shape, precisely, which is easily found on the Sardinian beaches: its function is, like that of Sabegias [Sabazius], to symbolize a good eye that cancels the evil eye. (I've also seen a shell shaped like this one sold in California under the name "cat eye.") Unlike the previous amulets, though, Santa Lucia's eyes can be both worn as jewels that are kept hidden.[168] Interestingly, one of the symbols used in Reiki is a spiral shape, and I have used it quite often to protect myself from troublesome spirits over the years.

"The other basic defense system consists of a whole series of objects such as amulets and apotropaic gestures designed to undo any possible evil influence from others. Among the amulets [...] the goldsmith tradition, [...] using specific stones and special machining [...] in Sardinia [...] is the black stone [...] onyx, obsidian; round, always embedded in [...] silver, because it was believed he would lose his power if tied in gold."[169]

There are more than twenty rituals against the evil eye, but in all cases there are always the following elements: "the "brebus" prayers such as "our Father, Ave Maria", the acting of the faith, often with the use of wheat, water, salt, oil, barley, rice, stone, muflone horn, deer or ox, Saint Lucia eye, coal and paper. To achieve healing, the rite must be repeated from a minimum of three to a maximum of nine times. For the resolution of the most serious cases, three different operators are usually involved.[170]

Two other amulets used in Italy to prevent "il malocchio" are the horn "cornetto" and the chili pepper "pepperoncino," "a habit mostly present in many homes that are in the country, a ccording to an old popular belief the animal horn cast out bad spirits, gave courage and protected from bad luck."[171]

However, the history and meaning of why people use "cornetto" and "peperoncino" proves to be based on ideas that are more modern and don't have a parallel root in nature and are rather indecisive in the way "do it yourself" explanations are, in that they try to give a meaning for the idea, rather than the idea being born from the meaning. Here are some examples:

1) "An important amulet function is also that of the hand that imitates the horns [a fist with pointer finger and pinky finger erect, with thumb and middle fingers folded in], also linked to fertility, as the gesture is a symbolic substitute for the erected male organ, according to folklore scholars."[172] This is untrue. Firstly, comparing the phallus to the hand (which displays TWO finger-"horns") it is a mis-match. Secondly, horns exist in nature in a pair. The pair of horns rather resembles also the female uterus and ovaries, which exists in nature like a mirror-image of the animal skull which has the horns (a center skull with horns on either side) which is why the bull skull, the "bucranium," or bull skull, is one of the most enduring symbols of the Divine Feminine's founding language of symbols whose purpose was to point to objects on the physical earth that are parallels to the spiritual world of energy, Universal laws of energy, and the Divine Mother who gave life to all.

2) "The habit of touching a horn is probably tied to the sharp shape of the horns, an analogy with defensive weapons. According to some, however, their phallic form would recall the idea of fertility and abundance and thus of the metaphor of the fertility of the earth and of the messes."[173]

As for the phallus being a defensive weapon, first, throughout history, the phallus has always been an offensive weapon used to rape women. The phallus has not been traditionally used, in nature nor in society, for protection, but rather as an invasion against it. This attempted comparison is clearly a male directive here. In fact the most ancient ways of living were harmonious; there were no weapons until separatist groups of men created them and used them to oppress and enslave other people and animals and control the food supply.

3) The horns, in fact, represent the anatomical sign of the sexual vigor of animals."[174] Symbolic language didn't ever express "sexual vigor," especially not of animals, until the patriarchy usurped Divine Feminine symbolic language to make "man" seem like the "Source" of all life. Animals have horns on their heads, both male and female, in fact. The horns, in the founding symbolic language, were a mirror of the uterus and ovaries and fallopian tubes, and therefore one of the symbols of the Goddess on earth, connected also to the moon. These things became symbols connected to the Goddess' life-giving ability because they show the parallel in earthly women; they point to life-giving anatomy.

Additionally, the peperoncino (red pepper) is from nature: it is not a weapon but an edible cure and something that maintains health: it is a gift of nature, from the Great Mother. The "cornetto" is a two-horned shape, just like the crescent moon and all horn-bearing animals which are just a symbol of the Goddess because of their uterine representation. Therefore, these amulets of protection are invocations and prayers to the Great Goddess, to whom all ancient people prayed since time began.

This is common occurrence, evidence of when a "new" system wants to get rid of the "old one." The reason for these particular mixed-messages is because their "generation stories" are traced back to Greek and Roman times, which are not that "ancient," at least when you consider that the original symbolic language (and its evidence in statuary, votive offerings, temples, and the origins of plant curing knowledge, metallurgy, clay work, burials, tombs, temples, and magic have an origin that shows all of nature: plants, animals, people) comes from the Great Source which is Divine Feminine energy. This was universally accepted, honored, and celebrated. The original language was symbolic of the world of energy and its parallels on earth; a psychic language if you will. This Language of the Goddess was so pervasive that it was THE founding language; since prehistoric times; her symbols of Universal energy and its parallels in nature in humanity (mostly through women) were everywhere, they are consistent and interconnected, not just in Italy but in all of Old Europe. This is where we come from, but we have forgotten because after the separatists' patriarchy invaded communities, it tried to hide this and turn the world "male" and created "male gods" in their image.

Profoundly, this founding language was also a psychic one that facilitated Mediumistic communications between the Spirit World and the earthly one. This is another reason the church targeted "witches," psychics and mediums: because of their ability to directly connect with higher conscious beings. This ability interfered with the church's directive of being the "go -between," or medium between humans and God, but not for the purpose of answering questions but rather for keeping people in line and punishing society when they were not. One of the important pieces of knowledge that had a parallel of spiritual power "brought down to earth" since most ancient times has been water: both life-giving, and cleansing, it's another natural gift from the Goddess, and early statuary showed the other life-giving fluids which her body was capable of producing. Even the church subsumed the use of water rather than to eradicate it; evidence of the truth of its power. This water, naturally, is used in curing "il malocchio." It's already been blessed by the Divine Mother who created it and gifted it to us on earth and does not need a synthetic "male blessing."

WATER

Water is used as a conduit of healing throughout Italy. In Emilia Romagna, water is used to "wash away evil" and 'throw out' evil and it is used in secret lineage methods to cure specific physical ailments. Handmade crosses are put into water to diagnose the cause of an illness so the appropriate lineage cure can be utilized.

Water and oil are also used throughout the region of Tuscany to remove "il malocchio": olive oil is dropped into the plate of water. If the drops "break," then it means the evil eye is present. All of the water methods for removing "il malocchio" involve using secret prayers and channeled energy.

Within the region of Campania in Guardia Sanframondi, a tradition that differs from both Silvia's mamma and Filomena is: When experiencing an annoying and persistent headache, people often addressed some elderly person who was able to check whether the state of malaise depended on the "il malocchio." The elderly woman poured a little water in a pot (piatto) and while approaching the head of the unlucky person, added some drops of oil in the pot of water, scrutinizing the movement of the them. If they widened, he meant that the person under observation had been the victim of the "evil eye," of someone's aroused thoughts, envious and malignant, and it was necessary to send away the evil. The old woman recited appropriate formulas, accompanying them with cross marks on the face of the unfortunate person, tracing with the same finger used to drop the oil.[175]

Throughout the northwestern Ligurian region water is used in the "pignatta/pignattin" pot and pan along with pins pushed into fresh lamb livers while secret prayers are recited. These actions not only remove "il malocchio" but they also cast out any malignant spirits possessing a mysteriously sick person. Some healers can simply look at the boiling bubbles to discern the problem or "who" caused the problem. In this method, the water is brought to such a strong boiling point that often two men must hold down the lid so the energy doesn't escape before the procedure is completed. Once the water is used for diagnosis and the chosen rites are used, "il malocchio" is released and is transferred to the objects in the water and into the water itself. There is an element of exorcism (outside church methods) involved in this procedure. To complete the cure, a burial of these things is required by some healers.

You won't find many "documentations"of these cures, and the reason has nothing to do with mystery. People don't document aspirin fixing their headaches, nor when other doctor-prescribed pills fix something. While these Italian cures may seem strange to many of us, for them they are quite literally natural. The point of the cure anyway, is to not hold onto it for some "proof" nor glory but bring life back to balance, then to go on with life. However, I did find a couple of older ones from the Valle Argentina in Sandro Oddo's book 'La Medicina Popolare Nell'Alta Valle Argentina," (Popular Medicine in the High Argentine Valley):

"In a local documented story from 1953: a family's young daughter was stricken with unexplainable pains. She had surgery to her adenoids but the pain remained. Her family took her to many expensive hospitals and tried various treatments, including visiting psychiatric specialists who prescribed calming drugs which just kept the girl in a sleepy state but didn't lessen the pain. After many months and in addition to pain in her nose, the poor woman began to complain about increasingly rapid breathing, as if someone was holding her neck to choke her. So her family sought the help of a male wizard ('mago') to help their their daughter. They met the healer ('guaritore'), a man in Val Nervia. The family was instructed by the healer to prepare a lamb's liver intact and a pot of new earth. He then heated the water in the pot and placed it on the tripod over the fire and asked to see the liver. He took a handful of pins and with almost majestic gestures began to stick them one at a time into the liver, pronouncing incomprehensible words, similar to a prayer, alternating the sign of the cross with other bizarre gestures. After about ten minutes, [...] he took the liver with his pins, introduced it into the pot, which was very hot when it came to the contact of the fresh meat, which was raised and abrasive, producing scratching noise. At this point the magician said, 'Perhaps at this moment the sick woman can feel the pain even stronger because the evil spirit that entered her body fights with all his strength to remain in his place but we are superior and therefore he will be forced to leave!' The magician then asked the family to take the

pot with the water and liver and sink it into the earth at least 60 feet from the house.[176]

Ultimately "il malocchio" is considered to be the "magic" that is used to curse; it's vehicle is the eyes. Because of the magical aspect to "il malocchio" and the negative campaign the church made against women healers for over 500 years, I found the resonance of that propaganda when I was repeatedly told local legends of the curses of "il malocchio" and their resulting illnesses being blamed on female witches, while male wizards are considered the ones who cure "il malocchio." One of the most common family stories (currently modern and also from the past) is that babies are targeted by "bad witches" who harm them with "il malocchio."

Silvio Falato from Guardia Sanframondi a folklore expert, etymologist, and author told me, during our interview, one of the main targets of the "Janare" (regional witches) was babies. While the many tales he told me sound imaginary, people claim they are real.

In fact, Silvia from Guardia Sanframondi (the commune in the Province of Benevento which resides in the Campania region) found herself in one of those legends. Silvia told me that when she was a newborn, her mother reported that whenever she'd eat she would also vomit right after. *"Every time, eat, vomit, eat, vomit. So my mamma went to the doctor and was told 'Oh your baby is ok, don't worry about her, we examined her, everything seems fine.' My mamma gave birth to me when she was 17, so perhaps the doctors didn't take her seriously, because this continued: I would eat, then I vomit. I got skinnier. I am a baby, so I was very very skinny, and of course my mamma was very, very worried. It was very difficult also for her to hold me in her arms because I was very skinny and also very contorted. In the end, to have some contact with me without embracing my bony little body, my mamma kept me on a pillow because there was no other manner to manager me. She was worried to hurt me since I was so fragile. I was with no strength in my bones nor muscles apparently, but the doctors keep on saying 'She's fine,' despite all evidence to the contrary. In the meantime, on the pillow, very little pieces of my skin were falling off onto the pillow as the skin all over my body began to peel. My grandma ('nonna') in that period knew there was a man and it was said about him, he keeps away 'fatture' (spells). So my grandma and my mom decided to take me to this man. He poured water in a bowl and then he washed me in the water. I don't know if he immersed me or just washed water over me. They brought me three or four times to this old man to do this. He was around 65 or 70 years old. After these 3 or 4 times, my mamma said I started to eat again, and all the bad stuff went away. So it's useless for me to say 'it's true,' or 'it's not true'"* Silvia tells me, *"because the truth is that I'm here. You have to consider it's not a tale or story that someone told me like a myth or legend, it's something that happened to me."*

One of the most interesting sights I've seen is the variety of ways the oil moves in water to offer consistent diagnosis. In one Lineage, the water does indeed make swirling "double image" oil patterns that look like coiled serpents. In another technique, the oil will always break to show "il malocchio," but in another tradition it will instead always spread outward into a larger circle shape to show the same thing. The oil also moves consistently to show whether men or women have sent "il malocchio" to someone.

PREVENTION AGAINST IL MALOCCHIO:

In the Valle Argentina in Liguria, some women make a bath of "Madonna grass" (erbe la Madonna) by boiling the plants for a few minutes and then putting them in a white bowl. Then they bathe their hands, passing them from head to toe. This tones the body and prevents the evil spirits from entering. This ritual is to be performed in the odd hours, three or five times. (note: Antonietta mentioned in her interview that this herb can fix any problem the body may have. She says it has "7 virtues" which perhaps relate to the 7 chakras).

Rue, if taken in secret or better if stolen, put in a canvas bag and worn on the person, prevents one from envy and therefore the "eyes" in Benevento, the "city of witches of the south" in the region of Campania.[177]

In the region of Tuscany, garlic bulbs and leaves of rue intertwined and brought to the neck or anywhere on the body are used to prevent "il malocchio." Another tradition is to carry in your pocket some hemp that was twisted on Christmas night.[178]

In Sardinia, *"in the folk tradition we find a system that involves sending a flower for nine consecutive days to the person who hurt us. The method works only if the flowers are sent with a feeling of sincere friendship. Also in Sardinia the saber, 'La Sabegia' symbolizes the ocular globe, in this case the good eye that contrasts with the bad eye, drawing its gaze; Its function is to save those who have it, splitting instead the heart of the 'guarded' person who is watching them. The saber was hanging on the cribs, while the older children generally wore it to the wrist, tied with a green ribbon and was traditionally gifted by the grandmother or the godfather of baptism. Women, on the other hand, wore it on the neck or hanging on the corset."*[179]

While in Italy, I "met" many people through their eyes, and they also "met" me this way. In Rome (and in Venice) I spent a lot of my time in the train station. I observed there were many gypsy women begging for change. While occasionally I saw one of these women looking genuinely sad, most of these women were quite psychic and very strong, very smart hustlers. I felt them trying to send me messages through their eyes "pay me or something will happen to you." Instead of fearing this, I recognized it and sent them messages back. And in their eyes, I saw they received my return message, and often we ended up laughing and embracing. In effect, with my eyes I said "I caught you! But I still really like you!" There was no money exchange, but a communication much more valuable was had.

Often, while interviewing people around Italy, my group and I would be outside gathered at a small cafe table: my laptop recording, my translators translating my guests, and my guests talking. While this was happening, sometimes women nearby would be drawn to me, and would come towards me, showing me their eyes. Even writing this now I can remember each one showing me this deep and almost overwhelming sadness, grief, and weight of invisibility, as if they'd been waiting for someone to "see" them, and I was the one. Often these women would tell me I came along to brighten their day. We'd briefly stop the interview to dance, or I'd give them a reading, and whatever trinket I had in my pocket so we'd have a remembrance of this moment.

Ultimately what "il malocchio" teaches us is that "thoughts are things," and that everything we do hasan affect on the world around us (inner and outer). This is a very ancient idea, one that resurfaces in each new time's period's mystical teachings. The parallel often used to explain how it works on an unseen "energy" level is: when a butterfly flaps wings, air moves not only around the butterfly, but through the whole neighborhood, and it keeps moving for miles and miles after each flap of her wings. These are actions which can just be subconscious (like breathing or walking) or conscious (I will breathe 8 times in and 8 times out, releasing negative energy and drawing in the golden light of abundance with each breath.) We can just let ourselves have mind chatter, or we can watch that chatter and focus it...into positive or negative thoughts. We can be active or passive, but no matter what we choose, our thoughts are moving our from our mind and affecting the world around us. The more intentional we are, the more we see evidence of the world around us supporting our thoughts... because they are supported both in the positive and in the negative.

"Il malocchio's" envy can also take a more focused turn, and one even more desperate. In Lucania, (also known as Basilicata, a southern region of forests and mountains and thousands of years old cave complex dwellings which touches parts of its borders with Campania and also contains the peninsula now known as Calabria), we can find a type of magic whose methods are more advanced (using just the mind in combination with naturally occurring "movements" and therefore the "energy" of actions) and simultaneously or rather ironically, more negative.

Described by author Ernesto de Martino in his book Sud e Magia, *"the themes of magic, forces of fascinations, of possession, of spells and exorcism are without any doubts in connection with the immense power of the daily negative that whoever lives there has to deal with from the birth to the death. The immense power of negativity along the entire life of an individual born there, and the connected fragility of anything that is positive is the root of the magic of Lucania. Similarly, the magic ideology connected with being pregnant, delivering a baby, feeding the baby, and the risk that a child is prone to, are things that are mostly at the root of the practical magic."*[180]

"In Valsinni, a mother that is plagued with lack of milk hides a tiny bit of salt in the kid's blanket and asks a friend to go with the kid to visit a luckier mother. Coming back from the magic expedition the mother without milk will prepare for herself a soup using the salt from the wrapping that one hopes absorbed the milk of the victim. After the rite is done, the milk starts flowing from the breasts of the thief. If the woman that got robbed discovers who is the responsible one, sends people to call her, the two women will have to show each other the breasts spraying a tiny bit of milk out of it while the one that got robbed says 'I don't want any of yours. and I don't want to give you mine.' This way, the jinx is done."[181]

This is an example of magic coming from poverty; a method used to "get something from someone" when basic needs are not met. A mental focus on "the lack of" is a negative perspective. As with any "energy"or "spiritual" method, the mind directs the positive or negative outflow. Abundance is the gift of the Goddess; and she can provide all; but "where your focus goes, energy flows," so the outflow is dependent upon the perspective of the person or persons the channeled energy is running through. While poverty is a situation created by the people who govern the society within it, poverty stays in place with a limited perspective, which is very human, so that limit can spread into all thoughts, feelings, prayers, and magic. Evolve or devolve. Magic is the currency of the poor, but whether we place our focus on "expanding from where we are and rising up" with our magic, or "taking from someone else because there isn't enough," it is our choice. Our choices matter, because there is magic that is of the self, then there is magic that is assisted by the Spirit World. Spirit World partnerships can give us the ability to do something far beyond our current capabilities.

"Il malocchio" teaches us that everyday people are already "doing spells" both good and bad against each other by having thoughts and actions of: jealousy, bullying, envy, and more. Thoughts do have affects, just as physical actions do, though they are more subtle. Because, like a moving butterfly wing, once you put your thoughts in motion by adding emotion to them, you simply cannot foretell just how far your vibrations will travel. This is not so difficult to imagine either: when your friend or partner is in a bad mood, you may feel that mood too, and what was a good day suddenly dims, and you may be afraid to say certain things in their presence in that moment because their mood is so strong and you worry about it expanding. This is an example of sensing "unseen" information. The "vibe" is very real, and you are affected by someone else's mood even though it's not your mood. You are sensing intangible information that is accurate.

"The human spirit, even the most enlightened, always has a dark corner where the horrible chimeras of the credulous are hidden, where the bats of superstition hang. The same ordinary life and so full of insoluble problems, that the impossible becomes probable. You can believe and deny everything: from a certain point of view, the dream is the same as reality."[182]

Eighth Secrets

I have learned a lot about the Spirit World from a lifetime of intense experiences and I am well-protected. However, as I mentioned, much of my learning during this journey has been through sensing, feeling, seeing and "re-living" this history through the memories of the women.

I didn't realize the opposition I might come up against trying to honor the women who were targeted by the Inquisition and to also validate the modern women who are psychics, healers, and Mediums.

The ways spirits of Inquisitors and other spirits who didn't want me to focus on this work created patterns that I could always recognize. At first, it was alarming at times, because the sensations were like giant waves of heavy emotions. I had to live in two realities when this would happen: knowing that I was fine, that my life was wonderful and this this would pass…and then being overwhelmed whatever sensations they sent "over me," draping them like shrouds. The best way I can think to describe what I can discern as a Medium is that at times I can feel the emotions, thoughts, self-esteem, personality and perspective of someone else as if I had "tried on a piece of clothing" that was full of these intangibles..almost like stepping inside someone else. I am aware of the difference between me and that person, but it doesn't make the sensations less dramatic.

The patterns of oppression I felt were:

- Feeling a "brain scramble." When I'd be at my computer translating documents or writing about the Inquisition in particular, I would see my vision become blurred and my mind would slow down and become sluggish. It was as though I were in mental quicksand. The feeling of weights being on my hands, my legs, my shoulders, felt like I was being immobilized, and my mind would scramble: mentally I am naturally quick and sharp, but when this would happen suddenly thoughts became stretched out so far it was difficult to follow them. As a result I would "lose time," often "paralyzed" in this position for a couple of hours until I could mentally move myself onward. This always occurred as I was discovering something very important, like proof of the evils of the church against women.

- Feeling waves of emotion come over me that were larger than my own emotions. I would liken this to being like having a marching band show up in your bedroom, the way you would feel hearing all that music around you, confined in a small space but instead of sound you experience feelings in that enormous way.

- Hearing male voices oppose my thoughts. If I was opening my mind to something new and positive related to this material, I'd often hear male voices trying to interfere by saying something that would conflict with my emotions. For example, if I felt excited about something they'd say "you don't enjoy this, this is a waste of time." After I'd complete a chapter and took a quick moment to pause and reflect and be grateful for progress, I'd hear male voices saying "No one will care about this. You are not worth anything. Nobody cares."

  These experiences were always trying to lower or slow down my vibration, my energy, my thoughts. I always knew what was happening, but these were the strongest battles I've had to fight to date.

- Being pulled into memories. These were moments that actually scared the oppressive spirits away, interestingly, because they showed a parallel between a person in my proximity and something the Inquisitor spirits wanted to hide. For example, I was on the bus going to work listening to my ipod. A man sat next to me. He seemed strange, so I began to pay more attention. He was seated very stiffly, and as I looked at his clothing, he was dressed like a small boy but he was an older man. As a result, he looked very stiff and neat and tidy in a way that was unnatural. He began to twist his fingers together in a way that struck me as "obsessive compulsive" and as soon as I had that thought I began to see this man's secret: he had some very dark sexual perversions. For some reason this opened a door into the memories of Inquisitors and I saw that they were also very sexually perverse men. The spirits were not happy about this and ran away, The man moved from his seat at the same time. Later I discovered some research that documented Inquisitors having sexual obsessions with women who they would capture just to torture for this reason.

Chapter 8:
Le Stregone, Le Maghi, Le Guaritori
(The Sorcerers, The Wizards, the Healers)

"The art of the sorcerer consists especially in making harmless the influence of hostile men or evil beings. He is called in severe cases, if the disease is caused by hostile people, or rather that the cause of it is a demonic entity …"

from "Sud e Magia" (the South and Magic) by Ernesto De Martino

"I was always encouraged to go out and listen to nature and talk to animals. When I was younger, I was just having fun, but knowing what I know now, I think they were training me for something, or giving me the elements to where they could see what I was or what I had. I think when my Grandma found out that I had received "it," there was confusion because I'm a man, and the lineage for so long was female[...] So when she sat me down she said, 'There is a heritage, a lineage you're born to. You are in a line of very misunderstood women.'"

[from my interview with Alexander Braboy, 2017].

The air of mystery that surrounds Italian female witches also swirls around the even lesser known male witches. This smoke-and-mirrors is borne of church instigation and perpetuated by way of folk tale, but is also likely is attributed to the very real and unique characteristics of male witches. To assist this understanding, it's helpful to suspend your ideas of what male "witches" are as well.

In many villages of Italy, male witches are called "stregone," which translates to wizards and sorcerers, rather than "male witch." "Lo stregale"is a name in folktales (who is considered in Benevento, for example, to be a male assistant to Satan in folk tales and is similar to another word "stregare" which means "to bewitch"); and "mago"(which translates to "magician") among others. These names mix function with superstition. Whether they are healers who cure with hands and prayers, ones who release "il malocchio" in various ways, or ones who exorcise evils spirits, they are the ones people go to for cures when sorcery is believed to be the cause of an illness. Beyond dealing with just "evil spirits," they are also Mediums who communicate with the Spirit World of passed-on relatives and other earthly people, and can also divine the future or peer into the past.

In Italy's popular belief (the folk tale side) it is the female witches who create illness, especially ones that target newborn babies, and it is male witches who are able to"undo" the harm done by female witches. (In reality, this "anti-propaganda" confesses the church's knowledge that women have a vast and deep understanding of illness in ways that educated male doctors and monks never came upon. And yet, the goal in the 1200s was to turn people away from the women healers they'd always been cured by. How to do this? Create fear.

Use them as scapegoats for what is still largely considered unexplainable and mysterious: the cause of illness, and even more terrifying, the cause of illness in newborns. Then, turn these fears into easy-to-remember stories so they remain in-memory and easy to pass along. Back up these ideas with public punishments of women, i.e. the Inquisition, and you have a socio-political way of controlling society's caring for themselves versus using your created industries. These ideas have remained part of the culture in Italy, and I met many women who believe them.

When a baby is sick and can't be cured by other means, families take take their baby to a male wizard to be cured. This is not a story from long ago folk tales, this is something that is still done today. I met quite a few people who, as babies, had become strangely ill and whose parents took them to see wizards (often in the mountains, incidentally, where female witches live and cure too) to be cured by magical means, even after standard doctors were unable to help. So whether or not the illness can truly be blamed on an "evil female witch," the reality outside of the folk tales is that the male wizard time and time again has in fact been able to cure illnesses of mysterious origins, and still does.

This peculiar belief in duality is very Italian: this confusing division of female witches = good and bad; male witches = good, is found throughout Italy. It is one aspect of the lasting effects of the church's ironic campaign against women. This is why you may meet old women doing "things" that look like magic, such as instantly curing illness in particular ways that might easily be called "witchcraft" by modern observers. You may find these very same women fervently denying any connection both witches and magic. This duality extended to men as well: psychic men who performed acts of magic outside of church associations were also punished. Oddly enough, the church was practicing magic also, but they were claiming to do it with help of their business' mascot "God," which made it "ok" to do spells and have rituals.

Because more than this instigation of the "feared, evil woman" is a church-driven deterrent from spiritual practices where women and men are in direct connection with Divine Intelligence (through psychic phenomenon, Mediumship and its practice of channeling, and also natural unstudied intuition.). It's also part of the religious "divide- and- conquer" aspect to social control. Keeping men and women divided from each other has its benefits for a governing social body (by instilling competition rather than cooperation) , and keeping people divided from their psychic abilities has its benefits in forcing people to rely on other people (the church) for answers.

Natural "magic," on the other hand, or more precisely in Italy's case indigenous shamanism, puts the power to receive abundance (health, food, herbs, babies, knowledge, guidance, cures) in the hands of the people (and their relationship with the Spirit World), which is a revolutionary idea in the face of governments and religious establishments who are in "power" and control over the healthcare, food distribution, money flow, and right to religious beliefs and practices of the people in societies. And do not forget that men were also killed during the Inquisition, for bearing "witch-like" traits of their female "counter parts." Imagine a world when men and women supported each other's connections to nature and the Spirit World, and a world where all genders were seen as natural...it would be a very different world to try and control socially, politically, and economically. It would be the world as it began: as a psychic and Mediumistic one full of witches.

Returning to male witches, this popular belief in duality extends to them as well, though it's less heard of. In Italy's southern region of Campania, for example, specifically in and around Benevento is a living folk tale portraying "lo stregale" (the specific name for male witches in this popular tradition) to be the "devil's assistants," especially in particular group gathering-type holidays where once a year we see "streghe "(female witches), "janare,"(female Mediums), and the Devil himself gathered together.

Silvio Falatto is an expert on Benevento folk tales as well as an etymologist. He recounts one of the popular tales to me during our interview: *"Lo Stregale' is basically a helper of Satan. This holiday occurs on the night of June 23rd ('La Notte delle Streghe') The Night of the Witches, which is followed by the paired holiday day of June 24th, the day of San Giovanni (St. John's day). When this day comes, all of the witches are full of wine. The night before, they recite these the formula: 'sott'aqua, sott' abiende sott'a noce di Beneviende,' which is a very old spell in dialect that means 'Over water, over wind, take me to the Walnut tree of Benevento.' Then suddenly everywhere is a sensation of wind, and this wind is the 'Streghe' and the 'Janare' who are flying and also Peppinella (old lady witch) and also Christina, and Gilda the beautiful are flying, they celebrate themselves to each other saying 'you are so beautiful, you are amazing, such a flower, the night is shining, the stars are very strong.' You can smell a very strong sulfur smell.*

And from so far away you can also see one of them on a 'scopa,' (flying on a broom) who is Rosina the Death, who is also mute, who is the boss and who is hiding a very long queue of 'Streghe' (not Janare). The 'Janare' stopped before and they feed the 'Streghe' because they were the popular side, the 'Streghe' were the nobility side, so the 'Janare' have to feed them (for the gathering) they have to fly the whole night…they finally arrive to the 'Noce di Benevento' (walnut tree of Benevento), where there is the 'Stregale' (Satana's/Satan's helper) who is surrounded by 'Streghe' and 'Janare' on both sides. All around the little devils jump, the little demons. These little demons help the ceremony bringing the special oil in the bottles. Presiding over everyone is 'Satana,' (Satan) the devil. The 'Stregale' is nearby him and all the 'Streghe.' along with the little devils. As soon as they can they make 4 lightning and 4 thunders. You can see flames everywhere because it's an imaginary world, and an orgiastic ritual starts. Then after a bit, slowly the flames begin to subside. Then 'Satana' begins to make dates and orders, as has been discussed. For instance, they can only go out at midnight on Tuesdays and Fridays, etc."

Beyond the colorful and confusing imagery (as Silivo says, it's an "imaginary world," which is a detail lost on most people) here we see the addition of sexuality, because the attacks against witches were obsessively focused on female sexuality being "out of reach" for the regular men (of the church) , and we can find in Inquisition documents (mostly outside of Italy, because Italy's records are hidden or destroyed for the most part), church men obsessed with particular village women who they desire sexually. This hunger is what often drives them to kidnap women and put them in private "torture rooms," where they are stripped naked and fondled by the men while trapped in torture devices.

The church created the Devil, pairing women with a powerful supernatural man who is in control of their sexuality. We don't ever hear stories of male and female witches working together (neither one having power over the other). We only have stories about the male Devil having power over and sex with women, and this is where the church also connected male witches to their story: in a supportive role of "Satan's" dominance over the witches powers, once a year determined by Satan, who is also in control of the women's magical abilities, both on this holiday and for the rest of the year. They church is so afraid of independent, autonomous women that they even connected their own gender to witches...because the church is an all-male institution, so we can consider the church to be, simply, "men."

These stories are like "church pornography," and they are literally truth that has been "perverted." And yet, from these tales we mostly know more about the women of myth and not the men. These stories do pit men against women however, in ways that are parallel to the patriarchal material world's social values. And still, who are these "stregale?" What do they do? What are their powers? Just like women, the exist outside of the folk tales and are very real.

I haven't yet met one of these allegedly "diabolic" witches. This elusive, evil witch who is of the folk tales, in some partnership with the Devil, she is not to be found. Nor have I met yet any of these mystical wizards who are able to cure incurable ailments created by women. I have, however, met plenty of "witches" who wouldn't call themselves "witches," including men, who do incredible things on earth. Within earthly Italy, where "reality" is already magical, it is true that men can also come from Lineages. Their Lineages are frequently passed as male-to-male transmissions, but there are men within female family Lineages as well. Their Lineages seem to be less commonly found than female ones and there is a perfectly technical explanation for this: Feminine energy is receptive. Masculine energy is outwardly active. This is the foundation for conceptual ideas about feminine energy being about the inward journey, being able to see light within darkness...and where natural psychic senses are active. In parallel, the concept of masculine energy being outward, explorative, magnetic, applies as well.

Feminine energy is different from a "woman" and masculine energy is different from a "man." Each human being has both energies, in different blends. In a technical nutshell, it is therefore more natural for people with either dominant feminine energy (who've found balance with masculine energy) or for people with dominant male energy who've found a balance with feminine energy or even transformation into a dominance of female energy to naturally be open to psychic sensations and to communication with the Spirit World, which comes through the psychic sensations. Reception is the key here, and it is where expansion is possible; whereas will alone is limited by human capabilities.

The difference between female witches and male witches is how their unique relationships with the Spirit world are expressed. Naturally dominant male energy lends itself, in the spiritual expression, as psychic phenomenon (the movement or manifestation of physical and visible-to-the-naked-eye matter by energetic means with assistance from the Spirit World) such as levitation and transfiguration.

In levitation, spirit people lift an earthly person, defying gravity. The earthly person is not performing this act of their own will. Scottish "physical" medium DD Home levitated in front of skeptics, government officials, and others over 100 times, even moving out of a window and coming back in, demonstrating the limitless possibilities of energy versus the slower, finite and limited physical form. He was documented repeatedly during the Spiritualism advent in North America in the 1800s, along with other physical mediums producing ectoplasm (which often created a "mask-like" presentation of a spirit-person's face superimposed over a flesh-and-blood medium, called "transfiguration). Also documented were bursts of trumpets and other music and rapping sounds "in the air" where no humans could be found creating the sounds. These phenomena continue until today, but very rarely. These abilities are also found among Italian "stregone."

In brief comparison, dominant masculine energy, in partnership with Spirit World assistance, can demonstrate the illusion of physical matter overcome. Dominant feminine energy in partnership with Spirit World assistance can demonstrate the accessibility of vast technical knowledge gained without education, money, nor social status: something from nothing, which can change matter in the physical world very quickly.

MODERN DAY "STREGONE"

Yves B. is my friend Fabrizio's uncle. I met Fabrizio in Ospedaletti in Italy's northwestern region of Liguria. Yves' family is from Sicily, but he was born and raised in France. He is currently still in France, legally working as a healer in a large hospital. He has been photographed with red and blue lights coming out of his hands while healing a client. The photo is hanging in the hospital. Yves tells me his story:

"When I was 5 months old, something weird happened to me while I was in my cradle. My parents put me to bed, and in the morning they found me under the bed sleeping. My parents weren't able to understand how it happened.

"When I was 5 months old, something weird happened to me while I was in my cradle. My parents put me to bed, and in the morning they found me under the bed sleeping. My parents weren't able to understand how it happened.

When I was 8 years old, and I did my first communion, another thing that was weird happened. My grandfather put his hand on my forehead and started saying some prayers, claiming that he had to do it. No one understood what he was doing or why he was doing it. My grandfather was a 'pranotherapist.' I was 13 years old when he died. My father Joe was seeing my grandfather in his dreams, but he was also able to see him, his spirit, when he was awake. My grandfather was telling my dad that at midnight of Christmas (Christmas eve) he was supposed to put his hands on my forehead and then say a specific prayer. My dad didn't believe him and he didn't say the prayer. For three times he refused to listen to what my grandfather (his father) was telling him to do to me... so much so that the next time my dad had a vision, the grandfather said to him 'if you don't do what I tell you, I'm going to hurt you badly.' So finally he did.

Then, when I was still 13, I started to work [as a pranoherapist] with the people in the family: uncles, aunts, some of them had pain in the back or in the knees, for example, and even if I wasn't trained to do something from a medical point of view, I was helping them heal. After that

I then started to see my grandfather in my dreams too, in the same way that my father was seeing him. Seeing my grandfather [that way], those are not dreams but apparitions. My grandfather is appearing in the room as a spirit, during the day, not in dreams. Basically my grandfather was training me on using the gift he had, and I had basically become a pranotherapist. I constantly keep being in contact with my grandfather till this day.

I have a ring, the same ring my grandfather used to wear. I wear it all the time when I need to do some energy work. There's a big black stone in the ring. When my grandfather died, everyone in the family wanted that ring, but whomever was wearing it was getting sick. When I was 18, considering that no one was able to wear the ring, I decided to keep it because I didn't get sick from wearing it. Then my grandfather said 'Of course that ring is for you and you've got to use it to do your Practice.'

When I was 20, a Medium realized that I was gifted, so she did some tests on me. She put me with my back to one side of the room, and I was facing the window. She was facing the window from the balcony. She was able to space travel like a doppleganger; she was able to get out of her own body from the window [by astral traveling] and I was able to perceive exactly where she was traveling to in the house. Growing up I got a regular job, and the healing work I was doing was just reserved for family members. I wasn't doing that professionally yet. My wife didn't believe me nor my explanation about my grandfather. She was asking me to prove that all what I was talking about was real. She was asking for noises or for furniture to move.

I had a big Belgian dog, black, that had three cerebral attacks. I was able to heal him all the times. The dog lived to be 17 and then died.

Then my father had varicose veins and his legs were very swollen. He needed to do a emergency operation so I tried to work his legs in the same way I was working with the other family members. Things got so much better that 3 days prior to the operation, my father wanted to see the doctors because he was able to walk, perform, and do everything. The doctor didn't know how to explain how he got so much better. His legs were not swollen anymore. He didn't need the operation anymore. After this event, my grandfather pushed me to start using this gift for other people, not just the family members. So I decided to go to Paris and to start making a living out of this. I had a family at this time, I had kids, a wife, but I never really took this gift seriously until that time.

In 2000 I went to Paris to get a certification for my pranotherapeutic gifts in order for me to start officially working . They gave it to me, and I now practice in France where I am in the official National list of Healers.

Now I'm a Medium, a card reader, a mentalist, I'm able to take off the evil eye ("il malocchio"), and I do regressive hypnosis. My tools are: pendulum, hands, and prayers. I still use my grandfather's ring. To take off the evil from houses I also uses incense, and each prayer has its own purpose. To recharge myself I go into the forest and look for a particular type of tree (not sure of the name), and I hug that tree for ten to 15 minutes and that action takes off any negative attachments that I might have. If I cannot go to the forest, I work with a picture of myself and a pendulum to take off "il malocchio." I also take showers to take off "il malocchio," two showers per day to recharge. I rub my body with coarse salt before taking a shower, and I take up to three showers per day if the negativity is particularly bad. If I don't clean myself, I get very heavy attacks of coughing: continuous cough, constant cough, my body gets sick. I sleep 3-4 hours per night. Since three years, I passed some of my power to my children. One of the two is following me (as a healer) the other is not because he doesn't care. Sometimes to recharge myself I ask my son to work with me.

Between 1995 and 2002 I levitated seven times. It happened to me both while I was sleeping and also while I was awake. When I was in bed, I was basically feeling that my body was raising, going up to the ceiling, and I was able to see myself on the bed, then I was falling back down into my body. Every time I had levitation at night, the morning after I was feeling particularly energized, like a million bucks. The last time that happened in 2002, I not only was able to go up, but I also twirled around so much that I got scared and wondered 'how do I go down now?' and as soon as I touched the soil again I was hyper and full of energy.

`In 2003 I was invited to speak on tv because a person I knew was in contact with someone who had a tv program about the supernatural. They did a tv report on me and they did two tests. They put me in one room. There was one other person in another room with a pendulum. They asked me to say how the pendulum was turning in the other room. I always said the right thing. The second test was with 4 people holding objects in their hands, one of which was an amethyst. I was supposed to find out who was holding the amethyst using my own pendulum. I was able to find out each time correctly.

There is a secret code between my grandfather's spirit and me: a special noise so that I know when my grandfather is there and not another spirit. If the following day I need to get some particular meaningful messages, my grandfather makes some peculiar noises at night. So when I hear these particular evident sounds, I know that during the day after I will have to pay attention so as to capture messages from my grandfather (they could be about anything). My grandfather makes his presence known this way to help me be aware. As soon as I get in contact with my grandfather, the houses are bombarded by loud noises." [end interview].

Within Yves' story are some of the most compelling consistencies I've found in my research that occur among Italian men of various ages who are being called into a lineage. Whether the legacies (such as Yves') are familial lineages, where a family member elder chooses whom in their family line to pass their abilities (not everyone in a family line receives the transmission); or whether these lineages are shamanic in the way they first were passed down to people on earth: the Spirit World elder (a Goddess/Great Mother teacher) chooses whom will receive the lineage teachings and transmission, and then unfolds the path piece-by-piece), the consistencies are there.

The compelling aspects of male lineage transmissions are:

1. Jewelry is important. They may have a special family heirloom ring which only one person in the family is meant to receive; or they have a natural inclination to find and wear a special ring or piece of jewelry.

Often the jewelry incorporates black or white (stones or colors) which are colors pointing back to our earliest spiritual connections on earth with the Great Goddess Mother, who passed down curing techniques. Knowledge of metals and how to use them were one of her gifts to the women. Stones represent her as "heaven coming down to earth," as meteorites. In Italy, many goddesses were considered to have "appeared: with the advent of black meteorites fallen down to earth, and it was not unheard of to find old women kissing black stones before they entered church.

Physical objects are important in general (or needing to be around ones that "feel" ok), being that they are a more external energy, in line with the masculine flow of energy. Male witches are often natural "feelers," able to sense the feelings of others, the "vibes" or a room or location, and the energy of objects (through psychometry. They are also channelers, and express this as musicians who create music and seem to write faster than others, or researchers who find information and connect the dots; any work that is manifested faster than usual and often while in a "trance" state where the "stregone" doesn't entirely remember doing the act.

2. They have a natural understanding with animals and an ability to naturally cure them simply through touch.

3. They display psychic phenomena of a physical nature that can be seen or experienced by other people such as levitation (which recharges the body and takes place instead of forced meditation and often when a male witch is overly stressed or "crowded" with psychic bombardment) and disembodied sounds (when a spirit person near the male witch makes loud sounds) and movement of objects (when a spirit relative moves objects around so the male witch will pay attention to it). This phenomena is performed by the male witch's relative who is assisting them.

4. A negative mindset can be detrimental to a male witch who has no spiritual practices in place for clearing his energy field or learning how to raise up his vibration. Negativity can can express itself as physical psychic phenomenon such as suffering the effects of spirit attachments such as seeming to have "multiple personalities" and depression. Negative emotions misdirected can express as eruptive telekinesis. For men, experiencing the emotions of others (during healing and from empathetic nature) is more difficult and challenging than it is for women. Water becomes an important natural cleansing element for them, energetically.

5. Being "watched" by living-on-earth relatives to see if they have "it" before they are trained.

6. Passed-over relatives remain close by to "train" their living-on-earth relative, similar to a shaman who has a Spirit healer work through their body, guiding them in their healing practice. However, family members as Spirit guides are rare and special because usually this assistance is offered by Spirit people who've dedicated themselves to being teachers and are no longer reincarnating into life on earth as an earthly relative would.

Alexander Braboy is an American I worked with for several years. I recognized, in his personal story, so many similarities to Italian "stregone," that I prompted him to find out if he in fact had an Italian heritage. He does, but he also has another lineage.

I was curious to know about him also because whenever we would be near each other, I saw (in spirit) an old woman with a pillbox fur hat and capelet and jewels, with a strong, stern face and I sensed that she was a "witch," but not in a modern, romantic sense, but rather part of something much older. She also had, I'd learn through out interactions, a great understanding of the Universe and its laws. She would also often push me to teach specific things to Alex (who is very stubborn). This would be his grandmother.

Perhaps the most telling part of his story is that both his mother and his grandmother have remained close to him to train him from the Spirit World, just like with Yves. They have both completed their death transition processes (they are not "ghosts" trapped in the astral realm avoiding their live review, etc.). Also, he is a gay man in an all-female lineage.

"I was born in Franklin, Tennessee, which is outside of Nashville, in a very affluent, white, southern area, but because it was so near Nashville, it was very open. It wasn't your typical southern town. But I was very sheltered. I was raised very properly. Because of my Old European heritage, both the Russian Jewish and the Scottish, and me being the first generation, there were a lot of aspects that for a long time weren't talked about, especially on my moms' side."

My father's family is from Scotland, very well-off, and they started coming over [to the U.S.] during the civil war. There's a side that is from Italy, my father's mother's side, from somewhere in the south.

My mother's family were affluent in Russia, but because of their Jewish heritage and their escape, they lost everything and had to start over. They did become super successful in Kentucky, but perhaps because of this there was always this weird tension between the two sides of the family.

During the time of Hitler, the Nazis were going into villages saying "we're going to take care of you," but some people in the villages found out this was a lie and tried to warn people, but for some reason people believed the Nazis. But my grandmother, she intuitively knew what was happening, she sensed it, and she told my grandfather, 'We HAVE to go." But it was so quick that my grandfather just…the only thing they could take was a suitcase, and they put all my grandma's jewels in it. They lost everyone because none of the family wanted to believe the Nazis were lying, so my grandparents were some of the few who escaped. My grandmother got sick on the trip to America and somehow they landed in Kentucky, learned English from the radio, and my grandpa would sell her jewels on trips to NYC when they needed money. He started working in coal mines, because it was the only thing he could do, and eventually, because he was a good businessman, he came to own the coal companies. That's basically how my mother and father got together: because they were still old School European, it was almost a fixed marriage. My father's people were in the TVA, Tennessee Valley Authority, which is this huge electrical company, so my one set of grandparents in electrical, the other set in coal, and the marriage didn't work out very well.

I grew up in a mansion. It was a little isolated, not on farming land, but there was acreage around all the houses, so your next door neighbor was across the lake. I was surrounded by nature, very sheltered. There's this beautiful waterfall on the outside our property, and I was always attracted to it and would go there often. I was always encouraged to go out and listen to nature and talk to animals.

My mother was really apprehensive about my grandmother spending time alone with me. My grandmother was always watching me and testing me by getting me to look at objects. She would do it in a way that was like games: she would set something on a table and say, 'Let's see if we can move this.' Or she would place an object in my hand and then say 'well, tell me a story about this.' This was when I was 4, 5 and 6 years old.

My grandma was a beautiful woman, like my mom, and was always "all done up," so it was kind of funny to see her in the woods all glamorous. She'd take me out to the woods and if I would pick up a rock, she'd always say, 'Tell me a story about this, or 'Can you make up a story about this?' And she'd take me to this place in the back of our property, near where the waterfall was, and she would walk me out into the woods and say 'There are happy places and then there are bad places. There's certain things that live in the woods and you need to respect those.' And the first thing that she showed me…I don't know if you've ever seen it…but where a lot of trees are growing, especially in the south, there will be a ring of mushrooms around the trees. I don't know what it's from, (and the weird thing is that there's a ring at my house right now in front around the tree, there's always a ring of mushrooms around my tree) and she'd say, 'That's a fairy circle. So if you're ever out in the woods and you feel that something is wrong, you look for one of these and you go inside and sit in the fairy circle.'

'I have always seen people who had passed ever since I was very very young. I think when you're that young, you just think they are…regular people…you really don't know. But there would be times that I would be really scared. And my mom would always come in and she's say, 'Play in the rainbow." When she first explained it to me she said, 'If you play in the rainbow, then all these colors are going to protect you. And then, if you're in these colors, nothing can ever get you. So if you're ever scared, just play in the rainbow.'

I was closest to my mother, of course. My dad and I only resurrected our relationship probably about 10 years ago, and we're really really close now, and he's super supportive of everything (my Medium side) which is really cool, but I was always a Momma's boy. She protected me in a way but she wasn't overpowering, and she always let me needed to do what I needed to do. But if it wasn't my mother, it was my grandmother, and they were completely polar opposites. The bond was really strong between me and my mom and my grandma, and there was always this battle between my grandma and mom: not in a bad way, but in the way they were watching over me. My grandma was always pushing, and sometimes in a very pushy way, because she wanted me to go and explore and learn and build on "it" [abilities] , where my mom didn't. Because my grandma and my mom were so intuitive, that I think my Mom experienced things that she did not want me to experience as a child, and gram was also pushing her to learn more…because the lineage goes so far back.

I started having a specific dream when I was very young: I would be standing next to a lake and there would be a silver snake with black jeweled eyes. It would swim in and out of a fallen tree. Across the lake there was a little island and I would see a blurry figure there. After that dream, someone I knew would pass away.

Later, when I was about 16 or 17, I was talking to my grandmother and told her about the dream. She told me that generations of my family had this dream but all of their snakes have ruby jeweled eyes and the figures they saw were not blurry but clearly seen. She told me, 'You still have to be handed the gift of sight.' A while after this, I had the dream again, only this time my mother and grandmother were in the dream and they told me, 'Now you share the gift,' and they lifted the snake out of the water and I saw that the eyes had changed from black to red. I've had the same dream ever since.

When my grandma found out that I had received 'it,' initially there was confusion because I'm a man, and the lineage for so long was female. I think that's why she was so ecstatic when she found out I was gay. My mom brought me 'out.' But when my grandma found out, she called all her friends because she had the first gay grandson, and she was so happy, 'Ok, he has a very positive female energy and male energy,' so it clicked with her. Since I was born they had to know I was gay, but it was never a big thing. I was 16 that's when I was outed, but I think it's why she was so excited because it finally clicked that 'this is why he has such a strong female energy and male energy, and so this is the Lineage.'"

One of the first things Alex's grandmother showed me (clairvoyantly) was that he had a ring that was coveted by someone else in his family. In our first talks years ago, Alex had been talking about wanting some pieces of jewelry that had belonged to his mother that his sister had taken (after their mother's passing). Alex's grandmother, however, was telling me the ring that he had was much more important and was meant for him, so I asked him about the ring again now:

"There was always talk about 'the ring, the ring, the ring.' My sister wanted it. I guess she thought she'd get it on her 16th birthday. But when I turned 16, after I 'came out,' my grandma brought me into her beautiful bedroom and she had this beautiful dresser and she sat me down and she sat down in the chair and she said, 'There is a heritage a lineage you're born to, you are in a line of very misunderstood women,' and she started talking about 'there were three stones that were gotten and formed into a ring.' When the ring was actually formed it represented my grandmother and her two sisters, and then it was going to be passed down. When my sister found out, she was very very upset. And ever since then…the relationship was never fixed."

"Do you think she knew about the Lineage? " I ask.

"It was never really talked about, but of course my sister had to know about the Lineage, and she was always very jealous and very bitter…that's all that I can explain about it," he tells me. I can't keep the ring in a box, it wants to be out. The only thing I can keep it in is this little silver tray that I found at some little antique store, and it has Jim's and my wedding rings in it, and I can keep 'the ring' in there too. This morning when I woke up , the ring box was on that silver tray! So I was meant to bring this ring today."

Alex lets me feel the ring, and it looks just like the vision his grandmother showed me when we first started talking about these things. As he places it in my hand, I feel my own vibration become so light. The diamonds and the silver are so light and bright and clear and sparking: I've never seen anything like it. It feels like an elf ring or something otherworldly, hiding in plain sight, although there's nothing plain about it.

'Whenever I get really upset, or there's just too much, I can just turn it in my hand, mindlessly turn it, to relax,' Alex continues, showing me it's so tiny that it barely fits up to his first knuckle. 'I do things like this because I cannot meditate. My mind just won't shut off. I've tried it, I've tried yoga, I've tried everything. So the thing I do now is that I have a cabin up in the Sierras, and I go there, and I go out into the woods and I still don't meditate, but I shut down, which is different for me. I completely shut down...sitting or standing. I'm not a tree hugger, but I'll walk around and find a spot, and then I just shut down. I don't hear anything, no wind, no birds, I feel nothing, I just shut down...in nature, and I levitate.

My husband has known for a while, and he's seen it twice. The first time was at the cabin. He didn't know what to think. I was levitating, but it wasn't like I was floating like 15 feet up in the air in a big bubble, but he noticed I was physically off the ground and he didn't know what to do, I wasn't aware [during] so I thought he was lying when he told me. So we researched it together and you [Karyn] explained it to me which helped a lot.

After the first time I felt completely drained. The second time I was at the waterfall at my house and Mitzi, my cat, was there. Jim was watching me through the window. And again, the only reason he could tell was because he could see a shadow underneath me. That's when you [Karyn] had first started talking to me about the 4 corners, sort of coaching me. So this time while I was levitating I saw the elements: air, earth, fire, water, and I even saw the air..the only way I can describe the air is that there were like water droplets in it. It was like shimmery. And that's when I realized the reason that I shut down is because I'm supposed to receive something at that time. So it was very calming. And the more I do this, the more I sense a combination of my mom, my grandma, and Mitzi with me, bringing in visualizations.

Water has always been something comforting for me. My mom said I was always in water. As a kid I'd jump in our pool and just go sit on the bottom, and I still often do this as an adult. Water has always been so comforting and silencing and enveloping for me. My family members know that now if we are all on vacation and all swimming and if I disappear that I'm ok and just spending time under the water. I have water features everywhere around my house, and even a pool. I always have to have water around, and it's odd because I don't like to drink water and I'm not a water sign.

The summer is also important since I was born right around the summer solstice. In the past, my grandma was always 'taking me out for my birthday,' but interestingly she would always be 'busy' on my birthday and unable to meet up, so we'd always have the day together on the 21st. She would reserve that date every year. Usually it was going into the woods, where she'd say, 'Tell me a story about this object or that.'

I've always had animals growing up, and was always encouraged to have animals. I can go up to the biggest dog and they just roll over and give me their belly. But when I first got Mitzi, that's when everything started coming together. I know it was grandma helping from the Spirit World, because Jim and I were walking through the animal shelter after having just lost a pet. I was just bawling, Jim was looking at little cat and I turned around and saw another little cat at the back of the cage. The woman who worked there told me they were having problems with this cat because it's very anti-social, and it doesn't want to be petted. I told her, 'I want that one.' She said, 'you can't pet it, it doesn't want to be held, it scratches.' I walked over, opened up the cage, and she walked out and she was so little. And she went into my hand, and then she crawled up onto my shoulder and just sat in that nook of my neck and shoulder, and I was like 'this is it.' Since then, she patrols.

She's just so super protective. She's like a little guard dog. If I feel something tugging at my heart or something, she wants to be on my heart. If there's so much going on in my head and I sit down, she'll lay across my neck.

And then she'll put a paw on my arm or my leg or will sit there and look at me like 'you need to understand this RIGHT NOW,' and she'll have this look, slanted eyes, and her ears flat: 'come on, pay attention.'

Alex and I have also found each other in the dreamworld-like place of astral travel. Dream time is often an active time for Alex, and often Mitzi protects him when he's having very active nights. "I will have dreams, but they are not really dreams, it's a training of some sort, and what I'm doing in each one is a little different and more elevated. I don't think it's exactly a healing training, because I don't consider myself a healer. I'm too inquisitive to be a healer, but I was told in one of these training dreams [referring to a particular night where he and I found each other in the astral plane and remembered meeting this way. In fact, we embraced. He thought he was comforting me, I thought I was comforting him] 'this is what you can do if someone needs you or if someone needs you to be there and you can't physically be there, and this is how you can do that.'"

What Alex hasn't said in his interview thus far is that he's now a semi-public Medium: while already a natural born Medium, he frequently gives people messages from their passed-on relatives, loved ones and friends. Sometimes perfect strangers just feel magnetized towards him and come over to speak with him at the local grocery store...or at a winery...and sometimes he approaches people. He will often have healing messages from difficult cases: like a daughter who killed herself but wanted her mom to know she was ok, who gave him this message while he was waiting to pay for some swimming pool tablets, standing in front of her mother in line. Alex and I have shared many experiences 'half in this world, half in the Spirit World' when we worked the retail floor together. There was also a lot of interference around Alex and I when we would talk at work. Often the phone would ring repeatedly, just as we were discussing something important of a Spirit World nature, or the lights would go off and on, or the registers would inexplicably beep: whatever could interrupt us would...and this was all before opening hours at the store.

It was during these early morning times when we were sharing experiences that turkeys began appearing on Alex's forest property in large groups, forming circles around him. Eventually they began to appear at his east bay home as well Often they'd be found eating his newly-planted flowers!

"I have never seen turkeys until we got our place up in the mountains. Massive amounts of turkeys would come into our yard. One of the first times I levitated Jim said, 'The turkeys were all around you. You were in the middle of all these turkeys and they were not making a sound, they were just enveloping you.'"

Turkeys can be considered "guardians of the forest," in Native American culture but also the "community bird," and therefore, a call for Alex to share his Mediumship more.

"It's awesome to have that support, because growing up when you see things you don't understand, it's frightening. Especially when you can't communicate it because you're so young and you don't know what it is."

Alex refers to the way his husband and extended family have accepted him. They accept also that his training continues, and they know his mother and grandmother are instrumental in this. His father really understood when Alex found out from a talk with his mother-in-spirit a few years ago, that one of the reasons she was protective of him is because she had a miscarriage before he was born. Alex brought this information to his father (because it was never shared within the family) who was shocked and demanded to know how he found out. But his response was ultimately positive: he connected Alex with an Italian Medium his wife knew, who also explained a lot of Alex's abilities to him as related to his mother and grandmother's lineage.

Jim also really understood when his mom passed. He woke up in the middle of the night, and I remember him waking me up and asking, 'What's that smell?' I was half awake but I knew, 'Oh, it's mom's perfume, it's my mom.' I just went back to sleep but then the smell just got so intense that Jim said something again because he had awakened from a dream that my mom had come to him to tell him that his mom had passed and that my mom was going to take her over. And that's when Jim really got it, because he later found out his mom had in fact passed at that exact moment.

I tried [learning from] books, and I get really irritated. I'd start to read a chapter and I'm like "no, this author isn't right, this doesn't feel right." I'll look at the back cover and see the author proclaiming they are something (like a witch) and I can tell 'no, you're not.' So I got really disillusioned with that, and I think that once I started trusting what was coming in, I find that so much better than books. Or if I just go inside myself and trust myself and trust the voices that are coming in and the feelings that are coming in..they're there for a reason, they're there to show you what's right. Not every person necessarily comes from a family lineage, but to know it's ok and they're not alone is important, to trust themselves is better than to have some person who calls themselves something they're not, like a 'witch,' authoring a book telling them who they are.

Being 'inside the experience' is different from taking a class as I've learned, too. Taking a class or workshops you gain the vocabulary of what to call things technically, but learning from the inside out, 'in the dark' you really live the life, which is the interesting thing about growing up inside the experience: you really don't know what to 'call' things you experience or always what to do with your abilities until you are taught."

One additional aspect of Alex's story is that people around him, like friends and family, have called him "golden boy" because whatever he has an interest in, he learns quickly and thrives. He began his career as an award-winning drag queen in his teens, combining the glamor of his mother and the feminine power of his grandmother. While he still gives highly-touted drag performances, he's also a successful sommelier.

One of the reasons I have included Alex's story, aside from the connections to all the Italian men I've known or count as dear friends who have similar experiences, is that it illustrates a very modern lifestyle. And even though Alex's family lineage is in the Spirit World, as with Yves', even though his life is very modern and in a city, it shows that if it's someone's time to step into their lineage, it will happen.

And among over a dozen Italian young men I know, this is a constant. The common age...early to mid thirties.

Fabrizio, the nephew of Yves, I'm sure will find more of his own magic if he ever goesto Sicily, which is where his grandmother-in-Spirit told me his Lineage is from, which he laterconfirmed.It has perhaps begun already: he's had is own dreamtime initiation that was like an initiation I received many years ago:

"Often at night, usually right before I sleep, my body starts shaking, like tremors. One night he saw a very bright white light at the side of the room that was getting closer and closer to me. The light got so close that I felt it enter in me and that woke me up."

I ask him if since that episode he feels that something change in his dreams, and in his awareness. He shares with me a car ran into him and injured his hand very badly. He is a musician, but the accident was so bad he thought his career was done due to the surgeries and pins in his bones. At the same time, he has a very positive attitude and feels that he helped heal himself faster than what the doctors though possible through positive thinking and making electronic music while in the hospital.

He also shared with me that he had levitated when he was a small child. He was at home with his grandma at the time, but he was in the living room and wanted to go to his grandmother's room. He saw himself, from above, in the hallway walking to the room. As soon as he entered the room of his grandma he saw black and woke up on the floor. As he opened his eyes he found he was on top of a completely broken chair that he landed on because he had fallen from the ceiling onto the chair. He was ten years old.

Even my husband...his mother is from a Lineage. Someone married into this mother's family who was not of a Lineage but was initiated into the Janare lineage; a man initiated into a female Lineage. And even though my husband has not chosen to follow that path, he cannot help that who he is expresses itself: a Medium since a small child, and this has only become stronger in him. His ability to read people has become very quick and precise. His ability to channel music, to create protection spells, to connect with animals and read the energy of places and things, to connect with nature, and to heal as well.

It is a part of you, if it is your path, that will come out whether or not you want it to.

I hope to travel to Corsica for Volume 2 of this book to meet with the men called "sciatica cutters," who use a special metal spoon with a hole cut in the spooned part, in which they insert a metal pointed stick, which is heated, and then pressed into both the hollow of the ear and a specific toe of the patient suffering from sciatica. This relieves the pain. These men learn also through Lineage transmission, a "passing down" of the secrets on December 24th eve. As one of the interviewed man said, "we remain connected to the spirits." You can read more about this in a wonderful article [http://reportages.corsematin.com/les-gurisseurs-au-del-dela-science] which I read on author Paolo Portone's facebook page, a never-ending source of information.

The challenge for men is that they are men. This Lineage, with Mediumship as its cornerstone, is ultimately a receptive art. Masculine energy is outward and active. Men tend to flock towards magic, because magic involves simply the will and action. Magic is to desire. Mediumship is to receive. Magic is about 1 person, Mediumship involves one to an infinite number of higher consciousness beings working in partnership, so the resource and the results are much greater. Magic is essentially from poverty; channeling is a gift that brings only abundance, and it is from the Great Mother.

So men do struggle on this path, with "receiving." They know how "to do." In Mediumship, one must allow the Spirits to guide. In magic, a man can reach, and he can reach as far as his skills allow, but he is also limited. In Mediumship, he needs to allow himself to receive, to wait, to surrender; all things opposite to masculine energy.

Masculine energy is outwardly active. Feminine, inward and receptive. These energies work well together when in a balance: the inspiration is received within and the inner creativity births an idea, then external actions are taken to make it a reality in the physical world. After all, lineage healing isn't about gender: it's about service, and it's about the people who are receptive to a life of service. However, the ability to receive communications from the Spirit World and become more psychically aware requires the feminine energy to be at the forefront of someone's awareness: it is receptive, and it receives subtle impressions in the form of visions, temperature changes, intuitive and informational downloads, and more.

Male energy is deeply connected to the ego and the will and therefore a force of action acting independent. Communicating with the Spirit World, the higher guides is a partnership. Beyond this, communicating with the Spirit World requires a willingness to be receptive: to listen to the silence, to trust to be guided in the right direction, to become aware of the subtle conversations emanating from nature, the health speaking about its root imbalances, and more. Spirit World communication is not simply: a spirit person speaking very clearly as though through a megaphone from the "other side." Rather, the spirit person makes an effort to communicate with a sensitive earthly person in the way they will notice most quickly, and the communication goes "both ways."

After all, our foundation as people on earth had at its core of functioning a relationship with the Spirit World; that's what not only kept us alive but also thriving. Communication as

Mediumship which channels information through the psychic senses. Women since earliest of time have received knowledge that way, and are the recipients of all that advanced knowledge that was laid as our foundation. We all come from witches.

But the most underrated, and often criticized, power of feminine energy are our emotions. Emotions connect us to other people but also to Spirit people. Even the higher guides use emotion as a means of saying "This is it! You are connected to the right person!" They would give these emotions to me each time I would meet a person who had something to do with a Lineage or any pertinent information for this book. It was as if I were seeing the people through the loving eyes of the Goddess proudly saying, "This is one of my children."

The turning point for men to embody their path as "stregone" is to learn to receive, to turn towards and embrace the feminine energy within themselves, or to simply surrender to their path and be willing to be guided. For some men, that includes meditating with one of the Goddess guides, to be "mothered" in a way that is both healing and empowering.

After all, men did build temples to Goddesses...and for sure she made her presence felt there. The shortcoming of those temples were that they were male-designed in both structure and in spiritual practice, so they were still about masculine directives, rather than surrendering to the Divine Feminine way.

Ninth Secrets

A habit I was inspired to pick up in 2009 when I stayed in Tuscany that I've continued has been to take pieces of the earth with me from places I visit. This habit became more focused when, in 2013 I began to have visions of Italy's history of Witches. I would spend my mornings researching, simply out of my own passionate curiosity, and often I would find evidence that my visions were giving me correct historical information.

I began compulsively collecting black rounded stones from the street, from the beach, wherever I'd find them.

I asked friend to give me jars of soil from Benevento, Italy and Salem, Massachusetts.

I began compulsively collecting pine cones form Golden Gate Park, near where I lived Judah and 32nd Street in San Francisco. Each morning I'd wake at 5am and go jogging in the foresty part of the park, often stopping at my two favorite pine trees and just communicating with them. At first they just gave me a sense of peace, but after time, this evolved into something I'd do when I needed to organize a lesson plan for Mediumship classes. I taught Mediumship at Spiritualist center at the time, and my classes were quite popular. I received the ideas for these classes while standing between these two trees, listening to what they had to say and writing down the ideas they shared with me.

I began collecting little ceramic bowls to put water in as part of my meditation altar or for divining messages from the Spirit World. The simpler the bowl, the better, the more handmade looking and imperfect, the better.

In 2006 when I started my training as a Reiki healer, I also began collecting minerals and gemstones. One I purchased was a round black onyx. It had a unique feature on one curve of the stone: a bright white perfectly circular spot that reminded me of an eye.

I remembered reading somewhere that witches used to give a stone to a potential initiate, and they'd have the possibly initiate carry it with them for a week. At the end of the week, the potential initiate would return it to the teacher, and she would use "psychometry" to "see" what the stone revealed about the potential initiate.

So I tried this on someone's photo…someone I hadn't met in person and felt I shouldn't trust. I placed the "eye" down on the photo and waited for three days. Then, I took the stone from the photo and placed it on my forehead. I was immediately transported into this person's apartment, moving through all the rooms, seeing the furniture. Then I saw this person in their bedroom in a moment that involved definitely "too much information." It shocked me so much "peering into" this person's private space, that I jumped up, coming out of that astral experience, and never tried it again. It did, however, prove my instincts right because I'd caught this person in a dishonest act.

I received, a few years ago before I returned tot Italy, a special stone: a chip from the street around the obelisk of Iside with Benevento's hieroglyph on it. I began to meditate with this stone each night, falling asleep with it on my forehead, working in my dreams this way. It was originally a light tan color, as sidewalks are. Over time, it began to change to a darker brown…Then it began to turn deep, shining black. Now it is completely black except for a small patch of dark brown to remind me it used to be a different color. I took photos of the evolution.

My onyx stone also has turned completely black: the white eye has completely disappeared.

I have a stone from the Tempio di Diana. It's natural color is a pale, sandy tan color. I bring it to my lectures so that people can pass it around to feel it. After the first lecture, I gathered the stone back from the audience and at first I thought someone had kept my stone and left another in its place because it was a blackened stone.

Chapter 9:

"Possession, Channeling, Ecstatic Trance, Exorcism"

"The human spirit, even the most enlightened, always has a dark corner
where the horrible chimeras of the credulous are hidden,
where the bats of superstition hang.
The same ordinary life and so full of insoluble problems,
that the impossible becomes probable.
You can believe and deny everything:
from a certain point of view, the dream is the same as reality."

"Sude e Magia" by Ernesto De Martino

All illnesses are traced by indigenous people to outside influence, such as: demons in animal form, or in natural phenomena (i.e. in the malevolent winds) which can approach humans and result in damage. That means men, with the help of black magic, claim to be able to cause the death of another individual.[183]

The art of the sorcerer [however] consists especially in making harmless the influence of hostile men or evil beings. He is called in severe cases, or that the disease/illness is caused by hostile people, or rather that the cause of it is a demonic entity.[184]

The gift of the sorcerer and the Medium is to know how the Universe operates, to know that even evil beings are subject to the Laws of Energy, and in this knowledge, to be able to clearly see the weaknesses of the evil beings without becoming one themselves, and even more to realize "evil" isn't really a "thing" but rather a state of mind.

Artemis was known as an exorcist, and then in Christian times Jesus and other men replaced this feminine procedure (feminine because women were taught the secrets of life and death by the Great Goddess Mother, the Signora di Gioco, and all the Goddess helpers who appeared time and time again in Italy). But of Jesus we find the accusation that "a saint or Jesus first punishes then releases an inhospitable woman, we almost do not notice the shift to a lesser degree of "low" of magic:[185] "In other words, even a saintly mythical person like Jesus was described as able to on one hand cure, on another, to punish. So even in the best of examples, it can be difficult to discern between high and low magic.

We must keep in mind the double-meanings of words and "things" and their inter-connected meanings in the Italian language to understand how fully beliefs in the Spirit World are naturally woven into not only Italy's history, but also indigenous practices and daily thinking. "Sinistra" means "left" and also "sinister," and refers to "the left hand path." However, the left side of the body is considered to be the "feminine" side, the side of the mother in many healing energy modalities. Herbs like "l'iperico" (St John's Wort) cure both wounds on the skin as well as healing the body on a physical level. But with its nickname as also "scacciadiavoli," it is believed this herb chases away devils, and devils are considered the ones who cause illness.

Illness that affects the physical body is considered to be caused by "evil thoughts or evil spirits," whose home is in the "world" of non-physical form.

Therefore this herb works on both the mind and Spirit, on the physical body and in the Spirit World of energy, in scientific ways and also magical ones. In parallel, the skin is also considered a barrier between someone and the world, and often results in rashes or skin ailments which reflect an emotional "irritation." Digestion registers the "processing" of a person's mental and emotional experiences. Illness that affects the physical body is considered to be caused by "evil thoughts or evil sprits," whose home is in the "world" of non-physical form.

And the eyes, they are not only doorways to one's soul, but also passageways for other spirits. As we bring to mind again the Campanella quote at the beginning of the chapter about "il malocchio," with the reference to "spirits escaping out of eyes," we find another double-meaning way to describe "spirit attachments."

Spirit attachments are lowly ghosts who try to influence humans in ways that offer the ghosts some semblance of experiences that they used to be able to have while living on earth in a fleshy body. The more aggressive and lowest spirits will also try to "jump in" and try to "see out of our eyes," which is another way to describe what happens during possession; the "attachment" part of this term.

As we learned from "il malocchio," the process of receiving the eyes as well as sending them or curing them involves a rather advanced philosophy of thought, and at the same time a natural one. Therefore, the power can be used positively and miraculously, when in tune with higher energies, and it can also be used on a lower level of focus, and can therefore be focused into a "street-level battleground," which can attract even more darkness.

Exorcism in Italy can be performed with oil and water and an old woman's hands as "medicine of the people," powerfully but lovingly curing by releasing the negative energy, also with the channeled assistance of the Grande Dea. While at the same time there also exists exorcism performed in the Catholic manner, which is the "medicine" of the ruling class, in this case the church. "Occhi" releases negative spirits naturally: using nature and channeled energy, to bring relief immediately and peacefully, with also an understanding that a person is responsible for their own happiness of mind and spirit: unhappy thoughts make an unhappy spirit, and illness is the result. Very natural, not alarming, and the patients are also empowered in knowing the cause of illness is negativity, they have a choice to release it, and if they choose, the negativity is cured right away.

The church's exorcism is torturous and for those people who are very far gone into self-denial. The church blames an intangible "devil" for the possession, thus rendering the patient powerless. Demons are accused of causing the possession illness, patients are disconnected from their own responsibility for emotional and mental health, and a huge war, a battle of good versus evil ensues, very much holding a residual practice from the first male tribes invading harmonious natural communities. The result of a church's exorcism: no healing... instead, a battle.

My husband has a relative in his mother's side of the family who's an exorcist, retired now. He told me that as a child he got to listen to some of the tapes of the exorcisms and how haunting and disturbing they truly are. Then again, possession is both natural and unnatural. The church's exorcism gives power to the invading spirit; Mother magic instead gives power to the individual seeking to be cured by connecting the patient to the energy the healer is channeling: The Great Mother Goddess.

There is both "light" and "dark" in the Universe, as well as in the light spectrum, and there can't be one without the other, and all the "shades and tones of grey" in-between. Benandanti remind us this is also natural, and keeping the balance is as old as time itself. All that can be accomplished in the mind can both rise and fall. Acts of magic and partnerships with Spirit World consciousness can expand into miraculous feats and delve into base and horrid darkness. The skills one psychic uses to cure, another can use to curse.

Spirit attachments versus Goddesses…possession versus channeling…ecstatic trance versus hunger for power…

The Spirit World has traditional ways of reaching out to the earthly world. Some of these ways are for positive, higher purposes that improve life. These are actions taken by higher consciousness Guides, Helpers, and Goddesses. Some of these ways are negative and only benefit the invading Spirit people who are trying to relive moments they had on earth or to live vicariously through still living-on-earth people.

the JUMP-INS

I've seen eyes of temporarily possessed Italian men, and they all become a strange, vapid dark glass…as if the color and pupils disappear from behind a lens, and something else comes to stand behind the lens, looking as if through a peephole. There is a discernible decrease in light. The eyes become not eyes at all anymore, but indeed a doorway. The original inhabitant is somehow still there but not "home." This is a surrender, but not of a positive nor beneficial kind. The "owner of the body," (if we call the body the "location" or "temporary home" for the spirit to have an experience on earth), becomes in this case "dispossessed" of his "home" while someone else takes over. There is not a partnership, and it is unpredictable. This is not the process that higher conscious guides nor helpers take either, because they take a partnership-with-permission approach, respecting the Law of Will.

What is most haunting in these cases is not the temporary disappearance of the personalities of the men I knew, but of the intense personalities of the male spirits who "jumped into" their bodies and started at me from behind their eyes. They seemed to want to own me, that it would not be enough to reach and grab for me; one looked at me with much hate and wanting to have me feel its deep and endless extent. Even though I know it's not technically possible for the "jump-in" spirits to function for long in the body of a person on earth, so the danger I'm near is short-lived, it still feels unpredictable. What I also learned, behind the technical theory of possession, is that in those situations there was nothing I could do for those men. When they did not want help, when they did not mind, for some reason, to have another spirit use their body, there was no pulling them back from "the background." Even at a distance, through the telephone and the internet, peoples' spirit attachments can reach out to intimidate someone else.

When I was translating a particularly dark part of this book, the Inquisition period, a male friend of mine began to send ominous messages to me. He was just the channel, but a spirit was jumping into him to intimidate me. In all these cases, the men were also very psychic and Mediumistic, but rather "untrained." Being a natural medium, no matter how much one can psychically see and sense, does not mean that one knows the protection protocols, and this was the case here in these situations.

These "jump-ins" are the temporary possessions. They can happen as several spirits "jumping into" the same person in a short period of time, like a revolving door, or it can be one person who's holding on, clinging as an attachment, not ready to complete their death transition.

An Italian man I know had a person dear to them pass away. My friend was devastated, but also the spirit of the person who passed was not accepting their death and remained near earth, in anger and regret. This spirit began influencing my friend to feel unsatisfied with his life. The spirit did not like me, and when this spirit "jumped into" my friend, he looked at me with contempt and hatred. I tried to help this spirit cross over into the light, but he did not want to, and my friend was jumped many times, in the presence of his friends as well. Because the "jump-in" allows the host to be functional, my friend carried on with his regular day, but at times would suddenly fall quiet, become "dispossessed" of his own body, and I'd find a cold, black stare boring through me with disgust and contempt. It was chilling. I tried speaking with this spirit, explaining the harm it was doing, offering it some help, but I finally had to let go of my attempts, because it was clear neither part was willing to give up this symbiosis. After some time passed, before falling asleep, I thought of trying one last time to open the transition point for this spirit to move onward towards the light. In the morning, my friend reported that he saw the spirit pass into the light in his dreams and he drew me a picture of what it looked like.

I met another Italian man who, at my first sighting of him, had bright white hair and had the slightly shrunken appearance of an old man. When I met with him on a later occasion, he had black hair, was taller, and looked considerably younger. And yet, his secret came out as he, several times during our visit, became quiet and still, with the lenses of his eyes turning black, while a variety of "jump-ins" took turns in his body, one even claiming to recognize my hands. Although he claimed to not want to experience this, I felt a duality there: a hunger for power and an allowance of this, because he felt it made him "special."

In Italy, ghosts and spirits and the "supernatural" are a daily part of life for many people, in one form or another. One of the first things my Italian mother-in-law said to me after we met in Northern Italy was "there are ghosts in my house, tell me what you see." After I did, and she confirmed that she sees the same male ghosts, she said, *"I'm not afraid of them."*

IN THE POSITIVE

A person can choose to share some of their body's "space" with a spirit. This can happen subconsciously, as in the above story. This can also occur intentionally, as with Mediums who are also healers. This can become a practice, such as with the Trance Medium whose story I shared. I have friends who are healers who feel their healing spirit guides as a cold chill and tingle on the back of their neck, and also a tingling sensation in their arms where they've reported it feeling as though *"the arms of the Spirit helper are moving through mine, as if I were the jacket and they were the arms going into the sleeves."* The benefit of this can be having a Spirit healer who has much more curing energy than the healer, work on the patient, resulting in a much more powerful and precise healing.

POSSESSION

Possession, rather than a "jump-in," is an almost complete takeover of a human being's body by an invading spirit. This does not last long for the simple reason of technicalities. Each human body is built from the "inside out" to house only one consciousness, or Spirit, per lifetime. "You" and your body are a perfect match. Whatever illnesses you may show symptoms of are from your own thoughts and emotions which "sprout out" through whatever is weakest in you (immune system, digestion), and those weaknesses have to do with an inability to process specific emotions and accompanying thoughts that are related to specific organs. It is not possible for some other spirit to permanently "take residence" in a physical body. The results are dysfunction, failing health and death. This is simplest to see in people on serious drugs like junkies whose speech is jumpy and jerky, odd changes in their voices which make them sound like monsters, bodies that don't move smoothly, but rather jerk or move constantly, and their overall health is compromised. Over longer periods of time, the body simply must decompose: the original spirit separates from it, the invading spirit must leave, and the damage is done.

Arriving to this point of being possessed is most interesting. To illustrate, your body is like a balloon. Your personality, your integrity and vitality, your emotions and thoughts are the "air" which fill your balloon. When your vitality is lowered (self-esteem issues, a desire to escape from physical abuse, drugs and alcohol, anything that lowers your sensations, thoughts, and emotions) you lose some "air" that fills your balloon and subconsciously give off a "space for rent" advertisement such as "this person is not fully here." If your subtle messages also are "life is terrible I don't want to live, I don't want to be here, I hate myself," there's even more vitality seeping out of your balloon. These are the conditions, especially over time, that allow another spirit to "plug in" and try to take over. This is rare and only seen in extreme cases where a person does not want to live anymore, often because of abuse, or something they simply can't face and continue to live: for example, a young woman raped by her father who is pregnant as a result. This kind of abuse can cause serious trauma, and the resulting repeating thought in her mind may be: "I don't want to live," but there is no disease rotting the person to release them from life, nor is there an accident causing their death, yet they do want "out"...there is a decrease in vitality from these messages being repeatedly vibrated, so an invading spirit can use this as an opportunity to "take residence" in this person who no longer cares to be alive and therefore surrenders their boundaries, surrenders their will to live. It is not expected that a person so far into full possession can be pulled out-it would take a tremendous turn around in their own mind- a determination to live in the face of an already accumulated result of a determination to deny their life.

Possession, therefore is being in possession of: negativity, someone else's energy, not empowered. Possession is the host body is dispossessed of their personal space: their spirit is not "kicked out" of their body, but in "the background." Only upon death is a spirit detached from the physical body, and the result is physical decay. Full possession is not functional for the physical body. It's like having a radio built for a current to pass through but the radio keeps getting blasted with other types of currents it's not built to receive, so the circuit board burns out.

Possessed-to have

Dispossessed-to have lost

SPIRIT ATTACHMENT:

Spirit attachments are like "tag-alongs," spirits who follow a person around for a little while or a long while, getting something in return. They are influencers. They are not all negative in personality or desire, but the fact that they haven't completed death transition means that they are technically "energy vampires:" and will plug into or influence other humans to maintain an energetic sense of remaining on earth. The spirit attachments seem the most natural in their symbiosis. People with spirit attachments often seem "like themselves but a bit off."

Spirit attachments often get their influence through most successfully when they find people drunk, under drugs, or "dabbling" in the Spirit realm without knowing the rules, such as playing with the oujia board and creating spells when done in an irresponsible way. In some cases, they are spirit people who don't want to be forgotten and are trying to teach something to someone who can notice them:

Shortly before I left for Italy for this recent journey, I was researching Triora Italy, which I had previously been uninterested in. I was focused on Benevento. However, after I contacted a friend in Liguria and we arranged that I should fly into Genova because as he said "the Inquisition started here," my journey took on a new shape. Interviews and meetings were being arranged for me all around the Ligurian region. So, I began to search for some photos of Triora to get a sense of this place. Often I see information "under the surface" through photographs, or memories of the past.

I somehow found an image of a mannequin in the Ca'botina remains of Triora, a place where poor women and children lived, often midwives, healers, and alleged prostitutes and "witches." The mannequin was of a red-haired woman behind bars. Suddenly my belly was twisting and turning, and the spirit of a woman appeared, told me that was supposed to be her, and that the mannequin angered her, that it was wrong and the clothing was wrong too. She hated seeing her effigy in there. She was enraged by seeing a likeness of herself "trapped" behind bars forever. She showed me some images of where I needed to go, including one where she was burned as a witch.

This would he the beginning of my "relationship" with Franchetta Borelli. She would teach me a great deal of important information: her own magical practices, who taught them to her, a place in nature she loved to enjoy alone, the truth behind some of the old stories, and more. However, her way of teaching me at the start was to get my attention through my belly area, which is where, on our "double" energy bodies, we have a psychic receptor for "clairsentience," or clear-feeling. She was intense, and this would make my belly feel like I had indigestion..in fact my breath would go sour, my intestines would gurgle, it was terribly uncomfortable. The way to instantly relieve this was to take a pen, my journal, and write down what she wanted to tell me. ..which was always advice for me, from parts of her life. She didn't want this information lost nor forgotten, and she was very opinionated about the way she felt I gave up my power to men and how to keep it for myself. She was "taking me in," teaching me the Feminine Mysteries, but she physically affected me in a negative way. And as the year would go on, as she would come to me to tell me more information, her affect on me became increasingly more full of despair, grief, and it would overwhelm me at times…make me literally immobile. I felt more grief than I believed was humanly possible to feel and still live. I was aware this was she, that these were not my feelings, but I also had never let a spirit person get so close to me before. I had always prided myself on clean and clear boundaries. But this book would have me learning in new ways, not just in my mind by "through" my body. While she didn't live vicariously through me in the technical way spirit attachments do, she was indeed having an affect on my emotions, so I would classify her as "attaching" at times rather than just "communicating", which is really not the proper way to engage. She would have liked to influence my life much more than I would let her. As a result, I had to set those boundaries, for my own health, and end our relationship.

In general spirit attachment cases, there is a "thievery" going on of space and emotion. The result is that the people with "attachments" can devolve into thievery and other acts against humans. Mental denial is what keeps them feeling comfortable in this, which is what sets the stage in the first place for a lowered vitality.

These occurrences are not random. You won't simply catch a spirit attachment like a leaf in the wind. Consciousness is involved: subconscious or very aware choices.

To illustrate, there was a case where I was communicating with the spirits who were attaching to and bullying a man who was also in spirit. I asked the bullying spirits, "Why are you trying so hard to fit in this man's body when you know you can't do it properly? You know you can't really live as you did when you were on earth this way?" They replied "fuck you," and left.

One does not simply "fall" into possession, and negative spirits are not "unknown " species of special demon that are a separate form of consciousness. These are very low, devolved consciousness belonging to irresponsible "people" who no longer have fleshy bodies, or perhaps never did, who don't care about the free will of other people.

LIMITED FUNCTIONALITY of the ATTACHED

My Guardian angel once asked me to buy a book. My husband and I were seated on the train, on our way to Ancient Ways, an occult bookstore in Oakland, California. We sat next to each other facing two seats that were facing us rather than being positioned in the same direction. The seat across from me became occupied by a woman who was, to the general observer, very mentally disturbed: moving in jerky motions, talking in scrambled and aggressive sentences, often using only curse words, speaking very fast and very loud.

I turned my attention inward and began to listen to my Guardian who was talking to me about ceremonial magic. My husband suddenly turned to me and said "what did you do to that woman?" I noticed that she had in fact calmed down considerably.

My Guardian explained that the woman had a spirit attachment, and if I were to speak to it instead of noticing her behavior, I would notice things that made this evident. So I did: when she would get revved up and super aggressive, I told the spirit attachment I could see him. Suddenly the woman would calm down, and she even apologized, she "came back into herself" for a few minutes, until the spirit was allowed to take over again, and the disjoined language returned.

Several more times I talked to the attachment and the woman was calmed, in the same way.

MAN ON STREET.

One night I was leaving work, a place I worked with Alex that was, in one direction an affluent shopping area, in the opposite direction where junkies, addicts, and homeless thieves populate the street. It was nearing Christmas time, so the sidewalk was very crowded, and within this crowd there was only enough room for the width of one person to move in the direction I was going: to the train. In this single-file line of us walking through the crowd, I noticed up ahead a tall man obviously under the influence of a spirit attachment: he was pointing in peoples' faces as they passed him, shouting obscenities and jumbled words, and flailing his arms. So I began to tell his spirit attachment to back off. As it came to be my turn to pass the man, he put his arm down and said "oh, it's you," very calmly and quietly. As soon as I passed he began cursing and yelling at the rest of the people in the line.

FREAK MAGNET SYNDROME:

I used to think I was a freak magnet, noticing that from a very young age the only people to approach me in public seemed to be the mentally disturbed, the freaky scary men, the junkies, and the general type of people I wanted nothing to do with. It took some time to realize there wasn't anything wrong with me, but there was something consistently wrong with these people: spirit attachments, jump-ins, and some on paths to full-possession. When I finally realized this, all I had to do, as guided by my Guardian angel, was to speak to the attachment rather than the person. Like having a conversation "underneath or in-between" the spoken conversation. This usually calms the host person down right away, and temporarily allows them to come back into themselves, which would release me from their attention. This is one of the many tools my Guardian has provided for me.

ECSTATIC TRANCE

In Italy, traditions of trance are woven deeply into the many cultures who have left their traces and imprints in land. With quite the cross-cultural mix: Scandinavian Longobards, Celts and Druids, Phrygians, Egyptians, Greek Sikels, Persians, and more, and all these traditions come from much much older time periods than paganism, although the patriarchal invasions have warped some of them.

Many of these traditions began as healing arts to solve "medical issues."
For Benandanti, the trance is for a purpose, to accomplish responsibilities that aren't in the earth realm, so the trance "transports" them to the battle realm to keep the wheel turning for the rest of us. This trance is not an individual experience, but rather for groups of people who meet in the trance and experience the what there, together, each playing their specific role and carrying out their assigned duties.

In "tarantella," we see a formula for ecstatic trance: A combination of violin, frame drum (larger than a tambourine which also has a hide stretched across it) and accordion, played in a traditional rhythm that acts as the musical trance induction for the woman, who dances in step, or runs in a circle, or spins like a whirling dervish, until her trance mind is induced and she takes a step "backwards" while a spirit temporarily possesses her body, continuing to move it in strange motions. She rolls on the floor, sometimes screams, and rocks back and forth to the music. For periods of time she is in a motionless "asleep state," then at times perhaps diving answers from a beloved saint. The movement is the release and the surrender to the trance and the "shared space" with spirit.

Then, there is ecstatic trance that is similar to tantra, but specifically for women to connect intimately with the Divine Feminine: sexual expression that is not earthly sex, but between a woman and the Divine Spirit. The trance is induced by The Divine Feminine and her helpers, and the sexual connection is woman-to-woman, for the purpose of restoring feminine energy, to heal abuse, and to feel a love for the universe, rather than an attraction-love for humanity, and to learn to embody the Great Goddess Mother. The duration of this procedure is entirely in the "hands" of the Spirit World.

It is not possible to completely understand these things without experiencing them. The path to knowledge involves experience. Experiences which offer growth require a person to go into unknown territory: otherwise, it is not an experience at all but rather but a mental calculation based on what the mind already knows. The ego prefers to keep the mind in comfortable spaces, in places it already knows so that it feels safe, and so it doesn't "look dumb."

Going into the unknown is exactly where the "new" is found. And there's an endless amount of "new." But in order to go into the unknown and not become a toy nor a tool for someone else, one must be aware of the mental and emotional disposition and how like attracts like.

To give an example, a schizophrenic person who is imbalanced and expressing himself as "crazy" to the outside world is also often channeling the words and thoughts of other spirit people who are "jumping in" and "attaching" in a veritable mental "free for all." Because human beings are built to be channels, even a schizophrenic person is still a channel, but because their mental integrity is "given up" or "out of their hands," a spirit attachment has much more freedom and room to plug in.

I experienced something like the tarantella for 13 years while in perhaps an unlikely place: singing as front woman of a metal band of men with middle-eastern musical influences. It was, in effect, a modern day tarantella template. As a former introvert, I felt this music allowed me to open my raw heart. I found myself singing in a melodic voice and a growling and shouting one, thrashing about in a very physical way onstage. I was not in my body for most of the performance. Once the music started I mostly felt like I was inside the electricity and was not aware of my body. Mostly I felt I was curing myself, shaking loose my pain and, in catharsis, becoming bright light. After the performances, I was in a very positive mood, very loving, and over time I'd find that people would want to embrace me and in some way, be healed. I always called it "summoning" rather than "singing," and I felt my most empowered self onstage. In fact, I wished I could take that sensation and plug it into my daily life, where things felt much darker. For me, it was a ritual. I felt the band was the mountain and I was the climber, and this was the challenge.

MEDIUMSHIP, TRANCE, CHANNELING

Proper, functional trance mediumship takes conscious preparation and inner journey, so that the physical body of the Medium is safe and healthy while her consciousness shares space with another spirit. Because the body is meant for only the spirit who was born into it, even with careful preparation and arrangements the sharing of space takes time to recover from. This is participatory and not spontaneous.

Mediumship is the regular practice of being a mid-point of healing energy or transmitter of knowledge from the Spirit World to the earthly one, and to do it with awareness and discernment of consciousness and energies and information. Trance channeling, intuitive channeling, and ecstatic trance are all forms of Mediumship.

Channeling is the natural ability to be the mid-point. Channeling is a result of reception, and when living in nature, this naturally occurs. Many young people I met in Italy feel this occurring naturally in their lives, especially the men, who seem to have an aversion to Spirit in human-type form, preferring to let nature teach them while in the nature itself. Women in Italy, naturally, are more aware of what they are channeling, experiencing, and sensing.

Channeling is the natural process. In Italy, the Lineage healers are all channeling spirit conscious energy…this energy is focused into the marks and actions that are specific to each Lineage. The humility of these healers is what attracts this Divine Feminine conscious power.

Ecstatic trance can be induced from the human side, in terms of "getting into the trance," but the trance itself is guided by the Spirit World. It is not of the making of the human beings, the human beings cannot change nor control the trance. The realm of trance is real. It is not like lucid dreaming where the dream can be controlled. In trance, a person has freedom of actions, but not without consequence. Ecstatic trances are for specific reasons: battles, healing, repairing and restoring sexuality, channeling the Goddess into a body or bodies, expansion of love or higher learning, bringing the ancient into the real-time.

These forms of channeling are beneficial not only to the channeler, the Medium, but also to the people who get to experience what is being channeled. These are expansive practices, and they are feminine traditions.

Tenth Secrets

My friend Christian, who lives in Milan, sent me a large box of books from Italy last December. They were focused on Triora, Franchetta Borelli, the Inquisition in the Valle Argentina, herbal cures and magical practices. A very interesting document he found for me is called "La Pace Impossibile," (An Impossible Peace) which is a study of documents written by two priests who visited the Argentine Valley (where Triora is located) and reported back no sightings of evil witchcraft, which was curious, since they both were suspicious of witches. This was a document I was unable to translate on my own because it was a mix of "Old Italian" and Latin.

So one day I was taking the bus to meet with a friend from Italy who was going to help me translate a portion of this information from the1500s , including letters of protest from the village elders towards the treatment of prisoners.

To meet my friend, I needed to take two buses with which I was well acquainted: one of the buses I used to take every day to and from work. However, this time period in my life was what I call the start of the "brain scramble" experiences. The first time I experienced this was in Guardia Sanframondi: this was the Inquisitors, from the Spirit World, trying to interfere with my efforts. The result was that I would feel confused and emotionally oppressed.

On this day I decided to meet him to work on this document, and from there everything went downhill. I had a strange miscommunication through an email. I felt a lot of fear for no reason, and I got lost on this bus going only a few blocks past streets ordered alphabetically. I got lost on the second bus too, which was only going in a straight line. I was losing my perception of where I was. I was becoming confused about where I needed to exit. I was becoming more irritated that I was spending all this time to meet my friend and I began to hear "this is a waste of time" in my head. I went back and forth on the same bus trying to figure out where I was. It was as though I was lost in a maze.

I finally arrived to meet my friend and was very upset. I tried to maintain my composure. I kept hearing as my "you don't want to be here," in my mind and it was making me feel more irritated and impatient.

We ate lunch, and my mood cleared.

Then we began to translate a passage. It described 13 women and one man who were put into a prison without a trial. They were accused of being witches without there being any evidence of them doing anything wrong. They were not documented: no one took their names as they were locked up, and would languish in this prison for 2 years while the Inquisitors who put them here waited on instructions from Rome as toto what to do with them. One woman jumped off the balcony to her death due to fear of the tortures.

Suddenly I didn't feel so well so we stopped translating. I needed to get out of that apartment. My friend and I decided to go visit another part of the city, but I became irrationally irritated at the change of plans. I tried to search for a bus route to take but suddenly I couldn't understand how to use my phone. It was like my part of my mind disappeared. I just kept fumbling on my phone, unable to use it.

I shouldn't have even needed to use my phone for this because I knew the neighborhood we were in: I had lived just a few blocks away for a a few years. And yet, as we went outside, I panicked because I couldn't understand where I was. I could see, from my surroundings, that I knew that this place, it was familiar, but my mind couldn't calculate where I was or where to go from here to get downtown (which required basically taking one bus in a straight line). I also lost the ability to put sentences together as well, so I couldn't express to my friend what was happening to me. I would try to talk and instead just tears would come out. It was very embarrassing. I tried to leave him and run away so I could be on my own until this passed, but he came with me and as we got on the bus my mind began to clear:

I was experiencing the panic that the imprisoned women felt in those documents, and how they were losing a sense of who they were over tim, going mad as they languished in this prison. It was a slow and gradual warping of reality. I later learned that most of the women who were kidnapped and tortured weren't even healers nor sorcerers, so it must have been even more confusing for them. Someone involved in sorcery or magic would have some kind of philosophy to hold onto as well as an understanding of human psychology, but a regular woman being accused of having sex with the Devil and being tortured for this would surely scramble her mind.

I realized this in a sudden moment but also was unable to communicate to my friend until some time had passed. How to explain this invisible whirlwind to someone who can't see it?

The way I found out it was Inquisitors who were behind this interference was having to share with my friend, explaining to him the specific black outfits these men wore. He confirmed they were Inquisitors. These men also appeared in my dreams.

Chapter 10:
"CACCIA ALLE STREGHE:"

(The Witch Hunt)
Europe's 500 year Inquisition, and it's fiery trail through Italy

Boiling down over 500 years of Europe's Inquisition history to tell the story of Italy's Witch Hunt, "La Caccia alle Streghe," is a task that deserves more than a chapter. Therefore, here I will highlight just the most important things you need to know to introduce you to what you've been missing. Hopefully this will spurn your own desire to research this matter so tens of thousands of innocent people who were murdered don't remain dismissed, degraded and forgotten because of fake propaganda.

1   The Inquisition had a different impact on the regions north of Italy versus regions of the south.

2. The aim of the church's directive behind the Inquisition in Italy was to turn people away from female healers and midwives towards male doctors and church healers. Economic goals and industrialization of life-for-profit was behind the propaganda that created "the witch and her Devil," a relationship that never existed.

3. Women were scapegoats at this time for many industrialization efforts that went wrong, such as in the fields of food where fake famines drove price increases and angered populations, newborn deaths by inexperienced male doctors trying to take over midwifery created panic, and of failures by monks to cure diseases.

4. The numbers range from 50,000 and up of documented cases in Europe. In Italy, many women were kidnapped and thrown in jail undocumented and remained there for years or died before their trials, so there is no record of their kidnapping and demise. Local people, hyped up on fear and paranoia created by the church also killed their own neighbors. Women simply disappeared. While the church kept precise records of their crimes against life, a sort of private pornography, they remain mostly locked behind church doors, that is, the ones which weren't burned to protect the church's reputation.

5. A perverse obsession with female sexuality and occupational jealousy of female healing abilities drove male Inquisitors to create wildly abusive types of torture, invading all parts of the female body.

6. The devil who is written about in the trials never existed: the church created this specific one along with the rest of their propaganda purposely using symbolism of the Great Goddess of ancient times.

7. There is absolutely no evidence that any one of the 50,000 plus people killed in Europe, and the numbers documented in Italy, were guilty of the absurd crimes they were accused of, but they were killed anyway.

8. This is a typical tale of "mob mentality" being inflamed by a governing body "in power."

9. The feminine perspective is surprisingly absent from the historical documents about the witch hunts, which is odd considering the documents detail the strange and sexually perverse tortures of accused women. No one seemed it necessary to interview "survivors" of this genocide and try to learn from those hunted.

10. The Inquisition didn't come to just one village but many. According to author Fabio Garuti, in some places so many women were killed, adult men and boys were the only ones left.[186]

11. The lasting affect is that healers don't want to talk about what they do, and their Lineage traditions are being lost. There is still a public fear of these invented, so-called evil "witches." More than that, people largely connect being psychic or mediumistic with the "devil's evil." Being psychic and communicating with the Spirit World, or simply being intuitive, is natural and has been, successfully, since ancient times. The "devil's evil witches" were wholly invented by the church, and that is what's "unnatural," as is the church itself.

NORTH and SOUTH

One of the most interesting aspects I learned about the Inquisition's storm through Italy is the different ways it affected the north versus the south. Benevento author Enzo Gravina tells me:

"In Triora, we had women who were burned on the fires. In the south of Italy, such as in Benevento and Calabria, we didn't have any women burned. We have women burned in places in [the central region of] Umbria going upwards, but not going downwards towards the south. Why? Because the economy of the north had something that was like a shared economy, and what it meant during that time period is that if something belongs to your family, the rule is that these belongings [property, etc] have to remain in the family all the time, you cannot sell it or give to others. And on a juridical basis, the proper name of this kind of arrangement is: 'Maso Chuso.' It means: 'closed land.' In the south instead, when the head of the family passes, all the belongings of the family pass to the first son. Only the first son has the right to inherit. The others in the family, if they were women, they then had to become nuns or get married. If they were male, they became messianic soldiers or priests. What result does it bring to us? That in the south of Italy, every family had at least one priest or one nun per family. When the Inquisition came against the women they wanted to accuse as witches, obviously, it didn't work in the south because of this. It's logic. The accused and their families would say the inevitable: 'that accused woman is my sister and she's a nun, or that's my brother he's a priest.' So in the end they were not inquisited. The attack against women was less successful here because most people were also part of the church because of this family property local law. While in the north, the families don't have these ecclesiastic figures. So it makes sense in a historical reason. That's why, in the south of Italy we have not had women burned."

But they did suffer other fates.

MAGIC AND MEDICINE

According to the many Italian people who shared their country's history with me, during that period, the local populations didn't care so much about whether witches did or did not exist. It was the church who kept pressing the idea, and it took some time, so the tortures helped convince people more than the religion itself.

Many unusual ideas existed in the "popular tradition," (which means the "traditions of the common people") such as: werewolves ("lupomannari") and moon sickness ("mal di luna"), and there were many shamanic traditions still lingering outside of original lineage witchery, having been adopted in part by pagan traditions from other lands that found popularity in Italy. The church structured itself in mimicry of these practices, before Christianity and paganism basically morphed into the same structure (only the church completely eradicated the feminine divine figure, whereas paganism "kept her around" as a wife figure, baby-maker, and war-supporter. The church copied both the women healers and the pagans (rather unsuccessfully in terms of offering cures and ecstatic experiences), and there were many types of magic that were part of daily, mundane lives.

It is difficult to overestimate the importance of magic in the ancient world. Whether you wanted your crops to grow, your lover to yield [...] there were rituals and incantations to suit the purpose. However, it was especially in the area of health that people were most liable to invoke what we might call the "magical."

If you were suffering some bodily ailment, a wide variety of choices were open to you, but none of them much resembled modern medicine."[187] For example, the most enduringly popular male healer figure and longest running competitor to Jesus was Aesclepius. To seek his cures, people would go to his temple, ritualistically bathe in water, and then often sacrifice a cock and smear its blood on part of their body.

This was not without logic: menstrual blood has life-giving nutrients, and is also connected, spiritually, with regeneration of life, so often in male-based magic we find animal sacrifices, synthetically emulating a natural life-giving, life-generating fluid. We must remember that the word "pharmakeia," or pharmacy, signified not only drugs and medicines but potions, spells, and witchcraft. The two were quite inseparable.[188]

Magic was everywhere in Italy. It was part of daily life for many, and it still is, having extended itself from the Lineage healer hearth and homes to those trying to emulate it with crafty spells and "psychic" work.

The psychic version, outside of Lineages, was where the magic devolved, being limited to human ability instead of the greater assistance of Spirit World teachers, but to some extent it still works.

The ancient Egyptians have collections of spells and exorcisms in the papyri, which stood alongside medicine and surgery.[189] Likewise, in the Italian church, "words of God" stood alongside spells, alleged psychic phenomena like "miracles," sorcery, and herbs...only the church was failing at using them to cure people.

In "La Signora del Gioco," author Luisa Muraro (a rare female literary voice in this field) writes, "The church is and has always sought to present itself as uniquely beneficial; but it is significant that even the priests were suspected by the peasants of being evil.[190] Medicine was practiced by Priests but also spells and exorcisms and invocations.

Manuela Saccone, Responsible for the didactic activities at the Archaeological Museum in Finale, told me in her lengthy interview, "the church used the same tools that were usually used by the women accused of witchcraft, such as crosses and prayers, and yet the Christians were accusing them of being something evil even though they used the same exact tools." As far as healing practices and customs, in the practice of folk medicine we face two categories: ordinary people (grandmothers using home remedies) and the healers: "settimini" (sons of seventh sons), those born with amniotic sac, healer family lineages, and priests through the intercession of the saints.[191]

This previous passage refers to "saints"being channelers, "intercessors" who are able to channel healing powers of the spirit It might be easy to have this mention go unnoticed if you weren't aware that men who worked for the church became "saints" only after their deaths. So here the church is saying the priests get assistance from the Spirit World of "saints," from church men in the Spirit World. This is likely an attempt to copy the Mediumship is Lineage healers, because it is well known the church wasn't able to cure people.

This idea of men being "sainted" is a more egotistical version of the Divine Feminine shamanism the church was copying. The church ha discovered a feminine tradition of women reporting a "Good Lady" visiting them at night, telling them factual "secrets of the Universe" such as how to cure diseases with indigenous herbs. The "spirit woman" who appeared to these earthly women was often accompanied by a group of other spirit people in an "oneiric," dreamlike procession mixed with animals and human-animal hybrids, denoting something special and "other" that earthly people. Those cues are that she was seen as part animal, part human, that she often had other "dead people" with her, all symbols simply pointing to the Spirit World reaching into the earthly world, which were considered distinctly different types of "people."

The church made the mistake of presenting a much more egotistical and earthly version of this by "sainting" their own regular men post-death. While there has certainly long been a belief in Italy of ancestors "living on after death," it is generally agreed that Goddesses and Grande Madre and Madonnas and other Spirit people who cure disease and teach advanced knowledge are not like earthly people. The male "saints," however, were just regular men who followed the Christian God and who then died. Simply because of this they became "saints" and simply because of this they acquired miraculous powers only after death. This is not the natural order of things: it was created by the church for the purpose of "elevating" their "men" to legendary status. Some of them are alleged to have made miracles while on earth, and those few were highly "advertised" in their day...whereas peasant healers were curing diseases every day, without being elevated above their peers. Peasant healers are humble: they don't claim to own the miracles. They lived among other people; the church saints lived in comfort, protection, and financial support of the church, coming into the populations only to give public performances like speeches.

PROPAGANDA

It was the church, however, who was trying to capitalize on healing and magic, to "corner the market" if you will. This is what all the propaganda against women was covering up: the church wanted to be "the ones," the Big Business, so people would be persuaded to only come to male doctors and the church for cures, to seek out the new "male god" in town. The problem was, people were dying in the hands of monks and doctors. And with magic everywhere and female healers readily available, how do you turn people into "customers" for something they get from their neighbor that actually works? By using a successful advertising campaign which, as we see in modern times, focuses on destroying the "competition" (and punishing those who don't convert).

Romans were masters of propaganda, developing powerful visual tools which extended beyond the use of vivid folk tales and their symbolism. Examples are: the "adventus" procession which presented the new emperor to his subjects, his likeness being stamped into new coinage, statues, murals, and a visual connection between him and his pagan god of choice. As author Thomas F. Mathews writes in "The Clash of Gods, A Reinterpretation of Early Christian Art," *"Art historians have been slow to address the power of images, but the fourth century witnessed an unparalleled war of images and it was the strength and energy of the winning images that determined the outcome. We are more accustomed to narrating events the other way around, describing the winning images as a consequence of the political fortunes of one or another party. But this is to imagine that art is chiefly decorations and illustration, that it merely echoes decisions made in a higher court of activity without taking part in the events of world history."*[192]

And at the same time, the church was engaging in imagery battle, using these techniques to portray Jesus in a way to catch the same attention new emperors did: [the composition of] Christ entering Jerusalem to the acclamation of the crowd is seen as recalling the images of the emperor being received at the gates of a city in the "adventus" ceremony.[193] Christ ascending in an aureola of glory is supposed to have been copied from images of the emperor on shields.[194] In this manner, it is believed, the repertoire of Christian images was gradually constructed.[195] Interestingly however, Jesus' image was continually changing: young to old, masculine to feminine. Unlike many historical figures of antiquity, Christ had no authentic portrait tradition.[196]

Socrates' visual history, in contrast, [is that] portraits of him were made shortly after his execution, and these became the prototypes for a very plentiful tradition of sculptures of the philosopher in Greek and Roman art.

No such tradition exists for portraits of Christ.[197] Images of him may therefore be said to be pure projections in the psychological sense that is, inventions corresponding to what people needed or wanted from him.[198]

At the time Constantine challenged his brother, the structure of the church was already in place and quite visible, with its cohesive communities organized under bishops, priests, and deacons, [...] and its strong financial system, which enabled them to *"send large sums of money to ransom captives" during the barbarian raids of 254 and 256, which "was a responsibility that the Roman government was not able to assume."*

The downfall of Jupiter and Eugenius [...] opened the way to the violent destruction of pagan sanctuaries in the following century.[199] Along with Jupiter, all the images of the ancient pantheon came tumbling down, and instead there appeared a strange collection of saints and angels that would rule the religious imagination of the West for at least the next millennium. But, the "strangeness" of these images didn't come entirely from them being new ones, but also because their presentations were visibly copied from others and mistakes were seen in comparison with the traditional visual language of that historical period.

In the early fourth century Christians were expanding their repertoire of succinct, unconnected images, adding new scenes of Christ's miraculous cures.[200] Generally these new images were placed side by side with the older staccato images, disregarding programmatic or chronological connections. Christian art was struggling to enunciate a more complex and nuanced message. Jesus didn't seem to have his own style; and he appeared to be copying other healers and magi around him. Most notably he is depicted copying Asclepius in a specific seated pose, wearing a specific dress which leaves his chest and right shoulder bare and therefore Christian artists were competing Jesus with Asclepius' healing powers. Christ was also regularly depicted with the wand.

Historically the wand as a wizard's sign originated in the Middle Kingdom Egypt.[201]

This lack of style and personal characteristics was not the norm in imagery propaganda: each new emperor and his chosen god had specific symbols, postures, and clothing styles which represented them. In fact, most of the Christian art depicting Jesus was mimicry and therefore competitive. Most importantly, this imagery did not present him as being different from other magicians and healers in visual art at all, but rather just like them. Christians chose to join their "leader figure," their "spiritual parallel to a Roman emperor" to the world of magic intentionally and calculatingly. They did not separate Jesus nor themselves from this world, but rather competed neck-and-neck with magic's most popular figures through visual stories. Christian art sought to show that "not only was his magic effective, it had ancient roots in the two great traditions of magic-that of Egypt and that of the Chaldeans.[202]

This competition from Christians with other magi did not go unchallenged. Christ was persistently categorized as nothing more than a common sorcerer in his times,[203] like other "sorcerers who profess to do wonderful miracles and those who are taught by Egyptians, who for a few obols make known their sacred lore in the middle of the market place and drive demons out of men[204] [...] said Celsus (c.A.D.178) referring to Christ's multiplications of loaves. After all, magic was commonplace in these days, even though Christian propaganda would have people think that Christ was the only one doing these "miraculous" things. Celsus (the author of the first comprehensive philosophical polemic against Christianity[205]) asked, "Since these men [other men besides Christ, and those who came before] do these wonders, ought we to think of them sons of God? Or ought we to say that they are the practices of wicked men possessed by an evil demon?"[206]

Whether Jesus was real or not in the modern mind, historically he was depicted as being a magician by the Christian church itself. That wasn't enough for them, so also, historically, the church promoted Jesus as the ultimate magician and healer among other healers, and they did so by usurping the symbols, poses, and styles of other magicians and healers. Because whether or not Jesus was alright co-existing with the plethora of other healers and magi, the church wanted to destroy all competition. While the emperor "adventus" was a military parade designed to impress his new subjects through awe and even terror through a display of power, the imagery of Christ's entry is not. However, behind all the imagery, the church's other "agents" like priests called for violence and hatred and destruction of their competition in fiery speeches, while the imagery propaganda of Christ was a process of "takeover by usurpation."

This confesses that the church didn't think magic nor healing were evil after all, since they championed Jesus as their "magic man." It's important to acknowledge that even though they called him the "son of God," they portrayed him exactly as all other healers and magi, and not as something new and different. The priests, with their speeches, are the ones who began to divide and conquer through words of hatred after they established Jesus as a magician and healer.

In order to separate him from other healers and magi somehow, even though they advertised that he was just like them, they developed the "heresy" charge that Paolo Portone mentioned. They, like all other socio-political groups, began the comparison game.

While the extent of this propaganda by the church (good cop/ bad cop) with " good guy magician" at the front and "bad guy Priests" behind the scenes is much more detailed, these few bits are here to show that propaganda isn't an "alleged idea," but rather this was the way of the world in 4th and 5th centuries, and the church used it to form "la caccia alle streghe," (the witch hunts) in Italy, as well.

These centuries mark most important transitions in time which show a line of continuity and development between socio-religio-political changes in Italy (and Old Europe). These changes must be acknowledgedand brought to light to show the reality behind the Witch Hunts, especially since the lasting effects of the hunts are the created hyper-fantasy stories and the damaged reputations of women. It's the cunning calculations that have been protected from public view, and they are the true evil, not the women and men accused of "joining with the devil."

Constantine is one of a handful of figures who for better or worse have unalterably affected the course of human history.[207] Would the emperors have been less cruel to women had they not supported

Christianity's rise? We'll never know, but likely not. Invasion was also part of their directives. After all, even their spiritual stories are about wars. In contrast, there are no original goddess stories of goddesses killing their successive goddesses (that weren't created by men).

The church was quite successful in their elimination of other magical male figures who stood in their way of the magic monopoly they desired. However, that still left them "in competition" with female healers and magicians. They didn't have a competing female figure to use to subsume and then to wipe out Italian peasant women in the same parallel way as they did male figures. So they just worked on the destruction part, through creating a story.

Even though women weren't valued by the church as peers in these fields, they were still a threat because of a most beautiful reason: women healers, the real ones who cure specific diseases do so mysteriously, and seemingly simply. They are not elevated on a social pedestal, they don't buy their cures from the store: they channel a higher power, and that higher power can't be learned in school because "it's" neither a craft, a skill, nor a spell." "It" is the Divine Feminine, the Great Mother Goddess consciousness, and She chooses who She'll channel through. And, She chose largely uneducated women, poor, and humble then, and She chooses the humble now. The ultimate miracle of channeling: boundless knowledge. However, this ability to channel the Divine Mother can't be recognized from the outside, so these true healer women remain often anonymous, (then and now) as did the mystery of their healing abilities...which often they take with them to their graves if a successor isn't chosen, even in these modern times. And that's the beauty of their healing power: it's borrowed, it's intangible, it's not a thing, and no one can steal it because "it" has a consciousness of her own.

Women have mostly been written out of history, and repeatedly exterminated and relegated to the shadows in the physical realm as well. But these two important parts of history: invasions of harmonious gylanic communities by warring male tribes, and the church rising to financial heights and propaganda power with their warring ways, directly led to their attack of female healers and creation of "la caccia alle streghe."

THE CHURCH CREATED THE WITCH'S DEVIL

Paolo Portone is a Roman researcher and published author whose passion is in untangling the diabolical stories from the real women who were targeted as witches. He has worked to reclaim Inquisition documents and historical truths for more than 30 years. As science director of the newly opened "MES" in Triora, (Ethnohistorian Museum of Witchcraft), whose inauguration was in December of 2016. He shared with me in our interview:

"We have a lot of differences between the north and south of Italy. The 'heretical' period in the north was more severe, because in the north there was more control from the church on the society. The south was a bit different, there was not the heretical target by the church." Paolo explains to me is that the accusation of "heresy," is how the church found a way to target women healers and not end up condemning themselves too, which was to extend the accusations beyond just "witchery'" (because to many people "witchery" meant magic and all sorts of things) to "heresy."

Paolo explained that heresy was an accusation of being "unorthodox:" a woman using prayers to cure diseases was "unorthodox" according to the church. In other words, it was a clever way to accuse people of doing something "different," since the church was now going to accuse magicians and healers of being evil, even though they had been advertising Jesus as a magician and a healer. Thus began "the Hunt" the to find "different." Interestingly, the church did find "different," and the "different" that they found actually exonerated women from evil: they found a female lineage of knowledge being passed from the Spirit World to the earthly world of women, for the purpose of caring for life through herbal knowledge and more. A still-living link to the ancient gylanic, pre-Greek, Roman, and pagan times.

Paolo continues, "*The trials were in the north, and the 'heretical' problem existed in the north of Italy and northern Europe. In the aristocratic 'Borghese' social class at that time they developed a sense of criticism against the church, they didn't agree with the church, and the church fought back. In the south, we have two main big cities: Napoli and Palermo, the rest was countryside. Here were different traditions, mostly agricultural. In the south there was less struggle against the church, even though there was a big magical tradition. In a certain specific period of history and exactly when the church started to fight against heresy, around 1200 AD is the period when the Inquisition was introduced around this issue of holding control of the society. They started to think maybe something was out of control so they enlarged their accusations to include anything unorthodox so they could accuse more people. In doing that, they put all the things we're talking about in something like a frame.*"

The "things" Paolo is referring to is how the "witch" became connected with negative imagery and how the ancient history the became attached to superstitions and negative propaganda. All our original, founding symbols were instead a language in harmony with life and depicted the divine feminine as source for all life.

This is the female lineage shamanism that Italian witchery comes from. "*So this frame,*" Paolo continues, "*is the 'diabolical' one, the one they created.*"

Manuela Saccone adds, "*What really marks the border with the witch-hunt is the devil's invention by the church. When we think of sorcery usually we relegate it to an area of very ignorant people, and in doing so we make a huge mistake, because 'witchcraft' was born in the cultural field. If there were no law-makers nor church men, the witches would not have existed. They had formulated this hypothesis, (based also on the latest Bible books) of the figure of the devil. People already believed in the devil, but the fact is that this obsessive presence of the devil explodes in the 1400s. This fear of evil explodes, because there was the plagues, because they did not know how to explain many things. Who should we blame? The devil of course. And who was in bed with the devil? Witches of course. They [witches] were already people who did not really live in orthodoxy. Because maybe these women were carrying on their rites in honor of Diana, in honor of Isis. So this figure of the Goddess was not gone [from peoples' minds, even though she was not part of the new patriarchal myths in original form].*" Today, there is this holistic idea of life, there is not just medicine to cure but you have to cure the soul beyond the body, because the diseases obviously start from the soul. That's what the ancients already knew.*"

Today, there is this holistic idea of life, there is not just medicine to cure but you have to cure the soul beyond the body, because the diseases obviously start from the soul. That's what the ancients already knew.

So we have at the beginning of the witch trials a competitive nature of the church with other male magicians and healers. We have the church creating an accusation of "heresy" to separate their acts of magic with acts of magic considered "negative." The next development was turning towards being competitive with female healers. And this is where the mysteries were: the church had no women as part of their organization, so they had to "investigate" to find out what was happening in the feminine world. As they did start to investigate and inquisited women, some interesting confessions came out:

"The start of the witch hunts In Italy," explains Paolo, *"were two trials of the same women, tried [or processed," as they say in Italy] 10 years apart. The two main women accused in these trials were Sibilla Zanni and Pierina Bugatis from Milano. What was found, when these women were Inquisited by the church was that these women confessed a 'Good Lady' would visit them at night, telling them how to use herbs to cure, telling them good things that were true. Maybe these practices were related with night life cults of women, or 'culti nottourno.' In these type of rituals we know they spoke about: the the Lady of the Place, 'Signora del Gioco,'(Lady of the Game) like Diana Oriente. We have several names to call these nighttime female figures, depending on where you were. So the 'Buon Gioco' wascwhat the church used to accuse the women of a non-Orthodox practice (not in line with the church). Socin the first trial, the women were accused of practical, non-orthodox methods. This first trial finished conly just with a warning 'Ok, don't do that again.' The women were given just a warning, no tortures."*

The first trial didn't stick basically, because of the all-too similar practices between natural 'witches' and the church's spells and sorcery. But there was no devil attached to them yet, and it would take ten years until we find the church having created and established symbolism to express the diabolism: they were "seeking," or rather, accusing women of.

Manuela adds: *"In fact at the beginning the 'sabba' was not called 'sabba' [the church eventually began accusing women of meeting the Devil at their Sabba], it was called 'the game of Diana.' In some processes this name comes out in the trials sometimes, in some areas during the interrogations and subsequent "confessions" of the women. At first, a specific name, especially in the first trials for witchcraft, was given. The women called her [this Lady of the Game] as 'Signora Oriente,' which means 'Eastern Lady.' [the name of the woman visiting young women in villages by the light of the moon and teaching them advanced knowledge] It's beautiful this thing here, because Diana was also called 'Signora Oriente." [The name was "oriente" because it was part of these cultures like Egypt, Mesopotamia, and also the culture of the Greeks, in other words, not originating in Italy."*

When the church began Inquisiting women in the beginning, searching for something "unorthodox," all they found was something that sounded natural to the way women were already learning to cure disease: a woman was teaching them. This particular story, featuring the "Good Lady," was a little bit different because she was outside of the family Lineage of these women. She was one Lady traveling around teaching women. And, she was a Lady from the Spirit World.

At first, the church couldn't make the "heresy" charge stick because this relationship they found was simply teacher-and-students. It didn't have a diabolical edge to it. And, the stories of these women were consistent. Additionally, this is a story that had been long in existence already. The church set about trying to find a way to create something diabolical, and ironically, the violence they were exacting didn't count. It was the church, actually, who gave the name "Diana" to the "Good Lady of the Night." The women who had been visited by her did not call her "Diana." The church, knowing Diana was a Goddess embraced by the Romans at that time, decided to add her to the story to inflate the "divinity" competition, and that was their angle of success: a Goddess competing with Jesus, the "one and only son of God." But they didn't stop there, because this is a story that until this point was only "unorthodox," but not much different a story than Asclepius, Jupiter, and the pantheon of pagan gods and goddesses.

Manuela continues, *"And even the figure of the devil himself that we have at that time is a collage created by the church from the God Pan, who was symbolized as half-goat and half man, a God of the forests. Originally he didn't have goat horns. He was not God of the Universe. The church put on the horns which was actually the crescent shape moon of Diana."* So in this way the church said: Pan belongs to Diana the Goddess, he is a reflection of her, by using her symbol as a "logo" emblazoned on his forehead. The horns were not a male attribute but a divine feminine one, and although at this time the Great Goddess was "replaced and subsumed" by many male gods, her symbols were still known even by the church. *"So they created the devil with specific purpose, surely."* Manuela explains, *"The Catholic church was not always able to eradicate a cult because while people were Christians they still practiced in these pagan cults. So when the Catholic church fails to eradicate a cult, when the church cannot extirpate it, they place a Christian cult on it."*

The "Christian cult" was basically "the demonizing of what came before" and a subsuming of the cult they wish to eradicate. With the Good Lady, they couldn't subsume it because the Church had no female figures as leaders, like Jesus. They only had "Mary," the subservient one. And while all over Italy syncretism can be found where Mary is the outward Divine Feminine symbol hiding a pagan goddess who is being worshipped, what Manuela is referring to here in terms of "putting a Christian cult on it" in regards to The Good Lady and Pan is "devil-izing," or "placing the devil over it."

It's an important twist of fate, however, that they chose to use this ancient female symbol of the uterus, ovaries and fallopian tubes; the "horns" of the moon, because in doing so they left a trail pointing back to themost ancient times of Divine Feminine spirituality and reflective female shamanic communities in Italy and Old Europe. Even though their goal was to destroy and eradicate women, by admitting this symbol (the moon crescent and its connection to the bull skull and horns and all animal skulls with horns) are a symbol of the Great Mother Goddess and not the devil nor any man at all, they helped leave a very small but important trail to Italian Witchery's lineage and to what came before paganism.

Paolo shares how this development affected the Inquisition trials, *"So they had two different trials [in Milan] for the same accusations against these same two women. The first one was in 1380 and the second, ten years later in 1390. In the first trial they were bought in front of the court and the women told them about their night life rituals. And these night life rituals are ones that have nothing diabolical at all.*

Of the rituals, the women just talked about a female figure who gave them some instructions about herbs and how to use them. In the first process, the women were accused of unorthodoxy and told to change their ways. However, it was important for the church in their propaganda to demonstrate that the witches were actually diabolic, which they could not yet do. The second process [trial], 10 years later, the courts judged the women had a 'relapse,' which meant in Latin that they still had a recurring problem with the same unorthodox ways, so the second trial for the same thing would be very severe."

"They used this process, this trial," Paolo continues, "as an example, to make the punishment very strong and severe to prove a point, with propaganda, and in this way they started the myth of the 'diabolical witch.' The tortures were something very important, because they were shown to people, as demonstrations of punishments, to deter people from also being this way. Since that moment, all the subsequent trials had that trial as an example so were all very severe. So that's why the witch hunting is like a process of violent acculturation. This process of acculturation obviously doesn't take just one year, it takes centuries, a huge process, over 400 years or more, and you can consider these years like one big continuing trial."

Manuela adds, "So the issue is that witches become persecuted when the church [and then the people] associate the devil figure to the witches. Without the devil, no witch is dangerous. So, it was created, built in the field. This was surely misogynous, because the Christian religion, like all religions, is misogynous. [And then] if you go through a plague, you need someone to blame, Jews, Jews and witches, it made a difference. They became one, all the people at margins of the society, or those who did not live properly in orthodoxy, were exposed."

ECONOMICS

Concurrent to all these things developing in the 1200s and into the 1300s, the same time in which the church was spreading the "heresy" accusations, the first medical doctors came into competition with "levatrice" (midwives). More precisely, the church and the doctors created a competition *against* the women that was also partly economical.

Manuela explains, "Even in Roman times, the witch is the one who cared for the herbs and healing, and who also made some sorcery for lovers. People weren't bothered by witches since they helped people.

Then we arrive at the Middle Ages. Witches already exist, but consider in a medieval society there were not any doctors at the time, there were only the witches. However, around the end of the 1200s and in the 1300s the first schools of medicine began to appear in Italy. And the doctors are only men. They would not allow a woman to become a doctor, and there were very few of the male doctors at the start.

As the figure of the doctor, obviously male, begins to develop, all these women with their medical knowledge are bound in their home. They are the midwives who help children to get born, and so on.

Let me say briefly that in the late 1300s and into the 1400s if there were any witches who *were annoying and disliked by people, they were kicked out of the area. But until that point there are no stories of any stake. If they were burnt, it was as heretics and not as witches.*

In the 1400s, instead, these women start to become a bother because they take jobs away from doctors [truly, midwives had always been women, it was the male doctors who tried to take their own natural jobs away]. And yet they are often women who live a bit on the margins of society [they were not part of the economy nor were they affecting the society's economy]. Most are midwives, and although the midwife is the one who helps you to give birth to the children, if we're in a time of famine and in a time when some plagues take place, and children begin to die, who should be blamed? The midwife; why not! Not the doctor surely, but the midwife."

So we have the doctors scapegoating the women for their own failures as medical doctors, and we have the church creating a diabolical story about them, and along with these attacks, the already covered-up divine feminine symbolism is being turned into symbols of diabolism.

Also during this time, in 1406, parallel to and slightly north of Umbria, we have San "saint" Bernardino of Siena, who was a hate-filled Italian priest, a Franciscan Missionary, public speaker and a systemizer of Scholastic Economics. His attack on witch women was fiery, hate-filled and street-level. He spread his blackened thoughts through public speech events, inciting fear and disgust among already powerless people in communities, and turning them against each other. As was already mentioned, people of this time were not worried about "witches," but the doctors and the church and their "agents" like Bernardino made a powerful 3- pronged attack to convince them otherwise.

Bernardino's public, fervent speeches made him popular, attracting crowds of 30,000 people. He also targeted sorcerers, homosexuals, and Jews. An economic jealousy was at the root of many of his speeches. He was specifically outspoken about the Jews for their use of "usury," an interest on loans. In fact, His greatest contribution to economics was a discussion and defense of the entrepreneur. His book, "On Contracts and Usury, " written during the years 1431–1433, dealt with the justification of private property, the ethics of trade, the determination of value and price, and the usury question.[208] One of his contributions was a discussion on the functions of the business entrepreneur, who Bernardino saw as performing "the useful social function of transporting, distributing, or manufacturing goods."[209]

In addition to "Big Business" goals, he emphasized (the Bible's) Mary's obedience to her husband, he tried to keep women "virgins" but had no condemnation of men who had sex before marriage, and he called for homosexuals to be banned from society and to be killed in public tortures. His homophobia, his misogyny, and his attacks against Jewish usury were ideas that he obsessed over, poring over his notes, writing and re-writing his speeches until he felt they were perfect; a man obsessed with destruction. He also targeted prostitutes. While churches cry "morality!" against prostitutes, they were not a problem for society at this time, and in fact were seen as "keeping travelers happy and harmonious," especially in the areas of Triora, which was an important crossroads for travelers from other lands. They were not seen as a problem. However, considering the church was forcing arranged marriages around this time, prostitutes were a symbol of freedom, and that was a problem for the church.

While in modern times we have been conditioned by the church to condemn women who are prostitutes, but in this time period in Italy, often it was older women who lived alone who earned a surviving wage this way, having little other "use" in the masculinized society. So condemning them for this was literally relegating them to nothingness and no resources. In contrast, Enzo Gravina tells me that many healers were making a very good living, not all were poor and in remote areas. Healers were, however, often called interchangeably both "whores" and witches and healers during this time period of the Inquisition. While on the surface we have been conditioned to see "errors in morality" in these lifestyles, the true targets were economic stomp-out of independent women. So as we expand our vision to what was going on around the Inquisition itself, the economic target becomes clear.

As for Bernardino, he was a man obsessed with destruction. His effect was that his speeches inflamed hysteria. For example, he preached on this subject in Rome and Siena in the summer of 1427. After the Roman cycle (May-July) of his homilies, in the city of the popes there was a huge number of complaints of witchcraft.[210] He thus became a major exponent of what historian Robert Moore has called "the persecuting society" of late medieval Christian Europe.[211] following St. Francis of Assisi's admonition to preach about "vice and virtue, punishment and glory." For this, he was canonized as a saint after his death.

As his lasting legacy, there are some interesting churches standing who bear his name. Notable, a tiny one I visited in Triora, Italy, is a testament to his polarized and judgemental view of the world around him: To visit Chiesa di San Bernardino, one simply gets the key from the museum and walks down the gorgeous and peaceful foot trails to find a little one-room church built onto a mountain side, whose apse is literally on the cliff's edge; it can't be accessed on the ground around the church, begging the question..is there a secret chamber underneath? The outside is an interesting mix-match of columns, which I'm told is common thing to see architectural ruins from one place re-built in another; a collage of sorts. Entering the church, a soft and diffused light shines into the apse and onto the walls. To the left and from floor-to-ceiling are painted saints (all men) with golden haloes and bright light and colors. To the right, from floor-to-ceiling are scenes of the fires of hell, burning witches, and bloodthirsty demons of all types devouring various men and women. While the room itself is small, square-footage wise, the ceilings are high: they reach almost two stories, and the full-walled murals and their scenes of heaven and hell are inescapable. It seems the church at this time was not advertising so much of the benefits their God had to offer, but they more clearly showed the torturous pain that would be inflicted upon people if they did not worship him anyway. That's where their power was: inciting fear of torture, making people feel unsafe and insecure and under watch at all times.

SCAPEGOATING AND MOB MENTALITY

"San Bernardino was one of the first preachers, among others, to accuse witches for dealing with the devil. He insisted that people denounce the witches, claiming they eat baby flesh during "sabbats,"that they feed themselves with the meat of the children pulled out of the tombs...the worst accusations really.

Hearing this, people start to become afraid. Also because they start to wonder if all those things were true as they coincided with the plague and famine and other problems. Who's to blame? People started accusing each other so as to not be accused themselves, and it became a chain reaction. At that point they even accused a noblewoman from Triora, then a collective delirium began, and that's when Triora's killings started happening," Manuela explains the "mob mentality" factor.

"The way," she continues, *"to accuse someone back then of witchcraft was: having your animals dying, having problems with kids, etc. If these things happened to you, you would look to point the finger at a woman who made that happen, a scapegoat. So, accusing 'someone,' even an imaginary figure like the devil, was powerful, because of the idea in Italy of consciousness being responsible for illness."* Relationships with people were important: whether someone was throwing "jettatura" (the evil eye) at another or someone was curing that action, or a neighbor was delivering your baby or divining a future, "people" were considered responsible for good and bad happenings, not random acts of "god."

As Manuela says regarding health, *"Because the diseases obviously start from the soul,"* and the soul is conscious. *"We cannot understand it with our minds, but if we put ourselves in these peoples' minds, both the educated and the peasants...they really believed in the devil. They were quite convinced that the devil was there and he needed to be eliminated as much as possible. And through these witches both men and children were also burned, because then the witches' sons were considered to be witches too. Those accused of being witches were condemned to death in Italy."*

"Other accusations about women being witches," Gerry Delfno adds, *"arose from competition with modern medicine, with the doctors who fixed bones. These [professional accusations] came from Genova. We also have an example of Inquisition actions before it "officially" started back in 1250 in Liguria when a woman was accused of being a witch. It was discovered that her husband accused her, but even though it seemed like a domestic dispute, in the end anyway she was burned by fire. Many people were accused of worshiping the devil and were killed in areas where the body couldn't be found, such as in between two mountains in a deep ravine. Bodies were thrown down there, and no one could help you if you were thrown, and people simply disappeared because it was too treacherous to go down and identify the body. There were women who got burned in this area, like at the river near in Badalucco, but there are no documents recording their names." I was also told of women being burned on the rocks at the river from younger people in the area who regularly use the river in the warmer weather."*

So women were not just killed in courts, or languishing in jails because even villagers took the power of judgement and death in their own paranoid hands, and death could come from anywhere. *"But there were intelligent people who also had good sense [among the accused witches],"* Manuela claims. *"These women, especially the first, they knew very well that these accusations were based on the neighbors' envy. And it was just a matter of time, if you were unpleasant to the neighbor...then you could find yourself in a trial."* In fact, Antonietta had told me that if she were alive during the Inquisition, that surely the bad witches would have turned her in.

She is not the only woman to have told me that witches turned each other in to protect themselves.

Triora was one of the places hit hardest by the Inquisition as well as the frenzy that spread around it. It is a place inseparable from earlier historical claims which paint a desperate picture as author Sandro Oddo shares in its signature "legend:"

"Between 1585 and 1587, Triora was the victim of a serious famine, which brought the population to the brink of collective death. In a climate like this and in a country as isolated as was Triora, yet "superstitious" and "backward," it is obvious that tempers warmed themselves in the worst way. Therefore, in the country, they began to suspect that the cause of the famine was not completely natural, but there was the hand of someone else: the witches.

The culprits were immediately identified in some women inhabitants of Ca'Botina district, the area outside the walls of the poorest across the country." [212]

But after recent research Sandro told me that *"It is true: the famine was probably a speculation by existing noble families in Triora (Borelli, Capponi, etc). [speculation here means: engagement in business transactions involving considerable risk but offering the chance of large gains [...] in the hope of profit from changes in the market price. The rulers of Triora,"* Sandro explains, *"in a letter dated January 13, 1588, says that the people had been given to understand that the famines in Triora for two to three years was caused by the witches, but at that time there truly was such an abundance of provisions that they didn't know what to do with all the extra food. It all seems really clear. And the losers were the poor women ... and one man!"*

Writer Francesca Bezzone reports in her article "The Triora Witch Trials" from lifeinItaly.com,

"Historians very much agree in saying that, of course, there was no witchcraft behind the accusations, and that the reason used to justify maleficent activities in the village – the 'caresty' (famine) – very likely never took place, as all records of the time define Triora as the 'breadbasket of the genoese Republic." [213] So what happened? It is possible that local landowners wanted to rise wheat and, more generally, food prices to increase their income. Even though the maneuver aimed at getting more income from their sales to the capital, Genoa, locals paid the consequences more than the Genoese, as they became unable to buy food to sustain themselves and their families. Blaming the death of hunger stricken people on witchcraft was a perfect way out.

Among the most gruesome and horrendous accusations moved to the Triora's witches was that of infanticide: however, birth and death records of the time do not show an increase in infants' death in the area. More likely is, on the other hand, the presence of expert midwives, with great knowledge of natural remedies, who often "baptized" stillborns or babies about to die in absence of a priest nearby. This practice was common, but not well liked by the church, and may also be one of the reasons behind the accusations.

Historians have also underlined the possible link between the Triora witch hunt and the events, in those very same years, involving Triora's canon Marco Faraldi, who had been accused of producing fake money and alchemic practices: in order to divert attention from the scandal, Triora's most powerful may have fabricated the accusations, creating a situation that would eventually go entirely out of hand.[214]

CHANGES IN THE ACCUSATION PROCESS

"In some regions," Manuela explains, *"there were some special arrangements, such as with the diocese in Savona. Thanks to Pope Sixtus IV, who was from Savona, there was this regulation where no citizen of the Diocese of Savona could be tried except by the Bishop. There wasn't an inquisitor but a vice-inquisitor, the last word was the Bishop's one. That's why the Inquisitors could not inquire anyone. This was from the end of the 1400 and onwards, and Savona never deleted this regulation. In Finalborgo we are also under The Diocese of Savona. So these accusations against 'witches' were made by private individuals.*

This was the accusatory plant. That is, the legal system was 'accusatory' until the XII century.

'Accusative' means that 'I accuse you, that you are a criminal, you are a murderer, you had stolen my animals or you put a spell on me , and I bring you in front of the judge.' The judge is says 'Okay, bring me the evidence that the person you accuse is guilty and I will punish him appropriately.'

Manuela explains that responsibility was implied for making an accusation: *"If I can prove that you have actually hurt me, you are punished. But if I cannot bring the evidence and they find out that you are innocent, I instead have the penalty that you should have suffered. So I'll think about it carefully before I accuse you."*

"However," Manuela continues, *"in the XIII century, the legal system changes. The trials become about the Inquisitors and not the people. What this means is that even the private citizen can report a complaint of a 'witch' to an Inquisitor. But before the judge needs to accuse someone, first here's the inquisitor saying 'Let's go, I want to see, I want to investigate to figure out how these accused people are.' So then the person who's making the accusation is no longer the one who has to bring the evidence. [so there's less responsibility] You make the complaint but it is the Inquisitor who decides whether or not to investigate. And even if the accusation is found to be fake nothing happens to the person who made the fake accusation."*

In a day-long mountain trek that my two Ligurian region drivers and translators took me on, I would get to see this part of history in real-life: we walked along a winding path that would twist and turn like a serpent, taking us halfway up a mountain somewhere near Dolceacqua and and then wind us around another mountain past a few homes in the middle of a lovely nowhere, to find ourselves come upon an ancient church in the middle of another fog-drenched and deep overgrown forest green nowhere. The one-room church with its tell-tale medieval "arch" that was supposed to receive visitors and protect them from the rain even though the arch was only a few feet wide and too tall to block any weather: neither sun, rain, nor fog. At the front of the one room church was a metal "cassette" as Simone Scuri called it, which was simply a metal "ballot."

"They used it, often there were two cassettes at the church; one was for the charity and the other one where you could put inside the anonymous sheet in which you accused people of things, or accused people who were trying to accuse you. The inquisitor would then collect the sheets and used these accusations to begin to inquire."

Gerry further explains, *"The Inquisition over here in Albenga* [Ligurian Region] *has been really harsh and was connected with the order of 'Domenicani,' or San Domenico. There were Tribunale Courts* (where you are judged by a judge). *Back then there was a civil one and a religious one. Witches were judged in a religious court. The torture phase was over 200 years. There was a prosecutor who was put in a church even after everything stopped. It took a long time to end the Inquisitions* (similar to how after a war ends and soldiers are still in the cities) *When Napoleon came in power, he took over and people suddenly forgot about the witches. In Albenganese, the area not just the town, which goes from Finale to Sanremo where there are 92 churches, I don't know exactly how many were accused but for sure it's more than 100.*

The famous names [of the Inquisition] *are famous because they are the only ones who went through some processing, in documents. Most of the women, there were so many that weren't processed.*

They were jailed or tortured or killed without papers documenting their names, so there are no traces of who they were. Many times what happens is that it takes so much time to publish this news from the past, so maybe there are even more names out there we don't know yet because they are being discovered and haven't yet been published. The real Inquisition has then happened back in 1400s and 1500s where in fact we have lots of these Inquisitors, Domenicans were very strong in Liguria where we can find them in Taggia, Albenga, Genova.

So we have this cruel reality at the end of the 1400s and into the 1500s. The more famous acts are the ones that took place in Triora because they are the most documented ones. At some point even the state of Genova was trying to protect these women who were accused for no reasons."

Genova is from where the Inquisitors were sent out, essentially where the hunts began: it was like the center of the wheel and the spokes all radiated from here, though Rome had the final word on many aspects."

In contrast, Manuela tells me, *"However, the Italian inquisition was less dreadful than the German, French, Belgian inquisitions. In Europe it* [Italy] *was the most mild because there was the presence of the church which was still guarding. Where there were no Inquisitors, where witches were judged by civil courts, not one woman survived."* In other words, though the Inquisitors were hunting down the women, in some ways it offered some protection from the "rogue, deaths-by-citizen-arrest" that also did happen where the church was not in charge. The deeper we could go into these dynamics, the more they show that the "mob mentality" was the true plague.

"This figure of the witch at the Italian level is also present in Germany, as just the healer, midwife it is the same model that is being presented in this wonderful text: 'The Witch Hunt In

Early Modern Europe' by Brian P. Levack. In all of Europe the differences between one State and another are were about: in one the healers, in one the medics, there are those where you understand very well that there are more political rewards. There are those, especially in Germany, where the witch is clearly seen to have been born or rather 'created' primarily for religious disputes, between Protestants and Catholics. Protestants are the most terrible. In Germany it becomes a delusion, people died as flies, they were terrified by this idea of the devil. So the witch as intended is born in the 400s when the figure of the devil is established. Established ... let's say 'better enriched.' So in every State it [the witch hunt] was a peculiar thing."

Additionally, in Levack's book it is made very clear that male pornographic ideas about women's sexuality were at the core of the hatred that helped create the witch by those in charge of this propaganda. Helping to support the male church's extermination of women in Europe at this time was "The Malleus Maleficarum," basically a book that reads like a "battle plan instructional" for finding, rooting out, torturing and then killing women (and calling them "witches."). Its recommended procedures include torture to effectively obtain confessions and death penalty as the only sure remedy against evils of witchcraft.[215] all the while knowing that the "evil witch" was created by the church itself; she was never real. This is the work of truly mentally disturbed men. And yet, it is considered to be the most important treatise written on witchcraft and was more popular than the Bible during its time. It reads as a "warning against women," accusing them of the standard patriarchal criticisms: being too emotional, not being capable of leadership, too weak, etc. It's a guidebook for men that encourages perverted sexual fantasy and suggestions on how to have fun experimenting on women's bodies and gives them the feeling that it's right to torture women. It reads like they are creating an image of "women as victims," ones who are powerless. And yet, they blame these alleged "powerless victims" for alleged crimes committed with the Devil, mainly: sex and eating babies. They don't offer any criticisms of the Devil at all. It is nonsensical. The church didn't instruct people on how to eradicate the Devil from their lives, but rather how to eradicate women from peoples lives. So who is the real Devil here?

The real concern here should be the mob mentality's embrace of this fantastical invention of female supernatural evil and of history's willingness to embrace the "evil witch" story in the past and to hold onto it in the present. More important than folk tales, psychologically, is this male directive to destroy. While the church's actions haven't been so scrutinized nor criticized (in the way many corporations enjoy clemency and are able to hide themselves behind distraction techniques) their true intentions are there in their own documentation, left behind in the stone of history as recorded actions to emphasize how little the church truly cared for actually finding "the devil" and getting rid of his alleged powerful grasp over women. While many of Italy's records were hidden or destroyed their actions, or lack of actions, against the "devil" himself, prove that he wasn't their target at all. But then, let's remember the church created this myth in the first place, the used a collage of natural symbols and our founding spiritual language symbols of the Divine Feminine to create him and connect him to her.

Their accusations, after all, were pointed at the alleged evil women who were allegedly eating flesh of babies. Since ancient times in Italy, generations of women have delivered their own babies, while modern male doctors were failing at delivering babies. Why would women suddenly start eating babies? They didn't, but this was a successful advertising campaign used to turn people towards doctors, even if they were terrible at offering assistance to health. They had a business to run, and the only way to make profits is to have customers.

Because, as yet, with all this power these women allegedly had being alleged sexual partners of the Devil, somehow they were unable to stop the Inquisition kidnappings nor prevent their own torture, and the alleged Devil didn't save them either. Was he powerful or not? If he was, why didn't he protect his alleged clan of women? If he was weak, why didn't the church defeat him? The church, if truly concerned about the Devil, would certainly have made efforts (magical ones and also prayers to God) to "stop" the Devil from infiltrating the population. Additionally, in a show of love towards "god's children," they might work to rehabilitate the alleged women who were "in the grasp of the Devil" to free them of such "evil." Instead, it can be seen that the only "urgency" in the church's mission was to incite hatred among the populations through fiery public Priest-led speeches so that they would turn on one another and turn away from female healers and midwives and agree with their deaths. And then, there's the important part: the church created the Devil...so there was no reason to go after him since he wasn't real, and they had nothing to gain by killing an imaginary creature. The women, however, were very real and they were there for the killing.

MISSING DOCUMENTATION

A brief examination of the tortures reveal everything we need to know about the damaged psychology of the church, its Inquisitors and the other men involved on every level. In a situation of urgency, if we are to believe the church's claim that these women causing harm upon their communities, it would follow that actions taken to stop the "evil-doings" would be immediate and would also alleviate the problems cause. This was not the case ever. There was no relief (of famine, of drought) caused by murdering these women, nor from torturing them, nor was there any backlash from the alleged devil. Neither were women hurriedly put into trials so the truth could be found, nor were any quickly killed (so as to stop the evil, from the point of view of the church). In fact, the scripts written by Father Ferraironi, local priest and scholar, were absolutely important because they describe a trial in Triora that didn't see any people being judged culpable.[216]

Enzo Gravina tells me that in 1428 was the famous trial of a Matteuccia de Francesco in Todi, in Umbria and that there were trials even earlier. Some of the most well-known are the Milan trials, Nogaredo trial, and the ones of Triora because they have been documented. A Parish priest named Nicolo Mascardi was sent to Triora, and priests did document their Inquisition travels. Mascardi's records show that parish priest took part in the parishioners practices, so magic, in his records, was something the church was also doing at this time, but shows no records of evil witchcraft being performed. However, there are some preserved letters during this time (early 1500s) written by the elders of Triora protesting the way women were taken and held indefinitely in jails accused of witchcraft because their health suffering. So while Mascardi's notes show no cause for alarm, no evidence of evil women, the Elder letters show that actions were being taken against this alleged threat which bore no evidence in reality. ...Mascardi was apparently a meticulous note taker, but somehow his records disappeared and only 50 pages remain, locked away in Albegna in church records, away from the public eye.

There were four phases of the Inquisition that would scar Triora, The City of Witches of the North. It was invaded, in the first phase at the end of summer 1587.[217] Consider there were only 2500 people living in Triora at the time, and the other villages that had people tortured and killed also had populations that were small in number. One hundred people killed in an area like this would have a big impact. Of course, other towns in the Argentina valley and neighboring valleys were also taken and killed. We don't know, with one exception, how many women disappeared from the accounts of Ferraironi.[218] Thirteen accused people were captured and put in jail before a trial even was organized nor any proof was given, and not all their names documented.

Post-Inqisition, in Val Poschiavana, a Federal Judge, Gaudenzio Oligati, collected what information he could (which still remains unpublished) in the last years of his life from1880-1890. In his notes he fixed his attention on the 123 processes of witchcraft that occurred there, a list of witchcraft processes lost by Poschiavo's archive (108 processes); a list of people probably wagered at Po Slave and Brusio (27 mothers of famous witches and 44 people named as accomplices); Witch figures and other people mentioned; List of Appointments; Index of Processed Individuals and Other Mentored Persons. Often only the wealthy could afford to have their trials documented,[219] so this tells us records were careless at times, and even the wealthy were not immune to accusations.

TORTURES

We are informed again by the local elderly people of the city of Triora who wrote a very important letter of protest on 13 January 1588, in which they mention that also other women were in danger of life because of the consequences of torture. A great number of women were arrested after the other 13 were jailed.;at least 30 women. The other women involved in the deal were the ones who languished in Genoese prisons. The inmates were not in good physical condition of course, and it is likely that they would not resist for long. It was, in fact,with the death of three of them that the Doge and the Governors in February 8, 1859 would return to solicit Rome [for what to do with these prisoners since the jailers were waiting on Rome to proceed.

And while these women were left indefinitely in jails without being proven guilty, Christian men were paying a small fee to rape them. Fabio Garuti, in his book, "Le Streghe di Benevento La Grand Bugia" reveals from his research of Italy and Germany, *as bestial as it may seem, these poor people, often left to agonize in inhuman conditions, after days of torture were also raped violently by lords or powerful and wealthy locals, isolated or even in groups, who also had the economic possibility of giving a few 'tips' to the prisoners, with the justification that they were dealing with demonic beings, so no sin was committed and would not have been committed. They were demonic beings, and so they believed everything was lawful."* It should be asked, psychologically, why a man would want to force his body into that of an alleged "demonic being" and what kind of god he believes in.

Fabio Garuti explains: *"Usually the Inquisitors adhered to certain rules to submit poor things to torture, which often consisted of tearing, i.e. the suspension in the air with ropes, hands tied behind her back, and then violent release. The dislocation of limbs was the least that could happen, also because, once led back to her cell, the victim was left with dislocated limbs. You can imagine the pain and suffering they were forced to suffer, these women. The list is long, ranging from crushing of the fingers, the mastectomy with red-hot pincers, the red-hot spikes and chairs, to the rolls across the body to dislocate all the joints, the stripping nails, etc. A list that only to read it you feel ill. A frightening cruelty, inhuman."*[220]

The "pre-tortures" which were part of the tortures, is the practice of molestation of bodies: This procedure was referred to as "researching the marks." The "finding of the stamp" was when a so-called expert performed: The Body Visit and Examination on the naked and depilated body of the suspect, made with the use of long needles: the true bad stamp does not bleed and is insensitive.[221] Women were strapped down, all the hair was shaved off their bodies, and every inch was examined with probing male fingers who searched for "the mark of the devil," which could be any mole or any spot on her body that an examiner wanted to "research." The stamp or mark and the sign that Satan thinks is on the body of the woman who puts is in his service and the finding of the stamp, made by an expert, authorizes the court to use torture in interrogations.[222]

In the witchcraft trials of 1587, the Inquisition made use of the properties of herbs to prepare two powerful sedatives: deadly nightshade and henbane which in fact created inhibitory effects on the nervous system, forcing the accused to confess what they [the Inquisitors] would have liked.[223]

The Cavaletto was a wooden structure that looked like the roof of a house; a wooden table with two sides which came to a point, creating a triangle-like structure. The torture victim would have to sit on the pointed area, naked, so their genitals were being pressed against the point, often tied with weights so they wouldn't fall off. Their "crotch" would be destroyed so they could no longer walk . Another version rips shoulder and hip joints. While the device was designed for women, there are accounts of male victims as well.[224]

Enzo told me also his theory about why they chose to burn the "streghe" (witches) using fire, and instead of killing them in other ways: *"Because other ways of killing could be faster, but the other ways of killing, almost all of them, involve blood coming out from the body, such as stabbing and beheading. In this period in Italy, they couldn't kill ....the holy scriptures said that humankind has been made in the same form and same image of God, so you absolutely cannot waste God's blood. That's the reason why they don't kill in a way where the blood comes out...so instead they burned the women. They also had created different ways of torturing like burned iron cauterizing, so they could injure you but not have blood come out. Another way is where they used to twist your thumbs and then put some water on you: if you were able to let yourself free you were a witch. if you were not able to set yourself free you were a witch. They decided you were a witch. When the witches were burned, imagine how many woods they needed to burn them! Tons and Tons. But, the fire was a purification symbol and there was no blood coming out in this method.*

But, at the same time, you can say, if you know a bit of history of Italy and Europe, that obviously we know that the church killed a lot of people through the centuries in very cruel manners, but before the 18th century it was not a problem because the church was a political power, yes, but not with very real powers. In the 16th and 18th century they became a political and official power, so since that moment they had to follow the holy scriptures literally, so they had to change their ways."

DAMNED IF THEY DO, DAMNED IF THEY DON'T

It was not enough, for the church, that women were kidnapped and jailed without evidence nor trial, just based on accusations. It was not enough that they were tortured, often for days, and left to languish in jail, no one even knowing their names, and not enough that women didn't confess except under torture or hallucinogens. It was not enough for them to fondle every part of a woman's body looking for "marks" of the fake devil they invented while she was strapped down and unable to prevent being raped by fingers and watched by groups of men. So the church also used every natural motion she made to also prove she was a "diabolical witch:"

"During the torture, the accused can turn around the eye, or hold them in front of him. These are new clues. In fact, if she turns around the eye, they say she is looking for her lover, the devil; if she keeps his eyes fixed, it's sign, they say, that   she has already found him and that she is watching him.

And if, during the repeated torture, she continues to remain silent, if she stiffens her face against the torments, if she falls unconscious, they [...] she is protected by the spell of silence, and that this proves her guilt[...]

If it happens that an accused dies as a result of all these tortures, they say it was the devil who strangled her[...]"[225]

In Triora, Italy, we have the ultimate showdown between an accused female witch (a real-life successful healer and independent woman who, even at 65 refused to marry) and a madman Inquisitor named Giulius Scribani.

A MAN OBESSED, A MAN PERVERTED

On June 8, Giulius Scribani arrives in Triora and the second part of the trial process begins, characterized by the will of Scribani to extend the search and the trial of all witches, not just the 3 villages of: Andagna, Molini and Corte, but also to the surrounding cities/villages of all the Argentina Valley. including valle Nervia, SanRemo city, Porto Maurizio and other cities in the inner side of the land.Suddenly there are reports of witch sightings starting in the summer of 1588, and that is called "Grande Caccia le Streghe, " connected with Scribani. Basically Scribani was creating geographical terror or mass destruction. After a period, the Genovese government was starting to be embarrassed by him. So at the end of the summer of 1588 the 3rd and 4th Phase of the Trial, with the revision of all trials that will bring the excommunication of Giulio Scribani. He will eventually be absolved, unfortunately.. (they kick him out and then invite him back).

Basically now we have 18 women in jail in Genova. On February 18 , the Senate was writing to the congregation of Sant'Offizio saying that: "Those Poor women that have been in those jails for so long. They are consuming themselves, and three of these are already dead." 13 women in a jail in Genova and one man, 9 women died because of torture in the prison of Tirora and Badalucco. This is the result of witch hunting that started at the end of the summer in 1587, and finished in the autumn of 1588. The imprisoned people were still waiting for the end of a trial at the summer of 1589. So people were imprisoned and left to rot there, without a trial, and often without being documented. And no one was overseeing this process: Scribani was free to do whatever he wished. So just in this mountain valley area, 33 people were put to trial, but this is not a precise count of the total.[226]

Scribani was a very sexually perverse man. It was not uncommon in Europe for Inquisitor men obsessed with specific women to imprison them so they could be involved in their bodily searches and torture. They were free to do this. This is a standard abuse of power, where there is a central power (in this case the church and Rome as its center) acting as the core source of "word and law," but just as with a corporation, there are agents sent out into the field, and the Inquisitors were the agents. Each individual Inquisitor took the Inquisition as far as his needs were concerned, in whatever directions his perverse nature. So even though other men from the church documented a devil-free Triora and Valle Argentina, with Scribani, for example his sexual perversion and hunger for control were left unchecked for quite sometime as he got to imprison women and have complete control over their bodies, pubic hair, tortures, reputations, stories he made up, etc…to cover up his own perversions. Even the names for witches the church created, "streghe" and "bajiue" and "basura" have a negative sexual idea connected to them, helping to create a culture where everyone is afraid of women's sexuality.

FRANCHETTA BORELLI, SYMBOL OF FEMININE ENDURANCE

Franchetta Borelli was a powerful healer, known over quite a distance for healing poor people but also doctors and midwives. She was from a "powerful and rich family," one that symbolized, in a way, the time period so peaked at time of the Inquisition: she was a female healer, her brother a doctor, part of the same human family, oppositional ways. The natural vs. the synthetic.Apparently she liked to spend time away from her home in a difficult to get to mountaintop where she gathered herbs. At the time she was "arrested" on charges of being a witch by four witches in Andagna who were themselves imprisoned, she was 65 years old. She was known for her beauty when she was younger and never married, preferring liberty to local customs, which also garnered her to be called a "whore" more often than the "terrible witch of the demonic sect who "dances at night."[227]

She is famous because her name is one of the few documented, but also because she survived 21 hours of torture on the cavaletto without ever shedding a tear nor confessing to knowing the devil. She said a few things that also lived in in fame: "*I grit my teeth and they think I laugh,*" she apparently said while withstanding so much torture that another older woman demanded Scribani set her free because she would die. The other thing she said gave her away as an herbalist, a psychic, and perhaps a medium: "*the wind is not good for the chestnuts.*" That statement on its own might seem strange, and it might make you question how she was mentally holding up under torture, until you realize that in Italy chestnuts are a very valuable food, and one that could last people through the winter where little else grows, especially up in the mountains.

Chestnuts in Italy are milled into flour for break-making (which lasts a long time), and also to make pastas or cakes. It can be a substitute for potatoes and it can be used in deserts, can be candied and roasted. Considering the time of her torture was September 19th, it was a valid concern to be thinking of the chestnuts crop going bad.

She was tortured. She ran away only to come back.She was stripped naked and her body shaved completely by the Inquisitor who probed every inch of her, looking for marks of the devil. She was tortured again.

She never confessed.

A small list of NAMES of KIDNAPPED AND MURDERED WOMEN during "la caccia alle streghe"

Sibilla Zanni
Pierina Bugatis
Franchetta Borelli
Franceschina Ciocheto
Gioanina Ricolfa
Cattarina del Borigio
Luchina del Borigio
Gioanineta Guerra
Magdalena Guerra
Battistina Giauna
Battestina Stella
Battestina Augera
Agostina Carlina
Battestina Carlina
Domenegina Borella
Maria Matellona
Biagio Verrando

Caterina Ross
Orsola di Trodena
Margherita Dell'Agnola
Margherita Tessadrello
Ottilia Della Giacoma
Matteuccia di Francesco
Maria Salvatori
Domenica Gratiadei
Domenica Camelli
Lucia Caveden
Catterina Baroni
Zinevra Chemola
Isabella and Plonia Gratiadei
Valentina Andrei
Maddalena Andrei
Marchetta Bistagno

Eleventh Secrets

Perhaps it sounds a bit naive but I never really thought about a connection between "witches" and owls. For most of my life I haven't really paid much attention to the owl ("gufo" in Italian). It's not that I disliked them, but I just didn't feel a connection. I have always been drawn to cats, crows, ravens, and wolves.

While I was training at the Spiritualist center, I didn't tell anyone that I was being visited by the Goddesses. I sensed my life was changing in a huge way. It was a profound thing for me to see these visions and then find out they had historical truth. Should I tell? Should I keep it quiet? I'm not sure why I struggled with this so much, but I felt there was an air of unseen danger around telling people this, but perhaps that was just me fearing some of the life changes I'd experience as a result of these series of Initiations.

During this stretch of two years, my friend Lorraine, a healer, kept giving me owls: owl dish, owl candle, 3 brass owls, an owl journal, and an owl bell. I wondered, "Why is she giving me all these owls?" Then I discovered the owl has an important significance for the story of the "strega" in Italy. But more than that, the owl is an important partner for the Great Mother Goddess and is part of our founding psychic language which represents the Goddess' power to regenerate life after death of the physical body. Owls, in ancient times, were carved on standing stones which pointed to water sources, on grave stones, and on bones left in tombs. Essentially, the owl was a Spiritualist symbol.

Also during this two year stretch my cat died just two months shy of 21 years. He was my familiar-and not just in the "conceptual" sense. He brought me ghosts to help cross over, he helped me find things, he healed my asthma attacks by climbing on my back and kneading my lungs, he protected my head when I slept, and he made me take what I call "shaman naps" when I was working too hard: I'd make him a little tent by holding up the covers, and he'd channel information to me while I lay next to him on the bed. It was deeply restorative.

My cat passed while I was part of this Spiritualist community but only a few people knew about it. A couple weeks after he passed, a woman named Jacquie, whom I only saw once a month or so, told me she left me a gift in the Center: it was a brass crown, used in Goddess rituals, with a crescent moon which pointed upwards. In the center of the moon crescent is a cat.

Chapter 11:
"Young Witches in Modern Italy"

What I'm referring to by "young witches in Italy" are not magicians and not followers of Wicca. They are women and men, of various genders, who feel a kinship with the natural connections that Paganisms offer. They are, however, not keen on connecting themselves to a "group" name nor identifying themselves with modern titles, but instead respond to a natural calling to search even deeper back in history before the Goddesses were given makeovers and before our modern times created very organized and commercialized practices of spirituality. They are very aware of their country's own history: some from a studied place having researched avidly, some from the viewpoint of an "insider" observing the comments of the general population's misunderstandings about what "witches" are.

Some of these young witches I've met do train with a female Mother: a Category 2 community mother. While their groups aren't traditional Lineages, they do still have initiations from the Mother (not from the Spirit World) and receive special marks. They do, however, maintain a sense of self-trust, and their training does involve a great amount of work with the Spirit World: it's ghosts, Guides, and goddesses. Among a few of these anonymous witches were friends who realized their own teacher's integrity was becoming dubious and opted out of that learning experience, preferring to continue on their own, learning solely from their spirit guides and comparing their findings with each other. This is definitely a more challenging path to take.

A most refreshing attitude among all the women and men I met outside of modern practices was a reticence to be attached to Greek or Roman forms of Goddesses. By this I mean that men, in general, connect with nature and let nature be their teacher, in whatever form nature chooses to guide them. Ever more exciting for me is the women who've been experiencing Goddesses who are connected to the modern Roman and Greek names, but their power, their personality, their energy and presence is nothing like those modern "make-overs" at all. This is exciting because it means young people are getting to know the real, living legacy in the Spirit World and not cutting their learning short by following only what's been written by men or any people who've based their writings on history post-patriarchal mix-and-mashup.

In honor of the anonymity these people prefer, I won't write their names. They take their relationship with their spirituality seriously and do not seek attention for it: for them it's a daily way of life. These are just two interviews, not by any means an exhaustive list of the Italian witches I know or spoke with, but two official meetings that stood out the most.

INTERVIEW WITH FEMALES from the Friuli-Venezia Giulia region.

Karyn: What is a group called? Do you use the name "coven"?

Anonymous: *The few we were aware of didn't have a specific name, including ours. "Circle" is a good name, and so is "Comari / Comarato" where "Comari" means "close female friend, someone who you share something important with, not necessarily under a magical or spiritual point of view. In Cercivento, becoming someone's "Comari" needs a specific ritual in a specific time of the year, around summer solstice.*

K: Is there a specific number of members needed in your group ?

A: *As regards a specific number, the answer could be "yes and no." Any number that can preserve "balance" is a good one: three, four, five, seven, but there isn't any rule especially in a "work with what you have" condition.*

K: Why are the numbers you listed good for preserving balance ? I notice some are odd numbers and one is even.

A: *They are all symbolic numbers. We found out that the general strength and balance of the group improves when the number is "meaningful." In a few lines just to make some examples: 3 is a well known "powerful" number: the aspects of the god/goddess are three and it's the "completion" of the couple that "gives birth" to the element which has aspects of both the "parents"... 4 are the elements and the direction in the circle, so in can represent the material stability; 5 are the elements + the spirit: so in can be stability + consciousness 7 has always been a symbolic number in most cultures; in our view of the Group, it represented the 4 elements, Nadir and Zenith and a "free" element that could move where needed if something was going out of balance.*

K: Will you please discuss the ritual, as you can, about becoming someone's "Comari"?

A: *Traditionally, you have to ask your friend to become your "Comari" on July 23, sending her a bouquet of flowers with a specific traditional request. And she has to answer with a specific phrase. In our case we became "Comari" later during the summer, with a quick but meaningful ritual on the devil's bridge in Cividale.*

Linguistic note: later on, "Comari" in Friulian became a word with the meaning of midwife/obstetrician but also wedding witness.

K: What are the Initiation rites for Witches in your area like ?

A: *Historically speaking, a witch was bound to give her/his own power to an heir just before he or she died. The power was transmitted by touch, holding hands. In some cases this seems to be happened in modern times too but we had a specific initiation rite.*

K: Are you able to say if your initiation involved the hand -to-hand transmission ?

A: *Our mother didn't die after passing us our "marks" although our initiation marked the beginning of the decline of her power and consciousness But our initiation had a more "ceremonial" allure with a strong symbolic structure. It had traditional elements but it wasn't in itself, "traditional." It's quite hard to draw a line between what can be said and what cannot. I think it's safe to describe the rite as a strongly symbolical one, involving the image of the soul traveling in the otherworld in a path that leads it to being born again.*

K: Are rituals/actions of a witchcraft nature able to "work properly" without the initiation? In other words, is it the special power that makes the witchery work, or the recipe/ritual/actions ?

A: *We are not entirely sure about other people's experience under a statistical point of view but we can say that there is a solid difference in consciousness, ability to feel and manage spiritual energy and to see patterns in magic and reality with Initiation. It literally gives you more access to power (your own) and more tools to work with it, although it's important to remember that access to initiation is gained through a long process of learning and evolving. The process itself, though, doesn't give you the same "benefits" of a proper Initiation and, actually, as far as we know, stopping before the Initiation leads to a quick decline of ability and consciousness.*
This, of course, doesn't mean that somebody can't be powerful and effective without an Initiation: it just means that this is the way our path goes. It's a bit of a "everything or nothing" kind of arrangement, we don't know why.

K: Are there separate groups for Women's Mysteries and Men's Mystery Schools ?

A: *In history there didn't seem to be two different schools. Nowadays we don't know, we belong to a female tradition so it makes sense that there could be a male one, somewhere. Male and female approaches to magic can be very different.*

K: Do witches have both masculine and feminine teachers as a Priestess and a Priest ?
A: In traditional witchcraft there are no actual "priests," not meant as in a Wiccan coven. But you can learn different skills from male and female teachers.

K: Are witches made or born?

A: *In our opinion, witches are born with a special "something". But they still need work to actually become one.*

K: Historically speaking, what are witches called in your area ?

A: *Stries/Striis, which basically means "witch."*

K: Are there more than one "type"?

A: *Not of I'm aware of, except the obvious good/bad witches subdivision.*

K: How did they learn what they knew ?

A: *As we still do now, it's an oral tradition so they were taught by someone willing to "pass" the craft.*

K: How were they taught?

A: *We don't know for sure, but we don't think it might have been much different from any transmitted craft in rural areas.*

K: Who were they (career-wise, community-wise)?

A: *Basing our answer on history studies, they were regular women either known for being "evil"(envious, and wishing bad things to happen to people) or for being able to heal or help people (sometimes undoing what the bad ones did).*

K: Where did they live (hills, valleys)?

A: *Friuli was largely an agricultural environment so most people, including witches, lived on the countryside. Since most testimonies are from Carnia, an area of the Alps, we don't know much about "big city witches". Also, there are no big cities in Friuli, even today.*

K: Did they have practices out in nature, at specific locations (rivers, trees, caves) and what were those?

A: *We are aware of "special" powerful places in Carnia, where traditionally witches are thought to meet or have met. The most known is the "piano delle streghe" over Cercivento, but there must have been other places in the woods that we are not aware of. In Friuli there are a few places with names relating to places sacred to the Celts, such as "Nimis", meaning "Nemas," sacred wood. We can hypothesize that the knowledge of these "certain" places lasted for quite a long time.*

K: Did they use nature as an attunement tool/hear the voice of higher consciousness through being in nature?

A: *In rural areas they were as in touch with mother nature as other people were so we don't think this could have made a difference at least until halfway through the 20th century, when people started to leave the country for the cities.*

K: Were there hierarchies within their practice (such as a Priestess who channels the teachings from Spirit World, and then a different category of worshippers who keep the family lineage going, and others who do work out in the world such as readings or healing)?

A: *Not as far as we know. The only hierarchy is related to experience and age. Basing on what we have been taught and historical evidence, groups of witches seems to have acted as equals once they reached the same "Initiation" level.*

K: What Goddesses and or Gods were they taught by/connected to?

A: *Witches, like everyone else, were Christian. But there is much to say about the figure of Oriente/Habondia/Holle and so on, the lady hosting night meetings who seems to be the goddess of the witches traveling outside their bodies at night. Ginzburg talks much about her.*

K: Were the practitioners only female or also male?

A: *Mostly female, but not exclusively.*

K: Were there some considered more shamanistic and some considered more earth-guardians, herbalists, healers?

A: *Under an historical point of view I'd say mostly herbalists and healers (also under a ritual point of view in case the illness was somehow magic-related). Today there both a shamanistic approach and the earth guardian character are a thing.*

K: Did some use scientific approaches such as astronomy? Did some use minerals and crystals? Did some rely on spirit-world communication (channeling, Mediumship):

A: *We are not aware of scientific approaches in traditional witchcraft in Friuli. On the other hand spirit-word communication is a Benandanti thing, and Benandanti historically were from Friuli. We can assume, though, that the moon phase and moment of the year might have played a role as it does today.*

K: Did some of them have special purposes (dealing with disease, dealing with troublesome "ghosts") ?

A: *Dealing with disease, especially when thought to be magic-induced by an evil person. Troublesome dead are, as said, something Benandanti tend to deal with.*

K: What are some important rituals and their purposes?

A: *Most rituals that have been reported were about removing "il malocchio" and curses from people or animals. It was thought that what you did to a "symbol" or something belonging to the cursed individual, you also did it to the person who cursed them. So the chain belonging to the cow that ran out of milk was put on the fire until red, or jammed against the steps leading to the house. In one case a very small grimoire was retrieved (date is uncertain) in which rituals to send an enemy away are mentioned, too (it's a very small one, like only 10 pages).*

K: Are there separate groups for Women's Mysteries and Men's Mystery Schools?

A: *In history there didn't seem to be two different schools. Nowadays we don't know, we belong to a female tradition so it makes sense that there could be a male one, somewhere. Male and female approaches to magic can be very different.*

K: Do witches have both masculine and feminine teachers/Priestess/Priest?

A: *In traditional witchcraft there are no actual "priests," not meant as in a Wiccan coven. But you can learn different skills from male and female teachers.*

K: When did witches begin to have a "bad" reputation?

A: *There has always been a good/evil separation. But in Friuli we also say that witches helped the virgin Mary hide baby Jesus from the soldiers so there have always been both good and bad witches, and the good ones might have had some kind of religious "amnesty." Generally speaking, there are reports of priests "relieving" "il malocchio" from a person or an animal, and of nuns sewing sacred talisman bags for children using the same materials used by Catholic witches in the last century (church candle wax, Easter olive tree leaves and so on). In this, a very important role was played by geography: we are so far away from the centers of power that there wasn't much need for repression, while agricultural beliefs survived longer than in some other places. An important moment that got stuck in the collective memory is Trento Council, who is thought to have banned all evil from the country, exiling all the evil spirits somewhere far (usually a remote valley).*

[Historical note from Enzo Gravina: A very big event for the church was "Concillio di Trentino", the Trento Council, which was one of the first big councils where people, priests, bishops and cardinals were altogether to take decisions during a very hard period for the church. After the Concillio all these negative ideas about women came out. Before the council we were still Christians who didn't care about witches. After the Concillio the church put again a lie and negative attack against women, we started to have these witch hunts, the processes, the trials, all the stuff. And the legends and myths began. In Italy we were Christians since Constantino, so for more than 900 years before that we didn't care about witches and then suddenly, at a certain point, these are damned women.]

K: What association with "the Devil" did witches have?

A: *The Devil itself is hardly mentioned outside the Inquisition trials, in which people were forced to admit worshipping it, even when talking about evil witches.*

K: When did they church decide they were "evil," and if they were so "evil and powerful" why could they not stop their own demise?

A: *At the time of inquisition trials. Most people involved in trials weren't probably even "real" witches, just the wrong people in the wrong place, charged by their own neighbors.*

K: Were there witch trials in your area? If so, when?

A: *Yes. It was towards the end of 16th century and the first half of the 17th.*

K: Were the condemned imprisoned without trial?

A: *We have trial transcriptions but it doesn't look like people were condemned without "investigation." For quite a long time, Benandanti were questioned and released since it wasn't possible to find something to accuse them of as they very firmly kept saying they fought the Devil, battling during the night.*

K: Was there a perception of a strategy by the church and military?

A: *Not as far as we know but, again, we were far from the actual power centers.*

K: What were the means of punishment: burning, drowning, hanging, rape…

A: *As far as we remember most of them were imprisoned. Some were sentenced to death but escaped, at least one (a male) was executed but we don't have enough data to be sure about how, when or where. An interesting thing to be reported,though, is that many of the accused people were male and witchcraft was not the only accusation. It could also have been heretical behavior, eating forbidden food and some others.*

K: How did they practice healing?

A: *Some knew herbs, some other were good at fixing nerves and muscles or broken bones (some of these people still exist and work in small towns) some others healed by magic.*

K: How did they raise energy towards a higher purpose?

A: *No idea. Sometimes repetitive gestures and phrases are reported in books but we have no direct knowledge or how it was done in the old times.*

K: What were some important plants to use?

A: *I guess it depends on the purpose. We widely use local herbs such as rosemary, sage, juniper and so on. Consecrated olive tree branches were widely used in the past.*

[Note from the author: I was taught to use olive trees, leaves, and branches in Tuscany, Italy]

K: *Did they use menstrual blood for healing and fertility?*

A: *The only actual use of menstrual blood we are aware of is related to love spells (it had to be mixed with coffee and offered to the man you fancied).*

K: Were certain trees considered magical?

A: *Yes. For example Viburnum and hazelnut trees.*

K: Was there a difference between private practice and daily life usage of natural psychic abilities?

A: *We think that, much like the present, most of the practice was private or, at least, discreetly dealt with.*

K: Were there any famous diviners and/or healers in your area?

A: *There's a couple of people known to be good at fixing twisted nerves. There are a few people known for being diviners but we don't think they are genuine.*

K: How are witches associated with magic and sorcery?

A: *In history they were known for having "certain abilities". In some cases spell books were found (and very often destroyed).*

K: Was there any connection to the Druids in your area?

A: *Friuli has Celtic roots, but we can't say that Celtic traditions were willingly transmitted to witches. Many season rituals have a Celtic origin, though, and are still very common in the area (i.e.: solstice fires).*

K: Was there any connection among local witches and other cultural pagan practices and groups (of co-mingling)?

A: *We are not aware of pagan groups active in the area before the end of 20th century.*

INTERVIEW WITH A MALE from the Ligurian Region

Karyn: What are witches called in your area?

Anonymous: *"Streghe," which is the international and Italian name that belonged to these women. Also, in my dialect they were called "Bajiue, " in the Ligure dialect.*

K: Can you tell me anything about those names?

A: *"Bajiue" was a name given to these women to represent something that was out of the ordinary social life and perhaps out of the christian religion laws, so the main meaning was : whores or bitches. that's what it means. "Strega" is a word that comes from the Greek, I believe the way to pronounce it is "Stric." That means nocturnal bird, nocturnal winged animal. Which makes a lot of sense.*

K: Why?

A: *Because I think the night is the moment of the day when we get more sensitive, that's what I like to think. So it's easier to gain our powers and it's very silent, there's no noises, everyone is sleeping. During the day we are just bombed by other people's thoughts. At night we have the time and space to think in a different way. More freedom of thinking. So thinking means just being natural.*

K: What about connotations associated with the term "Strega", perhaps from the outside view? Is there a meaning attached to this name by people who are not "strega" ?

A: *The word "strega," I think, I'm not sure, but I think came out in medieval times, but [the lifestyle] it was a practice and a way of living that always existed since the very beginning of humanity. For example, like around this area, before Christianity there was Paganism, which was a nature - based religion and paganism doesn't accept the word "evil." The word evil is something that comes from human behaviors. The word "strega" came, when I think, which is where it seems, is when Christianity became more prevalent, because this was a pagan practice and because Christianity was trying to take over the past which was paganism. So they tried to convert anything that was existing and happening in the past; they were trying to convert that. So from that time is when people who were attached to nature and had spiritual practices were seen as bad people.*

K: For you is there more than one type of witch?

A: *Yes. For me there are different types of witches. There's the person who again is attached to the nature, which is the person who tries to gain his or her own powers connected to the nature or, there are other witches who try to practice and gain their powers taking energies or power from humans, so from people. So that's quite different. So if you think under just a human aspect for example, under the evil aspect, when the bad witches come in, trying to develop a knowledge of techniques that are generated from human feelings like in this case we're talking evil stuff.*

For example what are called the black witches, women who attached to human powers more than to the power of the nature. So, and at the same time, with this new religion there was Christianity, the "evil practices," (for lack of better term) of people who were trying to get their powers through human fears or doubts were considered to make alliance with the devil as well. For me the devil is just a different form of human's hate and fear. It has nothing to do with nature-based religion.

K: Who were they (what we call "witches") in the past in daily life?

A: *Well as we know, the witches were just really normal women who were attached to nature, so they had knowledge of what nature was giving to them, basically giving to anyone, but these people just had a different knowledge of what nature was. They were basically normal people, normal people but at the same time spiritual.*

K: And what about men? Were men also considered to be witches? Or was there a different term for a man?

A: *Well you can call a witch a man or a woman, so..it can be female or male. It's pretty much the same thing, you can use the same word for both genders.*

K: So taking this same question into modern times, how do you view people who call themselves "witches" now, in terms of types, place in community, etc.

A: *I think going back to ancient times I don't think people who were into this spirituality and practices were calling themselves witches, I think this was a term coming from people who could not really understand them, so they were trying to find a word to describe them and to judge them, but it was just a natural thing. You don't really think "I am this or I am that," you just do your own things and you just feel very connected to the nature. So it was a natural thing, you don't want to, I believe in the past, those people didn't want to associate themselves or to identify themselves with a word that was included in the human society, so I think the term comes form the people who were not involved in this type of way of living. No one was saying "I am a witch;" that's what other people were calling them. Since then of course "I am a witch" but the term WITCH was something that came from a different circle.*

K: Were witches everywhere? How widespread were they in the past ?

A: *Well in the past there were like different groups of people but always very small villages or very small communities. I still believe it was just a natural thing, because if you grow up surrounded by nature, you become naturally attached to nature, and that's how we call witches today, that's how I think of witches, people attached to nature. But in the past, I think everyone could be a witch if you want, to these people with the term "witch."*

K: In terms of your area or Italy as a country, were there certain places where the "witches" were living (along rivers, mountain tops, etc)?

A: *But yes, there were lots of villages up in the mountains , and they were all surrounded by nature, also it was safer to live up the mountains because it was more hidden compared to the coast. So I think that was the main reason why people were trying to settle up the mountains than up the coast.*

K: As far as you know, is the history of "streghe" all around Italy or concentrated in one area?

A: *No, I don't know historical things, but as I said before, in the ancient times, when communication was very little, there was no way to know that there were other people practicing your same things, so there were just small groups. When it had the chance to spread out it was because it was already in more modern times and that's when the big centers became places where witches were getting together. But before that how could you know there was someone else doing your same thing? If all these small groups of people were just in the mountains and small villages, there was really no way to communicate and there really was no way to travel in long distances. So in the very beginning I don't think there were any big centers, but then things have changed through the years and that is when may be people started to travel a bit more and that's when people started to know about each other a bit more, the relationship between north and south, and people started moving around and getting together in different places. But you know back in the day there was no way people could travel that much. Even around this area, not even like 100 years, just going back 200 years ago there were people who knew about the sea but they had no chance to go see it because they were living up the mountains and there was no way to get there. So all the big witches centers, I don't now how it really happened when communication was really little.*

K: Do you think in an ironic way that the Inquisition had something to do with that, being that the preachers in the church had this task to sort of be the "press" for the church, get the word out about the Inquisition and its punishments by telling it to people publicly, traveling around to spread the news, literally. Do you think in some way that spread the word and help connect the country in terms of helping other witches know about each others' locations?

A: *Oh yes, absolutely. They just helped to spread the word, that's the only thing they did, because they were against that way of living. The church took over a philosophy to cover a religion that was based here. So the church is not from here. You know? They came over, they took over, they killed people, forcing people to believe in something that was different to their nature. And through the years people just forgot and couldn't really understand why they were praying to a single god, or couldn't remember what the past was or where they were coming from, so that's really bad.*

K: How do you feel about natural witches versus more organized witches, such as modern witches meeting in caves, at rivers…is this something that happened in the past?

For a spiritual person, it's a big pile of bullshit, the one of getting together with other people. A spiritual person is someone who is really attached to nature and who really understands nature and communicates with nature. So when you're able to do that, you learn how to feel good with yourself. When you feel good with yourself, you don't really need to share this kind of spirituality with other people. You don't need to engage with other people to practice or to reach a state of mind of revelations, or whatever. I personally like the very lonely side of witches. the witches that are attached to nature, the witches who don't need rules, traditions, laws, who don't need to have a role in a group. Because when you walk through the forest, that's all you need, that's a beautiful communication.

It's just the way you feel, so you can communicate with the nature by yourself. There's no one telling you what to do, there's no one teaching you about magic, it's just a very natural thing. Growing up and just spending a lot of time in the nature you build a relationship, which is a relationship between you as a human, and the nature, which is just one thing, so you just learn how to communicate. I really I don't like the witches that practice the need to practice with a group of other people, or within a group who tell you what's best to do.
I believe in instincts.

You can have a master or a guide, there's nothing wrong with that. You can meet someone who has more experience than you do. There's nothing wrong with listening, and perhaps following his or her guidance, but I just don't like when a group of people, an organized group of people get together, putting rules and laws within a spiritual practice. For me, it's very unnatural, so I don't like it.

When you feel good with yourself, you don't really need to share this spirituality with other people.

K: In your area, or as far as you know in greater Italy, in terms of anyone who practices modern witchcraft, in terms of people practicing as a group, do they call themselves "coven" or have another name? Is there anything you know about that organized formation?

A: *No. I told you before, I don't think it's natural. It's forcing someone to do something that doesn't come naturally. And nature behaves just in a natural way there's no rules or laws, what happens just happens.*

K: I've had quite a few men tell me here in Italy that women naturally have an easier connection to spirituality. Do you find that to be true from your perspective?

A: *Yes, it can be true because we think of the ancient past. Women had a chance to spend more time in private places, by themselves, or in more quiet situations. Because the men were just going out there to hunt, to fight, and they didn't have the same time to find a spiritual side of their lives. So that's probably why women are closer to the spiritual world.*

Karyn's note: there was a time period where men went to female oracles to divine outcomes of their battles or building plans..so in s strange way there was a partnership: woman's ability to channel wisdom from the Spirit World was honored, and mens' duty was honored.]

A: *Because the spiritual world means: thinking. It means use your mind. If you have to fight [in battle] you use your mind, but in a different way, its's a different approach.*

K: I also think that spills over into the modern world. There is a this stigma from the church that's still there, it's still very alive.

A: *The church started to do what politicians and government do now, they just wanted to control people. They want them to stop thinking, to stop thinking they were free people, so they tried to create a business for telling people who god is, to stop free thinking.*

K: For me it seems like a divide-and-conquer tactic: divide people from nature, divide from yourself from your own intuition, and separate men and women into this perpetual battle. Like the story of Eve being evil. Since when is exploring and learning evil? Men have always done it…and have received awards for doing so…why would it be something bad just for women? I think it's a detriment to all of society, both men AND women. I know men who've had to find their own way to heal from an over-masculine father, and they may be afraid to accept somethings about themselves.

A: *If you think about the history of our planet, the planet earth came before us. So we are the ones who came into this world. But what happened, was mankind wanted to take control of the planet, which is very unfair. It's not respectful at all.*

To me, the secret of the success of a human being is to understand who you are for real, like, the person you are. That is the secret. You have to understand yourself before you can understand yourself within other people. That's why I was saying the connection with nature is important.

Twelfth Secrets

My train ride from Roma to Benevento was eventful. I didn't realize I had bought a ticket online for the correct day but the wrong date, until a man came with his friends into my section with the same assigned seat number. He was kind enough to advise me to remain on the train and hope the conductor would be compassionate towards my situation: people would be picking me up in Benevento at midnight, my phone wasn't working, and there were no other trains to catch. I had seen a conductor force someone off a train on my previous ride, so I was unsure but kept affirming a positive outcome.

I tried to sit in seat after seat as the train filled up, only to have to move again and again because someone else was assigned to those seats. Then, there was one remaining seat. Luckily, no one claimed it after I sat down. The conductor let me stay on the train but had to charge me an $89 fare plus penalty fee…in cash. I had exactly $89 Euros in my wallet.

The scenery on the way down was so lovely. I got to see some of my beloved Toscana again, but as we went further south the nature began to look wild, darker, and also bit ominous, like it was hiding things. I loved it. I realized I was coming to a very special place. I was mesmerized by the deep greens and twisting branches and the rough and jagged edges and soft rolling mountains. The nature seemed to hiss and growl, breathing into the train, warning me to not get too close.

The train dropped me off directly in front of the Liquore Strega shop, but it was closed.
I met Alecia, my American connection whose apartment in Guardia I'd rented, and Domenico, who would be my driver and translator for 2 weeks. For some reason, Domenico realized we were on a journey and not only didn't question this but also had a great passion for seeking the answers he somehow knew I was asking. With one cigarette in his mouth, another being rolled, we drove into the pounding rain towards Guardia Sanframondi.

It was raining so hard the streets were flooded, but that didn't stop Alecia and Domenico from telling lively stories of Guardia for me as we barreled through the water, the flooded streets, careening around mountains, all while Domenico smoked one cigarette and hand-rolled more. I'm sure there were times we had only two weels connecting with the pavement. "This is exactly what I needed," I thought to myself, smiling and feeling happier than I have been in a very long time. This was the south: going with the flow, braving the rain and wild winds, full of hope and laughter no matter what. As a workaholic, I don't relax much, but I sensed that right now, in this very moment, it was wise to commit to acceptance and surrender to whatever the Universe had in store for me.

I relaxed into my car seat, as much as I could for being tossed around the twisting roads, smiling in the dark…when suddenly I began to hear contrasting thoughts "you don't want this," in my head. I knew this wasn't me. "You don't want to be here," I heard the voice again. I began to search, quietly in my own mind, who this could be, try to get a sense of who this spirit was trying to turn me away from this part of my journey. Again and again the voice was saying "this is irritating you," and other messages trying to sway me from my enjoyment.

When we arrived at Alecia's, half past midnight, Domenico decided to make me a pasta, and it was spectacular. He and Alecia began to ask me about my "to do" list I'd emailed of the things I wanted to see and placed I wanted to visit. My mind suddenly went blank. I couldn't answer a simple question. "Karyn, where would you like to go first tomorrow?" Domenico asked me. I lost my ability to put words together. I began to fumble, mumble, and tried to turn on my laptop so I could find my list and not have to think. The voices kept telling me "look how irritating this is, you don't want to be here." I became flustered and was unable to tell Domenico nor Alecia even one thing I wanted to do from my own list. I could see my list in my mind's eye but was unable to make sense of it. This is a list I'd been dreaming of for two years. Compassionately, they said "ah, you must be tired from your long train ride. Don't worry, get some sleep, we'll start early and go to Benevento!" As kind as they were, it was no reassurance: was

I losing my mind? I had to figure out who these spirits were so I could get them away from me.

Alecia opened the door to my charming room and walked to the double doors at its end: "Look at this view!" She proudly showed me that I had a little balcony outside the double doors. And right in front of my room was an old church. "That's who you are!" I exclaimed in my mind, "you're from the church!" Immediately the feeling of oppression left me as the church men fled, having their cover blown. I was free to enjoy now, and I slept like a baby.

Early that morning we three gathered in Domenico's car and drove to Benevento, the city. Many of the museums were closed, and it began to rain again. "I want to find the obelisk of Iside," I proclaimed, "and I'm walking this way," I told them and took a left turn, right into Piazza Paolo Emilio Papiniano…and there was the obelisk of Iside. As soon as I walked up to it and touched it, thunder boomed.

This would happen, this boom of thunder, each time Domenico and I would find something I was searching for on my list…even when there was a sun-filled, clear-blue sky.

Chapter 12:
The Region of Campania

"The clearest way into the Universe is through a forest wilderness."
-John Muir

The city of Benevento (Beneventum) was founded 500 years before Rome and inspired much of Rome's layout. Benevento's Amphitheater was built before Rome copied their design and built the Coliseum. Originally it was called "Malvento," or "Malventum" (bad wind) and post-Roman colonization it was savagely destroyed by Tottila, king of the goths, and later put back together again by another invading tribe, the Longobards. Walking down roads with Enzo Gravina I learned the stones placed under our feet, which were unusually rounded, had been taken from the river by the Longobards and arranged here. The wall near San Gennaro's birth place had pieces of column and stone put back together after they were dismantled from somewhere else. Down yet another street, walls of homes were built around beheaded, robed statues who remained in permanent open stone caskets for passersby to wonder after.

Just like the spectacular and atmospheric architectural collage-work that makes up many of the walls and streets of Campania's city of Benevento, so too is its historical story a wonderful and mysterious blend of cultures. Once an important crossroads (in the way Triora in the north was) not just for Italy but for people traveling from other countries, we can find imprints of the Longobards, Celtic Druids, Egypt's Iside, Streghe and Janare witches, Greeks, "sea peoples" from Phryigia (ancient Turkey), Lineage healers, indigenous curing traditions, mystical legends of San Gennaro, the Janare who seem to be something similar to Benandanti, and a veritable cauldron bubbling with folk stories and superstitions. In the province of Benevento, outside the city itself, are hidden places that I consider to be the most important, sacred land that is still resonating with energy and presence of the ancient Great Mother Goddess herself, who allegedly manifested herself in a physical miracle in the past. This is also the land of Benevento's legendary magic walnut tree.

Because of a strange political twist, Benevento became a somewhat "safe haven," at least from religious persecution, for witches outcast from other villages. While it didn't save them from persecution from neighbors, it still was a place where orphaned women could come and not be kidnapped, molested, and killed by the church.

As Enzo explains, "*Witches were said to have come to Benevento, which means they weren't already there, and it is said they came in 1046 AD for a specific reason: When the Inquisition was in full-swing, popes and bishops would come to various villages and cities to impose the trials and punishments. But some cities wouldn't allow them to come in and take over. In 1046 AD, the people of Benevento didn't allow Eric III (Emperor of Germany) nor Clementine II the Pope to come into Benevento. Obviously, the Pope became upset and he banned the city. The news was spread out by the preachers, because in those days the preachers were the old-school journalists who spread the word in public about changes with the church. Otherwise, no one would know.*

But 4 years, later, in 1050 AD, Clementine II died and finally Leo (Bruno) IX became

Pope. He was very worried about a possible coming Norman invasion. So he offered a deal to Benevento to make an alliance to prevent the invasion, and in return he would lift the ban as a compromise. The news was again spread out by preachers.

So persecuted women began to hear about Benevento being a 'safe place', now that the ban was lifted. Every other city could be considered "unsafe" for targeted women and healers, but since Benevento was now declared 'ok' by the new Pope, it simply wasn't just that the ban was lifted, but that Benevento was an ally to the Pope, so no Inquisition would occur there. And in fact, many Benevento people told me that no witches were ever harmed there, nor were any women accused nor killed.

During this time in general, it was still a "man's world," and most women weren't in good social standing, and most of the women who were 'presumed witches' were just women. These 'Inquisited women' didn't know Italy's geography, they were uneducated, but still they knew to come to Benevento because of the lifted banishment. They were able to be free and more tolerated there, it was a safe place for women, whereas other cities could still be visited by the Inquisition or be banished. The oral traditions say: 'in Benevento we aremore free and tolerated, and protected by the lifted ban.' So they kept on saying they would go to Benevento. They were forgiven there, there was no threat of punishment."

CAMPANIA CURING TRADITIONS

Silvio Falato, whom I interviewed, is an etymologist and folk tale professor from Guardia Sanframondi. He has also written a book compiling folk stories of the area of Benevento along with the dialect texts called "Ce steva 'na vota…Janare-lupi mannari, filastrocche-indovinelli" (Once upon a Time…Janare, werewolves, rhymes and riddles). From his book is an "occhi" recipe tradition:

Formula Against the Evil Eye:

(Formule Contro il Malocchio)/ Formula Against the Evil Eye

"Fuggi, fuggi "occhio" funesto/ Get away, get away deadly eye
che or passa Gesu Cristo! / Jesus Christ is coming!
Gesu Cristo e passato, / Jesus Christ has passed,
gli "occhi" malvagi sono scoppiati! / the evil eyes have broken!
"Occhio", malocchio! / Eye, evil eye,
scoppi, scoppi e crepi / bursts, bursts and creeps
l'invidia e il malocchio! / Envy and the evil eye!

"Fuggi, fuggi "occhio" funesto / Get away, get away deadly eye
che in tre ti hanno visto, / who in three have seen you,
e in tre ti hanno guardato, / and three looked at you
Maria Vergine ti ha salvato! / the Virgin Mary has saved you!
Scoppi adesso questo malocchio! / Burst now this evil eye!

"When someone happened to feel a nagging, persistent headache, they turned to some old person who was able to see if the status of the illness was caused by the 'evil eye.' The woman poured a little water into a pot and, approaching the head of the unlucky, added a few drops of oil, scrutinizing the movement of the latter. If the oil drops widened, it meant that the person under observation had been the victim of the 'evil eye', i.e. of envious and ungrateful thoughts, and it was necessary to move away the evil. The old woman would recite the appropriate formulas, accompanying them with cross marks on the forehead of the unfortunate, and tracing with her finger in the dish."[228]

Enzo Gravina Rosanna Scocca shared, *"With a lot of illness, we heal with penicillin basically made with 'mufe,' a very wet and humid room 'mold' on the mushroom. So look at how when you know nature you can prevent and you can make something do something in a preventive way. For example, if you get a cut on your finger, there was not at the time alcohol or something you cannot put on, you can use a spiderweb twisted the web around the finger to stop the blood, and you heal."* Rosanna says of the "nonnas," for example, *"In the past grandmas were able to help kids sleep. That's because in the red poppy flower at the the bottom, you have things that you can use to make babies fall asleep. It's a family tradition that you were healing in the family, you didn't go to the doctor. Also a lot of herbs in the mediterranean area allowed you to cure many things such as l'Iperico, which was used for pain, for example."* And Enzo adds, for example, *"At that time if you were able to heal an illness, if you were successful, you were a Good Healer. If you were healing someone who died, you were a witch, because people think you used the Bad Stuff, the evil. But if you were successful in healing a person, you would not ever share the recipe either, so perhaps there was competition."*

"Herbs are now a trend," Rosanna points out, *"but in the past past, the women healed with no education. Then apart from the herbs, there are some people, still one alive in our area, who cures little warts, there were healers with the power who could heal your warts even if you weren't near them, so at a distance and from far away. The moon is very important in the magical rituals. It's also important in the popular way when you put the seeds for the plants and harvest in the soil, everything is connected with the Moon. There is someone also still alive who can heal sciatica..."* These are the Lineage cures: they target specific illnesses.

Excitingly, in Enzo's book "Streghe e Magia: storia, formule e rituali delle streghe di Beneveno" (Witches and Magic: Formulas and Rituals of the Witches of Benevento), he lists the only historical documentation I've seen so far regarding the usage of gemstones in healing. He gathered this information *"from the elders who retain these traditions in their oral memories: the list of precious stones has come from consulting several ancient books and asking the elderly, who've lived in the countries of the province of Benevento. Many events and facts, rather than from books, can be known through oral transmission, through questioning people who traditionally know these things because they were told by their ancestors or acquaintances. In ancient times, in the winter evenings, the families of our countryside, they gathered around the fire, and the elders told stories of witches and ghosts and many things connected with these!"*

"Amulets and Talismans against all the maladies:" it must be considered that amulets and talismans can be precious stones, minerals, metal objects, flowers, or an inscription written on wood or paper or even simple objects or parts of animals.

A truncated list from Enzo's book:

- for Asthma: cat eyes (impure quartz) and topaz

- for Poisoning - cyclamen, amber and a T-shaped cross

- for Convulsions- all kinds of rings are good

- for Digestive Disorders - amber, coral, and blood stone (hematite)

- for Intermittent fever - abracadabra (piece of paper or parchment with the magical abracadabra word written from time to time omitting the first letter, thus forming a triangle that must be carried to the neck for nine days) plus chrysolite, blood stone (hematite) and sarda (brown chalcedony)

- for nightmares: crysolites and stones

- for diseases of the kidneys-coins, moonstone and selenite plaster

- for sore throat - aquamarine, beryl, charcoal (a variety of ruby in color) and cat eye (impure quartz with asbestos)

- for snake bite- Agate, T-cross, onyx and emerald

- for madness-dust of pearls in distilled water

and Herbal Remedies from Streghe e Magia:

- for Intermittent fevers- It is a good remedy for decoction made with gentian or camembert ... or pickle . There's also the custom to apply on the parts of the hand (carpal and metacarpals) a pesto of chicory flowers. Drink boiled wine with pepper, carnations and marjoram, or apply vanilla, mint, garlic and rye.

- for Abortion- A plaster was used ... made with egg yolk or even turnip mixed with flour and applied to the lumbar spine; Another remedy was to make a pomade of carousel flour ... egg white and pesto incense that was applied to the kidneys of the pregnant woman.

- for Fractures- Poultice of St Lorenzo's Herb Root, spread on the fracture and bandaged to encourage bone welding, plus powdered leaves of horsetail, to be taken after meals.

- for Heart problems- we used the digitalis (digitalis purpurea) that is still used today, but it was advised to pick up the plant in the afternoon, because there were more active ingredients.

- for snake bites- decoction of echinacea for wound healing

- for Anemia- infusion of "strigonella" truncated grass leaves (also called Greek hay) to be taken several times a day, or strigonella mixed with a teaspoon of honey or jam."

About "Ungueni" (Ointments) :

Says Enzo, "*When they used to presume the witches, (because he always says 'presumes' he doesn't want to say witches), basically when they used to make these 'unguenti' (ointments) they were not actually able to fly, but they were made because a child maybe has a burn on the skin. So with that 'unguent' you put it on the scar. When you prepare, you use herbs: mandragora, some belladonna. These kinds of herbs, when you cook them at high temperatures their chemicals come out. You have to imagine at that time houses were not like today. They had the kitchen with fireplace and kettle on the fire in one room. When you cook something immediately all the houses were inundated by these gasses. So sometimes the women fell down when they inhaled the herbs. When they came to after having hallucinated, the first thing they saw was always the big goat. Why, because in the past people used to live with animals. If you have a goat you live with it... so first things you would see would be the broom and the goat ... or 'the goat or the witch moved the broom because she 'fly.'* [in fact, Antonietta from the north talked about owning a goat when things were good and they had some money]. *But if you use it, in very little doses, you become desensitized to it on the part of the body where you rub it in. If you ingest it, and you add some hot water, if you are suffering for something, it's going to make your pain lighter. The things that provokes us are very high sweat and it's very useful to calm down inflammation. But if you ingest it in high doses, you will hallucinate and with very strong pains to your arms and legs also, you fall down and faint..and even death can occur. Applied on the skin it provides a warm or hot sensation, if you have a scratch. or when you are spaced out.*"

Enzo mentioned this before, saying that "*Plants can be both positive and negative; can be both therapeutic and also very dangerous.*" He starts with high explanation of myth and arrives to the practical. About "unguenti" he said, "*In the past that women have more problems with hygienic stuff. So in the past, women often suffered a loss of A vitamins. This loss of A vitamins provoked some "malattie scroffolosa" or illness of your skin, when you have pimples and things like this, so they made "unguento" to cure it.*

In a male, if you have lack of hygienic stuff it's less dangerous, in a woman more it's more important. They used 'unguenti' to heal these things and not to fly on a horse or a broom. Enzo tells me that all of what he's saying is demonstrated in a medical way, and he's done many researches about this, so he wants to underline this, it's not just his words but also proof and evidence. "*So basically they try to make the 'unguento' to help illness, they cook the herbs, the herbs and ashes and fumes makes them faint, and afterwords they hurt, and then start to hallucinate, then come back awake to spread 'unguento', and some people may see her do this from outside her home and think 'she's a witch,' because legends are started like that.*"

"Noce" Tree, The Magic Walnut Tree of Benevento

Longobards in Benevento

When I first read about Benevento's magic walnut tree in the Carlo Napolitano's Book "The Bewitched Triangle: The Mystery of the Benevento Walnut," I was delighted, intrigued, and somehow not surprised. I've always felt connected to trees, and felt their life force. In times of need, I often stand among trees, touching them, asking for advice (and receiving answers), and this is how it's been all my life. In his book, Carlo speaks about many tree legends and their connections to Druids, Greeks, and Celts, all whom have left their mark in Italy. Carlo describes the landscape of the area of the original walnut tree in his book:

"We are talking about a very thin land that eventually becomes Stretto di Barba in the very spot where the mountain breaks itself but at the same time tries to put herself together. Today from the official papers, this location has not a precise name, but it is remembered as 'La Noce di Santa Maria.' It's an unusual scenery of natural beauty, dark but fascinating. It's been many times pointed to like the hellish location where the Bevenento witches were gathering under the shadow of a big tree, the walnut, to celebrate with the Sabbat the love and dedication that these beautiful Janare had with the master of Evil. A legend that Benevento's Bishop San Barbato affected by eradicating the walnut tree to try to stop the cult."[229]

Basically, it was believed this magical tree really existed, and it's a tree that was near a river where Janare witches would come together and do what they do. Historically, it was chopped down during the time when the church pressured the Longobards to convert to Christianity and give up their pagan practices which included venerating a Golden Serpent. They were also pressured by the church to give up their protection of the local streghe. The tree was allegedly chopped down by San Barbato, but you can find old maps which show it illustrated in its place of origin, considered to have been outside of the city of Benevento. It is also believed that another walnut tree rose out of the seeds of the one chopped down.

Enzo shares with me some of Benevento's myth of the Longobards, which are distinctly different from legends of the Longobardi from their entrance into Italy's northeastern area of Cividale del Friuli:

"Why the 'Noce' (Walnut) tree? There are many traces of the Tree Cults in Italy, and in fact in 139 BC the Cult of Sabazio was abolished, and it was a tree cult. Sabazio was a male Divinity like Pan, God of Nature of the Wood, in the 1st and 2nd century AD. This cult was re-activated in the Tempio di Iside in 88 AD (temple of Goddess Isis in Benevento city). And on the 12 panels of Traiano Arch (the 'crossroads,' the important passage people must go through to enter the city during those days), 6 of them contain trees. The witches in the south were associated with 'Noce tree' (yet Diana with the Oak tree), and the Longboards also associated with 'Noce' tree and a 'ritual of skill' that took place around a tree.

Longboards arrived in Italy (in general, in the north) in the 6th century AD, with a tradition that was similar to the church's much later Communion idea of taking in the body of Christ to become more like Christ. The Longboard tradition was to take in the 'body' of the tree to become invincible. The tradition involved a tree (but could be any tree) where upon were draped skins (of goat or lamb) , strips of meat, and serpents. The Longboards (with long hair and long beards) would test their skill in this competition, riding backwards on their horses, with a sword. They would try to cut the meat or catch the skins with their swords..and whomever was able to slice off meat was able to eat it also (like communion) to become invincible. It was a test of skill. This tournament allowed people to come and watch, took place at night, so there were large fires burning. It was like the 'super bowl,' with loud cheering and yelling by the onlookers. People who weren't close enough to come would still watch at a distance and of course didn't understand. The

Longobards even looked diabolical to the people, and they perhaps connected it with witches and 'Diavolo' (the Devil), because the men had long black hair and because of this were often noted as looking like women. When people don't understand they often idolize or mythologize, make up their own stories.

Back to the 'noce': the Walnut has many associations that are negative: It has been said for a long time that falling asleep under the 'noce' tree will give you a headache called 'mal di lupo.' Also, there is an Italian saying (Sicilian): 'Noce=Noci' or, 'walnuts = danger' The 2ⁿᵈ 'o' should have an accent 'nuoce , nosy.' 'Noci' is plural, but also means 'to hurt you', and it's a warning that the type you see like on cigarette package.

There is a resin that comes from the 'noce' tree called 'ungladine'. The 'ungladine' is produced during the intermediate process of when a tree begins developing the walnut fruit. It's a green sap that comes during this development process. The liquid made from it is called 'Nocillo.' It is still made. Nicollo heals stomach aches. The green part of 'ungladine' is also used as a dye because it turns black when it touches skin: old men use it to dye their white hair black, for example. Black hair, black beards. 'Noce'= singular, 'noci' = plural.

So, 'noce': Why the Noce and not any other tree? Because we know that where the women were meeting, the meeting was called 'Sabba.' In Benevento, there is an idea that the 'Sabba' is related with the Sabato River but, I don't believe it because the name 'sabba' was the same in other places (Triora, Valtelilna, Nemi)." But I must note that what I found in different areas of Italy, in regions not even connected to each other, was that rivers and lakes are always associated with "streghe," so for me it made sense that this Sabato River would be connected to the walnut tree, the legend of the "streghe" and "janare" down here.

San Gennaro and Etymology of the Janare from Enzo Gravina

JANARE/Januare/Gannara/ Janara singular/ Janare plural

On the entymologic meaning of the word "Janara," Enzo asked, *"How do you say January?: Genarro. Genarro is the patron of Napoli, but he comes from Benevento. He's still a very big personality, born in Benevento, has been Bishop of Benevento, and Genarro was his name. It's very similar to Janara because women that were born in Benevento were women born in the land of Genarro.*

So San Genarro, the Saint, is an important personality. He was martyrized. He was killed in a very bad way, punished first in 305 AD. And he was martyred under the Emperor Domeziano. There is something mystical and magical about his martyrdom:

First of all, they tried to put him in a circus for wild animals to eat him (lions, panthers, tigers) but the animals didn't eat him. Afterwords, they tried to burn him. He was put on fire but didn't burn. So,they came up with a strong way to finish his life (the Ecclesiastics did this, the Emperor). So they thought to cut his head off. And they did. But, his blood kept bleeding, running. His caretaker (in the past there were women who would care for a bishop or noble person. The would care for you all the time, from the time of your birth and until your end. Like a mom, but not), she collected his blood. This became a very big event in Naples every year, because the blood every year will run/melt, and this is considered a miracle. The San Genarro blood every year, is preserved in a church: if it doesn't melt there will be very big chaos and pestilence and earthquake for Neapolitan people. It's an oracle. Basically, if it runs, all will be well. 19th of September is the date. Be careful, the Miracle happened in Naples, BUT the blood that was on the stone melted, but not many people know about the blood on the stones where his head was cut. So these 3 miracles were more MAGIC, MAGIA, MAGICAL."

[Karyn's note: September 19th is also the day Franchetta Borelli/Borello's torture began by the hands of Scribani in Triora].

"There is another fact about his features too. At that time, the average height of people was 1meter (50 cm /4 .5 feet) BUT San Genarro was the tallest person, almost 1 meter (82/85), so very, very tall, taller than the average, something magical again. So the women from Benevento are the women of the land where San Genarro was born. Genarro people, Janare. Januarium is the latin, Janara. People who come from San Genarro's land."

In Enzo's opinion, this is why the Goddess Diana doesn't come into these stories. He explains, *"Because if the Myth was taken from a Dianic cult, then women all over Italy would be called 'Janare.' Instead what we find also in places like Triora and Sardinia that people refer to women only living in the land of San Genarro as 'Janara,' so they are known by people in different places as JANARA, and they are known as known as women of San Genarro. The name has a connection to the land. So the local name 'janara, janare' exists ONLY in the Benevento area, so that's why doesn't come from Diana, otherwise local women would be called JANARA in every neighborhood, but they are only called that in the San Genarro lands."*

"But, there has been someone who wanted to see Diana in this myth because of the connection to Jano/Janus. Janus is a double -faced god, both good and bad," says Enzo.

How would he describe a Janara in his words? *"A woman that knows about nature. Why? Because she can use in the good and in the bad, her magical powers."*

"Giano Bifronte" and "Janua Inferi"

What Enzo is referring to is what the "dual nature: on earth, in the world of spirit, so a reference to "mediumship." As Manuela explains, *"Giano Bifronte' (literally translates to "door, two-faced") is a very ancient god. He is a man with two sides facing one side and the other on the other side because he is the guardian of the doors: the gates of the underworld and the gates of heaven. These two entities, the world of 'hells,' which is not hell though [but often called that in folklore or in popular tradition], the world of hells is the world of shadows, it is the world of spirits, of ancestors, but not of hell, hell is another thing."*

So Manuela is touching an important matter that we find related to the most ancient Goddesses that have survived in Italian folk stories as well as the early pagan Goddesses and Gods: Mediumship; the Spirit World reaching into the earthly world. These early Goddesses and Gods, though already having gone through some changes by the powers that be, still indicate that the earliest connection with humans, as "Gods" or Goddesses was through Spirit World communication. The role o the God was this one, first and foremost, and provider as second. This is why Hecate is also referred to as connected to the "infernal," which is simply a fear-laced interpretation by the popular tradition of Mediumship, communication with the Spirit World. Even though in Italian folk stories, going back as far as we can find, the Spirit World's touch upon Italian people in villages is common and not just relegated to women visited by the Signora del Gioco as seen in the Inquisition documents.

Manuela adds, "Historically, we have 'Giano Bifronte' on Roman coins because you know that the Romans have taken the gods from everywhere, not only from the Greeks. And this 'two doors' concept was also connected with a most important date around Italy (and not just in Benevento), a holiday of June 24th called in the religious sense, 'the Night of St. John' followed by 'The Day of Ascension,' which were supplanted over 'la notte delle streghe,' the important natural marker or female herbalists to pluck a most important curative herb 'l'Iperico,' also known as 'St John's Wort.' After the June 21st solstice, in Italy June 24th is And so there is this two-headed Giano who is presiding over this night, and still to this day whomever wants to make the hypericum oil collects the herb that night there and not another time. This is when the sun reaches its maximum zenith, so this is when this herb should be plucked from the earth, while at its maximum potency."

"In that day and the night of St. John," she continues, "the two worlds meet together. These two worlds, the world of shadows, of spirits, and of ancestors, opens to our world. And at that moment it's like opening a veil and the two worlds come in contact. So the heavenly world with the world of 'hell that's not hell.' The above and below come into contact with St. John's Night. It is not by chance that St. John the Baptist is the only saint we celebrate the birth and not the death. If Jesus was born on December 24 and St. John, who is his cousin, was born 6 months before, that gives us June 24th."

And I'll mention here among these significant dates, once again, is the fact that from Corisca to Emilia Romagna to Benevento, Lineages are passed on the night of December 24th, and that women were curing disease miraculously long before Jesus appeared. As Manuela acknowledges, "There has been an overlapping of dates, because when the church could not take out a cult, they put another [their own] over it. But [in Italy] they melt together in the end. For this reason I say to you today, people often do not know the historical origin of why they do something anymore, but they still do it."

Carlo Napolitano also brought my attention to a passage in his book I'd forgotten: *"The Witch, the fortune teller, the spell- maker, "levatrice" (midwife), represented the umbilical cord between [wo]man and nature, between human beings and mother earth (to whom the culture of the Antique pagans was still heavily tied to). But being a woman she was also that being who was able to bewitch men with her body. 'Janua inferi' will be said by someone pointing at her like the person who, exactly like Eve, was [accused of] separating men from God, of bringing him to perdition. So 'Janua Inferi,'* Carlo explains, means also a *"woman open to the otherworld."* In other words, a Medium, which is what the spirits of the Janare had shown me in the vision I experienced a couple years ago in San Francisco while reciting an invocation about the Walnut Tree at the beginning of Carlo's book.

Considering we now have our eyes opened to another connection to the Spirit World, it will be interesting to give you a deeper explanation of l'iperico: L'Iperico itself is rather interesting: its technical name (Hipericum perforatum) is derived from Greek eikon and means "the plant that grows on old statues. It's nickname, 'scacciadiavoli' refers to the belief that it can "chase away the devils," and we know that in Italy illness is often thought to be the result of an unhappy soul under the influence of negativity, which could come from spirits. So in "chasing away these devils," it is used to treat depression. It is also used to treat bronchitis and cough, to cure wounds such as burns,it cures many skin disorders, heals ulcers, and can be used as an anti-wrinkle treatment among other benefits.

The petals of its flowers turn blood red when crinkled and can stain the skin, which is how it got the nickname "the blood of San Giovanni." Its grasses are often burned the night of the 23rd in order to "know" the future, and since medieval times, "Iperico has been dried and hung over doors and windows to keep away evil spirits and wicked witches.

In Italy there is always a confused blending of witches with their tools to cure and sprinkled by a dose of "evil." Often there are special holidays connected to both "witches" and "saints" who are often depicted as being on opposite ends of the "good and evil" spectrum. Usually the men get the "good' reward and the women, who cure disease, are deemed "evil" in this anti-propaganda, to turn away people from seeking out the cures of the women and turning instead towards the religious promises of the men

Depending on where you find yourself, from north to south, east or west, the folk legends change their flavor about the night of the 23rd, but beyond the tales, it's generally believed that women who cure with plants and who have supernatural connections with the Spirit World, collect their curing herbs the night of the 23rd (and of course, the church has added the imagery of the devil meeting with them to make important plans for the coming year, including the dispensing of herbal infused oils and ointments which would give the witches to power to plan revenge spells.

And in true Italian historical tradition, the 24th is also associated a male Saint. Male saints who have allegedly similar traits to women who cure with herbs and the supernatural are somehow elevated in Italy as being "better than." So near each holiday celebrating a gift from nature (such as plants who cure), we also find within a day or two another holiday where a male saint defeats some evil creature slightly supernaturally, in hopes that people will remember to fear the witch and honor the church.

In this case, the petals of the plant's flower, once rubbed between fingers, leaves a red stain named "the blood of St. John." The translucent holes on the leaves are also said to have been left by the sword with which the saint has defended himself from the devil, assisted by the archangel Michael.

This duality is a part of Italy and her history. But if you look past the often fear-inducing stories, the root reveals the same thing over and over: women who know the secrets of nature use them to improve life, while the saints allegedly defeat evil, though there is no proof that they ever succeeded. The interesting part , however, is that in real, earthly, flesh and bone life, women actually do cure illness…very quickly in fact, but the church has had no such success, which is why many of their stories of miracles become "ghost stories" which take place after the man, who is raised into a saint, dies, and is able to create a miracle from the Spirit World of "heaven."

Etymology of Janara From Silvio of Guardia Sanframondi

"This is another song called 'The Noce di Benevento.' In the song, on the 24th of June, St John's night, is the annual meeting around the Noce tree in Benevento. The meeting was made by streghe and janare, a general meeting where they had to take the most important decisions for themselves for their community of the 'streghe' world. This annual meeting around the 'Noce of Benevento.' It's the only occasion where 'streghe' and 'janare' are together.

What you have to know is that the 'streghe' in every tale is always related to an imaginary world, and all their actions take place in a world that is not the human world; these are actions in a magic world. 'La Janara,' instead during the day when it's still light and no dark, is a very common lady that has only one main characteristic: to not participate in the community life of the town of the Rione (neighborhood) in fact, she is always alone and apart and isolated. Then, in the evening when the dark comes, she travels, in spirit.

The main important difference is economical. In fact, in every tale of this world, about 'streghe' and 'Janare,' what we can see, that the 'strega' is always the ugly lady related to the very magnificent castles. That was symbol of political power and economical power (the castles). The 'streghe' world is a world that belongs to nobility. The Janara world instead belongs to the popular beliefs and popular traditions; to the folk, the world of domestic stuff, the poorest things that you can do, popular things in life, the poor population."

What Silivo mentions here is quite curious for several reasons: the Lineage healers, whom this book is dedicated to, are considered to be of the poor population, or from very simple lives. Many of them live in remote areas, cure for free, and while some I met seem to be in comfortable family situations, others are alone or living on very little.

Also, Patrizia Costanzo, who was working at the Arcos Museum bookstore in Benevento, spoke to us and said the Janara were part of the cult of Diana, and the 'streghe' myth is connected to Isis, but many Italians consider this the same myth, just from different cultures. For example, it can depend on the area and the cultural influences there.

And in reality, the temples were not always for "the people." The temple to Iside in Benevento did not allow women into the inner sanctuary. So it would seem strange that a group of women, known collectively as "streghe" witches would be part of a Goddess cult that they weren't allowed into. In this case, however, it may be possible to search historically to find if women of wealth were allowed in. However, Silvio's comments allude to the fact that these stories, in general, are simply parables of the socio-economic structure of the time and reflect the "haves and have-nots," in a way.

I asked him about these women, being a natural line of female healers, using nature with an energy that's "supernatural" who seem to be just like the "nonnas" but instead called "streghe" and "janare." and additionally they seem to be led by a man called "Diavolo," or the Devil. I asked him, then, if he feels they are a corruption of the "nonna" healers, and if they are corrupted because of man's presence?

He doesn't think they were corrupted by the Devil, and he thinks it was not important. He sees the Devil figure in this story as the symbol of the political power at that time. *"You don't have to think that these popular women who were in the villages were not strong women. They were women who were strong. We come from an agricultural world they were very strong women, so we didn't have time to think that the Janara were bad or corrupted. Simply people just pointed at them as devil collaborators. The male figure of 'Satana,' or Satan is like the personification of the political power that has been always headed by men in Europe history. But at the same time these women are not how they appear in the oral tales or in oral tradition as submitted person or persons who were with no rights. That was not absolutely correct. They were very strong women and made their own business. The woman is the real figure who holds this land for a very long time. For example, look at your family or family of one of your friends: there is always a good connection between your female cousin instead of two male cousins, because it's the women who are the glue of our families.*

'La Janara,' from an etymological view, according to Silvio, 'Janara' is just an evolution of Diana, the hunting Goddess. When the Roman Empire became less strong and Christianity arrived, this hunting Goddess becomes a popular Goddess for the domestic duties. From hunting to cleaning the house, and as the old proper name, they became nickname.: Rosa =Rosetta little Rosetta, Maria =Marietta... Diana became Dianula. Then for a grammatical rule Diana became Dianala. Then it starts to sounds Diana : Diana, Dainula, Dianala, Jianala, Jianara.

From the Divinity, the Goddess came the folkloric world of the 'streghe' world." I asked him, in these stories, if the Janare ever did anything good for the community? *"No,"* he said. "What about the streghe?" I asked, *"No,"* he replied again. "So the only healers were the 'nonnas'? *"The Nonna type healer has always been in families, not even really considered magic, nor witches, just accepted,"* he replied. *"Our grandfathers didn't go to the doctor, because the medicine, as we know nowadays, didn't start until the beginning of this century. We are talking about something much more ancient."* And the Goddess, too, is much more ancient than the Romans, who remodeled her to be a hunter.

But this brings up an important point: that the stories about 'Janare' are all quite negative, which I found perplexing at first, because my vision of them showed me they were not just healers, but Mediumistic healers, channeling a very high-quality energy. And I felt their collective grief, from the Spirit World, of being portrayed as "evil women," because they certainly seemed humble, regular, and definitely not living in luxury, which would be the result, one might think, of "evil witches only looking out for themselves," that they would use their magic to have a better life. But then, the church's propaganda was all about these women healers being baby killers, illness-givers, and devil-partners in sexual escapades. So the regular women, living regular lives who were yet able to cure miraculously, were painted in a most odd way that somehow people bought into. I thought perhaps that this was a result of public disapproval of women living unmarried, alone, and away from society perhaps in nature. And yet, the spirits of some Janare visited me several times, always consistently as family women, and very regular.

I asked them, one day at work when I was very impatient with my job and unhappy to be there, "why didn't you run away from people accusing you?" *"Where would we go?"* they replied, *"we didn't have choices like you have, we had families to take care of and people who depended on us."*

As far as all the folk tales I was told by local people, they are all negative:

Hair

A common story regarding hair from Patrizia: She told me, as did Silvio and others, that the witches were known to take peoples' horses at night to ride to the "Sabba" and then return them. She said that while this is a folk tale, it happened to her family: *"Every night that the witches would meet, they would take my grandfather's horse. He was convinced the took the horse to reach 'Sabba'. He noticed it because every night when they returned his horse it had a braided tail. He tried almost his whole life to capture the Janare who were braiding his horse's hair, but he never did. My mother (who is now 70 years old) remembers this because she was the youngest child in the family and her duty was to unbraid the horse tail, because it was considered a shame if you put out your horse with a braided tail. So every morning she had to unbraid the horse's tail. My grandfather solved the problem by selling the horse."*

When a Janare finds your children, she will put dreadlocks in their hair and send them back to you. If you take out the dreadlock the child will become sick. If you leave it in, they remain healthy. I was also sent depictions of Janare with red dreadlocks from part of Italy I haven't yet visited.

Janare Coming into houses at night:

"At midnight they enter houses...." this is what Filomena told me, but also Silvia and many other people, along with being told they will sit on you or lay over you and try to prevent you from moving and breathing

"10 years ago during Christmas time, in the house at night there was the tree and a lot of holiday lights, white furniture, and since it's wintertime we were going to bed a little early because of family events. My husband and I went to bed, and our daughter in the other room, but I woke up after a while. Our bed is in front of the door, so I was still able to see the lights coming from the tree in the other room. Our feet weren't right in front of the door, but facing in that way. Suddenly I noticed something "as a flash" something that came in the room very, very, very fast. Immediately after, I noticed I was not able to speak and not able to breathe..."

Ironically, at this precise point in our interview, which can still be heard on our audio recording of this, someone's cell phone started playing the exact lyrics "hello darkness my old friend...we've come to talk with you again..."

Sylvia continued, *"So I figured out there was something strange. My daughter was 15 at the time and in the other room. I wanted to go check on her but I wasn't able to move. Suddenly in that moment I felt someone jump on my chest and I heard some voice say 'si, si, si, si, si, si' (yes, yes, yes, yes...) like 300 times in a few seconds. The shadow I saw felt like a 'she' because of the voice and something else. The presence passed from me to my husband. We tried to talk about our experience but then the presence went to the other side of the bed and said 'si,' moving its shadowy head up and down, giving a satisfied nod of the head. When we felt it was finished we ran to our daughter's room, opened the door, and saw her shouting 'someone threw off my blankets!' We all three suddenly couldn't move or speak. We realized it wasn't just our imaginations. It wasn't even very dark when this happened with all the lights of the holiday tree."*

Janare swimming away like an eel:

And Filomena, who is a Lineage healer told me, *"I've heard about the Janare since I was born, so they were something old. I was born in 1933, so Janare come before."* When I ask her if she thinks they still exist she says *"Yes."* Then she told me, *"Dada Michele [Domenico tells me 'Dada' is ancient dialect work to say Papa], had an experience with one. One night while he was sleeping, he awoke and saw a a figure, a ghostly female person and he said 'she's coming!' And while he was saying that, as soon as she could get on top of him she smothered him. He tried to sit up, he grabbed her hair, in that moment she asked him 'what do you have in your hands?' And he replied 'I got your hair,' and the Janare replied 'And I escape as an eel...'" and she went away."* She told me he knew what to say, *"This is a question the Janare used to ask, it's like a ritual...so people know what to reply basically. If you reply 'I got your hair,' she goes away. If you reply 'I got iron,' she stays, she can't move. Because if you keep her, when the morning comes, you can recognize who she is (maybe she is your neighbor or someone you know)."*

My encounter with an eel spirit:

Not long after I returned to San Francisco and moved into a new room in an apartment, my dreams became vividly intense, and they were not usual dreams, but astral interactions. I would also have some interesting experiences with the Spirit World during awake times. One early morning (it was becoming a normal thing for me to wake at 5am, begin translating books, then write all day if I didn't have to work. Regardless of work or not, I woke early to write) I came to, sleeping on my back. I felt something to the left side of my face and slowly turned to see what could be seen: there was a very black shadowy face, with no features nor sensation of gender, curiously looking at me. It was level with my face, floating there, but watching another part of my body. This black shadowy head was looking at me, within a 6 inches of my face. It tilted itself, and then, with a little jump of shock, realized I was looking back at it and darted away...only as it turned away I noticed it had no body shape, only a black tail undulated...just like an eel.

As is common for spirits to use shadows to hide themselves, the form this one was in reminded me of styrofoam mannequin heads that have no features and are just smooth head-shapes. Even though this spirit was hiding itself, I felt a curiosity from it in those few brief moments, and surprisingly, nothing malevolent. Surprisingly because in my experiences shadow spirits are never up to something good. But this one felt mentally more open and less focused on doing harm. I've tried since to sense who this was, or at least to gather more information, but

I've never been able to, which is unusual for me. It immediately reminded me of all the stories of the nighttime Janare, but this one was not limiting my breathing nor my movement and made no efforts to harm me, in fact it ran away, quite startled, when it realized I was awake and watching. This is an experience that doesn't fit easily into my lifetimes worth of experiences in any way, so I've had to just leave it be.

Iron:

While in Italy, in relation to these stories about ghosts and succubi-type women, I heard a lot about using iron to protect oneself against a negative spirit (having iron to prevent them from coming near you) , and I heard that if there's iron in a home that's haunted, for example, it will be difficult to get the spirit to move out because the iron will keep them in place. So the iron, I am told, works like a kryptonite. So when Filomena told me this story, the iron makes sense.

When I'd return to San Francisco, and after I'd been working on this book for at least 6 months or so, I began to feel something was wrong in the apartment I was living in. I felt there was also something wrong with my health. I had been feeling a ghost in the house trying to intimidate me, regularly. Increasingly I was watching my housemates become darker, gloomier, and eventually angrier versions of themselves. I realized we were all being influenced. And, I knew they wouldn't be open to talking about it, so I made plans in my mind to move out as soon as possible. However, I was also experiencing some physical symptoms: I almost fainted a couple times on the train to work, having to steady myself by sitting on the crowded, dirty floors. Additionally, I was feeling weak regularly- no matter what I ate I didn't feel like I was getting nourishment. I began asking my body to help me, and as a result I found myself having odd food cravings. They were odd only because these were foods I hadn't eaten in years or ever: plums, spinach, molasses, sesame seeds, and other foods that were not part of my usual diet. I found out these foods were all high in iron. Eating them was helping the strength return, but the ghostly situation at my home was getting worse. I booked a reading with an intuitive psychic medium I trust and the first thing she asked me was "where has all the iron in your body gone? It's like you have no iron left..." After a follow-up it would seem I had indeed developed something like "thalassemia," which is not just a regular deficiency in iron. Thalassemia is an inherited iron issue common among Italians, (also Greeks and African people) but I'm not Italian.

As I researched even more, I found out that a loss of iron energetically has to do with a weakened system from many conditions, none of which fit me, neither physiologically nor spiritually. I discovered iron, associated with physical strength and energy, is also used to deflect negativity and protect against evil spirits, apparently this belief is why it was used to make fences for graveyards. Iron is found in meteorites.

Considering this was not the first time I felt spirit people trying to distract me from writing this book in many ways, it would make sense that they would try to pull iron out of my body so my defenses would be down. Of course the spirit was not directly reaching into my body and taking out the iron, rather instead influencing the environment around me, making it very uncomfortable for me to cook in the kitchen of this apartment...so I began eating out, eating from salad bars, having to change my diet to as to avoid the angry and irrational people in my home. In this way, a small amount of influence allowed a chain of events that altered my diet (normally home-cooked and very nutritious) to one that was nutritionally weak. And this is what happened.

I was eventually able to get my strength back through dietary repair and also holding hematite and pyrite in my hands and wearing it in my pockets when I needed it. But the true solution to these seemingly physical symptoms was an energetic one, and it was Benandanti who helped remove the oppressive influence and I was able to regain traction and return to my meditative self-care. I should mention here that as a Medium, these are not my standard daily experiences. I'm very strict with my boundaries. I don't leave my "doors open," I know how to turn off my spirit telephone, raise my vibration, know what's me and what's someone else and how to "keep clean" vibrationally, and yet, because of this book, there were things I had to learn and this is how I learned them…getting close to the darker things but not become part of them. And these experiences would have very interesting reveals.

Janare making people sick:

I ask Filomena if she has any connection to Diana, Iside…and to let you know, she didn't even understand who Diana was until Domenico explained. But I was convinced that all these women I was meeting had some connection to a much older version of the Great Mother. I had seen a poster for "Madonna delle Grazie" somewhere and suddenly had an intuition this might be a syncretized version of the Grande Madre she would have a connection to, and she said, *"Well yes of course."*

I'd come to find, more than a year later, inspired to do some research because of Filomena's comments about MDG and the Janare and a mountain. I found the MDG is venerated in all of Campania as a syncretized version of a pre-pagan Goddess as one of the feminine portrayals of Mary as a Divine Feminine being having her own healing powers. While connected to Jesus, not just as a mother, she's also considered the "strong woman behind the man," considered to be the one who drives Jesus to do the miracle. She is a Medium, in other words, so that the healing energies Jesus allegedly gave to people actually come through her…revealing a connection to most ancient past of the Great Mother Goddess as spirit healer and provider for all.

I surmised therefore, in my research, that there must be a mountain procession involved somehow, and there is. The church sanctuary dedicated to her is on a mountaintop. The modern procession for her begins in a cave and then proceeds up the mountain. The climb, called "la juta" in local dialect, is an ancient tradition. People climb to atone for their sins and to offer their hard work to the Madonna on her feast day. People still make this pilgrimage up this mountain where it is believed the Madonna was actually, physically here (or manifested herself). The day of celebration is September 11th.

This is why the Madonna statues have such a presence and power in Italy, because they are believed to be "mediums, conduits" for healing miracles. And while these beliefs, these Christianized versions, are outside of mine, I can feel the energy being transmitted through these statues as coming from Great Mother. Italy is a very Mediumistic country, even if people living here can't put this into these same words, and whether in more natural form or more safely tucked into strange, unnatural Christian rites and processions.

"The Janare were there," Filomena tells me, *"there is the mountain there, and they were there a lot of old ladies giving healing to people from Janara's 'fattura,' when they put a spell on you."* Filomena explains that many people, not just in the folk legends, believe they have been made ill by Janare, and yet, no one seems to know who they are. "Do you remember Domenico's uncle Michele I mentioned?" she asks, *"Michele was touched by a Janara. He used the word 'storto,' something crooked."* This "storte" is also an actual illness that Lineage healers in the Emilia Romagna region also learn to cure. *"Why it is called 'crooked,"* Domenico explained to me, *"is because when they put a spell on you, they push a lot on your heart and lungs area and your stomach so you get 'storto,' or "twisted sensation. So our relatives of her family, they brought 'Zio' (uncle) Michele up to these ladies up to the Mountain nearby Madonna della Grazie, in Cerrerto, to be healed."*

My experience of "storto"

I had this same sensation hurting me, repeatedly, even before I got to Italy. It wasn't a Janare though, it was the spirit of an Italian healer witch named Franchetta Borelli. She wasn't trying to hurt me, in fact she was telling me helpful and often urgent things about my own life and she was also teaching me her practices. This pressure, this "storte" against my belly and twisting of my intestines was her way of getting my attention (because after all, the belly area is a psychic receptor for clairsentience). I would be able to relieve this sensation as long as I'd sit down when I felt it, take a pen and paper, and write down what she Franchetta was trying to tell me.

In the negative, I did experience this sensation from spirits of Inquisitors on more than one occasion both in Italy and also in the Bay Area. At first I didn't know the distinction between monks, priests, popes, and all the other male figures in the Catholic religion. It was after I told one of my Italian translator friends what kind of clothing they appeared to me in that he said, *"Oh, those are the Inquisitors."* I wouldn't learn anything directly helpful from the "storte" they made me feel. I did, however, get to see their memories which were very ugly and revolved around sexual perversion in the tortures. They did not like that I could see their memories, of course.

My dream

While working on this book having returned to the Bay Area, I would have many dreams that weren't "dreams," but were instead astral experiences doing work: the work I was doing was either discovery, where I caught people stealing from me in different ways, where I exposed the spirits who were trying to influence me and those around me, and also sort of "test battle" dreams that I've long had. This one reminds me of Zio Michele's "storto" experience: In my "dream" I was in a downstairs room sitting in a chair. The chair was a high-backed antique one of stuffed fabric. I was watching myself sitting in the chair. The chair, and thus myself, had its back facing the wall-papered wall. Between the chair and the wall was a wooden bannister and stairs. I felt someone come down the stairs behind me and then suddenly they were going through my hair. I turned, startled also because it didn't seem possible that someone was reaching through the chair. I saw an old woman with a pale pink cane descending the stairs, staring at me intensely, and then slowly coming towards me. She saw short, dark hair, definitely in her 80s by the way her gnarled hands were curled around the cane, and she was intense. She then tried to touch me with her cane as I faced her and I started demanding "who are you who are you." It was as though she was touching me without actually being able to reach me, into my belly and chest area, and I tried to grab the end of her cane. This was weird, because in these types of dreams I am always quick to use my secret symbols and marks of protection, but for some reason here I did not. My only way to escape her was to get out of the dream, so I woke up.

From my perspective, these are all examples of how the Spirit World reaches into the earthly world…specifically spirits who were once earthly people living on the planet. These are not abilities limited to "Janare" by any means, and they are employed by spirit people: people who have passed out of their bodies and into the spirit realm. Spirit people can only communicate with us this way, or through visuals deceived in our "mind's eye," or in rarer cases through our "inner ears" or even as sound in a room that others can hear. We have psychic receptors here known as "clairvoyance," "clairaudience," and near our brain we have our psychic receptor that combines many of these into "intuition." It would be very physically challenging for local women, still living on earth, to spend so much time traveling in the astral plane harming other people. It would also require a great knowledge of how to affect the energy bodies of others and how to affect the physical world from the energetic one. And while Benandanti are part of something even bigger, the battles, they only happen 4 times a year. While they do a lot of work in dreams, they are not regularly doing the exact same thing in the astral plane as the Janare have been accused of. But, until I experience more, I'll have to remain undecided.

Preventing Janare from entering your home:

The folk stories continue to insinuate that the Janare are poor: to prevent them from coming in your home at night the stories say you can:
Put a broom outside your door. The Janara must count all the fibers of the broom. It takes them a long time to count because they are uneducated, so while they count the morning comes and they must go away without entering.

It's the same procedure with salt: if you leave a pile of salt outside your door, the Janara must count each grain, but she loses track because she can't count well and the sun comes up, so she must leave.

For anyone familiar with the Vampire stories of Europe, they all stemmed from those patriarchal invasions already mentioned in this book: of turning people away from the female healers and midwives, and turning people away from a belief in death and regeneration to instead see death as a failure. This failure was blamed on women, and deaths of babies were blamed on women, whom they also accused of killing through eating the flesh and blood of the same babies. So here, with Janare, we see them compared to lupo mannaro and Benandanti (people who can astral travel and people who used to be born on December 24th) as well as with vampires. We know vampires are really just female healers and midwives attacked by male businesses (doctors and the church). So these folk tales give us some clues, and they make me very very sad. I don't so far have any evidence that these women as a group are harming people in the way that lowly ghosts traditionally do.

A habit to note is that when I spoke with local people about Janare, they crossed their legs, crossed their arms, and even crossed their fingers to protect themselves. They explained there is a real fear about them, because at midnight certain night of the week they are known to enter into houses, in spirit, astrally traveling, and sit on people so they can't breathe and make babies sick or take them out of their cribs and place them in harm's way.

Being a medium, I regularly look at things "between the lines" and "underneath the surface." I find that "face value" is often an illusion. So from my perspective, I recognize the validity in these "crossings." Crossing one's arms and legs (and fingers, but also) is a way of preventing a loss of energy: it's a way of protecting one's own energy. In fact, these are techniques taught in modern psychic and Mediumistic practices. These are common techniques used when having to speak with people who naturally "use" other people "consciously or unconsciously" to drain their energy. This happens, for example, with the narcissist and victim complex person, and also with the the spirit attachment (same personality in the Spirit World). The results of being in contact with these personalities is feeling tired after listening to them, drained of energy, weakened, defenses down. We have all experienced this "friend" who does nothing but "take," and we don't have to be a professional psychic Medium to experience this.

So there is a valid truth behind these seeming "superstitions" the locals use. I'm not convinced it's the Janare who are entering houses at night and harming people, because these are standard things that all sorts of ghosts do, globally, not just in Campania. And the key word here is "ghost." Perhaps.

Lupomannari, Janare, Benandanti

Filomena also said that these women *"were Janare because they were born as a Janare, born at midnight of the 24th of December, so it was just a question of destiny. And whether a Janara or a Lupomannaro, they 'go out' at midnight."* She told me the story of a young boy in their neighborhood who was a lupomannaro. This date, of December 24th, is a date we see repeatedly among Bendandanti and their counterparts of male lupi mannari (which can also be female, by the way), Janare, and Lineage healers, all being mediums of one level of awareness or another.

What I can tell you is that I am connected to people who know Janare living in Caserta, and that this is a Lineage. The transmission can be passed outside gender and family lines, as happened with someone in the family of the people I'm connected to. These people are all naturally mediumistic. Additionally, when I was learning about how to align myself with nature, my Guides taught me a few things: they'd ask me to sit in front of my jars of herbs (which I never studied, somehow I couldn't find a deep interest) and pay attention to which one(s) grabbed my attention. For example, one morning after I'd re-dedicated myself to this research and to my own spiritual path, I was guided to choose my jar of White Willow along with another dried herb. I was instructed to make a little pouch of these herbs in a specific way: in a square shape, folding the fiber paper into itself in a specific way. I was to wear this in my bra for the day (each day would be something different). After I did this, I realized I was running late for work, so I ran to catch the train just outside my apartment and jumped on the train as the doors were closing. I sat and suddenly realized "I forgot my phone!" I decided to stay on the train but I also heard a voice say "but people are going to need to contact you today." I put on my ipod and listened to a song I needed to write lyrics for, took out a pen and immediately penned the lyrics, which remained exactly as I wrote them down with no adjustments. I titled it "White Willow" and the main chorus of the song contained the words "I reclaim." I later learned that the power of White Willow was to help people reclaim: their power, and their ancestry, for example. Before I left work that evening I got paged over the intercom by my manager to take a phone call at the register area. It was my mother, informing me that her mom (my grandma) had passed away that morning, exactly at the time I wrote those lyrics, and she'd been trying to call me all day,

I also later found that my mother-in-law's mother (from Caserta) put a packet of herbs in her bra on her wedding day. Ana would also sing to people a secret song that would cure a specific ailment. These were simple ways my Guides were teaching me old ways that were traditions, using whatever was around me at the time and "synching" them up with profound moments of meaning so I would understand " available herbs, grandmothers, heritage, lineage."

Caserta is a place of poverty, at least in part. While taking the train from Roma to Benevento, the landscape of the places we traveled through were lush and elegant, soft and country-like with whispering grasses, calming yellow wheat stalks peppered with Populonia pines, and even dark and wild rolling mountains , but then as we came through Caserta, there were skeletons of multi-storied buildings that either were falling apart and coming down, or were supposed to go up but for some reason remained uncompleted, rusting in place. So here can we find magic that reflects poverty? Likely. Are there also healers who are from Lineages? Yes. More than this I want to experience for myself, and will have to report back in Volume 2.

Cultural note: The Italian language doesn't have the soft "j" sound found in English as in the word "jam." They pronoucne "j" as "ya" so Janara is pronoucned "yah-nah-rah." "G" as in "Genarro" is soft like the "j" found in English.

Thirteenth Secrets

Last year, my San Francisco winter was grueling: full of cold and rain and the challenges of translating documents about Italy's torture of women from the 1500s. I'd wake at 5 am and begin. Trudging through the emotions of my own regarding this material, along with the added flashes of memories of Inquisitors and from Franchetta Borelli, my clairvoyant vision was overloaded with grief.

A welcome break was reading the book Language of The Goddess by Marija Gimbutas, recommended to me by Manuela Saccone. Looking over the ancient symbols I felt a growing hope: it was clear our foundation as people was from a female-to-female lineage: passing down knowledge through a symbolic language that anyone involved in meditation or healing or Mediumship or magic would recognize. The roots of these symbols, however, were chopped off by the patriarchy. Luckily, roots still have life in them.

During this haunted period a man named Ben reached out to me. He lives on the land of his Native American ancestors and is an artist who lovingly recreates ancient traditional artifacts from nature's remains on his land: discarded animal bones, shells, and river rocks. He creates his own dyes and paints naturally from plants and ochres. He makes his own glue from pine pitch, beeswax, and wood ash from ceremonial fires. He also occasionally incorporates pieces of ancient pottery found on his lands from Woodland and Oneota cultures.

"I try to create these items using methods the prehistoric peoples would have, using other stone or copper tools, water, sand, and other larger stones for pecking and grinding. On occasion, modern tools are used to help create my works, but this is kept to a minimum. Both in materials, tools, and designs, there is a blend of old and new."

He wanted to send me some gorgets, a traditional Woodland necklace style that features a circular centerpiece cut from whelk shell engraved with a specific symbol. When I opened his package, to find 4 incredible gorgets, I gasped. The imagery was so similar to what was found in the ancient pre-pagan times of Italy: serpents, crosses, water, bird motifs, colors of: red, black, and white. Later gifts he'd send me also had a correlation such as pieces of nipple fragments from Mississippian jars that looked like water vessels from the period of 5300 BC found in Old Europe's Yugoslavia and other countries.

I invited him to work with me re-creating artifacts for my Language of the Goddess lecture series where I present Maria Gimbutas' material and offer suggestions on how to use it for creating a Divinely Feminine practice of ritual and symbolic language as an option to the masculine magical systems that are pervasive.

Unbeknownst to him, I was writing the chapter "The Importance of the Color Black" when he sent me another gift that is truly "other worldy": he sent me the Moon and the Stars. It's a necklace made of a piece of the moon, surrounded by a "chain" of black meteorites; fallen stars.

Wikipedia footnote: "Mississippian and Oneota cultures from the Southeastern Ceremonial coplex, (formerly the Southern Cult) is the name given to the regional stylistic similarity of artifacts, iconographies, ceremonies and mythology of Mississippian culture…from 1200 to 1650. Other names were Buzzard Cult and Death Cult"

Chapter 13:
"The Importance of the Color Black in Italy's Witchery"

In 1626, a woman named Benedetta Carzolia from Finale Ligure, Italy, was accused of witchcraft when she was seen kissing a black stone in front of a church while having her back to the church. According to Manuela's documents (which are no longer in print) the black stone could be one of the ancient stones that were used in Pagan rituals. This woman was a midwife who used coins and the gospels, the same means as exorcist friars who did the same thing, in order to protect themselves against evil sprits.[230] In the records, Benedetta admitted kissing the stone, but, she said it's because it was Jesus Christ's feet. Also contained in these documents are an "affidavit" of sorts where she had to sign a statement of contract vowing to not practice any witchcraft and to "grow" the religion of Christianity in her grandson.[231] Because of this she was spared death.

For years now, friends and various people I've met have teased me about always wearing all black clothing, black eyeliner, and black stone jewelry. And for years now I've had a natural impulse to pick up black stones and pebbles I find on the sidewalk or at the beach. My backpacks and jackets are often filled with them, and some of them find their way into my laundry. They are like little pets, and I have bowls and bowls of them. It's been much the same with water and my need to have bowls that contain water, to take baths or showers at night, and needing to be near the ocean. My love of gemstones turned towards the black ones as well as I was guided to buy obsidian pyramids and eggs, onyx, tourmaline, and especially jet. I use the found black stones in ancestor group meditations with students who always remark on how charged with energy they feel. I use them as omphalos stones. I knew my Guides were leading me on a trail to understand something important from the inside-out before they would provide me with the evidence, as they always do, for the existence of the meaning beyond my own ideas.

I'd find out, in rather exciting ways, that my Guides were leading me to something very real connected with feminine spiritual history, and therefore, something quite hidden and buried. In Italy, some of these clues are out in the open, in often "in-plain-sight" presentation of magic, symbols, and belief in the "Grande Dea." There is a most ancient connection between the color back and the Grande Dea: it's part of the symbolic psychic, shamanistic language from our founding days. In the original founding Divine Feminine spiritual expression, black was considered to be the color of the Universe's womb, a place of potential from which all life comes, therefore it's connected to birth and death, the womb and the tomb. Death was not seen as a failure, but as part of a transformation from earthly life into the Spirit World, from which a person would "regenerate" and come back to life again.

Even more significantly, and in relation to Christianity's fight to "demonize" the color black belief before the rise to power, was that black symbolized the Spirit World itself, which was available to people directly, the poor and humble especially. With individuals being able to receive knowledge and intuitive suggestion from Spirit World through channeling, they'd have no need for a religious business institution to tell them who God is, nor would people need priests nor preachers to talk to God for them: they'd already be in connection with ancestors and the Goddess herself. In fact, this is what I found often in my Spiritualist training as a Medium:

people came to learn this skill because they told me it provides specific answers whereas when they went to church they received none. San Francisco's Sheila Medina encapsulated this ancient belief in a modern phrase "In meditation, we go into the darkness to find the light." The darkness was not considered evil, the Universe, being of the Great Mother Goddess, was considered to be abundant, and worked to assist us always.

Once the church came into greater power than the military in Italy, and war was the main directive of the patriarchy, it was natural for them to create a a war against these original beliefs that were in harmony with nature (and were still lingering, nevertheless in altered ways, in Paganism), so they could supplant a male-figurehead religion which had little to do with nature. So in order for their symbolic language to make sense, they had to create a new order complete with a propaganda campaign, one of "against" the "other," just as we see in modern politics. In evidence of this, mostly what we see in Italy regarding religion is the opinions of the church against others, pointing fingers at alleged "evil" and "enemies of the new morality," all the things they want you to know are now deemed "bad." In reality, we directly know more about what the church was AGAINST rather than what they were FOR because torture and punishment were always around the corner, marriages were arranged to keep people "in line" and dependent on the church for spiritual answers as social order was the focus. Because of the persistence of ancient spiritual practices that were surviving in one altered form or another, we have the allowance of "syncretism" in Italy. We see this, the marriage of pagan and pre-pagan beliefs and devotion to Grande Madre in a variety of sculptures that are in line with a church-allowed portrayal of the enduring portrayal of "Mary" but are, underneath, pagan Goddesses and even more ancient ones. We see this specifically, this link to pre-pagan Goddesses in the "Black Madonnas."

But first, before we delve into this, we must look back to our foundational past, beyond our modern form and beyond the the identity these symbols have been hijacked with by those in power.

Perhaps the most potent symbol of the Goddesses coming from a place of "higher wisdom" are the aniconic stones, or in Italy's case meteorites and black stones, venerated in the Goddess' honor. Something "aniconic" is a symbolic representation of supernatural consciousness. Rather than attach a human form, which inferior to higher consciousness, in "aniconism" a natural symbol, and the simpler the better, is used: "In many lands shapeless stones have been adored. Among several ancient nations the idea of Divinity was symbolized by a rough stones. That "aerolites" should be revered is not surprising, since they, as the idol stone of Ephesus, came down form heaven."[232]

I have maintained for years that what has been categorized as "anthropomorphism" is not what it is historically believed to be at all (primitively making everything seem to have humanity), but rather a way to say that "Goddess, that higher consciousness energy" is in all nature, plants, and animal. So for shaman to create symbols of her, all those items can be used including a physical human body, to represent when a human body can "embody" her wisdom and energy through channeling. Her energy was believed to be the Source energy from which all life forms come, and this is what the statuary represent. With "aniconism" I liken this to comic book drawing styles: the more details an artist uses to create and express a character, the more the character seems alive to us, as having that specific personality that the artist created, in direct relation to the information connected with its form. The less lines and details and colors the artists uses, the more we have to use our imagination to fill in the blanks, so to speak, to allow the character to naturally develop and come alive. Less form means the subjects is more open to interpretation (and exploration).

Despite the "blackout" of women and Goddesses from history, these stones have remained in historical records as part of public events. This color black is actually a key to our history, because it relates to nature and natural events that marked supernatural events (such as meteorites coming down to earth after which human consciousness received an upward and expansive growth). These types of symbols were given to the human race by the Spirit World. Human beliefs are often limiting because they are connected with people in power, so traditional symbols become connected with beliefs that often have nothing to do with their origins, the same symbol can be largely accepted as "positive" during some centuries and then "negative" thereafter.

Meteorites, which were making their way down to earth, were largely black. The meteorites, literally something alien, spiritual from the Universe "coming down to earth," are often honored and placed at spiritual temples and sites. These rare but repeating events marked changes in spiritual perception on the planet. We know this from religious propaganda: In the story of Jesus, traveling "magi" or "wise men" are said to have seen a bright star or light appear in the sky that guided them to find this "magical boy" having just been born in a manger. We know historically the church copied Roman emperor propaganda techniques, and we know the church was also practicing magic and attempted shamanism (and failed) and was aligning their modern magician competitor, Jesus, with other magi present in Italy, and to do this they were using the symbols used by other magi. Forbes Leslie conceives that many figures represented on stones "are disconnected from any Christian symbols,"[233] such as the zigzag and comb[234] which were from the founding Divine Feminine symbolic language and which represented water and its life-regenerating force.

We see here ideas taken from these much older occurrences: a "heavenly body" falling to earth and some corresponding events that caused humans to connect this event with advanced learning, spiritual awakening, introduction to a spiritual teacher (a "savior" in Christianity) or some other energetic event that demonstrated to them a higher consciousness at work. Pre-Paganism and Pre-Christianity, the Universe was considered Divinely Feminine and all within it being from her "womb". The meteorite descents marked the global appearances of female Goddess teachers appearing to women at night from Italy's indigenous Goddess the "Signora di Gicoo, also called "Buona Dea" among other "good Lady" names. She taught women the secrets of nature and more.

Cibele (also spelled "Cybele"), a Phryigan Goddess and one of the older Goddesses in a lineage of Spirit Goddess Teachers who has an important place in Italy's history is reported to have had a black stone venerated in her honor at Pessinus in ancient Greece among other locations. However, the stone was moved to Rome in 204 BCE after the Cumaean Sibyl, an oracle, urged that she be embraced as a religious protector against invaders in Rome's second war against Carthage. Additionally, it was believed the priestesses of Cybele had the gift of prophecy of seeing into the future a psychic gift transmitted from the Goddess to the earthly women. Thus, Cybele became 'Mother' to the Romans. "*The personification of Cibele was the largest iron meteorite known in the ancient world. It was a 16-feet-conical object worshiped as the "Simulacrum of Cybele" and weighed several hundred tons.*"[235] Alongside Isis, Cybele retained prominence in the heart of the Empire until the fifth century CE; the stone was then lost, although it's rumored to be in the possession of the Vatican (as it is also rumored that the Vatican is built on top of her temple). Whether or not this is archaeologically correct, it is conceptually factual, as synthetic religions like the Catholic one subsumed Matrilinear ones). Her cult prospered throughout the Empire and it is said that every town or village remained true to the worship of Cybele.[236]

Female Divinities associated with "aniconic" black stones are many: Aphrodite at Paphos, Astarte at Byblos and the famous Artemis and also Diana of Ephesus, to name a few. The most ancient sculpture of Diana, it is said, is carved from a black meteorite. There are many "black virgin" statues in Italy, many stories of black stones in secret places being venerated by old women in the countryside, as well a story I learned about black jeweled heirloom rings that can only be worn by the "chosen one" in the family line of healers. My own intuitive years-long habit of collecting black stones took its own historical and fortuitous turn when stones my husband gathered for me from the street near Iside's Obelisk (in Benevento, Italy) began to turn black after I started to meditate with it. Originally it was a pale tan-colored stone, and the dramatic change prompted a new direction in my own research.

That the Universe's wisdom is associated with Goddesses as Mother of All is further evidenced in the ancient customs of honoring "Omphalos" stones, symbolizing the center of Great Mother's body; the "navel of the Universe" from which all life comes. While the "Omphalos stone" is an actual "thing" housed in a museum at Delphi, it's also a multi-layered concept. As for the stone itself, it marked the place of the Oracle at Delphi. Centuries before the birth of Christ, seekers form all over the world were journeying to this sacred shrine on the slopes of Mount Parnassus to ask questions of the pythia. Delphi was considered the center of Greece as well as center of the civilized world. This "center" of Mother Earth was marked by a cone-shaped stone which stood in front of the temple, but is now in the Delphi museum. The Delphic Oracle herself was there as a Medium. to [help]"overcome this estrangement from the gods[sic][desses] and their wisdom[footnote have u been to delphi].

As a concept, the "omphalos" was a marker of the Goddess' touch on earth, a marker of her "center," where she could be found in some expression. At Delphi, her touch was expressed as a mark on the earth over which sat a psychic medium female"pythia," or"oracle." Pythia were exclusively female. As every ancient nation regarded its own version of the Great Mother as the cosmic spirit, so its own capital or chief temples was located at the center pf the earth, marked by the stone omphalos that concentrated the Mother's essence. [womens'ency]. In other places around the world and in Old Europe especially, stones were used consistently to mark the Goddess' life-giving properties of water in the forms of rivers and wells. At Delphi and everywhere there was an Omhalos stone, it represented the center of her conceptual body from where all life comes. Again, we have the macrocosm (Goddess and Universe) and microcosm (earth) again; the navel on women's body having the similar capability of life-giving (which is separate from her ability of fertility). A parallel that naturally makes sense, in contrast to the stories of gods "birthing" children in ways that are not possible in the natural world-even in these folk stories, the men reach for feminine fluids and life-giving properties to attempt to tie their stories to some natural phenomenon; they use drops of their blood (since they don't have life-giving menstrual blood with its nutrients), they sometimes use sperm (without a womb) or bones and dust (remains of a lifeless body) to "create life," albeit synthetically, whereas everything in a woman's body or Goddess is life-giving, nurturing and naturally supporting of life.

In addition to black stones and meteorites representing the Goddess Great Mother's wisdom coming down to earth, and the Ompahlos stones representing the center of her creatrix universal "body," marking her touch upon the earth, we also have the temples celebrating her teachings of life, death, and regeneration. These temples celebrate her higher wisdom and her earthly parallel: the female body as representation of the Universe's wisdom, nurturing, and navel center from which we all come. Subsequent structures have come to symbolize man's accomplishment in the world and his ability to conquer it: what were once rounded structures symbolizing the body, the womb, and the tomb (natural cycles of birth, life, and death) are now square buildings and structures which impose themselves on the land around them, at odds with natural shapes.

The most notable temples built in her honor bear a striking resemblance to the curves of her fertile body (as they have also been represented by clay figurines with large breasts and large buttocks, but it's important to acknowledge that fertility is only one aspect of the Goddess as it is only one aspect of women) and also display complex mathematics, (another gift of the Goddess): the megalithic temples of Malta. The oldest freestanding temples on earth, they predate the Egyptian pyramids and the ziggurats of Mesopotamia.

Malta is a Mediterranean island of Italy situated 80 kilometers south of Sicily and 370 kilometers east of the Tunisian coast. The temples have largely been buried under heated debates as to the origins of their builders as well as the dates of their origins. While some researchers claim Malta appears to have been first settled during the early Neolithic period by a wave of immigrants from the island of Sicily, there is no evidence connecting any other Neolithic structures to these temples, and yet there is outstanding evidence and research proving a much earlier settlement occurring in the Paleolithic period and perhaps even pre-historic. While I'm not a researcher and I'm not interested in entering the debate of validation via documentation (as a female spiritual practitioner most of my history has been decimated, buried and burned, and my ability as a Medium connects me to the knowledge I seek), it doesn't take an expert to see that the "professional handling" of these temples in the hands of excavators, researchers, historians and archaeologists is suspect, to say the least.

While it's been documented that some 7,000 to 10,000 skeletons of bodies were found be found, in equal amount male and female, as well as elongated skulls, Goddess figurines representing her various aspects, and more, somehow every piece of potentially radio-carbon-datable material has disappeared.How do over 7000 bodies just vanish? Graham Hancock documents the name-recognition battles of archaeologists and researchers who get to claim, in their name, what they discover and who allegedly fight to keep their discoveries as the final historical truth, even if contrasting truths come along later. Some of the archaeological battles, political battles and document tampering are alluded to in his book "Underworld" as well.

Such a hotly debated set of remains with such obvious underhandedness must mean that these temples are more important than we can imagine for the whole of this planet. Perhaps this is why they are largely unknown outside the academic world, in the same way witch hunt truths are unknown, hidden under the distractions of the smoke of the perpetually burning bodies of real women who have been tied to the stake "ad infinitum" of negative propaganda created for political purposes to set in-motion the decimation of women with curing powers and knowledge of nature's wisdom. At Malta's temples were found elaborate underground chambers, like caves, with artifacts and spiritual artwork and often the color red.

Outside of Goddess temple structures, literally, are individual stones or collections of stones (in the shapes of circles known as "henges") which mark and point to her natural conduits; live-giving sources of water like rivers, wells, and also energy vortexes. In Lithuania [...] along waters there still stand menhirs, called "deives" (meaning Goddesses) full of mysterious powers, as late as 1836.[237] Slavish Goddess Mokosh , name connected with moisture.: "mok-"or "mokr-"meaing "wet, moist," and her ritual called "mokrida," and the root "mok" is also a name for stones.[ibid] Additionally in Lithuania "mokas" is [also] a "standing stone" always appearing in legends associated with lakes or rivers.[238]

Throughout my travels around Italy, in each area where there were longstanding histories of "streghe," there were also rivers associated with them. They were always powerful rivers with unique rock formations around them, a bit hidden and not easy to get to, considered to be places of power where women *washed themselves and performed their rituals.* Most interestingly, my translator and driver Domenico (from Guardia Sanframondi, a medieval village in the Benevento region) and his "Nonna" (grandmother) who lifted a very old "Malocchio" off of me, used a word when talking of specific legendary witches of their area: *"Manavana,"* Filomena said of the "Janare" witches of the San Genarro region in relation to the river. *"'Manavana' is a very interesting word, Domenico told me, because it means 'they put themselves there,' at the "fiume (river) Sabato."*

The Greek surname of Artemis was "the Stony One".[239] While she is associated with stones, she is also connected to childbirth as is Diana and also Brigid. In Ireland and Scotland Brigid is considered the midwife to the Blessed Virgin and thus the foster mother of Christ.[240] In Ireland, the Holy wells (recorded by the hundreds in 19th century literature), mostly became St. Brigit's wells, all visited on the first day of spring.[241] From both Caserta and Benevento, villages in the southern Sanniti region of Italy, comestories of women gathering around wells, "streghe" who gather around wells, and the curing power of the waters in wells, often build of stone.

Back to modern times, consider this connection to the color black to be a call to return to the Great Goddess Mother, for the purpose of receiving her abundance, for becoming empowered. It's not the only call, but it is an important one, and one found in cultures who embrace the "modern witch."

Something funny happens in the documentation of spiritual artifacts around the world that look "primitive"- they tend to be written about in a discrediting way, assuming the creators didn't know what they were doing or had limited ideas and abilities. Anthropomorphism is one example. Another example would be the temples on Italy's island of Malta: they are megalithic free-standing stone structures. Enormous. Built in the shape of female bodies, which is hotly contested of course by male archaeologists and historians, and seemingly disconnected to the rest of history (invasion, war and subsuming will do that). Some of them bear very intricate carvings which show great craftsmanship-not only in their actual execution, but also in the symmetry of their designs: repeating rows of animals which look identical, spirals moving both clockwise and counter clockwise and often connected. These were created by artisans, to be sure, and there's nothing primitive looking about these designs. At the same time and in the subterranean chambers of the same temples were found statuary of bodies that look like the creators didn't know how to depict a human being skillfully: there are shapes accented.. sometimes the belly, sometimes breast, often lumpy and exaggerated beyond what we see in nature, the torsos engraved or painted with spiral lines and chevrons marking the belly, pubic area, eyes and breasts ad mouths. Some bodies are clay, some are carved from bone or alabaster and look stiff, like a simplified body frozen in "cross shape' pre DaVinci's "Vetruvian Man" These are found not only on Malta but also Sicily and in Ligurian caves and elsewhere in Italy. These representational human-like figures were made by the same people, so if they were skilled enough to be exactingly symmetric, how could they be also primitive as to not be able to carve a human body that looked like us? Because this was intentional and symbolic. This founding language symbolic after all.

This only intentional design only increases with the modern ages in Italy's art, such as with the Black Madonnas in Italy (and found throughout Old Europe). These statues are associated with different Goddesses, depicted as very fine statuary, with highly detailed and modernly recognizable female features. These statues are very decorated with often intricate woven colored fabrics, an array of jewels, gold and gold leaf, modernly recognizable clothing, highly ornate and crafted crowns, and often with babies (like the baby Jesus). Leonard Moss at a meeting of the American Association for the Advancement of Science on December 28, 1952. Moss broke the images into three categories: *(1) dark brown or black Madonnas with physiognomy and skin pigmentation matching that of the indigenous population; (2) various art forms that have turned black as a result of certain physical factors such as deterioration of lead-based pigments, accumulated smoke from the use of votive candles, and accumulation of grime over the ages, and (3) residual category with no ready explanation.*[242]

But these Madonnas haven't been depicted with brown skin nor tan-like skin color. Some of their depicted "fleshy" parts are entirely carved out of walnut wood or pressed from black metal, and are uniformly colored so, unlike the rest of their adorned parts. Some statues are entirely made of black metal-so that the skin, the hair, the fabric, the jewels are all blackened. These are made by obviously modernly skilled craftsmen who could have easily depicted brown tones of skin in the same way all the other details of these statues were created. However, they did not, and this was intentional.

What we have here instead of a literal depiction of an earthly woman is an upgraded "aniconic" representation of the ancient Great Mother Goddess. In Italy the Madonnas are a Christian-friendly depiction of the pagan Goddess as well as the even earlier ones that were "safe" to worship as such, because this worship could remain hidden. It's well known that as the church all over Italy was was supplanting pagan holidays with Christian ones, they did so by placing their holiday date right next to the date of the pagan ones. A young male witch from Italy's northwest told me *"On the top of the mountains in Liguria you find the saints and monuments that were planted by the Christians over the who killed people who were accused of witchcraft, destroying pagan culture and symbology while taking over with Christianity."* They built their churches on top of pagan temples and mystery schools, such as with the Mitra Temple in Rome and on many mountaintop locations that once displayed temples to Goddesses. These Madonna statues mark the black stone advents, or rather, her natural marker in time when her knowledge came "down to earth" as represented originally but he "aniconic form" (the actual meteorite itself) then black stones (as meteorites were not readily available all over) and then this developed into statuary as this representational form became more popular, as we see especially in Greek and Roman times where statuary didn't represent anything, it was portraiture for propaganda.

It should also be noted that there are many churches in Italy adorned with spectacular art that depicts saintly men, Jesus, and other all-male depictions of the "godly." There are also churches which only have female iconography, as with the Madonna statues, Madonna paintings, and for the ones who are holding a baby, the baby is not given a great deal of attention: it's all about the feminine.

So the trail back to the original feminine spirituality, the shamanism that connected women to the Spirit World has in its symbolic language: black, black stones, water, rivers, symbols representing the way energy moves on earth as it does in the Spirit World. Feminine energy is abundant, represented by black and gold, and feminine energy is regenerative, as represented by blood red, and the ochre red painted in the Malta temples.

I remember reading years ago, but I cannot find the source, that witches used to give a black stone to potential initiates. The hopeful initiate would be required to carry the stone around for a week or so, and then give it back to the Teacher. The Teacher would then read the "psychometry" of the stone to know what it revealed about the hopeful initiate. So I tried this. I was just learning about gemstones, and so I used a black onyx stone I had that was rounded, like a pebble, with a perfectly circular bright white spot in the "corner," which reminded me of an eye's pupil. I placed the pupil down onto someone's photograph. I wanted to know if I could trust this person. I left the stone on the photograph for three days, and then I laid down on the floor on my back and rested the pupil of the black stone on my forehead "third eye" area. I was instantly transported inside of this person's apartment, able to see furniture and wall color and details as if I were really in the room. I saw this person with another person, and what I saw shocked me so much that I jumped up and never tried this again. I had an astral travel incident rather than just a psychometric reading of the stone, and I wasn't expecting that.

Not long after my husband-to-be and I moved to San Francisco, having returned from Tuscany, I was training as a Medium and trying to come to terms with "outing" myself. I had begun to notice the dreamy and atmospheric blogs of young artistic women who seemed proud of the history of witches and were aligning themselves with this world. I, on the other hand, was living this life in secret, but trying to become more comfortable with living it out-loud. During this time my husband gifted me a necklace by one of these young women designers whose jewelry company is named Bloodmilk: the necklace is a black bird claw. When I first put it on I felt a little "pulse" within it, like a heartbeat. This necklace would be like a living crow, often warning me of danger, or helpfully pointing me in the right direction for my research.

When Diana first appeared to me and began teaching me, through my meditations and in other ways, she appeared to be wearing black clothing, but with a non-specific form. She was so very tall and "robed" in black, and there were horns at first. Over time, she would "appear" as white light, but the way she presented herself to me at first was as "black." During this same time period, I was training as a Medium and my Guides were communicating with me through imagery and emotional sensations before we moved into full on conversations. Like everyone's Guides, mine were aware of what "visual language" I was most familiar with: colors and what they meant to me versus what they meant to everyone else; which animals I was inspired by, what songs I had recently listened to or movies I had recently seen. They use this easily recognizable imagery with me to show me they are trying to "speak my language" by using things I would recognize quickly not just from the image itself but also because of the thoughts and ideas I had connected to these images. For example, when I trained as a Reiki healer years ago, I would often clairvoyantly see illness in the body (breast cancer, liver disease) as "black, non-moving energy," marking the places where there was illness. But as an artist and in my own philosophy, the color black always represented something peaceful, expansive, and full of potential…that is, in more recent years as a result of an experience I had in 1991.

At this time I was asking deep questions about how the Universe worked and why I often felt so lost within it, a friend took me to his family's home near the beach of Manasquan, New Jersey. We went to the beach at midnight, and I walked out only a craggly jetty of big black sharp rocks that extended like a pier into the ocean. I walked carefully out, being splashed with powerful waves crashing through the rocks, until I came to the end. As I was looking out to the ocean and the night sky, both were equally black and I could no longer discern where the sea ended and the sky began. I felt weightless, I felt free from the physical world, in this great void that was somehow not frightening but instead felt like a giant womb, and I heard a voice that said "Home." I felt a great peace. After that incident, however, would spurn my search for a "home" on this earth that I never felt rooted in. The color black would lead me there, over many years, as I found who had been with me all along, guiding me on my search: The Great Mother.

Fourteenth Secrets

Before I went to Italy in 2016, Neapolitan author Carlo Napolitano graciously responded to my many overly-excited emails about his book "Il Triangolo Stregato" and my life stories that seemed to match up with his documentations. "You must come to this land now," he told me, and offered to take me to the places in his book. As he told me about the area, he said that in one particular place, he would only be able to take me so far: I would have to continue on by myself if I wanted to venture further.

We chatted over the internet about his book, and he told me he was writing another one but had not concluded the process. He didn't tell me the subject of his second book, but suddenly I thought to ask him, "Carlo, in places that are said to be connected with Goddesses, is it common to find caves nearby?" To which he responded Oh yes."

That night, I had a dream that he and my husband had taken me to the Stretto di Barba and we were walking through the trees. I was leading the way. We came upon an old stone structure that looked like a door on a circular platform. The door seemed to have a small room behind it, like an old telephone booth, only made out of ancient, pale marble stone.

They both told me they could go no further. As I approached the door, Carlo turned into a grey stone gargoyle and perched himself on the circular platform's edge, as if he was protecting me as I went into the chamber.

Waking up in the morning I discovered an email from him which told me our conversation had helped him help decide the name of his book. He revealed it to me as "Il Guardiano di Pietra"… The Stone Guardian.

Chapter 14:
"Carlo Napolitano's Bewitched Triangle of Benevento"
Benevento, Ceppaloni, Petruro Irpino and Avellino

"Unguento, unguento, mandame alla Noce de Benevento,
supra acqua et supra ad vento, et supra ad omne maltempo."
-Invocation used by the Janare

Potion, potion, send me to the walnut of Benevento,
above water and above the wind and above my misfortune.

Reading Carlo Napolitano's book " Il triangolo stregato: Il mistero del Noce di Benevento" (The Bewitched Triangle: the Mystery of Benevento's Walnut) is one of those fantastic synchronicities that make you realize that timing can be everything. This divine timing can open your eyes to truly wonder at how the lives of people can weave together. Carlo's own research and journey into discovering this material and writing his book coincided with it being in a bookstore at the exact time my husband returned to visit his mother in Italy. At this exact time he'd been telling her what I'd been discovering about Italy through Mediumship, so they decided to drive down to Caserta to see her family, and she revealed to him that she's part of a Lineage family.

He found out on this trip, that his "nonna" cured people with a song, and that there was a town full of psychics and mediums: for example, if you needed relationship advice you went to a specific neighbor. When you went to the doctor for an illness, he gave you a piece of meat to bury in the soil, instructing you to know that as the meat rotted into the earth, so too would your illness leave your body. He met uncles who were sad they never got their "marks." My mother-in-law gathered things I'd asked for without blinking an "occhi:" black stones, white stones, walnut shells, pieces of wood, a jar of soil from the area, Lire coins, and she also added dried lavender, sewing pins form her mother, a thimble and more.

He, along with his cousins would take him to see the Obelisk of Iside where he'd take a loose piece of the street for me (which over time went from a light tan color of cement to a solid deep black shiny stone) and then to a bookstore where his cousin pulled Carlo's book and one from Fabio Garuti for me from the shelves. His cousin would pass not long after that, with the photo of the obelisk containing Benevento's hieroglyphic he took that day being the last image he'd take on his cell phone.

In Carlo's book I would find evidence of all the visions my Guides had been giving me about Italy: about Scandinavian men with long beards meeting with streghe and exchanging information and forming alliances, celts, druids, healers, Iside, Cibele, and a Goddess Lineage, rivers, mountains, stones, trees, serpents, and more.

My husband and I arranged to once a week translate as much of the book as we could in a couple of hours. He'd translate it verbally from Italian to English and I'd transcribe it into my computer. This was no easy task- the spirit people who wanted me to know about the contents of this book were very high-frequency and powerful, , so I found myself falling into trance while I was typing what he was translating, fighting to stay "awake." The book is full of legends, folk tales, historical ones, and a lot of dreamy atmosphere.

There was s special moment among so many eye-opening ones that charged this entire process: we were sitting on the wooden floor, and he read the invocation "Unguento, unguento…" and while he read these words I saw some spirit women appear in the room. They were dancing, holding arms, moving around a fire. What was extraordinary to me is they were creating an energy field : golden light that was two strands entwined, like the DNA helix, forming the circle around the fire, and in the enter where the fire was, a golden ball of light was expanding. What was so exciting is that I'd seen this energy pattern before during my training as a Medium…not in the giving of messages, but in giving Mediumistic healing! This is the exact pattern of energy I see consistently when giving healing as a Medium, that is, channeling not my own energy but being a conduit for a higher conscious, more powerful and positive Spirit Healer Guides). During my training, Spirit Guides explained how the energy was moving. The energy always appears as golden light forms a golden circle around the patient with the DNA helix, sometimes moving vertically into their head and down through their body like a DNA helix column, with the ball of glowing light expanding in their chest area. I had only seen this when I trained as a Medium, not ever during Reiki sessions (I've given over 1,000 hours of Reiki to people and animals). Here I was seeing it being created by a group of old women called "Janare" in Carlo's book.

Through tears I exclaimed "Italian witches are healers!" And then I felt the grief of these women consume me and I began to cry. They told people made stories about them being evil, that some of them were hunted, hated, and they still feel great despair in being forgotten. In that moment I determined to return to Italy to let them tell me their story.

The Sacred Triangle

They taught me, in spirit, all along the way-leading me on an exciting trail of discovery. But, coming to these areas, of Benevento, Ceppaloni, Petruro Irpino and Avellino is where everything came together for me:

This area, as Carlo shows in a map found by Jenny Capozzi, points to the place of the original Benevento walnut tree, within a precise triangle which is formed by the locations of 3 apotropaic magical "churches:" Maria Santissima della Pieta, Chiesa di S. Bernardino, and Maria Santissima di Montevergine.

This triangle reminds us of the pubic triangle emphasized on all the early pre-pagan spiritual statues representing the Divine Feminine Goddess combined with the 'Goddess-come-down-to-earth in the human female:" the life-giving, life- regenerating, eternal bed of divine fluid of creation. The life-giving and eternally life-regenerating power of the Divine Feminine was recognized in nature, whose symbols of her energy are stones, water sources, trees, the moon crescent and horned animal skulls that make the same shape as the female reproductive organs, the colors black, white, red and the gold of the sun.

Here, in Carlos' triangle, in which it is believed the original magical walnut tree originally grew, is an important water source: fiume Sabato (the Sabato River), life-giving waters. On each side of the river can be seen curved mountain peaks making the gentle sloping shape of crescent moons..like the Horns of Knossos..but naturally occurring in these mountain peaks rather than carved of stone.

At the first "church" which protects and marks a place where the Goddess physically manifested herself. In front are two trees flanking the "church" which is not used as a church. The trees have spiraling trunks. Trees, in the ancient and founding Divine Feminine spiritual shamanism that Italy's witchery came from, represent the Great Mother Goddess' "column of life," her literal channel for wisdom "come-down-to-earth," which is why women gathered around trees: to receive knowledge. At the back is dense, impenetrable, wild nature which also encroaches its sides. it is a small one-room square building. This first "church" is not used: there is a locked, gated door and artwork can be seen inside which represents the Divine Feminine. It is the "center" point of the triangle. Carlo reports in his book this church, which is literally on the road, there is no place to park in front, is the most haunted. He documents reports of people driving by at night losing sense of time, of their cars suddenly not functioning, of people who try to go see it at night and becoming very ill, of all sorts of apparitions and frightening experiences. I knew I must go here. I didn't believe it was a place of evil, as has been alleged: I sensed it was a place being guarded from those who don't belong here.

At one of the far points, where the river bends, is an oddity: a church dedicated to San Bernardino. This is the only one actively operating as a church, with a smoothly paved parking lot as well. Intuitively I did not want to visit this church, not knowing at this time who S. Bernardino was. Carlo told me allegedly this was the site of an alleged miracle. Apparently Bernardino arrived here on a trek and asked for some food, but was told they had none. He told them to go inside, and apparently there food had appeared. The most ironic thing is a specific compilation of statues in front: at the center, a representation of the Divine feminine. Flanking her are two spiraling stone pillars, each with one potted plant on top which look like tree tops. Bernardino was responsible for fiery hate speeches against women, witches, homosexuals and Jews. Why would he have a church here? If we remember males of church were supplanted into female miracles, both into their stories and built onto sites where Divine Feminine miracles occurred, then we can recognize that this church and this story was stamped over something very interesting, and rooted in the Divine Feminine. Perhaps that discovery is yet to be made.

The third, and most special church, where literally "X" marks the spot, is another one like the first: slightly larger, locked gate, built right into the "sidewalk" cobblestone walk, this church has a little more walking room around it, with another room to the side, Divine Feminine paintings inside, with a thin and curious trail leading from its side and moving through the forest. I only followed it a certain amount of the way because I knew Carlo would be coming back for me but I wanted to know where it led. The way this church is literally on a path going further up the mountain, passing in front of someone else's property makes it look like an oddity, out-of-place, just like the first one. On the face of this church is a little half-circle window near the top of the pointed roof. Carlo told me it is a "site" window which points directly to and faces the remains, on a mountaintop in the distance, of a temple to Cibele. I kept my video camera rolling, but in this gloriously sunny day I suddenly felt I should meditate, facing the mountain.

Oddly, my guides asked me to do a specific "opening" procedure that involves visualizing a cross of white light intersecting my body, after which I raise my vibration up to meet my Guides. This was odd to me because until this point I recognized this as part of male, ceremonial magic, but it was also an action of "raising up" the vibration, so I agreed. For some reason, as I was done making this sign, I happened to look at my feet and see that I was standing exactly in the center of a cross of white stones laid into the cobblestones on the path!

And then it happened: I got "electrocuted" with an electric charge of white light that expanded me beyond anything I know how to describe. Beyond what Reiki attunements offer, beyond what I've felt through Mediumship. It was what I'd felt before from Cibele, but so much stronger. I was pure electricity. The closest way I can describe it is to liken it to when you fall in love…and you feel those tingles inside and out…and all your cells seem to open at their core and expand…and you become weightless…you don't even think about your body anymore, just the sensations you feel that make you aware your physical borders separating you from others have dissolved and you're flowing in this wave of love…and even when that person you love is not around, you dream they are…and you are alive in that dream somehow…maintaining a sense of expansion…and hope and love for just being alive. It's true that it feels like being in orgasm from head to toe that doesn't end-but make no mistake, this is not an earthly orgasm stimulated in response to a person; it doesn't have an earthly conclusion. It's rather it's the natural feeling of our lower charkas blended with the highest Universal love. This is not human love, this is Divine. This is one way to describe how I felt, but there was no person who was the object of love, I was just feeling a love for being alive. I'd felt this before: Cibele. I understand why she is misunderstood. I could see drums and bells and women dancing in circles. This is strong: walking around as this beaming energy could easily make people who were not aware of what's happening, to want to express, with great affect, what they were feeling, because it's the way life usually does not feel. This is being in love with being. This is feeling the source. Nothing matters in this state of expanded love and bright light except to be. This was my transmission. I'd already learned the marks and the secret invocation and the Mediumship at other times, and now, in this triangle, this was the Great Mother Goddess deciding I was ready: this was the Spirit World choosing me. When Carl picked me up he was a little alarmed. *"Karyn, are you ok? You are electric!!!"*

That night, after a spectacular pizza, I asked Carlo to leave me alone at the first church, the haunted one. This would be the only night I'd be able to do so, and it happened to be a full moon. He reluctantly agreed, worried that I might get caught by the police. As we drove up, there was a solitary candle burning, so I asked Carlo if this was something someone regularly did, considering this church wasn't used, to which Carlo replied, *"They only burn a candle on November 2nd, the day of the dead. They must be expecting you,"* (it was June). I did indeed feel invited, so I was not worried.

I waited alone in the dark, nowhere to go. Though it's a full moon, it's beyond the trees now and I'm a lot of darkness. Behind the one-room "church" was dense forest, whose darkness absorbed my cellphone light, so I turned it off, and my phone wasn't getting service anyway. There was the road, which was right up against the "front door." I was instructed to hide from any cars that would come by. Over the other side of road was the railroad tracks then the Sabato river, where the "Janara" witches allegedly held their "Sabba" in the past…And then, I felt them.

One by one, dozens by dozens, I felt the presence of what must have been hundreds of spirit people. Due to the work I've done as a Medium, and having died once already, there's much I've experienced and little that scares me. But on this night, in this very palpable moment, I felt fear. And then I felt terror. But I also noticed that not one spirit was trying to hurt me nor scare me, and none were moving towards me past the place where they initially appeared. I knew they wanted me to feel this, and they wanted to speak with me.

I feel this wild, feminine, Goddess energy, and also the women. Very intimate, just between women. It feels like this is a place of sexual healing for women, a safety in being wild and free just among women. Now that I'm here in the dark, I also feel their somber sadness, and they tell me,

"As women we have to live so much of our lives alone, whether we are with a family or a lover…so much of our inner world must remain unspoken if things are to be easy, especially with the emotions…a woman's world of emotions is vast and undulating and serpentine…our bodies are like radios picking up all these energies in response to the environment around us…if only we'd listen to them more and accept they are trying to guide us instead of feeling a sense of struggle to release our emotions, worried that if we release them they will be problems for others and trouble for us…often we feel a sense of loss doing that publicly, like we are letting go of our power as they fall on deaf ears and cold ears…letting go of our own vitality…we forget our emotions are our vitality because we are always getting the message that our emotions are something we need to keep hidden and contained, that we need to not express them for the sake of other people…it's a sad and lonely kind of fate for women…we all struggle to find women with which we can unify and feel close to…because we know as women we have times where we all struggle, where we feel there's never enough to go around, that there's never safety, never what we need to really be free."

But out here in this land, I feel these women have found the secret to be free: some of them were forced to, forced out of their homes and had to live alone in nature. Talk about a terrifying way of being vulnerable and exposed. But these women found a way to do it, and found a true power in that way. They had to walk into terror…walk and be hunted…walk into the groves…try to survive. Those women had to walk into their fear, they had to truly be alone, with all of their emotions, with whatever it was they could do to survive. And in that, they found each other, a circle and community of women. And the Spirit World helped them. And this is the legacy we have of women moving forward; trying to be our authentic selves, and still maintain a sense of community. Because our world is an internal one, we can raise our vibration up from one of need and one that puts us more in the power of our femininity, to come to trust and rely on our instincts. The more we trust them the more we can trust them, as we become more fully ourselves in face of all the change around us

When I listened, they told me they were hunted women. They told me the nature and the darkness had protected them and gave them shelter, but at first they had to walk into that darkness and into their fears, all alone, into their terror, and let go of everything they had… only then the illusions of the world fell away. They told me that's where a woman's power is: walking straight into her terror, into her fears, and into her emotions. These feelings are what connect us all as human beings. They are part of what makes us so alive. And if you're alive now, it's your time.

The Legendary Walnut

The next day, Carlo drove me back to the first church so I could jump the barrier and cross the railroad tracks (without getting caught by the military police hopefully) and make my way down to the Sabato River. The Sabato river is perhaps the most mysterious and legendary rivers of all the witch legends in Italy. I've been looking at this river for a couple of years now and I can't wait to feel the powerful waters. I hope to cross the river to find some walnut trees that have allegedly regrown from the original one. The waterline has recessed from what it once was, as have many water sources in Italy. In Liguria I climbed a "mountain" so high I couldn't see people on beach below, and yet the "mountains" were not hard rock at all but crumbly, dusty pink sandy-like stone embedded with seashells: this was once all underwater. Diana's Mirror, or her lake "Lago di Nemi" as well, no longer rests at the temple ruins as it once did, but has receded and been manually drained a few times before being refilled.

As I walk, following the railroad tracks that move with the seemingly impenetrable wall of nature protecting the river below, I can hear the noise of the waters. I try to push into the brush but it seems that the drop is a sheer cliff wall, and I decide it's too risky. While I could get down, perhaps, how would I get back up? I try again and again and it seems to be the same thing. But I refuse to give up. I'm just so happy to be here. I decide to keep walking and I keep filming my walk when suddenly I notice a walnut shell in-between the tracks. I pick it up and put it in a bag and keep walking…till I find another and another…and I notice someone has left me a trail. There are no walnut trees here, and in fact there are no trees close to this wall on my left side which rises up into the road, the railroad tracks are clear of plants, and there's the wall of nature, more than 6 feet away, on my right side. And yet, as I keep walking, I find more walnut shells until suddenly there is a pile of them! I crouch down, gathering the pile, and look t my right: there, on the lowest point at the grass, is a small arch of just enough space to be an opening. I decide to go look and I can see that the "cliff" here is more sloping. I decide I will descend this, and I get on my belly and begin to crawl like an army soldier into this brush. There seems, once inside of the dense plant life, to be a faint trail that has many branches grown over it, but I decide to follow its twists and turns and eventually snake my way down to the river! Once I get down there, a small patch of sand is waiting for me at the water's edge…with a solitary walnut shell resting there.

While the other side of the river was impossible for me to get to without a boat due to the deep and rough waters, as for the Legend of the Walnut being there? Well it's true that the walnut shells led me here, I have the video to prove it. And this was enough for me. I remained here for a couple hours, just singing into nature around me. I left an egg-shaped pyrite as a gift, and I laid some onyx eggs as remembrance gifts from other Americans to Janare of the past, and to the nature here now.

Carlo and Jenny discovered this "womb" of the Goddess reflected in Italy's nature and generously brought me here, and I was renewed, regenerated, here, just like ancient Divine Feminine art claims her energy will do.

Fifteenth Secrets

The Weather

A phenomenon that became a topic of conversation during my criss-cross travels through Italy would be the ominous fog ("la nebbia") and drizzling rain that would follow me everywhere.

Before arriving in Italy, Italians repeatedly told me "you made a great choice to arrive in May, it's absolutely the best weather Italy has to offer." That is, until 3 days before my arrival when I was told that a storm was coming to Liguria, which would remain for two months, and it would follow me around all of Italy.

The first time I came to Italy, I was almost stranded in Germany while awaiting my connecting flight because there was too much fog for my small plane to leave the ground. This time, I was worried about the same thing. In fact, in when we, slightly delayed, ascended into the night skies in the little Air Italia business plane from Munich , just as soon as the stewardess began to wheel out the drink service, she wheeled it back, stumbling, unable to perform the service. The captain asked us to all "hold on for a very bumpy flight." The small plane bounced and shook and tossed about more than it flew. It was both incredible and terrifying to look out the windows and see blackness and then a swarm of slithering and strange narrow stripes of cloud formations. In swirling tones of grey smoke like the "cartoonish" Tibetan cloud depictions in religion paintings, these were real and most unusual. They reminded me of witches on brooms, and as soon as I had that thought I could hear their cackling voices and see faces smiling at me, daring me to enjoy this out-of-control plane ride.

I felt my heart swell and tears streamed down my face joyfully: the Ladies (as I call my Goddess guides) really got me here and now they were bringing me in! And finally, when I saw the lights of Genova's rolling hills, I knew I'd found my treasure In Italy again at last, where my heart has been since 2009.

This fog would follow me every day, and I came to love it. Sometimes people would joke and call it my "Fantozzi cloud." Everywhere I went I'd be told, "Karyn, the weather was great just yesterday before you arrived." I came to know the gloomy weather meant there was important work to be done, and there were important discoveries to be made. The only full day of sun to touch my skin was during a 3-train-connection day trip I took from Udine back to the eastern Ligurian region through Venezia.

Looking back this was, in fact, the same weather I would experience the year prior to returning to Italy, when I would run at night to the beach under the moon, or through the forest in the early morning mists. I lived near Ocean Beach at this time and lived like a nun, and this was when my daily morning and evening meditation times with the Goddesses and my devotional work with them began. This was a time of intense learning for me, when my Spirit guides were sending me initially confusing cross-cultural information about Italy's history.

Chapter 15:
"Goddesses in Italy"

"Vedermi
nella luna,
al sole,
tra gli alberi,
nella pietra,
nella tua riflesso"

-Karyn Crisis

Italy's Feminine Divinities

In Italy there is not one singular Goddess and God pair that is accepted throughout Italy. Nor is there a God and Goddess couple in Italy's shamanism. The Goddess/the Grande Dea/The Grande Madre is not connected to a male partner. Throughout Italy, whether in modern Catholic religion or in the pagan past, Goddesses and Gods are quite separate. In Italian churches, there are paintings of male saints and other "godly" deemed men along with, sometimes, angels. But within this masculine representation there are rarely women present. In some churches I visited, such as in Campania, the only art was representational statues and paintings of Mary, the Divine Feminine, sometimes depicted with her baby. There are also many religious processions, such as the Riti Settenali in Guardia Sanframondi, a religious ritual which takes place every 7 years, where a Mary statue is venerated as a Goddess with healing powers, but she is not partnered with a male. This goes also for other cultural Goddesses who had passionate followings in Italy such as Egypt's Iside (Isis) who was worshipped alone without Orion and Phrygia's Cibele who had no male god counterpart. Diana was only connected with Italy (and sometimes male Gods) during the Roman and church-coming-into-power period that led to the Inquisition, when marriages were being arranged to form relationships into binary "male-female" structures, and the paganisms also followed this structure of pairing the Goddess with new male gods. Someone(s) somewhere along the times have written stories, as myths, of Goddess and Gods paired like marriage partners, but in Italy this is not expressed in the visual propaganda which dominated the public perception and was relied upon more than storylines. The myths seem to be disregarded. There are also other Madonnas, but those belong to a separate category of religion, just as magic is another thing.

The most commonly embraced Divine Feminine figure among Lineage healers (called "streghe" witches by some and not others, called "guaritori-segnatori" in some regions and not in others) is the Grande Dea or Grande Madre, and she is accepted in a more formless state, being the most anciently "named" Divine Feminine figure. Italian people also haven't tried to make her fit into a specific form, which I find to be a wonderful thing. Our human need to define and delineate and categorize everything to make us feel "comfortable" that "we know" limits our learning, especially with the Spirit World. In Italy, you won't find a statue of the Grande Madre wearing stylish Roman clothing, nor with a modern hairstyle, looking like the many Roman statuary depictions of the Goddess Diana. In Roman art, Diana is depicted as being a beauty, sometimes wearing war armor with sword drawn and with a dog at her side, or a lady with many breasts: always some very modern human depiction that is like a lady from a fashion magazine of the times.

But among the minds of the Lineage healers of today, they let her be whomever she is and they don't try to give her a specific form nor force her into an idea that makes them comfortable. There is an innate understanding that "she" is as big as the entire Universe, and while the Universe has energetic shapes that are parallel in the earthly human body, this doesn't mean we have to force her into our idea of what she should look like.

This is why, in order to understand Italian witchery you absolutely must come to Italy and walk on the land. Avoid the tourist areas and let yourself walk in nature…and just listen. Walk around small villages, eat the food, and just be. Listen to people talking to each other on the trains. Let the locals watch you walking around and wave to them. Don't look for anything, this is the secret in Italy, to just accept what is and go with the flow. In this way, you let your heart lead the way, and it begins to beat with the pulse of nature, and in this connection you will come to understand.

This can be the antithesis to our American way of life where we have to work hard to find what we're looking for; we push ahead, we seek and search, we boldly explore…as we try to find our roots. But we can also stop our learning process too early by a need to know, to define, to encapsulate, to name. Honestly, ask yourself, if once you know what "to call" something or someone," do you often just relax, thinking to yourself "now I know" ? And in knowing "the name," do you then stop wondering? Or do you let the person or place behind the name and behind the concept make itself know *to you*….?

Indigenous Goddesses

Being that Goddesses are Spirit guides and can therefore visit whomever they choose anywhere, (they are not relegated to a village or a country), it's even a little silly talking about "Italian Goddesses," but since Goddesses did appear in all cultures, and those cultures gave them names, it's important to make a distinction of what an "indigenous Italian Goddess" is. There are many "Roman" Goddesses, which have been re-named from other sources. The Greeks, Romans, and the Church used propaganda in their businesses, so it became important for them to homogenize "things" by naming them. During the Inquisition in fact, the Goddess was talked about in her older terms, but it was the church who gave this mysterious woman the name "Diana," because Diana was the en-vogue Goddess for the Romans at the time. In Italy, the names for their indigenous Goddesses are more like "descriptions" related to her purpose and the way she provides, how she appears to people, and what she does. The less we understand a name, the better, because that means it's many steps closer to our original founding expression of Feminine Divinity:

- Lady of the Game
- The Good Lady
- The Lady of the Night
- Lady of the Perennial Year

- Good Things
- Abundance

The Goddesses we could say who are Indigenous to Italy and their "names" make this clear and are consistent and in alignment with other ways of 'naming' things in Italy connected with the Goddesses and their gifts of curing traditions: For example, healers have simple names for what they do: fire cutters and sciatica cutters are what male healers in Corsica call their method to cure the pain of sciatica. "Making eyes," is what to call the cure for the "evil eye." If you ask other Lineage healers for the names of their cures, instead they tell you *what* they cure: "fuoco di San Antony, verrcuhe, vermi."

They don't have many technical names for healers either, among themselves, but rather call things by what they do. People call family Lineage healers often just "nonna"(grandmother) when it is the "nonna" who is curing, and it usually is an older woman. Guaritori-segnatori means "healers-scorers," referring to the ones who mark the affected body part with symbols as part of the cure. Things just simply "are," and whenever you find a name of a Goddess that sounds like a modern woman's name, it's a modern invention. When you find a technique that has a name similar to another modern modality, it's modern.

As Italian witchery naturally developed through daily connection with the Spirit World, which is alive in the Lineage healers today, Italy's Goddesses appeared naturally throughout time and for natural purposes: They are providers, helpers, givers of knowledge, teachers of cures, givers of protection…and largely, often fiercely, they are protective over feminine energy. This is basically what Italian Lineage healers are too.

There are many Goddesses in Italy in general, because the history of this land is so long. There are also Goddesses from other countries who've enjoyed impassioned followings in Italy. This is due to people experiencing them "reaching down to earth," being communicated to form them with and experiencing them ecstatically. These Goddesses are not myths and legends but real, living consciousness in the Spirit World. Their purpose is to be abundant providers for the people. And they have been, and they still are. This is something profound the Christian religion modeled their God after, as a "provider," but no one was experiencing this directly, and priests and pastors claimed to be the ones "in touch" with God, while the regular people were left waiting and wanting.

Human beings naturally believe in what they can touch, in what they can experience, and it's true in Italy that many Goddess [sub]cult[ures] were very difficult for the church to stamp out, even with torture, and that's because people were experiencing the abundant, providing assistance of Goddesses, and often many at the same time.

A Modern Re-modeling

On the other hand, what is most readily available in terms of information about Goddesses is a jumbled compilations of stories created by the Greeks and Romans which supplant original Divine Feminine ones with new ideas about male leaders and "male gods as source of all life." These stories often retain some hints as to the original Goddess symbols, so as a means of attaching a truth to a new story and adding some relevance. Examples are: "gods" being born from "stones." In nature, this is not possible, but we know that stones and water were considered to be parts of nature with Divinely Feminine attributes: water was considered life-giving, and since the female mothers as Goddesses-brought-down-to-earth have life-giving fluids produced in their bodies (and the spiritual statues mark these places: eyes, mouth, breasts, vulva. Stones were used as "markers" for Divinely Feminine abundance, to built temples with, to point to rivers and water sources, to hold water with well constructions, and more. So in Greek and Roman myth, we see stories that pervert nature so as to make room for the "male supernatural" tale.

It's necessary to consider that, in the bigger picture, the Greeks and Romans are not that ancient and that, more importantly, they borrowed their spiritual symbols, myths, and ideas in-part from the original Divine Feminine spirituality of their predecessors. They used the parts they agreed with and collaged them into their new male philosophies and binary gender moralities. It's also significant to note, regarding the "age" of the Greeks and Romans, that myths and folktales began changing shape before they added their ideas, because of the patriarchal invasions that spread through Old Europe even before they joined the ranks of the new male philosophy that was being spread.

So while the patriarchy already began changing original symbols and their meanings, the Romans continued to masculinize all representations of earlier Goddesses and tried to cover up the evidence by taking over symbols and changing their meanings. Roman spirituality was enmeshed with Roman emperor propaganda and war. Therefore, continuing a process begun by invading patriarchal tribes, the Romans created gods and goddesses to support their efforts of invading and conquering.

In contrast, the original symbolic language from the Goddess is connected to nature and visually represents a parallel to nature, so there's no complicated code-breaking method needed to decipher their meaning). In this way, trying to trace a myth or story back to its original roots would be very difficult. The male leaders wanted to be seen as the source of the universe, so all their efforts to propagandize this would have to lead to this central idea, covering up anything that would hint at its derivative nature.

In this marketing scheme, anyone would think the Greeks and Romans were the originators of Divine discovery. While the earlier Divine Feminine spiritual practices came from the Spirit World as gifts to the earthly world (and therefore based on experience versus creations of the mind) the Greek and Roman ones were collages of stories and new philosophical thought; they were creations used to promote ideas, along with the propaganda of Emperors often coupled with the "support" of a mythological god. They were very stylish and targeted towards supporting war and invasions and other male directives.

The earlier Divine Feminine spiritual practices, symbols and language came from peoples' direct experience with the Spirit World, so the shapes, symbols, language, temple shapes, burials, and knowledge were given from the Spirit World to the earthly one...and as a result, they symbolic language from Italy and Old Europe at this time looks similar to other shaman practices around the world. There are few human attributes put onto the statuary.

Shamanism imagery from around the world, as it does in Italy's history, incorporates animal parts, plant parts, symbols such as spirals and triangles and chevrons, water and mountains, all pointing to the Great Mother Goddess' ability to give life through the earthly female body. All male created religions have a consistent man-only figure who gives life to all and punishes his "children" frequently."

"The language was tampered with in late Minoan times when invaders from Central Asia began to substitute patrilinear for matrilinear institutions and remodel or falsify the myths to justify the social changes. Then came the early Greek philosophers who were strongly opposed to magical poetry as threatening their new religion of logic."[243] And while myths over time became so very muddled and confused, author Robert Graves claims, *the study of mythology is based squarely in tree-lore and seasonal observation of life in the fields which points to the Great Mother Goddess. Myths frightened or offended him [Socrates] and Socrates, in turning his back on poetic myths, was really turning his back on the Moon-goddess who inspired them."*[244] And the tree symbolized the Column of Life of the Goddess: the connection between "earth and the stars."

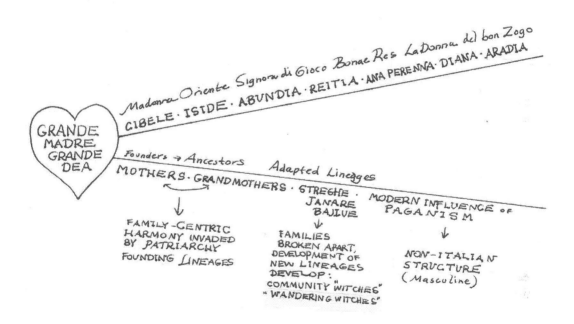

The Great Mother Goddess has created a lineage; a family tree parallel to our human lineages on earth as it is in "heaven") We have great great grandmas, great great grandmas, grandmas, mothers, daughters, grandchildren..and onward, who perpetuate the lineage of a family. Our founding mothers became the Ancestors who also helped guide the great great grandmas. And, your great great grandma likely would have some trouble understanding your current modern world. Her ideas and philosophies would still have valuable messages for you, but her practical advice may be different...not better nor worse, but partly a result of her environment, just different and likely not as applicable to your life in these days.

While all the Goddesses ultimately have the same purpose: to provide and teach, and they all come from same great Grande Dea, in order to perpetuate the lineage and for her offerings to adapt to modern times, she has different "children" or Agents, or "assistants," as I like to call them, appearing in every culture, in many periods of time. As humans, The Divine Feminine knows we are attached to physical form and seeks it representation even in the Spirit World. So, the way she makes us aware of Goddesses often is to make us interested in many symbols such as animals or cultural ideas that trace themselves back to "forms" of Goddesses. These are the "invitations."

Perhaps the best way to learn is through an interview I did with an Italian mother I met after one of my "Italy's Witches and Medicine Women" Lectures at Brid's Closet in Cornwall, New York. After the lecture Jessica Hoch Reilly contacted me through the internet asking me about the name "Ana Perenna."

Karyn: Jessica, would you briefly introduce yourself?

Jessica: *I was raised Catholic, then became a born again Christian, but I realized neither religion answered my questions of who are these [spirit] people walking in my room at night? And who are these [spirit] people talking to me?" That led me ultimately to my path. I did a lot of reading on Celtic practices, Wicca, and wound up just saying 'ok I'm pagan. I'm a Medium, I'm just going to go with it."*

But I let all that go when I had my baby 9 years ago, but after that I then found myself drawn to the Egyptian goddess Sekhmet, and that just opened everything again for me. I began reconnecting with the Pagan community, I started studying with a woman who started teaching me about ancestor worship and shamanism and things I was already doingbut I had no idea [what to call what] I was doing. So I became formally connected to my ancestors in a way that I hadn't before and that's where I am now.

Karyn: So you were a natural Medium, born sensing the Spirit World. That's exciting to me. And then at a certain point Sekhmet became present.

J: *Lion is my totem, and I've always been fascinated with all things Egyptian, so I was getting the nudge form her from a very long time without recognizing it. So when I finally accepted I was drawn to this goddess, eventually what I know now I was chosen by her to be one of her daughters, and she's helped me through so many times in a short period working with her, so she's the catalyst for where I stand today, a lot of the changes I've been through.*

K Fantastic, so she introduced herself to you.

J: *Yes. One of those things, I wasn't ready at first, I shut my things down with the kids, to not deal with spiritual things. But then I was feeling stagnant and things needed to change and that's when I needed to do something. She was there and guided me to where I am. She'd say 'You ned to go to this festival, you need to explore this...' She led me back into the path of working with my ancestors and mediumship, etc.*

K: So would you say your process of working with her is step-by step, where you were gradually aware of who she was and how she worked with you as she sent you synchronicities, for example?

J: *Yes I keep getting synchronicites. Lion-headed Goddess of Egypt kept popping up even in silly things like when I was reading a young adult novel, or talking to a friend who suddenly said one day, you know, there's a lion headed Goddess of Egypt.'*

Then when I was ready, I found a book from a temple in las vegas which spoke to me. I got the book and started doing the meditations and she [Sekhmet] laughed at me during my meditation. She said 'Why are you doing this meditation? I'm already talking to you."

Karyn's Note [I didn't mention it in this interview because I didn't want to affect her flow of thoughts, but the same thing happened to me with Archangels, with Aradia, with Diana, Iside and Cibele. In each case, these "ages" of Goddesses presented themselves to me forthe purpose of getting to understand who they are from the "inside" rather than from a book. When I did later read a book on Ceremonial Magic, for example, which gives a meditation on how to call in the 4 Directional Archangels (and which colors to imagine them wearing, etc) the Archangels were already around me and also laughed at me. They said 'We're already here, you don't need to dress us up in these silly clothes.' With the female Goddesses, each one of them appeared naturally, but they also appeared during meditations or moon rituals, and when they did, they always tossed aside my ritual tools and books I was reading invocations from, and told me things were "child's play" for them. So J's story really excited me because it shows that when the Spirit World reaches out to you, it may look more natural than you expect, and also be more magical…because you come to realize this consciousness is alive, she is not a "concept" nor an "archetype," but someone very alive in-the-moment like you and I are. Tools and rituals can be helpful to get us started on a path, but they shouldn't necessarily be held onto, especially if they prevent you from receiving communication with the real living consciousness the ritual is supposed to be about.]

K: The reason I was asking is that's been a lot of my experience..so it's important to share that with people who are naturally mediumistic, there is always that trust of what you're experiencing and then the worry of 'Am i making this up?' and 'Is it really true'. ? I find the path to be subtle, so you have to really pay attention to the synchronicities while the spirit person or Teacher or Goddess tries to help you understand who they are from these experiences, and that's also a way for you to learn how to trust this communication with them. So it;s important to share because often people I work with get discouraged that they don't see the name of their Guide or Goddess in big flashing lights. They expect to be able to know everything at once, but it's more subtle and gradual than that. The relationship is built through a process of trust, and the teachings come through a process of unfoldment…one bit of learning at a time.

J: *Yes there were times I thought 'I must be crazy.'*

K: Another important thing you mentioned is that you were led to shamanism. Do you feel like Sekhmet led you to that practice?

J: *She led me to the people I needed to talk to. I had no idea and couldn't even tell you what shamanism was. I met my teacher who I was studying with, and for me it was the connection with her [Sekhmet]. I wouldn't even have gone to the festival period, if Sekhmet hadn't told me this is where I needed to be. So she led me in away. I can't formally say I'm a shaman, but I'm getting there.*

[Karyn's Note : this is an important statement because Jessica is living this experience from the inside-out: naturally born, naturally connected with the Spirit World in various ways, and it's the Spirit World who teaches her and connects her with people, places, and things that help her grow and also identify who and what she is. It has been the same in my life: so many times people asked me 'Don't you know you're a shaman?' or 'Where did you learn that healing technique-it's shamanism,' when I'd use healing motions and actions that my Guides told me to use, not knowing there was a "name" for them. Italian Lineage healers are mostly the same, not knowing there are modern technical names for what they do, and likely never even having heard of shamanism as well.

K: Do you feel like the system of shamanism, I'm not asking you to qualify yourself a s shaman or not, but do you feel the system of shamanism feels very natural to you, like you're "remembering"?

J: *Not so much that I'm remembering but that it's very natural to me. When things are explained to me I realize 'Oh, I've been doing that all along.' It's just been a natural progression for me.*

K: Do you feel its'm more natural than applying a pagan system?

J: *I think I've always thought that we're all connected, it's just a matter of how you personally connect them or what resonates with you..whether Celtic or Wicca…I feel in the long run they're all the same.*

[Karyn Note: This statement made me very excited to read. Often women who come to work with Goddesses who have a reputation for being very ancient come to learn, from these Goddesses, the connecting threads , the commonalities between all practices, so they can eventually recognize other "daughters-in-the-making." There are many similarities but also significant differences: the differences tend to be those that simply reflect the "powers that be" at the time re-modeling older ideas in a way they are more comfortable with. This is the path of a different kind of teacher, a teacher who has come to know many specific styles of spiritual practices as well as the roots of all practices globally. After all, the Great Goddess Mother is a worldwide provider.]

K: Would you say with paganism are there certain aspects which make you feel really comfortable or resonate with you, and if you feel connected to specific path, or just the wider field?

J: *For me, just the wider field. In the beginning what attracted me was the structure , because I was coming from the Catholic religion where the priest does this on Sunday. So it made a lot of sense to me in the beginning that you put your "athame" (ritual blade) here, and this action there..so the structure of it called to me, but in the long run I couldn't thrive in the structure, which is why I had to seek other aspects.*

K: In shamanism, as you're exploring and learning about it, could you describe a few things about it that resonate with you?

J: *It's a lot easier for me to understand the concept of, from what I've learned, working with my ancestors, and respecting the earth, and healing, because I also started out doing a lot natural healing. So all that really worked with who I am and the freedom to do it my way. I feel like shamanism gives you more options, but again what really I've been working towards is dream shamanism. Otherwise I've been having a lot of discussion and theory discussion with my teacher. Since I'm a kid I've done the lucid dreaming thing. I'm very aware of what is a "message" versus what's not a "message," and what to pay attention to. Now that I'm studying I realize maybe I didn't pick something up back then, but it makes more sense now. Now I make dreaming into a purpose by asking questions before I go to sleep to actively work through my sleep instead of just letting it happen.*

K: At what point did you feel Ana Perenna and become connected to her?

J: *I had a DREAM. I went to sleep and I had a lucid dream and in the dream I was in a village or camp town. A giant sled with a donkey came down from the sky. We all knew it was an angry deity that was coming to punish us for no real reason. And when the donkey hit the ground it became an old man in a donkey skin vest. He was handing out punishments. Some severe and some not as harsh. When it was my turn he wanted me to "buy" all these random items from him and it would cost me all the money I had. I was looking at this wad of money and responding 'This is all I have, my family won't be able to eat,' and things like that, refusing to hand him the money. All the while he was getting angrier and angrier, and I didn't want to accept the punishment that he handed towards me because I didn't think it was fair. And then I remember the whole sky started to glow and vibrate and the clouds were making a whirlpool. I looked up and raised my hand and said "I call you Anna." Then the clouds created a cone of energy and it came to me: I was 'possessed' by Anna. I then pointed at the donkey man and then moved him with that same cone of energy, into a tree. I then turned him into a cocoon, which shriveled him up from man-size to cat-size. And I said "Now you'll stay there until you become a better person and learn not to be a bully."*

So then I started doing some research on Italian Goddesses named Anna, because I knew she was Italian and I knew that it wasn't me who did that, because that's not what I do. The research was limited, so I wound up finding "Ana Perenna's" name, that she was a Goddess but a Goddess of the people.

[Note: Jessica's comment in an important one: often people who believe in angels at the same time believe they are "off limits: because they "belong to God," not realizing their purpose is to help us on earth understand who were are as spirits and souls, in other words, how to be "of energy and of the earth" at the same time. Goddesses also are not for the myths and the Emperors-they are living conscious helpers for women and the men and other genders who are receptive to them. So Goddess were not for "temples and temple-worship" only; Goddesses were reaching into earth to the poor and uneducated women especially, to empower them. Often paganism's rituals often set their Goddesses and Gods "off limits" to people besides their designated High Priestess and Priest, just as the church places God "off limits" to everyone but the priests or preachers.]

K: What I can tell you is that when you talked about peasant people calling on her for protection, that this is the proper way to describe her relationship with people. She is what I like to call an "Agent" of the Great Mother Goddess. In Italy what you find out the further you go back in history is that there was both a matrilinear aspect to culture (tracing the family through the females) and a gylanic way of living (genders living in harmony with each other and without hierarchies. Women were given the secrets of the Universe but they cared for everyone's needs with them). The shared belief was that everything came from the Great Mother Goddess, who was simply called Grande Dea or Grande Madre. Her appearance was formless. Spiritual art depicted how her energy moved both in the Universe and on earth through people (women's bodies) animals, and plants, and even men.

But the Great Mother Goddess, in order to adapt to growing and changing cultures, sent out "agents," or helpers from her own lineage in forms that could be recognized by women, because heir purpose was to help women when they were under duress from patriarchal invasions and religious oppression in addition to their original purposes of assisting with: childbirth, curing, planting and harvesting. So from this larger female force came there were a variety of smaller Goddesses who were focused into more graspable purposes: assisting women in childbirth, teaching women how to cure with the herbs growing around them, teaching women how to plant and harvest flowers and food, and more.

Likewise the pre-pagan Divine Feminine "Agents" of the Great Mother Goddess" who were sent to help women during oppressive times in culture had simple names such as "Ana Perenna" which means: PERENNIAL, as in the origins of a new year, spring time, the beginning of the year and of vegetation. She was connected with celebrations of the ides of March and the Roman New Year. I was confused at first hearing "Anna," because the indigenous Goddesses in Italy tend to not have modern sounding female names. In this case, her name is "Ana, Perenna" of the Latin per annum, and that offerings were made to her "ut annare perannareque commode liccat" ("that the circle of the year may be completed happily"). She was [also known as Bel, who was a masculinization of the Sumerian Goddess Belili [...] so also the god Anu, a masculinization of the Sumerian Goddess Anna-Nin. Parts of her name are also associated with meanings of "heaven" "mother" "the fruitfulness," and "the fruitful (abundant) Mother."[244] While popularized by Romans, she is considered to be from the Etruscan culture[245] which has ancient roots in the area where Turkey is now located. In Ireland, Ana is known as "guardian of the dead."[246]

Being an ancient, pre-pagan Goddess she is associated with important markers of how Divine Feminine energy moves in the earthly world: through water and eternal vegetation, as protection, through stones, mountains, food, trees, and fountains. In the Parioli Mountains in Rome she was linked to water and he passage of time. Most importantly, and simply said: She is a provider: in whatever way the people, especially women, need help: cures, healing, protection, birth assistance, protection, feminine autonomy, planting, harvesting. Goddesses help the common person, not the powers not the military nor the authority or rich. This is another similarity between paganism and Christianity: the "middle-man" of a priest or a "high priest" standing between "the people" and the Divinity.

Years ago, when I was teaching Mediumship classes, I created a class for reading messages through "Psychometry," reading information through "psychic touch," based on the belief that items carry a memory and the energy of who has been in contact with them. I created a little aluminum strip for people to write a question with a wooden stylus. Of course, the message wouldn't be legible: it could even just have a symbol as its carving. More importantly it was to implant the object with a person't energy. Then, everyone rolled up their sheet metal carved messages, put then into envelopes, and into a basket. Then everyone would draw one out of the basket without knowing whose it was, so as to truly "blind test" their ability to read the energetic imprint. I was inspired by a brief National Geographic two-paragraph article about lead cylinders found at the bottom of a well with coiled rolls of prayers asking for protection and also curses against who a person wanted protection from. I didn't realize at the time, because the article did not state it, that these were found in the fountain dedicated to Ana Perenna. These curses are called "incantesimi e maledizione, magici e defixiones." These are not things from the Divine Feminine shamanism, but these practices were present in Rome at the time and were a large part of magical daily life. Magic is another thing.

K: What excited me, Jessica, about you bringing up your symbolic dream and the fact that you're a natural Medium is that you're connecting the way people naturally were connecting to the Goddess, in the older times, when the Goddess chose the people, the people didn't chose the Goddess. In general, all we can find about these connections are small references written by the ones documenting history (which were men) , so we find a lot of the documentations are reductive.

Her purpose is to provide what you need in the moment. She, along with other Goddesses like her, were really Providers, Protectors..everything the Christian faith (and other religions) claim their God is . The difference is that people experienced the Goddesses; help regularly and simply..like you, but no one was experiencing the Christian God. And this is still how it happens now, today. So the idea the Christians built their God, they built him in the image of the Goddess. They literally had business meetings that took place over time to organize this. They modeled their concept based on something "supernatural" that was already in existence.

The further back in time you look for depictions of the Goddesses, or as you look into the Spirit World, the more formless they become and therefore the more expansive their energy and power. They do maintain, however, a specifically feminine energy as helpful guides and teachers, and the greater body of them are female. They're all about learning together in earthly-Spirit World partnerships. They provide information directly and through synchronicity and dreams, unfolding a path that puts the puzzle pieces together. While they are unconditionally loving they can be very tough, very strong, and at times ruthless about protecting feminine energy. They all want women and female-identified people to be autonomous and empowered.

Even if their original symbols are no longer relevant in their original form in our cultures, they will still use them to give you a trail to follow and to recognize them (whether colors, shapes, animals who've been associated with them, cultural clothing) . They will find you naturally, not in ritual. In fact in my experience they often scoff at ritual and all the modern tools like candles and ritual blades and other objects…but, because they understand our connection with physical objects, l they will teach you their rituals (which usually they take care of, which means they bring you into ecstatic trance). The rituals I have experiences contain very few "items:" fire in a metal pot or from a hearth, menstrual blood, water, herbs and plant stems from the surrounding land. The majority of the "ritual" takes place ecstatically (energetically) bringing the Spirit World into the earthly one, and the earthly person into the Spirit World. There are many Spirit guides present and one singular earthly female.

Spirit can reach through anything…not tools are needed. But because we are occupied with physical world, and we notice when physical changes occur or when another person confirms what we are thinking, the Goddesses do work with what catches your particular eyes. Witchery has no ritual nor ceremony…the Goddess is a provider like "god" is supposed to be, and she is available daily and in every situation. Paganism, in contrast, created ceremony and ritual and procession for the public and as a formula to try to repeat experiences. Italian witchery is about the Goddesses being available to the people whereas Paganism's pantheon of partnered Goddesses and Gods are for the elite, select few to experience. The relationship of Grande Dea as Ana or Aradia is a private relationship. While it's common for modern day people to be drawn to ceremony, it's more important to pay attention to the subtleties in daily life and to ask questions that deepen our experience with the Goddess.

J: The thing is when you talk about with her, Sekhmet and Ana sound like the same people…

K:The Goddesses have specific bodies of knowledge, even through they are all connected and from the same source. They appear at different points in time, adapting to lifestyle changes, modern developments in culture, to help people where they are now, based on current needs. People do believe she is connected with Etruscans and Etruscan calendar. The Etruscans were known in Italy as a matrilinear and mysterious culture. They didn't write down most of their history, everything was orally transmitted, which means they were also a Mediumistic culture (like the Druids also).

Consider the interesting similarities in names here, as documented in the Italian language: "Culto DI ANA PERENNA and "Culto DI DIANA." Di Ana Perenna and Di Diana… DiAna

J: I found out there's a "strega" in my ancestry. She was the "strega" of the village. People would come to her but no one would would admit what she really was. She's been trying to get my attention for years, she's been trying to teach me for years…so this is like my first lesson [our talk] because other than my ancestor I have no reference. This is what led me out to Bernadette's,..the connection of it is very interesting. [Karyn note: Bernadette Montana owns Brid's Closet, a witch shop in Cornwall, NY who hosted the debut of my "Italy's Witches and Medicine Women" Lecture part 1 and subsequent workshops.]

K: One other thing I thought it important to mention is that in earlier references Ana was connected the Sow (Pig) which in the foundational Goddess spiritual shamanism language was a symbol of the renewal of life: pregnancy, life comes again (regeneration) the moon because she's a Medium and connects with people through Mediumship which is truly the cornerstone of all this in the first place. And we see that even in the more modern Roman times, many of her associations were retained by the new myths, but they were just truncated and changed and limited to support and reflect the new male powers. Male figures of power rode on Donkeys… as in your dream.

Goddess and Forms

DIANA is a name synonymous with Italian "streghe" OUTSIDE of Italy. Within Italy, it truly depends upon which area you are in as to whether or not any Lineage healers or practicing "witches" consider her an Italian Goddess…or even consider her at all. Her following seems to be relegated to Liguria region, due to the Inquisition including her in trial documents, and in the deep south where many practices were brought over from Greece.

Even with all the information these Goddess spirit teachers had given me about the origin of Goddess, it was still shocking for me to meet Italian women who were creating real magic and who were not familiar with Diana as a Goddess or who laughed at the idea of Diana being something real. It was shocking for me not as a Medium, but from a cultural standpoint: there's not much information in American about Italian witchery, but the way it's been presented has been largely: "streghe+ Diana= Italian Witchcraft."

The Italian women were not, I should make clear, laughing at the Goddess: they explained that the name Diana and her modern image is seen as a Roman creation. Many women believe Diana is part of the Grande Dea, but they prefer, as mentioned before, a more formless Divine Feminine energy. Names that sound like regular women's names once again, do not mean much.

In the Ligurian region of Italy, as well as in Milano, there has been established a strange connection with Diana: from the Inquisition process of Sibilla and Pierina we have their confession, as Paolo mentioned, that they admitted to meeting with a Good Woman at night. This Good Woman was often accompanied by a procession of spirits. This Good Woman provided truthful information about cures to Pierina, and she gave "Good Things" to people whose houses she found clean and in good order (and we can assume this is didactic material for keeping oneself "energetically clean and organized, a teaching from Spiritualism and other forms of Mediumship). This "Lady of the Night" was not called Diana, but rather: Abundia, Satia, Signora del bon Zogo, Signora di Gioco, etc. It was the church who stamped the name "Diana" into this story because she was more popularly identifiable at the time: she had "marketing" behind her due to the Romans celebrating her as their "hunting Goddess." So as times modernized, people re-created their own cults bearing Diana's name. Diana, in her Spirit form, is considered in Italy to be from other lands, a "Madonna Oriente;" a Spirit Guide connected with an ancient traveling group of people who created circular stone structures in Ireland before the Irish even lived there. The Cult of Diana co-existed with Christianity in Devon as late as the 14th century, when the Goddess was worshipped in woodland shrines even by monks.[247]

Nevertheless, Diana is an important part of the Spirit guide Lineage of the Grande Dea. Her name is not important, but her energy is and connecting with her will open doors to even older more formless Goddess forms, and that is the point of the Goddess Lineage... to pull us back into what and who the Goddess is beyond the names given and the concepts formed by modern minds with directives. She is, in many ways, a "preparatory" teacher; offering unconditional love to seekers, drawing them into themselves for self-love and self-knowledge before moving more deeply into a Mediumistic connection with the Universe.

I visited Diana's Temple remains that were once on the shores of Lago di Nemi (Lake Nemi) also called "Speculum Dianae" (Diana's Mirror). Due to the receding waters, the temple is now surrounded by olive trees and ferns as wild nature reclaims the area. Oddly as well, her actual temple site is on a small patch of "public" land surrounded by a farmer's "private land."

What is more easily reachable in the remains are the square structures "in front." The remains of these walls are exposed and there are tarps strewn about the interior parts. I came here to leave prayers for her from people, and while while I loved each and every exposed brick I could touch, I didn't feel this was the actual temple, despite my friend insisting it was. I followed my nose past a sign that said "don't come in here" to a wall with little "cave-like" archways. I intuitively picked one that I felt was important and read everyone's prayers into the raw earth there, cried tears of their despair and pain into that soil, and buried their clay offerings there. I sneaked into the interior part of this area, where sadly a farmer is growing crops. This is the main temple area I would find out. At the exact point where I buried the tears into the earth, but inside the wall on the other side, is the place of the original altar for Diana. Despite this temple being build by men, I felt her loving embrace here.

I was inspired to come here after reading a passage in a book that I can no longer find, that told of women bringing clay effigies of body parts that needed healing and leaving them at the temple with their prayers. Women also came here asking for protection during childbirth. Diana seemed, from these accounts, to offer specific support for women. It seemed odd to me that then these temples were often "off limits" to average people and also to women.

Legend has it there as once an oak grove, a sacred "nemeton" protecting her temple, guarded by an escaped slave. Apparently anyone could become the protector, as long as they were an escaped slave and killed the previous protector. Allegedly also at this time period was the rumor that Diana was disgusted with men. While this is a very confused story, I have found it consistently true that energetically, spiritually, Diana protects the feminine energy, so that even men finding her appear to them in their meditations must surrender a certain amount of masculinity in order to receive her support and care. An "inner" death perhaps, but because the Goddesses provide abundance for the improvement of life the "murderous devotion" story seems unlikely. In truth, Diana is a Master Teacher and has nothing to do with war or killing animals. References to her being part of the "wild hunt" is actually symbolic language; a nod to her being a Medium, that she comes from the Spirit World. This is demonstrated in her many legends that portray her as making "processions through the forest at night" with a trail of "souls of the dead." The old legends claim the oak tree, the same tree sacred to the Druids and their mistletoe, was what composed the sacred grove here that protected the temple. I found no oak trees nor walnut trees here, only olive. I was not able to find any topographical information about this area from around the time the temple was built, which was over 2,000 years ago, nor any information about its more modern history of trees…at least, not yet. In Benevento, the longstanding legend says the Janara witches are connected to Diana. Silvio Falato also mentions that Diana has a bigger following in the north, and that in the north there is a Celtic population. He also refers to the Celts when talking about Benandanti. But in the south, the story is: "Janara+Diana, Streghe+Iside." But the Janare legend says they in fact gathered around walnut trees, and the most magical walnut tree of all. So, I can't substantiate the truth of these trees in the legends. However, Diana's spirit does come here, and this area is surrounded by olive trees. And during time In Tuscany, it would be through the olive trees that Aradia and Diana would teach me.

ISIDE (Isis)

Not long after I began training as a Spiritualism Medium under the guidance of a certified Medium Minister at a Bay Area Center chartered with the NSAC (National Spiritualist Association of Churches), I was giving public platform readings and healing demonstrations. The focus of Spiritualist training is to become adept at gathering specific information…so that life of the consciousness (spirit) can be proved to continue on after death of the physical body. In other words, it's a way to not only communicate with your ancestors, but also a scientific way to test the validity of these communications. So for example, if you are curious about your Aunt Joan in the "afterlife," I would communicate with her, and then present to you information that she would give to me: specific things like dates of birth and death are of course important, as well as city or state she lived in, and other factual details about her life such as names of relatives. Beyond data, other important identifiers are: personality quirks, favorite memories, mannerisms, objects of affection, perhaps personal jokes or hobbies and other emotional, intangible things about Aunt Joan.

For a period of time I did receive very factual information, but then my communications changed. Spirit people were communicating more deeply the personality aspects of themselves: their quirks: grudges, sense of humor, illness, mental weakness, regrets, sense of pride, favorite phrases, emotional insights and philosophies. Often I'd be told I would hold my body in the posture, of Aunt Joan, for example, or know what kind of clothing she preferred to wear, or make a facial expression that was distinctly hers, or know her favorite expressions and songs. I also always felt a great amount of emotion that signaled "we have made connection" and often a mix of joy and pain. Often I would be communicated very personal memories, beliefs, and also cultural traditions. My communications were really getting "inside" the personality of the spirit people, and deeply into their emotions…and I was able to sense all of these things about the earthly people I'd be giving the messages too. I would be able to see peoples' expansive possibilities; their potentials and talents…even in cases when the person I was reading for was someone I didn't personally like. This is due to the higher perspective of Spirit guides and relatives offered during this process: any spirit people who are loving and encouraging will encourage the positives. My public readings became quite popular.

And then, my reading styles were changed once again. Rather than communicating with relatives and friends who had passed on, I was being visited more frequently by cultural guides from around the globe, healers of different types, other philosophies and ancient people sharing their practices. This was also exciting to many people I gave readings to in public. I was often told "my grandmother was a shaman but, you know, we can't really talk about that here." In general, the Spiritualist community doesn't like to entertain talk of angels or Goddesses or any other spirit people who can't be substantiated as having lived on the earth before.

In my case, however, my teacher decided the quality of information coming through my messages was high quality and valid enough to "be allowed." This approval didn't come without embarrassment for me, however. While training in our traditional Spirit Circle, I gave many messages from Spirit guides of all sorts as well as from relatives and they were all validated by the receivers of those messages. During one class, however, our teacher asked us to connect with someone who had lived on earth who had passed…and to ask them what their death process was like and how life in the world of Spirit was compared to life on earth. Then, we'd share with the rest of the circle the information we received. The "person" who communicated with me was "Metatron," a person who was "turned into an angel." My teacher was visibly upset by this, and repeated his instructions to me, but I held my ground. The message I gave from "Metatron" was a beautiful one that was hard to argue with. The next week our teacher asked us to do the exact same exercise. Guess who appeared to me again? "Metatron!" So, out loud, in front of the circle, I had to admit this again, cringing at the criticism that would come my way. At the same time, I trusted my abilities and I trusted what I had been communicated. And, not along after this class was when I became a public platform reader for this Center.

And then soon after this, the Goddesses would present themselves to me and remain a part of my daily life. Anyone who has given a message to someone from the Spirit World has had doubts in the moment. No matter how clear and precise the message coming from the Spirit World is, no matter how full of emotion the communications are, there is always a worry of falling short or or a fear of just imagining things. But for me, after being aware of the Spirit World since childhood, and training as an adult, and now experiencing Goddesses (whom many people consider to be a myth) in the same way I experience Aunt Joan…everything was too consistent to be discredited. I was too far into this way of life to disbelieve it now, even though I continue to keep a skeptical mind full of questions. The Spirit World had truly opened the "veil" for me further and deeper with each step of trust I displayed, and I chose to honor our relationship even if it made me nervous.

First, Aradia and I consciously reconnected in Tuscany. I became aware after she first presented herself to me with visual form in Tuscany that I'd always felt her presence in my daily life, but now I had a specific reference point for "who" she is, and how she wanted to teach me (and how she chose to "look" to me). Aradia then brought Diana to me. I wondered at a lineage here, because the concept of Daughter and Mother seemed applicable but didn't quite fit…then Iside came into my meditations as part of this circle, also connected to Italy…along with Celts, Druids, and Scandinavians.

Iside appeared to me regularly after these beginnings, and showed me that she has a connection to Italy. I didn't understand this connection at first, but I accepted it, I accepted her. She was also pointing towards more black stones and water sources and serpents and trees, as did Aradia and Diana.

After my husband gave me Carlo Napolitano and Fabio Gruti's books, this became more clear. But, after I arrived in Guardia Sanframondi and then ventured into Beneveno, I'd see why:

"The "Cult" of Iside was brought to Benevento by Emperor Domeziano (Dometian) between 88 and 89 AD," Enzo Gravina would tell me during one of our interviews. "In my opinion, Domeziano basically fell in love with the Goddess Iside, and as Emperor he decided to devote his relationship to her in this way. Obviously this is my personal theory. Here in Benevento they found some remains yes, but they never knew where exactly the temple was. Whatever was found, as in traces of Iside, was found near the Traiano Arch. The important think about the Iside temple here in Benevento is: while in other places in Italy we find Iside artifacts, like Nemi, the pieces are findings coming from Egypt. Here in Benevento, the reality is different; they were made locally. So they don't know if they were made by Egyptian people who were brought here, or just by locals. Most probably there were people who could work that type of stone, so basically some Egyptians were here likely brought over by Domeziano. Benevento even has its own hieroglyphic: mountains that look like a face. All this stuff can inspire people to fantasize, but I'm a researcher and who studies, and for me fantasy is enemy of studies."

What's most interesting about the artifacts I got to see in Benevento, including a 3-D presentation by Giovanni Caturano which presented some of the elements of Iside's temple, is that even in these patriarchal assemblages that pay homage to Egypt's Iside are preserved some of the most ancient symbols tied to the Grande Dea: the bull, the moon crescent, water, ship or boat, chevron design, the sistrum and serpents, …as well as an autonomous feminine existence.

Lingering within Iside's statuary depictions in Benevento show her "age" in the Goddess Lineage to be much older than the Roman remodeling of Diana (who is certainly older than the Roman period, it's just that during this period she was given the name "Diana," so we can identify her modern reappearance under this modern name as coming from post-patriarchal invasion times.

The clothing in the Benevento temple artifact remains displays a figure wearing a dress with a particular knot falling in the heart center area of the chest, with fabric on each side making a specific chevron pattern. This is known as the "Isaic knot." What is significant about it is that in the founding psychic symbolic language if the Divine Feminine shamanism, female statuary was depicted the three phases of life cycles of nature; statuary was not attempting to capture a reflection of physical anatomy: breasts and buttocks were enlarged to show what cycle of life the Great Mother's energy was moving through the earthly female's body. When "death" of the physical body was being depicted in these statuary forms, the body was carved our of bone and white marble to look stiff, like a cross, with a masked face and slight breasts. Among many of these statues showing the life-regenerating properties of Divine Feminine energy, we see V shapes, often together forming a Chevron shape or an X across the chests emphasizing the Divine fluid that comes through the earthly female's body. The places where the fluid comes are marked on these statuary: the eyes, the open mouth, the pubic triangle, and as we see with Iside and moving into later Minoan statues: the breasts.

These statuary forms were symbolic and were not limited to showing "fertility;" this is a patriarchal reduction. These statuary are a symbolic sculptural language showing parallels between heaven and earth, and honoring the Great Mother Goddess as the energy moving between the two realms.

The bull is the animal that shows the power of the female reproductive organs (the bull skull is the exact shape as the ovaries, fallopian tubes and uterus), and was thus used as a symbol of the power of the Goddess,and earthly woman, as "heaven come down to earth;" to regenerate life from death. A bull skull facing a human skull is an arrangement often placed in tombs, such as on the Italian island of Malta where we have megalithic tombs and temples older than the Great pyramid in Egypt. Also among the symbolic language was a basket pattern which also represented the life-giving properties of water, a gift from the Great Goddess Mother... and in Benevento's Iside temple I was told there was also a "mystic basket."

The colors of Iside were white and black in the temple, and in the founding symbolic language white symbolized death, like it does in nature's bones. Black represents the great Universal womb from which all comes; therefore a color of the greatest potential.

The serpent is the bridge between earthly life and the world of spirit, or the "afterlife," a symbol of Mediumship and feminine shamanism. The serpent also represents life "comes around again," because of the shedding of skin which does not kill the snake but offers a renewal. It was Christianity who made the serpent evil and forbade Mediumship.

Also, most importantly for women, Iside is a Goddess of healing feminine energy lost to men; she is a Goddess of autonomy. Women were the first musicians, and the sistrum was given to women, not to men. These important roles were taken over by men when paganism subsumed the Divine Feminine. These symbols were all ones given to me in my meditations, and in Benevento they all came into focus.

Iside "is" in fact a Great Goddess for women; a protector of feminine energy and a teacher of Mediumship. Her teachings involve women (and female identified people) helping men (and masculine identified people) connect with their feminine energy.

Giovanni explained to me that, *"Entering her temple, in the approach, one would be met with a pool of water whose purpose was for purification. There were bull statues and lions at the entrance. There were life-size statues inside of people in a specific prayer position."* When I saw one of these statues I gasped, because this is the meditation posture that my Goddess guides had taught me to do, and it's the position I always keep.

Oddly however he explained, *"Priests played the sistrum. They would make an invocation to the Goddess Iside,* [often called the Queen and the Grande Dea], *with their voice and instrument. Only male priests were allowed in the innermost part of the temple."*

This is where much of what is written about her, from Roman times, is a jumbled mess. Iside is a Goddess for women, as they all were. They guide women to help men connect to their feminine energy. Public temples, such as this one however, were made by men and as such they were exclusionary. Women were the first musicians, and the Grande Dea gave the instruments to women: the sistrum and the drum being two of the most important instruments as well as instruments in the forms of waterbirds, all bearing markers of chevrons and V shapes, just like the "Isaic knots" that were formed from fabric , in later periods, emphasizing the life-giving moisture that comes from female breasts.

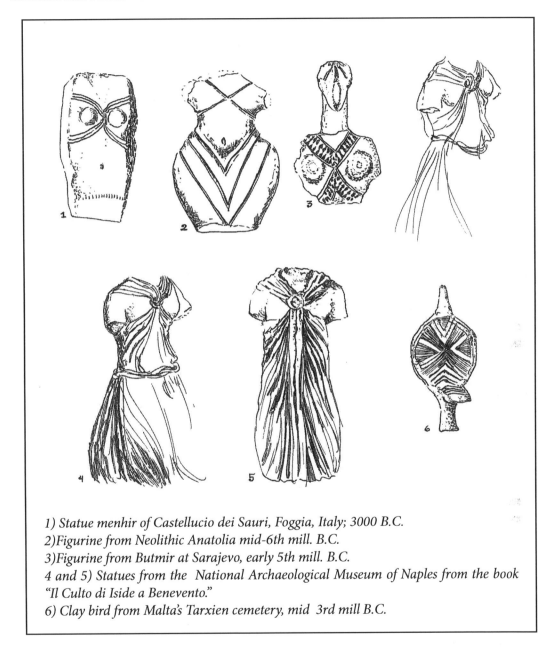

1) Statue menhir of Castellucio dei Sauri, Foggia, Italy; 3000 B.C.
2) Figurine from Neolithic Anatolia mid-6th mill. B.C.
3) Figurine from Butmir at Sarajevo, early 5th mill. B.C.
4 and 5) Statues from the National Archaeological Museum of Naples from the book "Il Culto di Iside a Benevento."
6) Clay bird from Malta's Tarxien cemetery, mid 3rd mill B.C.

A phrase form the Hymn of Isid from the Oxyrhncus papyrus n.1380, II Century B.C. as displayed in the Arcos museum reads: "Well skilled Goddess, honour of the female gender. Lovely, you let sweetness reign in the assemblies, enemy of hatred. You Reign in the Sublime and in the Infinite. You easily triumph over your despots with your loyal advice[…] You want women to join men. You are the Lady of the Earth, you have made the power of women equal to that of men.." We can read references here to channeling "your...advice," and we know from this she was a provide of love and sweetness as well. And we know that this was a poem written after the patriarchy subsumed spiritual practices, because pre-patriarchy women were naturally seen as equal to men and spiritually superior because women were honored as having connection to the Goddess and the Goddess' knowledge...men were not considered more powerful than women in our earliest days. Still, we have evidence attesting to the power and ancient age of Iside, that she was still venerated by the patriarchy and even with some of her original symbols.

It's incredible these symbols survived, considering that the Romans were doing all sorts of collage work among spiritualities they liked and adopted from other lands. For example, the Romans built a temple to Iside and included a statue of Dionysis there...two different cultural spiritual figures who didn't belong together. You can study the founding language through Maria Gimbutas' "Language of the Goddess" and from there, consistently learn to spot the signs of the Grande Dea and untangle the many masculinized replacements from the original practices.

MITRA

Mitra was a god embraced by the romans whose story incorporated the idea of a man/god named "Mitra" killing a bull. Without delving into the history, I have been intuitively drawn to Mitra for years. I never researched beyond a few surface sentences because I dislike this masculine show of power over the natural world in this practice, what I call a "Masculine Mystery School." It's seems to me ugly and ruthless and It is synthetic. At the same time, my Goddess guides encouraged me to notice that this practices was also a Mediumship practice. I sensed somewhere in here was a connection to the Goddess, some sort of imitations going on with this blood sacrifice. I intuitively felt this had to do with the idea of menstrual blood but I didn't have proof yet during those earlier years of my research, only a gentle and subtle guidance by the Goddesses to keep searching. but it took me a while to put the cookie crumbs trail into a solid road...which ultimately leads back to our founding Divine Feminine practice of witchery. I intuitively felt had to do with the idea of menstrual blood but I didn't have proof yet several years ago.

However, during my stay in Italy I was invited my Mauro and Diana to the Temple while en route to meet Paolo. So, I accepted their gracious invitation and I'm so glad that I did...and I can't wait to return.

I had a completely unexpected emotional "recognition experience" here, which dropped me to my knees in front of the sacrificial room, reducing me to heaving sobs of like that of a long-lost child being reunited with her Universal mother. This "recognition experience" is how I describe the way the Goddess teachers indicate to me that I've come in contact with a part of this feminine history: I feel it when I meet a Lineage healer, "nonnas," while walking on some ancient lands, and seeing the faces of female strangers. I felt the presence of the Great Mother there, in that place created by men, so that even though I thought the act of killing the bull was horrific, I realized that all the ideas that had been floating around in my intuitive mind were true; that this was a spiritual practice attempting to connect with the Great Mother's life-giving blood, and that this was a Spiritualist place of old. This came into focus for me as I saw the "classroom" where these channeling practices took place. Regardless of my own prejudices, I felt Her here, and this means that other people can too…and did, in the past, as well.

CIBELE

An even more ancient, and therefore more formless energy is this Ancient who is connected with the primal heartbeat of drums, ecstatic trance, and sexual energy used in a spiritual way, as a source of healing and joy for simply being alive: a oneness with Goddess (Source) even while being separated from the Great Mother by physical form on earth. This is the unadulterated energy we are all made from.

However, the stories most commonly found about Cibele are perhaps the most confusing ones, serving more to scare people away from non-binary genders and turn them away from her by connecting her to violent scenes "eunuchs and sex orgies.". This is the result of attempt of men to attach oldest from of Goddess with newer Greek and Roman propaganda which was against the female and against the homosexual male.

Cibele seems to come from pre-Turkish Phrygia, and if you read Roman accounts, she has a very confusing birth story, as is typical of Roman myths. She sounds terrible, causing people to have frenzied sex orgies and castrating themselves in public. If you take a quick search around the internet or research documents form Roman times, the accounts sound wild, uncontrolled, and frightening, featuring strange tales about birthing herself, and birthing her son who became her consort.

I have to note once again how silly it seems talking about a Goddess "coming from somewhere" on earth, when Goddess are Spirit, so they can be anywhere or everywhere without being limited by earthly geography. However, the "places" Goddesses are connected to show us a simpler beauty: that from all cultures is this same Divine Feminine shamanistic connection to the Spirit Word…it WAS the natural way of living on earth and rising to our highest potential in "partnership" with the Spirit World to create abundant life on earth and to cause "miracles" of healing when needed, but also create miraculous feats of building, arts, and music. Mostly, this potential is relegated to healing work and ceremony in our modern times, swept into the corners of society.

From personal experience, having unexpectedly felt her energy on several occasions, I can see the fright one could feel if not practiced in feeling the energies of others in one's own body. And, if one was not spiritually inclined, it is fair to say her energy could lead to a "frenzied" feeling related to sexuality, a needing to "have sex." Because we are not used to living in this great energy vibration of "joy" and "wonder," when I felt it too, at first I wanted to run around like a child, yelling at the top of my lungs how great it felt and then taking a private moment to myself to connect with my lower chakras. I would find out, however, that it's not possible to remain in the flow of her energy and be the one making the decisions on how to use this energy. She has a very strong guiding hand, and she demands this energy remain focused on Spiritual aspirations. The truth of this energy is that earthly sex is less and lower than its vibration and therefore "lowers" the expansive sensations; it dissolved the "miracle." However, for women, remaining in the flow of this energy is what Cibele's tantra is calling out for: a sexual recharge and repair between feminine energies.

When I was experiencing her, I can tell you the man closest to me did not castrate himself, but he did confess a "feeling" of abstaining from sex..and even considering to give it up, in the way a monk focused on "inner work" might do. This to me seems closer to the reality: sexual energy and creative energy do come from the same "energetic organs" our chakras) … they regulate this energy in the way our kidneys perform their function of regulation in our physical bodies. Therefore not using these energies to have sex with human beings means that it has the opportunity to be used in other ways, such as in creative expression.

Cibele, being divine feminine autonomy for repairing women and independence form men, would certainly then affect men in a way that would connect them to inner femininity… which would mean also a "giving up," at least during the experience, typical masculine actions.

As far as gender and Cibele are concerned, as we know in pre-pagan times, there were not the standard "male-female" relationships that "lasted forever." While there certainly there was sexual intercourse between men and women, there the moral standards of "family planning" and religion were not in place because paternity was not known, so men didn't "claim" the women and children as part of their property yet. But as far as only two binary genders, it seems unlikely. Those roles came about when the church imposed a scathing "morality" based on controlling populations in medieval times, arranged marriages enforcing this, condemnation of homosexuality, and harsh criticism of single women. From this we know homosexuality is natural and was already a natural part of life: all genders are natural. And we know from more modern shamanism (or accounts of shamanism) from cultural lineages that there are many genders accepted as natural.

So in these feminine communities, going back to most ancient times, women birthing babies, caring for the food and land, growing herbs to cure, caring for animals and their own bodies pre and post pregnancy, being natural healers…it seems reasonable to figure that a part of spiritual practice would be autonomy for women. Even in our modern days many of us as women or female identified persons who are natural healers attract relationship partners who need healing, but instead we try "make them happy" and we forget our power and lose ourselves.

In a spiritual practice guided by a strong Goddess teacher such as Cibele, it would make sense that she would change the sexual partnering dynamics: Goddess-to-female identified person in a tantric relationship. Men to refrain from regularly performing sex; a separation so women could become clear channels. Only with some autonomy can women be teachers to men, or channels for this energy, so in this way men have potential to reach the Goddess as well.

Cibele is also associated with the pine tree. It is noted that the Etruscans, who embraced Cibele, imported pine trees in the area of Etruria.

As far as the many other Goddesses known during Roman times, there are many: Albina, Carmenta, Mefite, and the more formless Vesta (which we can ascertain is older than Roman times because of her lack of anatomical portrayal), and many more.

Reitia, a Goddess of Italy's northeastern region whose temple in Este near Padua was active in the 6th-4th centuries B.C., is considered a health-giving Goddess whose specific assitance to women was in the form of helping "restore women to health after childbirth." She is also a Goddess who gifted writing to the people. "Raetic" is an actual language with runic expression that existed and is listed among five other main historical languages of Italy: Venetic, Etruscan, Greek and Latin. There many dedications inscribed in the Venetic language, mostly in the form of bronze writing tablets and styluses. The majority of these inscribed dedications to Reitia were made by women, and their dedications seem to be giving writing itself back to the Goddess.

Among the Hitties, priestesses known as Elderly Women taught the art of writing, kept records, advised kings, and practiced medicine. In Babylonian times, the noble art of tablet-writing [...] belonged to the special scribes called matyanu. A similar Egyptian word for scribe was Maryen or Mahir: "great one" or "mother". The triple Goddess of Fate was incarnate in three Gulses or "writers" corresponding to the Germanic Fates called Die Schreiberinnen, the Writing-Women, and the Roman mother of destiny Fata Scribunda, the "Fate who Writes." In pre-Hellenic Greece, the original alphabet was attributed to the original three Muses, who were identical with the Fates of Graea, eponymous mothers of Greek tribes.[248]

About the followers of Abundia, it is said they were often falling in a sort of catalepsies before starting in Spirit their trips crossing walls and doors [passing through them] which takes place on the night of the 24 of June, the date where in Greece is celebrated the birth of Artimede and also the night where in the tradition Diana manifests herself in the visible world together with her procession.[248] This date is known in the Latin world also like Notte Delle Strega. It is also the time where in the tradition , the fruit of the walnut tree are collected to prepare a liquor called "Nocillo".[249]

When we tread into Greek and Roman territory, there are Goddesses for everything: for writing, for charms, childbirth, protection, luck, war, love…whereas in Italian Witchery there is One Goddess who provides all those things.

While there are pagan stories of Goddesses and Gods as couples, these are modern inventions made to fit social changes, to be used as didactic material. Even here, in these stories, beyond copulation and arguments, these couples are really not doing anything here together, especially not anything supernatural. Beyond the stories and into the practical places of "worship, the Gods and Goddess were segregated. Italy's indigenous Goddess (as well as her adopted) ones were not venerated alongside a male counterpart.

Essentially, however it's clear:

Goddesses in Italy are often providers just for women.
Goddesses provide for peasants.
Goddesses teach and assist solitary women.
Then, women can help men.

Italian Goddesses, or Goddess adopted and adored in Italy, are all believed to be traced back to the Grande Madre. It's the Greek and Roman remodeling of them that make their biographies sound outrageous and fictional, as well as all the other human dynamics added to their "birth stories," and other jumbled tales.

The Indigenous Italian Goddess, Signora di Gicoo (also called Diana di Gioco and Aradia di Gioco) didn't have all this man-made confusion attached to them in their earlier stories until we find more modern versions.

The tradition is that the Spirit World reaches down to earth: the Goddesses choose us. Hathor, Diana, Sekhmet, Iside, Cibele…my advice is to seek them out and let them introduce themselves to you. Be aware of the invitation and when it comes, take it.

Sixteenth Secrets

While researching the Signora di Gioco, who was brought to my attention by Paolo Portone under the name "Buona Raes," I found some incredible connections to the names of the people involved in this story.

I can't help but wonder if then Universe has played an historical trick on everyone, however.

Considering the Signoria Di Gico, Italy's indigenous Goddess, was called "Lady of the Game," referring to the learning circle in which she taught women how to cure disease, etc, and that Goddess teachers often teach through synchronicity and leading breadcrumb trails to information, it seemed that she played a fun and factual game with me and with Italy herself.

The trick, the game I'm referring to is a trail of names.

Sometimes names are arbitrary, especially if we acknowledge the human need to put so much emphasis on naming things, naming Goddesses even...

The most famous documentation in Italy's history which refers to the Signora di Gioco is from the two Inquisition trials of Sibila Zanni and Pierina Bugatis of Milano.

Basically, in this story these two women describe their repeated visionary experiences with the Signora Di Gioco, who is a Spirit Goddess teacher, a provider. In order to communicate with a Spirit person, an earthly person must "channel" information through her natural psychic senses.

In Italy and in Greece, there is the historical tradition of the "oracles;" professional women who channeled advice from the God (often named as a man instead of the Divine Feminine) to men (Emperors, etc).

They were more recently called Pythias, such as the Oracle at Delphi. The Delphic Oracle was there to overcome this estrangement form the gods and their wisdom [ftp.11] She was, basically, that "Medium" between Spirit World and earthly one. Or, as author Roger Lipsey so eloquently put this channeling-of-information process into energetic terminology: "Unfolded into Light Through a Woman: the Pythia" in his book "Have you Been to Delphi?"

Near Naples there was also the Cumaean sybil whose cave was in Cumae, a settlement of Greek peoples in ancient times. This "Sibilla" and her cave called "Antro della Sibila" (cave of the sybil. Sybil is the English spelling, Sibilla is the Italian spelling). The Sibilla was an oracle; a channeler; a guide to the underworld.

So we have a tradition of a channeler called, technically, a "Sibilla."

And also, we have a character called "Zanni" in folk tales who was a male Medium, related to the Arlechhino figure, or the harlequin, who made contact with the dead.

We also know the Goddesses are connected to stones and meteorites.

And in the Inquisition, the Inquisitors accidentally "uncovered" a female spirit circle between women in Milan and the Signora di Gicoo who was a Spirit teacher appearing to young women. Two of the young female members: Sibila Zanni and Pierina Bugatis.

The name Pierina means: a rock or stone.
The name Sibiliia means: oracle.
The name Zanni means: Medium, one who communicates with the "dead"

So we have:
Pierina: rock or stone of the Goddess
Sibilla Zanni: Oracle Medium

SIBILLA ZANNI AND PIERINA BUGATIS

Chapter 16:
La Signora del Gioco

This is the most important central figure in understanding how Italy's witchery began, how it has been passed down, how its loss due to invasions has been repaired, and how it continues to exist and be transmitted in our modern times even outside of Lineages: the Signora di Gioco. She is Italy's Indigenous Goddess.

This is how the secret Lineage knowledge was given to women in Italy, and this is how it found them again and again: whether invaded by Patriarchy, invaded by Inquisition, or broken from female communities through general gender gaps in the quality of living. While the realm of (more formless or named) Goddesses as Spiritual teachers is deeply internal and often conceptual and subjective and based on an individual's communications, experiences, level of understanding, the Signora di Gioco is the Indigenous Goddess Mother of Italy's people, of her ordinary, uneducated women, living openly among society. This is Italy's "feminine magic in plain sight."

The Signora, also known as "Buona Res," as "Lady of the Night," (La Donna delle Notte), "La Donna del bon Zogo," as "Lady of the Good Games," as "Good Lady," as "Madonna Oriente," as the "Bona Dea," and in other cultures "Habonde," "Richella," "Abundia" and the "Matronae." It was later that her names became like modern female names such as "Diana" and Aradia di Gioco, largely due to outsiders re-naming this Divine Feminine being, such as when the church added "Diana" to this story during the Inquisition, as well as creating a male evil consort for her: the Devil.

The Signora di Gioco is a provider, appearing at night time to women, helping them in practical ways. She may be flanked by a procession of spirit animals and other spirit people, but she never has a male counterpart "Signore." So even as in the paleolithic era, when the Universe was considered to be a Divine Female being who provided all to people on earth who had no male counterpart but from which male energy comes (and the forms of women and men), in Italy's indigenous Goddess we see still, in more modern times such as the 1500s, this tradition continuing as a solo female figure provider from the Spirit World bringing her knowledge "down to earth."

The Signora di Gioco, known in the same way in other cultures as well, is the "opening of the door" to the Spirit World. She is the Spirit Mother of the "practical Mediums," and her teachings were on the level that the young women of the times could relate to: she instructed them to keep their houses clean and to keep good manners. There were respectful greetings between La Signora and young women she invited to her night time circle, and one woman confessed she was not allowed to return to the circle because she disrupted the event by throwing a rock. In modern times we are taught in many spiritual practices that keeping our house clean also keeps our minds clean and our energy clean. Among these practical steps, La Signora also taught women how to cure disease with local plants, and other magical ideas "brought down to earth." In the Milano confessions we are told La Signora always told the truth. *"Health to you, Lady of the East"/Salute a te, signora Oriente"; And she replied, "State bene, brava gente," All is well, good people.*[250]

This is where the Italian Lineages come from (and likely the Lineages in other cultures) Aradia and Diana are some of the Signora di Gioco, as is Ana Perenna. These are the teachers-in-action appearing to women at night or in dreams.

As Paolo told me in our interview, "*In the first trial of Sibilla and Pierina what came out in the confessions of the women was a series of beliefs that describe a feminine tradition in which maybe there is also a propitiation; a ritual for making rain or some act to appease a Spirit in return for something. The Spirit is the Woman of the Game. This could be the tip of an iceberg.*"

Even in the Como (Comasco) the Sabbath was superimposed on a layer of similar beliefs: the nocturnal gatherings, such as registered by the Inquisitor Bernard of Como, there were called "Game of the Good Society" "gioco della buona societa"(Ludum bonae societatis).[251]

Also Burchard of Worms, 500 years later, stating that the table was set with three knives, intended to the Fates: probably corresponding to "Matronae" Celtic, long revered as a good ladies (bonnes dames, bonae dominae).[252] The "Matronae" is the "Signora di Gioco" of the Celts.

In the documents of a Diocesan council held in 1280 at Conserans in the Ariege region, she is called Bensozia (probably a corruption of "Bona Socia," good partner)[253] In other instances we find[,,,] Perchta, Holda.[254] The presence of these variants indicates that similar traditions […] were found in different times and places[255]

"Behind the women (and the few men) linked to the 'good' nocturnal Goddesses we glimpse a cult of an ecstatic nature." Of the followers of the Lady Habonde it was said that they fell into catalepsy before undertaking their journeys as spirits, passing through doors and walls."[256] Via a temporary death [astral travel] one accedes to the world of beneficent female figures who bestow prosperity, wealth, knowledge. Their world is the realm of the dead[257]

What's most exciting about Italy's documented history (from Inquisition records) are the "confessions" of these spiritual experiences which are the type that simply don't arrive in documentations. They are experiences, and as such, often defy verbal descriptions. Even in our current modern days, there are limitations to describing the inner experience, and in fact the "language" used to do so often turns people off or on to spiritual ideas. While describing the same idea one can sound "new age," "hippie" "occultist" or even be labeled as "crazy." And the documents in Italy, from an outside perspective, sounds like a jumble of thoughts. Often, women confessing to have these experiences in fact deemed "mentally unwell" because the church and Inquisitors simply had no frame of reference with which to understand or process their claims.

Regardless, this feminine tradition has carried on over lifetimes and ages, Italy's Indigenous "goddess" taking visual form to "come down to earth", to also provide knowledge to women outside of Lineages, to women broken off from their power: this is the Bona Dea.

Sibilla confessed of her experiences: *"every Thursday night, she had joined [Madonna] Oriente and her "society." She had paid homage to Oriente…she would bow her head as a sign of reverence saying "Be well, Madona Horiente"; Oriente would answer "welcome, my daughters (Bene veniatis, filie mee)." Every kind of animal communed with the society. Oriente answered the questions of the society's members, providing information and instructions"*[258]

"Gioco" and "Ludus" in Latin, and "Zogo" in many Italian dialects: all three words mean GAME, and the GAME is the most ancient name of the feminine Sabba.[259] Originally the the Italian "sabba" was about women congregating around a Divine Feminine Spirit teacher, otherwise known in Italy as La Signora del Gioco. It was the church who changed this story into what you see in woodcut drawings: women dancing in a circle around a male Devil with whom they will have sex and plot revenge spells.

"In the processes [Inquisition trials] in Val di Fiemme we still find traces of the female figure who commands the Game, but no woman who owns up to having participated, (only admitting vaguely know of people who have done it), although some admit during interrogation that she had seen this and try to describe it."[260]

This is how the Goddess came down to earth: not as a human being, but as a Spirit Guide helping earthly people "appearing as" a woman.

And frankly, to put this in American cultural terms, she's like a real Santa Claus: riding through the stars, coming down to earth to gift women with knowledge of all sorts. Often this is how she's described, age after age, but instead of riding reindeer and sleigh, she's accompanied by other spirits and animal spirits…a more natural procession. Instead of leaving wrapped presents, she offers gifts to improve life through having conversations, teaching cleanliness, giving knowledge of curing plants, and more. Cleanliness leads to high vibration and organization, whether energetically or physically.

"In the culture of Pierina and Sibilla, the frontier between dream and reality was not rigid and could be crossed from one side to another. Their existences usually took place on two floors, that of dream and ordinary life, with an alternation similar to night and day. But between the two worlds there was a very strong connection: domestic care, for example, daytime work of women and a criterion of value in the world of the Madonna Orient; The concern to maintain a demographic balance, suggested by the rule of being replaced before dying; Medical and divinatory art, practiced in reality but with the foundation in the universe of the "Game."[261]

All other Goddesses around he world, with their the various names are really coming from this Spirit World tradition of the Signora di Gico, a Spirit World Female teacher who exists in every culture, and those cultures had their own names for her.

Iside was one of the first Goddesses to appear in Italy from another country to be so specifically personified as a deity with a human likeness in statuary and artwork, depicting her as more relatable, all while keeping many of the symbolic language that people already knew was still signs from much older times pointing to the Great Mother Goddess. During Iside's time of popularity in Italy, anatomically correct sculptures, paintings, and coinage, (anything that captured a human likeness image), were very popular marketing and propaganda tools used by the Greeks and Romans to market their new philosophies and to promote men as spiritual leaders and emperors; leaders in power. So this is also a time where we see Goddesses having new images that reflect humanity-in-divinity in the same vein.

This is the real reason Signora di Gico stories were "left in superstitious dust" as history and culture developed in Italy. Because Signora appeared to women at night (and also during dreamtime astral travel, it is important to note) and was inaccessible to men, she was not "available" to put into statuary nor in public temples. She very clearly demonstrated, albeit mysteriously, to be a real intelligence but very in control of how she appeared to people in visionary form. "La donna del bon zogo protected, with its mystery, the secret of others."[262]

She very naturally appeared in very specific and similar form to earthly women looking like a regular woman, wearing a dress and shawl of the times. Always present were some other visual cues that she was an "otherworldly" visitor: a common example in the confessions of women who had this experience is seeing La Signora accompanied by many [spirit] and a procession of other dead people, and sometimes she herself had animal parts such as furred hands [like the wolf paws described by Benandanti as a signal they are now in the astral realm]. In other words, La Signora is accompanied by nature: earthly nature symbols and Spirit World symbols.

She taught the art of curing disease with herbs, she taught people to keep clean and orderly, and she taught positive manners. For the Romans, however, she was too practical: their statuary was to be powerful and magnificent, and the image of a housewife, the image La Signora took, was not an image that was seen as powerful.

Apparently in Italy the idea of La Signora is a debated one: many people think her validity lies in whether or not she was a physical human being. Ezo Gravina shared with me that, "Basically the tradition says that if a woman is a witch, from her comes her daughter who is a witch, and from her daughter comes another witch. The "oldest" woman in the lineage is the "boss" the one who helps other women to give births, and helps with house issues. The social contract is that. It was a patriarchal society as a social structure: in the patriarchal structure the oldest men are the boss because the oldest is the wisest." So Enzo's proposal is that in the groups of witches it was the same, and that these groups were open to everybody.

I do think this structure, an "older or at least wiser" woman teaching others is the natural form, but the advanced knowledge to cure and improve life in harmony with nature didn't ever come just for "human beings;" this advanced knowledge comes from advanced consciousness, La Signora di Gioco, the Grande Madre, the Grande Dea: the wisdom is from the world of Spirit; the application of it takes place on earth.

The Spirit World is one where energy is form, there is no physical matter. Spirit beings can takes on different forms recognizable to us so as to help us with whatever it is we need to find out, and so we can relate to them. Some of these forms are kept and used again and again to remain through the ages as a way to identify who from the Spirit World is passing down knowledge.

In this day in age what I'm finding so interesting and exciting is that people who are searching for their roots   especially in Italy, have shared with me that they are finding these these older forms of Goddess reaching out to them. It is my personal belief that we are being led back to at least acknowledge the foundational Divinely Feminine spiritual symbolic language of our earliest history. This great legacy has been covered up since a change in social structure due to the repeated patriarchal invasions, so it's more difficult to find, but it's there.

In Inquisition times of the church's extermination of women and men, people ultimately were persecuted because of their beliefs and not because they did anything wrong nor evil. This is why the church's deterrents from connecting with the Spirit World through channeling and Mediumship are still banned with strong hellfire: to control minds, to control beliefs, and to make people afraid to independently seek "god," because in doing so, the finds will be natural looking and make sense within nature, and they will be not at all church-looking. This is what the church is afraid of: individuals being in communication with the Divine.

Seventeenth Secrets

June 7, 2017

I've fallen into a fast, hard, deep depression. And, I know it makes no sense...my life is good, I am blessed. The weather is wonderful. I am appreciated at my new job. And yet, this sensation is like a heavy weight and it's slowed me down, and my writing has taken a hit. This has happened before when working on this book: I've sympathetically taken on illnesses and now, I'm feeling immobile. I'm thankful that I have to go to work. The 30 minutes walk to and from work isn't delightful: usually this walk, listening to music is a joy, but now it feels endless. Once I arrive at my job and get to work temporarily I am lifted because I am busy; part physical labor, part paperwork, part lovely co-worker people.

Anyone who knows me knows I am terrible with dates. I don't remember anyone's birthday, just ask my mother.

But on the 8th, I wake up early and decide to post a picture of Triora on my Instagram. I choose to post the one of me standing in an alcove beneath Franchetta Borelli's unmarked grave. I write as the caption "There's no place like home X3 in Triora, Italia."

I have two espressos. I can't get this sadness to go away. Instead of a full moon ritual I find myself sobbing, as if I'm experiencing a great loss. It reminds me of a relationship break-up when it's raw, and deep emotions well up and you feel helpless to them, and they just overflow. My shoulders shake, I sob. My stomach is upset again and bloated. I try to write, forcing myself to stay awake even though I want the comfort of the temporary unconsciousness of sleep to be away from this thick sadness that has moved into an overwhelming feeling of grief. I simply can't identify it; I know it's not mine, I know i am perfectly ok. I know my life is abundant. I know there are more wonderful things coming my way. I know in this moment all my needs are met. I look at the beauty outside my bedroom window and give thanks. I hear my housemates having a lively conversation and I'm so grateful for this joyful atmosphere, how wonderful I live in a house where people like each other. I give into the sinking despair, knowing at some point it will dissipate.

On the 9th, my stomach is even more twisted and bloated. The sun is shining. There are colorful and lush plants, ...and I am desperately sad. I'm aware it's something I'm feeling but it's not making sense with "me" nor with the reality around me.

I go home determined to write. I had some success this morning from the tremendous brain fog. The deep waters are there, however, and the closer I get to my home and the desk in my bedroom the more I feel myself drowning under.

I give up. I just cry. For some reason I feel like I should go on facebook. I don't spend time on facebook in general, and I don't have the app on my new phone so I hardly check it anymore, it's just so full of ugliness, I don't need more of that. But I log on, and the first thing I see in the "news feed" is a post by an Italian woman that says "June 8th...Scribani arrives in Triora."

And suddenly, my stomach explodes in the way I know Franchetta has gotten my attention before.And the depression is lifted! This is the reason for what I've been feeling! She's telling me this now, and I understand. The part of me that is so connected with her from the past is mourning this passage, living it over and over again...Ah I can breathe again now that I've identified the source of this grief. My stomach burps and belches and suddenly all the air goes out. I am overjoyed ..because I found the treasure: Franchetta's been pointing her finger at this date and I finally "got it." I am relieved of all the emotions she wanted me to feel, that she wanted me to know.

Chapter 17:
"How the Goddess Became the Devil"

At this point in our journey together it's been revealed that the church created both the "witch" and her "devil." This is historical fact. These creations were used to control people and as an excuse for sexual abuse and murder.

As Manuela explained, the church created a specific "devil" whose marks symbolized that he belonged to the Goddess so that this "evil" they were creating would "stick" to women and Feminine Divinity, emblazoning "her" as the ultimate enemy. The church, you've been shown, also created a very strong campaign against female healers: this was a business plan of theirs to overthrow peasant healers and replace them the up-and-coming male doctors whom the church had control over. Prior to this, it's not that women had such a better standing in Italian life, but female healers and sorceresses co-existed with male sorcerers and healers without being hunted and killed. It was the church who instigated this genocide, and the full-bodied way they went about this attacked, with last affect, women in general, healers, psychic and mediums of female identified energy. This is a lasting effect today: the church still has a hardline against mediumship and psychics and women's sexuality. And, female Lineages and also magical practices remain secret or hidden in-plain-sight.

What I've presented here is just the tip of an iceberg full of information I found.

On the more uplifting side of this is a treasure trove of information from Marija Gimbutas showing that Divine Feminine spirituality created not only our founding symbolic language in Italy (as well as the ability to count the passage of time, to cure, to build, to make music and more) but in Old Europe as well. In her book, "The Language of the Goddess," are figurines and drawn symbols and carvings all showing the movement and physical expression of the Divine Feminine's energy "on earth as it is in heaven" in parallels. These earthly survival tools "unfolded into light through a woman," as author Roger Lipsey wrote it so well.

The evil devil existed for long time before the church's campaign, but it was the Italian church in Inquisition times who made the devil into someone who was connected to women and even had sex with women. The church's focus, in fact, is on the negative and therefore they are a symbol of negativity. They had wanted to find something "diabolical" about women they could use as evidence of "heresy" but what they found instead was a feminine tradition of specifically Italian shamanism which was a tradition of abundance and positivity, which remains today, alive in the Lineage practices.

This tradition of the Spirit World reaching down to earth has been in existence since our earliest times. The sculptures, symbolic art in tombs such as Malta, and water bowls found throughout Italy and Old Europe testify to a symbolic language that shows the Goddess' energy come down to earth in the form of nature: water, earth, trees, animals, stones, and in people and animals. Most important to understanding how the Goddess' energy moved through life in cycles of abundance is the parallel of the cycles which take place in the bodies of earthly women; the earthly parallel of the Goddess in "heaven."

This is reflect in the belief in life after death of physical body: regeneration. This is reflected in the belief in the cycles of nature and how to grow plants for nourishment and cures in harmony with those cycles. Birth is part of these natural cycles. These are in opposition to the synthetic industrialization of life created by men: intensive farming methods which harm the earth and forced-birth through animal husbandry.

The truth is, the Italian "witch" which we can't identify with one name, really is truly special, and her ways truly are secret: the healing Lineages are set up this way. Healing is available to anyone and everyone who needs it, for free... but not everyone is chosen to be a Lineage healer.

Perhaps this is what set the patriarchy in motion, a simple jealousy: not being able to accept something is free but can't be "owned." Maybe this gave s sense of rejection to men who wanted to "know."

The Spirit World can be known, as human beings we are built to communicate with spirit because we are also spirit...we are just spirit housed in a physical body while on earth...and when we pass out of our bodies we will return to being just spirit. But while on earth, physical matter has different forms. And, the female body has a form that can give birth to new life from her body; not from outside of her body...the babies come from INSIDE her body. The earthly woman's ability to be life-giving is why she is a parallel example of "heaven on earth;" it is natural.

The following symbols show are our foundational ones which show 3 cycles of nature, as Maria Gimbutas categorizes them:

Life Giving
Renewal and eternal earth
Death and Regeneration (life after death)

There are many more symbols and much more information in her book. Here I will share just a few of the ones which have been usurped and changed from their original symbols of abundance into symbols of "evil."

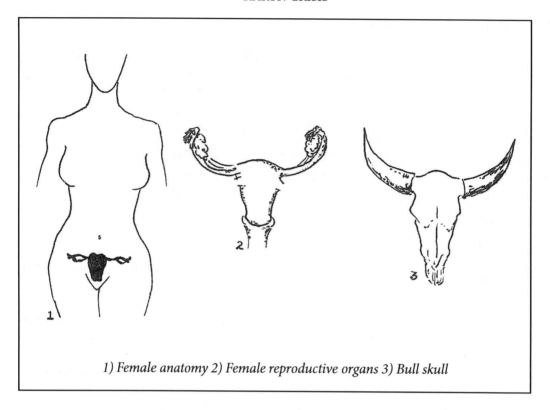

1) Female anatomy 2) Female reproductive organs 3) Bull skull

From these diagrams we ca see why the bull and the bull skull were a symbol of the Great Goddesses (and earthly woman's) life-giving abilities: there is a visual parallel. This is nature. This symbol was usurped by men and turned into the image of an evil man with horns, but this evil man with horns does not exist in nature. This is a synthetic creation.

As part of the ability to give life is the importance of water and bodily fluids. This is why water birds and other animals associated with water are symbols of feminine life-giving abilities.

ANIMALS who share characteristics with female anatomy's life-giving fluids and ability to give birth: hedgehog, serpent, bull, water birds, sow, female cow, fish. Horned animals all have this same parallel to the female reproductive organs. Female cows do have horns, but they are often cut off, so this parallel is often synthetically erased.

WATER and bodily fluids are also celebrated as being life-generating gifts of the Great Goddess' abundance.

The FISH was a symbol of the Great Mother Goddess' gift of life-giving water, and also as the female bodily fluids on earth. The fish's scales and image were caved and painted on water bowls and other objects related to these properties.

USURPED: The fish is a symbol that the church connected to Jesus' miracle of creating "abundance" through his magical multiplication of fishes to feed people. What was once a parallel of nature: the Divine fluid providing abundance, became a symbol of man's synthetic ability to control matter and manifest.

The BULL (and the cow and horned animals) whose skulls look like a parallel of the woman's reproductive organs became a symbol of man's dominant control of nature (Mitra). Horned animals also became the symbols for the male devil (who had a dominant control of women, allegedly), and also became a symbol of male divinity-in-nature when Paganism came about and decided the Divine Feminine wasn't capable enough of taking care of the Universe without "man."

The SUN and the MOON were both energies of the Divine Feminine.

USURPED: It was men who "took" the sun as their symbol and decided it was superior to the moon.

The SERPENT: The serpent was a powerful symbol connected to water, the regeneration of life and healing, and the Spirit World messenger, and the Divine Feminine.

USURPED: the serpent maintained its symbolism of healing in paganism. In Christianity the serpent became synonymous with their devil.

DEATH: Death was a positive transformation in this belief system because it was known that the Spirit continues to live as consciousness after death of the physical body. Death was simply a transition point from the world of matter to the world of Spirit. Death in nature was seen as a natural cycle of abundance: the old disintegrates and the new comes, reminders that there is always abundance because the cycles continue.

USURPED: Death was seen as a failure, and as such, it was blamed on a scapegoat: the witch.

TRIANGLE: The triangle originally represented the pubic region of the earthly female and her ability to provide life in a parallel way to the Great Mother Goddess, also the fertile soil and often connected with the Four Corners showing that the Great Mother Goddess works through the entire Universe to bring abundance to all life forms through her natural "clock:" the natural seasonal cycles.

USURPED: The triangle is used in masculine magic to represent men and manifestation and it is also seen as an evil symbol by the church because of its origin as symbol of the female reproductive organs.

TREES: Symbol of the Goddess' wisdom come down to earth.

USURPED: Trees are our most widely attacked natural resource along with water and are often connected in folk stories to the masculine discovery of wisdom.

CROSS: The cross represented the 4 directions and the 4 seasons, nature's cycles and therefore the Clock of the Great Mother Goddess' heartbeat; her pulse of life brought down to earth.

USURPED: The cross came to represent the persecution of Jesus, a story of injustice intended to end all injustice stories.

COLORS: White: represented death of the physical form, frozen in place while freeing the Spirit from it. This was represented by cross-like "stiff female shapes" carved from bone and white alabaster, showing no life force.

USURPED: The church turned this into a symbol of purity, and used it as a means to force women into virginity or suppression of healing powers and natural sexual expression, a "cover up" of her life force.

Black: Was a symbol of the great Universal womb from which all comes; it is potential, abundance, Source of light.

USURPED: Black became a symbol of death and of evil.

Red: Symbolized the life-giving properties of menstrual blood and ancestral lineage.

USURPED: red became the symbol of the church's evil devil.

OWL: The owl was an assistant to the death transition process, having all-seeing eyes like the Goddess' Divine reach, the owl, like the vulture, helped the disintegration of the physical body to release the Spirit. Often in the early symbolic spiritual language we find owls on tomb markers, we see owls carved into bones, and we see physical representations of the Goddess' Universal energy as a female body combined with owl feel and bird wings, symbolizing the death transition process (whereas water bird parts combined with the female body represented life regenerating once again).

USURPED: The owl became an omen for impending death when death was seen as a negative failure. Death in this belief was also blamed on someone else: the midwife, who became the evil old lady who ate newborn babies; the vampire, the witch.

In my interview with Paolo, he said that the words we give to things often come as a result of something happening: they are give from the outsiders. He is referring to the terms "strega" and "stric" and "strix" being ones used in connection with witches to owls.

"For example," he explains, *"The name 'strega, strix strigess, or 'witches' in the Anglo-saxon tradition, is another tradition. In ancient times, 'strix' are birds, ONLY birds, not women. We don't have a connection between 'very greedy birds.' There is no connection between these birds the Romans called 'strix' and with the wise women about magical things nor the witches. There is no connection between 'strix' and witches in terms of historical facts. This connection between these kinds of animals and these wise women that are interested in magical things takes place several years in later in the late ancient times, so the beginning of the high medieval times. As to how it happened: when there is a myth, and another story, and they start to connect to one*

another...for example, in these ancient historical sources like Ovidio, certain Christian authors take them in the early medieval times and start to modify them in some way. So what happened to these birds is more or less very similar to what happened to the ancient Goddess... it's like process of demonization of them. Their destiny is the same."

In our most ancient beginnings, our "Founding Fathers," who lifted humanity up from what must have been an overwhelming sensation of being born into the earthly "unknown" with an abundant supply of knowledge (from a higher consciousness helper) for living life successfully in seeming earthly limitations weren't Fathers at all; they were Mothers.

More than that, they were shaman, witches, and healers to whom were given everything necessary to supported life on earth. This knowledge and the natural resources for life were considered gifts from the Great Mother Goddess.

This was our founding natural order of things: Mothers are founders. Simply, naturally. They had babies coming out of their bodies, so they naturally needed to know how to deliver them and care for their bodies and the bodies of babies. They also needed to know how to live on the earth around them, cohabiting with animals and plants. Naturally, since they spent so much time listening to their bodies and being intimately involved with babies, they became doctors, being naturally aware of the symptoms and signs of health imbalances. These experiences naturally helped them diagnose symptoms of others, and with the wisdom they received, Mediumistically, to know how to cure using the nature growing around them.

Naturally, they would need to know the passage of time: their own bodies menstruations and pregnancies. Naturally, they would need to know earth's passages of time, the seasons, to know when to plant and when to harvest. Naturally they would need to know how to communicate with others and with their children. They would need to understand the death transition, and that life continued on after the soul separates from the physical body. The Great Mother Goddess watching over them would gift them writing, music, symbolic language, and the art of making clay vessels, with which to mark the symbolic language for others, how to remain in contact with their ancestors, to point from earth to the stars and back. All of these abilities were guided into existence by the Spirit World, and in Italy in particular, the Bona Dea.

Their clocks were the sun, the moon, and the cross and their own bodies. These are marker of the passage of time of the 4 seasons and pregnancy. Though Christianity usurped this, Lineage healers in Italy still use it as well as a channel for spirit to work through: the X marks the spot that needs healing, the X also diagnoses the illness. It's a clock from nature, and since all nature is a conduit for higher consciousness, therefore it is a conduit as well.

But this symbol, as we know, was taken over by Christianity to become an enduring symbol of the suffering of Jesus, supplanted over the miracles of the Goddess. Gone are the connections to the 4 seasons, gone are the connections to nature, and in its place X marks the spot of a man to be worshipped instead. Christians used it as an ultimate symbol of persecution and sometimes, as an excuse to target others as "being the enemy."

All spiritual art in the beginning depicted the female body as an energetic source (not as a thing of beauty meant for mere decoration). a conduit between the Spirit World and the earthly one.

Paternity didn't factor into this representational art nor spiritual expression, not just because paternity wasn't know, but because naturally it is only a small part of the life-giving creative process. Because masculinity is only seen as a small but important role, there was no emphasis on the male body in the same way as the Goddess' parallel in the earthly female body. In fact, we see when Greek and Roman statuary reached realistic heights, the sculptures sought to portray man as having power and control over other life forms: so an exaggeration to overcome their smaller role in nature.

From "the stars" (the Spirit World), The Great Mother Goddess sends whatever knowledge is needed to improve life that can be used with whatever is immediately available in the environment. Having infinite knowledge of the Universe, she is abundance. The human woman is her parallel on earth, a symbol of the physical world's mysteries of life come-to-be in the form of birth and advanced knowledge applied. Man's role is important but smaller and compartmentalized, limited and temporary. The simplest and most natural way to see this arrangement is with pregnancy: the male has a role at the beginning, but after that and for the next 9 months, the female's body is the one literally feeding and nurturing what's growing inside of her, she must also exit this child out of her body so it can become an independent life form. However, it still needs care, and it is the mother who must feed the child and more. The mother's energy is ever-flowing into this new life. The father's was just a small part planted.

Both gratitude for and knowledge of this in our earliest days was expressed through spiritual sculptures and temple shapes and their decorations. Our founding language was a psychic and symbolic one that, rather simply and sensibly shows parallels between the earthly world and the energy (spirit) world. This psychic language is the route that enables advanced knowledge such as midwifery, herbal cures, and food production was received through a mediumistic process (called channeling) from the Spirit World. This is Old European Shamanism.

However, most of what we know in documented historical form (including interpretations) are from the patriarchy's establishment. So what used to be a symbolic language that showed parallels between nature and the Spirit World (Universe's energy, how it moves and manifests), became a confusing mix of ideas that are difficult to understand and were described through a masculine perspective which is already removed from the internal process of life-giving. The link to nature was broken, so the meanings were lost. This was the start of synthetic religion and art that subsumed Feminine Divinity, and also connected her with the idea of her biggest rival man: The Church's Devil. This has also affected magical practices. In Italy, we find both the female shamanism and the masculinized magic.

From my interview with Manuela Saccone:

"The first statues representing the Goddess are from the Paleolithic, the oldest one is 40,000 years old. This statue is made in Mammoth ivory and represents a woman with huge breasts and with her vulva precisely marked because life was there... it was the natural cycle of life. The woman

creates life, the woman feeds, and then the earth, when you die, takes your body back in your mother's womb and then to the Mother Goddess who welcomes you again. It's is a miracle if we think about it. So the woman is basically a creative figure of life. The man still did not understand the mechanism inside the woman.

These were first engraved in bones and stones, because pottery wasn't yet known. These female statues always had her vulva in evidence if you look. Now these statues are found throughout the Mediterranean.

When we come to the Neolithic period , and then we start farming and there's agriculture and we're no longer nomads, this cult does not end but turns into the so-called 'Neolithic Venus.' These also are small statues. They are always the same, they can be fatter or slimmer but what they represent, they're strictly related to fertility and they are made in terra cotta.

When we talk about Mediterranean Europe, there were the 'gylanic' societies, at least this is what some studies say, and was really a balance of nature and between man and woman, that is, it was not patriarchy or matriarchy, They are called matrilineal societies. This means 'of a female, maternal line'. If you say matriarchy it means the woman prevails over the man, just as in patriarchy the man prevails over the woman. These societies, on the other hand, were a kind of balance. So we have the God of vegetation and the Mother Goddess procreating fertilized by the God of vegetation. They had to be pretty peacefully societies, dedicated to the agriculture. There are thousands of these statuettes, scattered all over the Europe, representing this development.

This is also the thesis of Marija Gimbutas, who is a Lithuanian archeologist. She wrote 'The Language of the Goddess' because observed these ancient traditions, the local traditions, peasant traditions, still alive in Lithuania. She studied them starting from the traditions she remembered as a little girl, dating back to the Christian traditions, previously pagan, that were all related to this Goddess. It is always the same Goddess who creates life.

What happens then, at some point from the north, these patriarchal societies who traveled on horses, who lived by raiding other communities, such as the Mongols invaded from the north and pretty much destroyed what gylanic society was, the balance between male and female. As a result, the role of the woman is then relegated to the home.

Women were certainly the greatest herb pickers because in the Paleolithic women were dedicated to harvesting, because it was one of those activities that could be done while looking at the children. It is thought that they have discovered agriculture because they knew the plants and the healing powers of the plants. Most probably, in prehistoric societies, were medicine women, not men, who already had that role.

*As far as what has happened to these Goddess, once the patriarchal society has come, they do not disappear, but become the wives of the gods. **The Goddess is no longer the principal but becomes functional to man.** This is my idea anyway and Marija Gimbutas also talks about it. That these gods, the Romans, the Northern Gods comes and they have a woman next to them at their side in their stories. So there is 'Diana the hunter' and there were the other gods of the Pantheon. **They become the supporters of man, they become wives, companions.***

Diana the hunter, is also Isis; it's always her: the Mother Goddess who takes a lot of names depending on where she is, such as the Mesopotamian Goddesses. So these figures of the Mother Goddess merge into all these historical Goddess. But, of course, becoming a patriarchal society, they become functional to man and become companions, the Gods' wives, but always the same Goddess.

The snake is the sacred animal to the Goddess. The snake, because it makes a spiral in a loop shape, and who changes its skin in a regenerative loop, a cycle, is a natural representation of the Goddess' energy of life, death, and rebirth (reincarnation and healing). Goddess was death and rebirth.

The was then transformed by Christianity into the serpent who allegedly tempted Eve. Everything that was part of the ancient religion is demonized. However, in this book titled 'The Witch and the Crucifix' by Paolo Portone is the explanation of all these pagan cults.

And then, when I had my first daughter while I was taking my clothes off the terrace [from drying] and my mom came and said to me, 'She retires the clothes that is evening and if the witches pass they put a spell to the baby.' I look at her and say, 'Mom, but do you believe what you are saying?' And she: 'No, however, my mom told me and I'm telling you.'

So the idea was that these women accused as witches were guilty of something above all with the children. Especially in farms where there was a need to be numerous because you had to cultivate the land and where you need help taking care of the home. And children often died. So even more than being accused of being a healer was the midwife, since both the healer and the midwife were doing good, the scapegoat idea believes that the boundary was always thin: the thread that divides the good from the evil. So sometimes people believed you were a wonderful woman because you healed someone, but if the church tells me that you are not in orthodoxy I will soon say that the baby has got the stomachache because you have done the evil spell. I'm not saying that there were no evil women and that perhaps women did kill somebody. But the accusation was always the same.

So the witch is not dangerous until she is paired with the devil. The accusations are Is defined as the cumulative concept of sorcery because of the association with the devil, which then becomes the accusation of the adoration of the devil against Christ."

Eighteenth Secrets

During my Spiritualist training, I learned that vibration can be changed at will and that both emotions and thoughts vibrate. Some vibrate lower and slower, such as sadness, grief, and depression, which seems to be not an emotion but a process that squashes all emotions into immobility. Other emotions vibrate high and fast such as love, hope, joy, inspiration and the mental thought process of seeking of knowledge.

The reason "raising one's vibration higher" is important is because: earthly matter moves much slower than energy. Spirit people such as Guides are comprised of energy which vibrates very quickly...so in order to communicate, we must attempt to blend. We raise our vibration high as we can, they lower down to meet us, and the frequencies become closer..so our "radio" with our tuning dials (psychic senses) can grab onto this subtle information and "tune in." to receive information.

Ways that we can raise vibration are: music (a gift of the Goddess) dance, laughing at a funny movie, smiling, meditation, color therapy, using gemstones and minerals, smelling flower essences, being in nature...and more.

The Signora del Gioco recommended to her students to keep their houses clean as a practice, to have good manners, and to also enjoy the spirit of "play" in learning.

People in many cultures burn herbs such as sage, to clean the energetic space around them by raising the energy, others purify with water.

In his book "Have you Been to Delphi?" , author Roger Lipsey interviews a Tibetan lama and scholar about the Tibetan trance oracles, "...There is no training at all because the person- the medium himself- is neutral in the sense that he is not directly involved in the process of oracular activity. But in the case of high oracles, the medium is generally required to go through Buddhist training, especially training in advanced yoga concerned with controlling inner energies, chakras, and the nervous system. People would commonly say […] that any oracle must have a special kind of energy within his body […]so that a powerful spirit can possess him and function appropriately.

He also tells the author "I have visited some of the female oracles. The system of transmission there was hereditary, form mother to daughter."[263]

Chapter 18:
BENANDANTI:

"GUARDIANS OF THE THRESHOLD"

Benandanti are a challenge to describe, and not simply because they are a secretive group which must remain that way. This is not a group you can choose to join, so likely you will never come in contact with a Benandante, knowingly. (Benandanti is plural, Benandante is singular). The challenge is in describing their roles and duties, because in order to understand those, you must have come to a place of understanding of "form versus formlessness." This type of understanding cannot simply be come upon logically; it must come from experience. So, if you are not regularly actively involved with the Spirit World, this understanding will simply be like vespers in the wind. I will do my best:

For example, if we look at life on earth, we know what we can see. If we look at people, we see: babies, children, young adults, adults, parents, aunts and uncles, grandparents, great grandparents, great great grandparents, the ancestors, and onward into generations past and even into past lives...

And then if we look, from our place on earth into the Spirit World, we can first find a "realm" of ghosts of all sorts: all forms of consciousness who haven't completed their death transitions so therefore are in a variety of "stuck, stunted growth" states. Some have "devolved" into parasitical forms, such as spirit attachments, ones people like to call demons but really aren't a separate category of consciousness at all; we have the regretting ones such as suicides and people who just can't let go; we have the lowly ones who love to bully and scare others; peeping toms and angry ones, manipulators, and people who've simply lost their way since they have passed out of their bodies and never quite made it to the light.

In this "astral location" near earth, like a layer of atmosphere, these spirits were all once earthly people who remember their earthly forms but who have also de-formed, rather than moved on in their transition: they grow almost backwards, becoming a manifestation of their fears, negativities, and irresponsibleness. These "ghosts" have a range of mobility that is limited, even though they are without physical bodies. They are literally "stuck" because of the Laws of Energy: they have not completed their death transition and so their territory is "close to earth" but not beyond. Because of the Law of Will, however, they can choose to stay here also, and drain energy off earthly people rather than grow.

In addition to the many "forms" consciousness can take, or the many more that can be accomplished in the Spirit World of energy that is not limited by slow-moving physical matter, there are many "realms" of consciousness, like many different "neighborhoods" for many different levels of consciousness.

In a more "mobile" range and "higher realm" the earth, we have passed-on relatives, friends, loved ones and those who have passed out of physical bodies, who have completed their death transitions and have ascended into the next phase of their lives without physical bodies.

This grants them more mobility: relatives can carry on in their realm, which may be just to develop more in Spirit World until they come around to earth once again, and they can also communicate with their friends and relatives still living on earth, as well as with their Guides and Angel helpers who may help them travel to specific realms for the purpose of learning, until they decide to temporarily be in a physical body on earth once again...and again..and again.

There are even higher realms, further away from earth and therefore more generalized, less specific in form, which offer the conscious beings who naturally "vibrate" in these realms to have even greater mobility and to take a variety of forms if necessary. Everyone who has passed out of a physical body has the choice of making themselves appear to have one form or another: the one they were familiar with while living on earth, or a younger version of themselves, or with the "devolved" ones we find "shadow figures" who want to hide their identity, or even others who choose to "appear" as monsters for the sake of scaring those they appear to, etc. Their chosen forms will always be in a range of "what they know," or rather are limited to their imaginations and therefore can't imitate higher conscious beings. We also have, in the realm of Guides and Helpers, higher conscious beings who can choose to have a relatively consistent form (like angels) so to whomever they appear they are recognizable as being a "specific type of being with specific type of knowledge" no matter whom they appear to and in whichever culture or belief system, all while not truly having a form such as this.

In these higher realms we find consciousness as "bodies of knowledge" who have chosen to assist humanity's growth and development, whether the humanity is on earth in physical form or has passed out and into the spirit realm. So we can find Helpers and Guides of all sorts in a variety of categories: philosophers, healers, native people, earth guardians, goddesses, doctors and indigenous medicine healers, keepers of world knowledge, animal helpers, angels, gods and more.

And then, as we get even further away from the "realms" nearest earth and closer to the "Source" energy from which we all come, we can find the formless yet recognizable conscious energy as the "Great Goddess Mother" who can just appear as collected light or can be experienced as a vibration, a frequency...and then onward into a formlessness from which all comes.

There is no singular man in the sky as god: there is simply infinite intelligence...the Source energy from which all energy comes. In order for all things to come from the same Source, the Source must offer a formlessness (that yet operates according to laws of this very energy, which keep it constant, operational, and consistent), a type of form that is all forms. Specific form is limiting, but also helps us to identify people, places, and things. From this Source energy comes all: ice cream, electricity, people, trees, colors, this planet, fluorescent pink, violins and musical sounds, ravens, coffee tables, the oceans, oil paint...

To simplify: there is consciousness energy and there is energy which consciousness can use to create form.

That's it.

So what in the Universe does all this have to do with Benandanti?

If we try to explain that Benandanti have a purpose, that their purpose is not that of parents on earth, nor as teachers, nor as Spirit guides, nor as Lineage healers, but those who have a specific purpose in a specific realm that is off-limits to ghosts and passed-on earthly ones, a realm that Angels and Guides are aware of but do not tread. A realm that has Infinite Intelligence watching over it; a realm that has its own rules and types of "form" that will appear to materialize for the purpose of "carrying out specific duties" in this realm which have a benefit for all realms, of duties that are ancient and largely indigenous to a specific area within Italy, and that are not widespread, we can begin to give some form to the duties of Benandanti.

So even now, we begin to try to examine a different type of hierarchy that's difficult for human beings to accept, because human beings like to put things in a certain order and categories, and if they can't succeed in doing so they deem it "chaos," which is technically not possible in this Universe which is ordered by Laws of Energy which are always in operation. We nevertheless come to say that in some way Benandanti are like watchers. But not just watchers, because they engage in a realm of the Spirit World that mostly none of us will ever become aware of. And they watch this realm and engage with it, intensely, and battle to keep a balance between the darkness and the light...like overlords, like universal parents... all while we are busy, like ants, focusing on such tiny things, often passively going about our days. Benandanti see, 4 times a year, the results of the thoughts and actions we all make and how these affect the Wheel. Benandanti can also be witches, and can practice magic, but those are smaller things than what they do. They are most certainly all Mediums.

In their own words,

"'Sense of responsibility' is the description that fits better the general attitude any practitioner has. Benandanti have been given special abilities and a training and it's their duty to put them in practice. For example, deliberately ignoring the call for the battle is almost a blasphemy. Being able of doing something, such as cure, protect, and solve and yet stay still is not conceivable. Sometimes responsibility is heavier than the pleasure of being part of the craft and in touch with the gods. You just 'do the job that is in front of you' and you are not supposed to find pleasure in it, except from the one you find in well done 'craftsmanship.' Duty is the main feature of the tradition, and we are very serious about it."

I had the privilege of meeting with Benandanti, members of a secretive group who will remain anonymous in the printed versions of parts of their interview I'm able to share. Why would they speak with me? We could perhaps say, as with my entire journey in Italy, I was guided to people and they were guided to me. It is my job to know systems, but not necessarily to use them. To put pieces together, not just for my own mind, but also to reconnect people to their histories so they can reclaim their spiritual power in full. I am like a train station, and many types of people from different walks of life come in contact with me. These are not my systems and I have no need to claim them as my own. Perhaps my beliefs and knowing my place are why they chose to meet with me. We surely "interviewed" each other, energetically, before we physically met.

From here, however, meeting them in person would be what gave me an understanding of who they are through experiencing their energy. As a Medium, this sensation of energy tells me everything, and it occurs in the process of "experience" not within "logical mental computations."

The best I can do is to describe the environment around Benandanti, because I haven't been chosen as one and therefore I do not travel to their realm.

I like to remain skeptical of many things: people, places, and things, including my own abilities. It leaves the door open for me to be proven right or wrong. It all starts with the act of questioning what someone, some place, or some thing truly is.

This skepticism is the reason, half a decade ago, that I went to experience an Italian-born, British-transplanted trance Medium at a Spiritualist center in San Francisco. I didn't know what a trance Medium was at the time. So, I thought it would be the perfect opportunity to observe, to pay attention to how I felt in the circle, to sense my reactions, and to learn more about myself in comparison. The experience I had made me a believer, and I'd return 3 other times to be part of this circle.

This trance Medium channels a group of beings who operate under one specific name. The Medium, a woman, has arranged a special working relationship with these beings: They "use her body" as the vehicle through which to speak to people, to answer specific questions. This is an arrangement to which she agreed under the condition that she gets to remain "conscious and in the background so as to still be aware of what is occurring." This is a relationship that takes great practice and organization internally for the Medium. This is in contrast to Edgar Cayce, a trance Medium whose own consciousness was entirely asleep while the Spirit consciousness who channeled through him gave people medical diagnoses.

This trance/spirit circle procedure is one that is arranged carefully for the public as well. To start, this Medium is already seated when we arrived. She has taken some time (an hour) to get into her trance. I noticed her head moved in a soft spiraling motion while she was going deeper into this trance. Likewise, when it was over, she remained in a state of "coming fully back into her own body" for at least an hour, and we were instructed to not touch her.

Her husband was the circle facilitator, and he spoke directly with us, welcoming all of us, explaining the procedure, and asking us to give our names and the question we wanted to ask the Medium. He chose the order of the names.

He told us it was very important that no one broke the circle of energy once it was created: he instructed us that, if we needed to use the restroom (the events are often 2 hours long), to please let him know so the Medium's Spirit guides could open the energy circuit of the circle in a way that would not harm the Medium.

Then, the event began. First, the Medium's Native American Spirit guide would appear and be the one to cast the circle, calling in the four directions, and speaking a few words through the Medium. The Medium's eyes remained closed for the entirety of the event. The

Medium's voice sounded completely different when channeling the Native Guide as compared to the group of Spirits who were operating under one name and answering the questions from people. However, her body would turn and face, directly, the person who's turn it was to ask their question even before they began to speak. She was "seeing them" without her eyes open.

I had the opportunity to sit directly to the right side of the Medium. When the Native Guide appeared and "entered" the room, I fell forward and was almost pushed off my chair with the force of his "invisible" power of presence. Additionally, I saw much more clearly than my clairvoyance allows normally, white smoky light in the shape of a circle for the duration of the event. It looked like a ring of white fire was enflamed around the room. When a person would ask their question, and especially if it was emotional in nature, the white fire would also form directly in front of them. The strongest sensation however, was the sensation of the vibrations of the beings who operated under one name through the Medium and the continued presence of the Native American guide.

Their frequency felt, against my own energy, so fast and high-quality that it seemed as though my own cells where shaking apart in their presence. It felt like the trance was trying to induce me, but because I was not used to this high of a frequency, my mind was not able to interpret the information coming through, it was scrambled, so it felt instead it was falling asleep because of the whirring of the frequencies...similar to being in extremely hot weather and your mind sort of melts. In this case, however, there was no sun energy melting anything; there was the energy of higher consciousness whirring so very quickly. So I had to try very hard to remain conscious, and I did, because I didn't want to miss a word, but surely my head was dropping and surely people in the circle saw me. I was told my main Spirit Guide is a Goddess of Abundance and very ancient that my life was like a dance: where Spirit wanted me, I'd be: writing a book, making music, traveling...

Later, the Medium and her husband informed me that I had been the only person to remain conscious while sitting in the right-seat position; that people always fell "asleep" under the vibrations.

In my training as a Spiritualist Medium I got to experience many different vibrations of spirit beings, (from low to very high) but this group of beings operating under one name as channeled through this trance Medium was the closest thing to "Source" I had ever experienced until that point in my life with the exception of one other time in class where I felt a little bit of that same "Source" energy and burst into tears. Similarly, I felt like by molecules were going to shake apart. I felt an immense beauty and love beyond human capabilities. It made me tremble and cry because of the beauty and also made me a little fearful, like right before a huge storm hits: there is an eerie silence and then a huge, intangible power.

After these experiences, the only other times I've felt this vibration was when my husband and I were translating Carlo Napolitano's book about the Janare and walnut tree of Benevento. The Spirits who were teaching me and helping me to "connect the historical dots" while I was typing what Davide was translating to me, were so high and fast that I was falling in and out of consciousness while typing on my computer. Somehow my hands kept typing, but my head kept dropping.

The other time I felt this sensation was in the presence of Benandanti.

So now, you can read as they speak for themselves:

Karyn: What is the practice of Benandanti about?

B: *"It focuses on four 'night battles' in four specific nights during the year.During those nights the Benandanti fall in a trance-like status and fight against ranks of "bad" witches. The purpose of the battle is to fight chaos and to ensure the right climate in that specific season. There is more of it, depending on the awareness of the single fighter and how long they have been part of the tradition, but it's something we can't write about. Outside the 4 nights, our job is to maintain balance and guard the thresholds (between the worlds, between life and death –meaning that we deal with ghosts and are supposed to help souls reach peace- good and evil and so on). We also are in charge of guarding our own land in a strong mutual relationship and are in charge of keeping the balance and keep our land free of dirty energies."*

K: Are there special purposes, specific things only Benandanti can care for and do?

B: *"Yes, and of course the main thing is the battle itself. The threshold guard and the purification/protection is the other one."*

K: Which parts of your practice are taken into daily life?

B: *"There is a series of small rituals and acts of awareness involving, in most cases, purification and protection. They are daily but not public."*

K: Which are left for private?

B: *"Our being part of the tradition is strictly private. Being an initiatic path we are not supposed to speak about it to people who are not involved in it (with some exception for very close friends and people we trust. In our case, our relatives don't know about what we do) and we tend not to trust self-declared Benandanti: we can also recognize each other in some ways so it's not easy to fool us."*

K: Is there an organized system?

B: *"In 'real life' we are equal, with the only obvious difference of age in the craft. On the 'other side' there is a military-like, pyramid structure."*

K: Is the path opened in-part (initiation) by the Spirit World and then by a human earthly teacher?

B: *"Yes."*

K: Are there initiation levels to Benandanti practice?

B: *Yes, but they are mostly linked to our "battle" plan of existence and are about our roles and experience during the battles. It's similar to military ranking.*

K: Who preserves the lineage?

B: *"As long as we know, a Benandante has to pass down his or her heirloom at a certain point. Not everyone reaches the age for having a heir and not everyone finds one but this is how it should work."*

K: How Would each of your describe Benandanti to an outsider?

B: *"They are warriors, and what they fight for is balance, to preserve balance. They fight 4 nights a year, and they try to not be overwhelmed but the negative side to keep things the best they can keep them so the wheel can keep going. [4 marks on the wheel of the year are the 4 seasons]. The wheel needs pushing, needs something to push it, a force.*

The battles are, from a shallow point of view, about winning, but we're saying that the most important things is that the others don't win. We don't need to win but we can't lose. The most important things is that you're giving your energy to the earth.

There is a chain of command in the pyramid, because it's a pyramid structure. You do not really have to beat your enemy, because light and dark have to be in balance. Too much light, too much dark... you have to keep the idea that there's something more complicated. We know what's below us, we have different jobs in the field and we don't know what's beyond that. Probably not two lines against each other, probably a pyramid, probably not a person anymore, an archetype, an invisible link. The important thing to know is that the battles will never end, they must never end.

So you retire your job after a certain time, but the battles go on, because you can't give your energy anymore. It makes you really tired. You start around 20 years of age and end around 40 years of age. Which was the moment of maximum energy. You are allowed to continue if you want to, you can sign up for more, but we don't know how much more, maybe another 10 years, probably not 20.

It's been 10 years so far, [for one of them] and I feel nowhere near being done with battles. I can feel it, I'm halfway through. It's a full portion of person's life. I feel I barely scratched the surface even in all of my times.

We are very aware when it's time that it will be like this. Maybe some people are not aware, but the battle needs every kind of person and every type of help they can give, every kind of help they can do. So maybe they're not fighters, maybe in the background doing small tasks, because a couple of friends of ours looked like they were doing something along those lines without actually fighting.

For example, a friend from Sicily feels the tempera, but she knows that she does something that looks like ascetic witchcraft all over Italy that has something to do with this. Even the Gioco di Oriente, Aradia's Game, her ladies left on Thursday, at the same kind of time, the same kind of state, but they didn't fight, but they eat and drink and play and be merry [in a realm like battle realm]. And maybe that's very useful too, because fighting is very strong and hard and sad and maybe adding some merriment to add in the mixture to make it work is useful."

In battle, while they have different positions and roles in the battle, they may see one of their group perhaps involved with logistics for the battle such as working on plans, and then late in the battle see another person they know with a different task such as fighting in the front lines. This is similar to traveling together in the astral realm and all being aware of it, at the same time, and seeing all the same things, and doing tasks together.

Something else I can tell you about the environment "around" Bendandanti is that they also work in dreams and can dream in groups in daily life, outside the battle times. They work together in the dream world, often to protect, where they actually see each other there and they see the same "things." In fact, the morning after my first night sleeping in their home as their guest, when we first met for breakfast I made some comment jokingly asking "Did you sleep well or cause trouble?" This type of comment and humor is not like me at all, I am much more polite and serious, but something compelled me. They brought this up at dinner to tell me they had in fact not slept well: instead they were protecting me from a dark-haired man who had followed me, through the dreamworld, and was trying to harm me. He was very jealous and envied my journey. So they spent their night in the dreamworld backing him off. This would not be the only time they would help me in this way.

When they are in a learning period:

"Sometimes you don't know you're dreaming, it's confused and shallow, just your mind unfolding and downloading the feelings and emotions and simulations from the day, And there are different types of dreams which cane be pleasant, or important or WORK. These are the levels in general. And you also meet people, we met Karyn in our dreams, there are just ways in which you have to battle something (Karyn's guy), or someone which links to what Benandani is."

You may notice that Benandanti also learn as-they-experience. This is because being Benandanti is not entirely a choice: Ecstatic Trance is not always something you put yourself into entirely on your own, although Benandanti do have techniques to induce trance. The Spirit World brings you into this trance as well. You can prepare yourself and begin the process, but it's largely an experience that takes place in the Spirit World and is conducted by the Spirit World. You don't have much of a choice in this realm. And as far as being Benandanti, of course your choice has been made by your spirit before this lifetime, it's an agreement, a soul contract.

"You feel pulled into it [the battle]. You can resist a little bit, but if you wait too long you're not able to get in anymore, even though you can still feel things moving around you like blows, but you're not able to see it anymore...so you can only hold off a little bit. If you wait you have the feeling of the battle but not seeing what's happening."

I am told about a particular battle where one of the Benandati was waiting for a bus and were pulled into battle: *"One other time me and my people had been promoted, and it was funny because I was waiting for the bus and the battle began. I looked to my side and I saw a row of garu wolves wearing super kitsch kind of armor and I saw my paws...where's my armor? I'm sure I wasn't imagining that because I never would have imagined something that tasteless (laughing). Other times, late at night you can feel it, anxiously, you start being nervous, just waiting for the time, and then the doors open and you can see the fields, and it's always a quiet moment before the battle when you're in line, and you wait...you actually are in the moment in which you're still waiting, but sometimes you are already started in the fight. I think it depends on many factors...*

One is the Moon, we find out that many times the moon is in an air sign like Libra. How you feel the energy, the place in the earth, you can be in the fight and not find out all the factors. And sometimes you don't see anything or dream anything too specific but you you have the feeling that the battle is going on, maybe because the time on the other side of the world [referring to the location of the battle], so you're already in a different moment of the awake part, and so on."

Note: Garu wolves are "werewolves," the wolves Benandanti transform into for the battles.

K: So in a way would you describe it as you're traveling in the astral realm or...is it more like this physical illusion falls away and you're there, in the battle?

B: "It's difficult to use terms I know."

This is the point of my book as well: insiders to these experiences are not part of the historical record, other than in persecution records where the people forced to confess are made to look evil or crazy. It's difficult to put into words the idea of the battle, the transformations that take place (becoming various animals) and more. Benandanti don't change shape except for when they are in battle, but never into snakes. Snakes, apparently, are a transformational form that witches take in the Udine region. They told me, "Benandanti are both sides of the tradition: ecstatic process on one hand, witchcraft on the other hand."

"It is fun to remember things. The last [battle] time I was awake I had a couple of very very interesting experiences. I was seeing everything very clearly. I was able to summon a few of our people, I was also awake enough to scribble down notes, then I immediately forgot about everything. But two or 3 of them have been with me since almost the beginning [of the battles]. At about 2-3 years into the battles I could summon them and see their faces, and saw someone with very long white hair, sometimes a male with wolf skin, and one time I was walking and entered the tent of my captain and I had a wolf skin on my shoes, and I don't like skins."

And another one of the team recounts: "There was one time, I saw another person I know and there were also gods who were not fighters, they are gods. I remember them fighting but not in the front rows, in the bowels...I remember them because I was bringing "news" form one point to the other and I stopped watching the fight and saw both of them with arrows, and I was thinking 'maybe if they moved better up the cliff...' because it was a dried riverbed, and I was thinking if they moved a little up maybe they could stop the enemies from coming down better, but then I thought 'well it's not my business, I'm not here to fight I'm just here to run there with the news. The battles themselves are not my business. I fight but I can bring messages,

I just do duties that are like spy sorts of things, logistics. I'm not in the front lines."

And another battle description: "I was around the camp of other people. The other people released their beasts, they had really big beast like dinosaurs kinds of things, and monsters behind their lines..."

"Another time in 2008 I had wings. I had an upgrade in my levels, so I could also fly then. This time, I'm in the front row...so it's much more exciting. One of the last times I was awake I was a werewolf, and I had to jump two feet and I was running like berserkers, cutting through with the tip of an arrow because I had to open the way so the others could spread around behind me...because I had to get to their biggest guy on the other side who was much bigger than I was. I had to get to him to touch him and then touch my direct superior, push them together and push them together in a side dimension because that clash was going to be so heavy they couldn't know what kind of outcome there could have been. And then I could fight in the line after I pushed them together .The other ones are always fancier and more elegant. That's the funny thing. Apart from the lowest levels, the higher you go the fancier they get."

Benandanti are chosen by the Spirit World and therefore are of a practice very difficult to understand: the battle scenes sound like a collage of visuals, but their own description of what they do is very technical. Unless you have a great understanding of the Spirit World and the Natural Laws that govern energy and of the universal systems in place, it may not sound as it should.

K: Is the inclusion of men and women done for a specific reason?: (i.e. in myths of Proserpine, only a balance of masculine and feminine energy opened the doorway of knowledge through Universal love):

B: "It's probably about balance."

K: Are there Spirit Teachers /Master teachers/ Goddess teachers who have passed down the way of Benandanti?

B: "Yes. And much of what we know is learned through insights, meditation and dreams of a special kind."

They explain to me that in their "work" dreams, they (the spirit teachers) try to find images they like and can relate to for the purpose of sending easily recognizable messages to Benandanti. As an example, they say if it's a supportive dream, "it could be a handsome actor from a movie or tv show, something we saw recently at the theater or on a tv commercial."

This immediately brought something to mind that my own Mediumship teacher told me: that when working with Spirit, the Spirit person will try to use visual vocabulary that you're already familiar with, because they will always try to use the familiar as the fastest way to get a message across and recognized: whether symbols, song lyrics, images from a movie you just watched, a tarot card you just pulled...something that will stand out as being recognizable by you and have a special meaning for you (beyond what it may mean to anyone else). *And in fact, this is what I teach Mediumship students as well, That's why it's important to know your reactions to things, your preferences, your desires, your instincts, your ideas, because Spirit will contact you in these ways until you build up a more steady and constant language.*

Another observation I can share with you is the "earth guardian" part of their duties that I find really wonderful. Each of them is very connected to the earth, even though they walk "in the Spirit World" as well. I've found that with other people I've met and known who "walk in both worlds," meaning their contact with the Spirit World is on a daily basis, is that it's hard for us to find ways to plug into normal earthly life like others. I believe this is due to "seeing too much." I can give a parallel example: if you are a character in a movie, but you know the ending of the movie, likely your path through the movie will change based on knowing more than the other characters. The other characters innocently go through their actions without being on the lookout for danger or for challenges. This is what it is like for those who are closer to the Spirit World while still living on earth: being able to see beyond the illusion can make it less interesting to be involved in mundane things that are repetitive: taking the train, going to work, coming home. But the sense of responsibility is much greater as well: knowing more deeply how significant is each choice and action and how these add to the bigger picture.

For example, they shared with me how it is to meet and recognize another one like them and choosing not to battle outside of the designated Wheel battles:

"I was trying to locate a group of people allegedly causing some negativity. When the group was discovered and "found" in the astral field, it was clear they were not just regular people but at least one was also Benandanti...

At a certain point I had a perception of the leader of this group...I was looking outside my window because I felt a threat coming, ...because he was hitting the ashes around my house. There is an invocation around my house, a firewall, and very powerful last resort solution.

So I was trying to understand where it was coming from and who it was.. and I saw him, and then he saw me, and we looked at each other, and we both realized we were at the same level on the other side and we looked at each other and were very respectful, and We said 'ok, we're not going to do that' [battle each other]. He extended his hand but no, I wouldn't shake his hand, wouldn't touch his hand because if I did, then his people would be at war with our people . I am in command of people under me, a hierarchy, and if I were to engage over something not part of the battles...then part of our line becomes personal and that's not allowed.

What could happen if we tried to battle with each other would be too much, and we're not going to do that. It was very scary...so we said 'ok, we're not going to do that. And that's very important because you have a responsibility.

He was very elegant. I know there are many people as powerful as I am in this area, at least in the area, but he was huge, and I had the feeling that we could go on battling each other forever, so we look at each other and say 'no.'

The more you are high in the chain of command...the more experienced you are the more perception you have of the structure and dynamics, the less you can do and the less you should do for yourself, the less you are allowed to do for yourself. Years ago I had the feeling walking on a very thin line between right and wrong, I had to keep a balance very very carefully, and that's probably around the time another person we know was going 'bad.' Because If you put hate in what you do or hope in what you do...you just have to do the job that's in front of you [objectively].

In our job you're not supposed to have fun, but in the beginning you're more naive, so you just go an shout and hit and smash [in the battles], and it is funny, but the more conscious you become the less fun you have because you know that everything has a consequence, especially for people after you or below you. You have more and more responsibility so you have less and less fun."

SECRECY:

Secrecy is also a matter of protection. Both as a self-protective measure from outsiders as well as a protective measure from other people who "work" in the Spirit World/astral plane, and in dreamworlds. It is a built-in safeguard to keep the legacies preserved in their original form.

They are guided by other higher conscious beings (directly or intuitively). And as such, the lifestyle and its accompanying knowledge is received through a process of unfoldment: bit by bit, as the person advances deeper into their path. There is no "guidebook," nor instant understanding of all. The path and the education on the path and the training is all in under the Guidance of higher consciousness rom the Spirit World. The training does involve dealing with light and dark. There is no escaping this. Because of the "unfoldment" process, there are things that cannot be understood by someone else who has not reached that level of "unfolding." Learning something truly new requires moving into the "unknown," which can be frightening for many people, and therefore the knowledge that is acquired from these brave steps is often frightening because it is unfamiliar. Secrecy of the unfoldment process keeps fears from becoming enlarged. As far as secrecy being important as a protective measure for those around Benandanti, I was told that "people we know who have perception can be an easy target for oppositional forces, so we never let any people know the real depths of our practice. It's very important that no one knows the actual extent of our abilities."

I shared with them a situation I found myself in, which wasn't the first time and wouldn't be the last. They gave me some important insight on this, and put it into an historical context:

I had become part of a spiritual community where I went to train as a Medium under a Certified Minister with the National Spiritualist Association of California. Due to the quality of messages that came through to people from my Spirit team, my messages became popular. I was invited by the teacher to also teach and to give inspired speeches to the group, to heal and give platform Medium readings regularly. So while I originally went only to train, I became a solid part of this group, I even was elected Secretary of the Board, and I became very public part of this community. Unbeknownst to me at the time, my readings garnered much interest and curiosity from other already established psychics and Mediums in the Bay Area.

When the Minister, the only certified member of the community left the group, trouble ensued. Over time, people began infighting over board positions and whatever "power" and territory there was to be had in this small group. Additionally, as often happens in a "Hogwarts"-type situation: competition. None of the other psychics and Mediums who were involving themselves in program scheduling here were trained by the Certified Minister, there was a lack of ethics and understanding of the systems Spirit World: people began bringing all sorts of "spiritual" groups into the place during one phase, which resulted in a "Spirit World battle for territory": because Guides and other lowly spirits do watch over "groups." The higher the guides involved, the better quality and harmony of the space. The more earthly territorial and ego-driven the group, the more instability and darker the energy of the entire place. In other words: competition. During one other phase, several people wanted to take over the group with their ideas, which were darker. They began to place objects in the community which changed the vibration, and subtle chaos was ensuing: students in the classes were feeling uncomfortable and nervous, attendees were becoming confused about what they could sense was "not right," and they couldn't put a finger on it.

As Secretary of the Board, it was my job to protect the Charter and ensure the bylaws were being upheld. I didn't know this at first- the Spirit guides of the community told me, and guided me. Thus, I found myself in the middle of two different territorial battles: the earthly people who were fighting to take over the space were being influenced by spirit people of a negative quality. I was seeing all the ugly details.

The spirits were trying to bully me through sensations of oppression and confusion because they saw me as the "protector" and I was also the only one who could clearly see what they were doing. I see well behind the shadows. Some of the elders in the groups sensed, in part, what was happening and supported the efforts I had to make, which, because of bylaws being broken, had to be made to the Board as well.

Nevertheless, I was the target of both negative groups: earthly people and spirit people. The spirit ones influenced the egos of the earthly people, pushing them to be aggressive with me and try to fight and discredit me, the only Medium who had trained under our Certified one who founded the community. They tried to scare me, they threatened me with legal action, they threatened me personally, as well as some of my friends…because those friends were supporting me. The negative spirits can see the weakness in humans, so to influence them they tend to go for what works easiest and fastest: align with earthly people who want power and inflate their ego. The earthly people feel "driven" to fight for the power, and an even be driven "out of themselves," going on an ego trip. However, because this is a literal battle for territory, the negative spirits know how to "gather troops," so in these cases there were people banded against me, but only the ones who wanted power. Additionally it seemed, through the threatening messages, that some of the earthly people had become obsessed with me, having seemingly studied my art and musical careers and using the imagery against me.

So I largely had to battle in private. Some of my peers did help, even if they didn't understand, but I was the only one who could see the details and locate the spirits. I was also supported by the Spirit guides associated with the Spiritualist practice. Even though I was on the Board, I wasn't properly trained to know what that entailed. So, the Guides pointed me to legalities, how to write the proper letters and leave a trail, and whom to ask for assistance. I largely had to battle alone, and keep balance in mind. Since there were negative Spirits involved, I didn't tell any of my friends or loved ones outside this group (nor even many inside) what was happening, because I knew the negative Spirits would try to scare them as well, and likely the earthly people would threaten them also. Because the way influence works, if you're one who is being targeted, is the negative spirits will use whomever they can wherever they can to make their target feel vulnerable and isolated.

We won the first battle, but In the end, and during the second battle, the board members and people in "power" were very much under the darker influence of the negative spirits, so it was best for me to leave. I attempted to explain what their choices were doing on "unseen" level, but I was laughed at-even though attendees and students were once again complaining about the strange vibrations in the community space. The members who insisted on maintaining not only practices that were against the bylaws and charter, but that also maintained negativity (and the ones who wanted new roles of power) were clearly being influenced and their egos pumped up: even after I resigned and left there were a couple of people trying to continue to fight me and make me look like a bad example through group emails and threatening texts to my cell phone. It was clear these people were ok with being influenced, and in order to protect myself, I had to leave the community. The spirits, after all, knew that I was the one standing in the way. I could have fought - gotten the charter taken away, dismantled the community in the physical realm and therefore sending the negative spirits elsewhere, but I decided that was not my responsibility. I should mention that between the first and second battles I had left the Board due to traveling for other work and also for this book, so there were many changes while I was away. I knew those changes had to take their course, so regardless of my efforts, the downward spiral had too much momentum for me to fight alone. And, I kept this secret from my "sensitive" friends, so no one would be a target.

It was Benandanti who and shared with me some material they label didactic which explains this phenomenon well:

They described to me author Terry Pratchett's "The Cunning Man" story about a man obsessed with a witch who then becomes, after death, a spirit obsessed with harming witches. Apparently his character is based on a German Inquisitor and not a medicine man, so the idea that his obsession was also a bullying tactic.

"When he encounters the objects of his aggression, he attacks them with fulminating vituperation, otherwise, he operates in the subliminal domain, persuading the general population toward suspicion, hatred and violence against the objects of his rage: Witches […] the spirit of the Cunning Man is capable of occupying a human body to carry out his agenda. Poisoning people against witches is quite easy to accomplish as they, by their nature, focus on doing the right rather than the popular thing, and are thus always at risk of a backlash."[265]

On a more positive didactic note is the film they recommended I watch "Doctor Strange." I saw the animated movie from years ago and not the film released in theaters in 2016. In this film the message is basically that "magic is in the mind," such as in the scenes where the "Doctor" learns that as he imagine he is holding a sword he comes to actually hold a sword. And they way the team "passes" from one reality into a battle scene, Benandanti say is done very well to show a parallel.

And even though the film "Constantine" has a heavy Christianized vocabulary, the essence of it, of "seeing what others don't see" is valid.

THE CUNNING MAN STRIKES AGAIN

Several months after I returned to San Francisco from my latest research stay in Italy and I began to translate many Inquisition documents that had been given to me in Italy, the "Cunning Man" was at it again, along with spirits of the Inquisitors.

Unbeknownst to me at the time, I had planned my first series of lectures in NY for my book material during the time period, back in the 1500s, when a particularly abusive Inquisitor named Giulio Scribani would come to Triora and become with a healer accused of being a witch name Franchetta Borelli, sometimes as Borello.

As I was learning more about her story from a historical point, and of the sexual perversion and torture by Scribani, these Inquisitor spirits and also murdered women began to appear around my writing sessions, drowning me in waves of grief, rage, and resistance. Franchetta was pushing me forward to speak up and discover, and Scribani along with other Inquisitors were trying to shut me down.

Fortunately, several people very close to me at that time could also sense this happening, so along with my Guides I had support and protection. It was my job for the time being, however, to learn about this hidden history through experiencing many of the memories, emotions, and sensations of all sides and players. Needless to say, it was intense and took a toll on my physical body.

I checked in frequently with the Benandanti I knew, to compare notes about what was happening around my energy, and how far the Inquisitors had infiltrated my energy. They hadn't, but the interference they were creating around me was palpable, and I had to hide my book work from friends so they wouldn't become a target of these negative spirits.

And also occurring simultaneously, I was renting a room in a haunted house with two people who had been abused in their younger years. Even though often very kind and generous, when dark moods came upon them, I began to notice that they were becoming influenced by the Cunning Man syndrome, we will call it. There were several ghosts in the house always who were harmless, if we can say ghosts living near earthly people are harmless (truly they are not-it's best to help them move along so as not to become an energy drain on the earthly people-earth is for the fleshy, the Spirit World is for those without flesh).

In my case, the people were becoming increasingly influenced by the negative spirits trying to scare me. I was in a constant state of alert and alarm, even while knowing I was truly ok, sensing alarm and danger. I knew this was illusion, but I also felt concerned for my laptop, hard drive, and video camera, because all my Italian transcripts, documents, writings, and footage was on these electronic devices. So I carried them with me everywhere.

The housemates were becoming increasingly angry and irrational, and it escalated to a point where the man began refusing to speak to me, instead standing with his feet planted apart, fists clenched, just starting at me. Then loudly saying things outside my door like "dirty, dirty, some people are so dirty" and accusing me of breaking things around the house (even though I did not break anything and was spending as much time out of the house as possible. My health suffered because I was avoiding the kitchen also, which was right outside my door which was at the back of the house because usually he was in there). It all escalated to a point of me feeling I needed to call a domestic abuse assistance and tell the police in case anything happened to me, which I truly knew it wouldn't. It was a matter of bullying from the Spirit World, and these people in the house were simply vulnerable because of their own wounds and were being used.

I did move, but right before I did I let my Benandanti contacts know what was happening. I told them I felt I needed to take care of this myself, but that they had permission to "take a look." However, when one did "take a look" while dreaming, the ghosts attacked, so the Benandante had to battle with the main ghost in the house and in fact backed her off, which allowed me a great deal of energetic relief during my last week of moving out. The Benandante did confirm just how powerful this ghost had become because of the extra energy she was taking from the others.

Mostly, the experience was not going to harm me, but it was a parallel, and I was learning a lot about Italy's current situation and its past through these "experiential parallels." I was learning what it was like to be a targeted woman who felt all alone and being in a danger that was invisible to others, learning how difficult it was in fact for women in Italy not only in that time period but also in our modern days when violence turns her into an orphan, an outcast, with nowhere to go. Because as much as I had friends who were concerned, I couldn't find anywhere else to move to, I was being held in this situation, and since both the housemates were under the influence, I was truly alone in my perception of the downward spiral.

In the Spiritualist world negative spirit experiences are not talked about. Even my Mediumship teacher wouldn't answer any questions about negative spirit experiences except to say He would say he never encountered any. He said he chooses to his raise vibration, and by doing this to then live in different "altitude"…and to a certain extent this is very true. You can choose to keep your energetic environment very clean and elevated and organized, which I learned how to do at a great relief. However, light and dark do exist, and there are some of us whose purpose it is to see all, and to learn how to navigate it as "watcher" but also be involved to protect people, places and things from these negative influences, such as Benandanti.

So, while training cleaned out my life for a long time of general "spirit traffic," and brought into new relationships with very high vibrational guides (even though some have been at my side since I was born), all of this natural ability and also organized training was beneficial as a "preparation" for the historical recovery work I was doing in Italy which was drawing resistance. It also helped prepare me to speak to so many spirits who wanted to share their stories of being witches, and also those spirits who wanted to give spontaneous messages to earthly people I met and interviewed. So much of my research in Italy was Spirit-led on a daily basis, and perhaps without a lifetime of experience and a much shorter time of training I would not have been aware enough to take in all the details, to be assisted, to recognize the resistance, and to keep it all in balance.

HOW BENANDANTI PERCEIVE MODERN WITCHERY…

"We think that is good that some people have now a chance to find their way to witchcraft. On the other hand, now the craft is accessible to many people who are not fit for it: they seldom are dangerous but we don't like much the 'anybody could be a witch' kind of approach. The craft is serious matter and many people don't even understand the basic frame of mind that's needed but just want to be accepted in a 'religious' system in which they live much like catholics do, often misunderstanding the relationship with gods and mother nature.

Some are just drawn by the fascination of power, bright colors and glitter. But among these some rough diamonds emerge, people with the right "mark" on their souls, with that "something special". They get tired of glitter and ribbons and start digging for the 'real stuff', so there is something good even in this 'witchcraft for everyone' kind of tide."

K: How does the outside world see the Benandanti?

B: *"As a lost rural tradition, a folklore legend. And we are ok with that."*

SHAPE -SHIFTING

The wolf and being born with the caul are both connected to Benandanti, as is the ability to "see the dead," or what we would term "Mediumship" in modern times.

In the Inquisition time period, where we find Benandanti transcripts of trials in Friuli, there are mentioned people born in the amniotic sac, or with a form of the caul. This was, as a Benandante told me, "the mark of someone special," or a way for nature to say "something is different here." This reminds me of the early days of Spiritualism, when on the east coast of the United States there was an explosion of Spirit activity in the form psychic phenomena occurring in "broad daylight," we can say, so that anyone could see or hear or experience the phenomena. Spirits were creating loud trumpet sounds or music, they were lifting furniture, helping people levitate, creating ectoplasm and transforming it into the form of deceased persons, creating a painting where there were no paints, and all sorts of "manifesting" as if to say "hey, we're here!" This physical psychical phenomenon hardly exists anymore, just like the caul. As a Benandante told me, "we are proof that it can work even without the caul. The way that these abilities are "distributed" no longer needs a physical sign of being exceptional. And the people that are needed to do our job are somehow found."

The garu wolf, as it is called in this Friulian region, or the "werewolf" is a natural part of Benandanti battles. Also called "lupo mannari" in many other regions of Italy, where I even met women who said were friends with families whose sons were werewolves. But nowhere else in Italy are werewolves connected with Spirit World battles of Benandanti. outside of the Udine region, werewolves are part of folk tales, but importantly, they are considered to be men born on Christmas eve, a belief that is the same for witches: women born on Christmas eve are witches. Men born on Christmas eve are werewolves.

As it was explained to me by Benandanti of their historical heritage:

"Herodotus, in the fifth century BC, wrote about the distribution of the myth of men turning into animals to fight battles related to fertility. It is a pattern found in Asia, Africa and America and it dates possibly as back as the Paleolithic era. People (also women) turning into wolves to take part of the fight are reported in Juergensburg at the end of 17th century, but up until 15th century werewolves where not considered bad creatures. After that they were tied to witchcraft and became the werewolf we know. This is also interesting because it is connected with all the other changes we know happened. In Russia and other Slavic cultures, anyone who was born wrapped in the placenta were bound to become werewolves, and had to keep the placenta on them. They would become powerful and glorious warriors. It was the same in Friuli, except that they were named Benandanti instead of werewolves and there was no glory in their future, but the pattern is plain to see."

Additionally, mothers kept the placenta, or the people who were born with it often wore it as a talisman.

But more on the history, *'Pausania and Plinio' mentioned temporary animal transformation in Arcadia. To Plinio it was a specific family, the Anthi. There is always an initiation element to the transformation. In Arcadia the werewolf had to put his garments on a tree and then cross a stream, water crossing being a recurring element, probably symbolizing death and rebirth.*

A last thing: Friuli is the only place where everything is present. There are women who fell into ecstatic states and met to worship a version of the Bona Dea, which happened in other parts of Northern Italy and further north in France, always during the tempora. There is the meeting with the dead, and of course there is fighting and taking animal shape."

Benandanti change form in the astral realm, in the very real battlefield. They can see their "paws," as one mentioned, and other clothing. Experiencing their transformation, they know, means the battle has begun.

My experience with shape-shifting was different and it occurred before I met Benandanti. I shape shifted on the earthly realm. I would preface this by saying I didn't believe in shape shifting, nor did I believe in past lives…that is, until I experienced them. When this occurred, I was with another person and suddenly changed posture. I began growling in a specific way that was not something I could do on my own…because I tried to imitate the way I sounded later, after I was transformed back, and I was not able to make the sound nor feel the emotion of the transformation. There was a distinct difference between me trying to "be" an animal and when I became one, in effect. I found myself in a protective posture over the person I was with, as if there were a threat against this person or both of us, and I began biting in the way a mother would bite to pick up her young. It happened twice. For sure my physical body remained, but my energy, my voice, my posture, and something more changed. The person I was with experienced the same as I did. And, the person I was with also said I changed into a wolf, which is exactly what my experience was as well. In our individual experiences there was no uncertainty that maybe I was a dog or a hyena or some other animal. Without discussing it, we both declared "wolf." While I don't believe this connects me to Benandanti at all, this is the way Spirit often teaches me or leads me somewhere: by giving me an experience regarding something I am skeptical about or something I need to become curious about.

DREAMWORLD:

Benandanti train often in the dream world, as preparation for their work in the astral realm. These are different realms. Some dreams are "work," some dreams are the mind unwinding, some dreams are dimly aware experiences in the astral realm, and dreams in the astral realm are real "happenings." But again, "dreamworld" and "astral plane" are not sufficient words to describe the differences nor similarities in these realms. Just as Benandanti told me that Carlo Ginzburg's books "Ecstasies" and "The Night Battles" are often quite accurate, or at least the closest thing to an accurate portrayal that can be found, nevertheless lot of the language in the transcripts and trial documents reflect language of the time period: certain plants mentioned that were growing in those days, such as "sorghum" are not a necessary tool for battle. In fact, as the Benandanti drove me around the area where they live, they pointed out areas along the drive where new crops, unrecognizable to them, were covering the fields. So much of the language used by Benandanti of the past to describe their experiences reflect the language and ideas of the time. And because they are describing experiences that are not easy to describe, because they don't take place in the physical realm, the language doesn't always apply to the relevance of Benandanti today in modern times.

It's important to note, however, as Ginzburg documents in his historical book: "The Night Battles," "[..]Benandanti [...] is a very special sect, whose ceremonies, in the words of the Benandanti themselves, had an almost dreamlike character. But actually, the Benandanti were saying something different; they never doubted the reality of those gatherings which they attended 'in spirit.'"[266]

BONA DEA, ARADIA DI GIOCO

Benandanti are also historically connected to the Bona Dea, the "Good Lady" of the night who appeared in some Milanese trial documents. In Milan, she was teaching young women, through Mediumship, true information about how to cure with plants, for example.

In the far east of Italy, and in Benandanti tradition, she was one who brought celebrations, joyful gatherings, food and fun. Being in the present moment of life, we could say. The Benandanti I know have never been taken to these celebrations but wish they had. They are "too busy kicking people," they laughingly told me.

Nevertheless, we know Benandanti have a hierarchy of roles, and this is another reinforcement of the "realms" outside of our physical, earthly one, and the fact that there is limited mobility for us: not everyone has access to every realm.

This is further evidence of the Mediumistic cornerstone that makes Benandanti life a real one, and it's one more way in Italy that the Spirit World is "alive" for people in Lineages still, in modern times, and not just in the ancient past. Even more importantly, we have historical evidence of yet another Female Lineage that has to do with Spirit World relationships with a Feminine Leader figure. There are no Benandanti reports of a male Leader anywhere nor a male counterpart to the Bona Dea/Signora di Gioco/Aradia di Gioco.

Perhaps also because they are Guardians, there is an awareness among Benandanti of how ancient they are, but also of the challenges of living very earthly lives.

Having a bigger perspective of "caretakers," for them other people are a bit like children that don't belong to them, caretakers of a bigger family than a nuclear one. Everything must be viewed with a detachment that offers the position to not judge with emotions, but rather to see balances and imbalances, whether in yourself or others also.

Nonnas take care of immediate family. Streghe, guaritori/segnatori, megdona, and levatrice take care of the community (as Mediums, family is anyone and everyone) Janara the same. Some women have the role of disseminating Goddess Teacher female legacies as a "Signora del Gioco" come down to earth, and this is role of devotional work. Benandanti oversee the balance of light and dark of movement of the universe all these women, and we, occupy.

PLACES OF POWER

K: Are there places in your area of importance, either older pagan sites built upon, or "power spots?"

B: *"Yes. One of course is the "plan da stries", where we brought you. Another is the "buse dai pagans", where a stream cut deep into a rock wall and created a narrow, circular space In southern Friuli there is a 'forra delle agane', where 'forra' means 'deep' like a small canyon and 'agane' are a kind of female water spirit. We don't know exactly where it is, though. There are also other places that bear the 'agane' names, like 'clap des aganes' in the Pordenone area.*

In Carnia there is the 'plan das furmies', where sbilfs dance.

Many places have now small churches built on them: like in Cesclans, which has a Celtic iron age grave cut into the stone, under a Roman tower, under a Lombard tower, under the church. It looks like there was a moment in which churches and shrines were built over any meaningful place (also, on every crossroad, rewriting Hecate's cult).

Some places have names related to Celtic Gods and Goddesses, other have names that derived from Celtic language like Nimis (from "nemas", sacred wood) and Gemona ("round hill"). Generally speaking all the places with names ending in –icco or –acco were founded during the Celtic period and can still be places 'of interest'."

Chapter 19:
"Magic versus Mediumship"

In Ernesto de Martino's book "Sud e Magia" we find a passage describing the Goddess Artemis having been known among people as an exorcist. This has been one of the "gifts of healing" the Goddess brought down to earth. We see this natural exorcism cure, the releasing of "evil" as negative thoughts, through "occhi" and other Lineage cures in Italy. However, just as the feminine purpose of communicating with the Spirit World was usurped by pagan gods in their myth stories (and the earthly men), in Italy the church's men also took over the role of exorcism.

In this same passage in "Sud e Magia" we find an accusation against Jesus healing with a strange double-sided cure as he "first punishes then releases an inhospitable woman, we almost do not notice the shift to a lesser degree of "low" of magic[267] "In other words, even a saintly mythical person like Jesus was described as able to on one hand cure, on another, to punish. So even in the best of examples, it can be difficult to discern between high and low magic.

To expand, the Catholic idea of exorcism engages in the lower world of energy battles. It goes down into those levels, entertains the negative spirits, enables them by agreeing with their idea of power. That is the real truth here-when you agree with someone's bad intentions, you give them power. This not denial, but rather an agreement that works against the higher possibilities.

The "occhi" curing procedure enables the patient to be part of the cure, it operates on the belief that a cure is inevitable; the patient can choose to release this negativity because it doesn't belong to them, and the cure's actions accomplish this. It is a positive procedure.

The church's exorcism

There is a difference between high and low magic. Perhaps not always in the external view: ritual tools can all look the same, invocations can all sound intimidating, movements of the arms and hands can look sinister and mysterious even if they are curing. And this is because of the more hidden element of these recipes: the unseen energy, and more importantly, the unseen spirit people who've become attracted to these events. Helpers? Higher conscious beings? Or lowly "joyriders" seeking an influential experience through an earthly being by a spirit who won't pass over but who can't be reborn?

More than high and low magic in Italy is a deeper level of truth: magic is from poverty, from the affects of male invasion, usurpation, and control of life the disconnect from nature (for the users) Masculine magic, we should say, is a product of the conquering, the hoarding of information, and the synthetic structuring of a spiritual practice that is "in action" only, devoid of spiritual partnership. Whereas women (and men) in our founding days relied on intuition and help from the Spirit World to handle childbirth, to navigate their landscape, to understand which foods were edible and had curing powers and how to plant and harvest with the cycles of time. The male warring tribal invasions put a stop to nature's spirituality and from 4500 BC

-2500BC instead implemented life under male control, forbidding of women to commune with the Goddess in her many ways (survival, spiritually, psychically) and worked to slowly change public perception from the belief that the Goddess would provide for needs with a reliance to instead one that relied on male figureheads in the communities as well as in the heavens.

Nature was the original conduit for Mother Magic: natural magic guided by higher consciousness (the Great Goddess) to improve life with indigenous nature.

When male tribes invaded Old Europe and Italian communities that were harmonious and spiritually led by women, they also usurped feminine spiritual practice, implanting male gods over the female ones. (Such as gods being born from stone and from the sea water... which are actually elements first connected with the Great Mother Goddess. In effect, they were claiming to come from the Life Source without saying the Life Source is feminine). They created stories of how men birthed the Universe even though there was nothing in nature to support this. They took head of the family and of the communities and hoarded the herbarium books and feminine wisdom. The symbolic language of "heaven on earth," or "goddess brought down to earth" was scrambled and disconnected from the knowledge the language was created to represent.

In this "taking control of," we have a "taking away from," as the tribes industrialized life through animal husbandry and surely did the same with women and their ability to bear children. Life changed; "others" came in and took control of food distribution and spirituality and more. In fact, "fake famines" helped enflame the "caccia alle streghe," or witch hunts, in Triora, Italy in the earliest of Inquisition days. So not only did Italian populations experience poverty due to industrialization of life, but then these tribes also disconnected people from their own natural currency: spiritual magic. Male magic is arranged and organized, it contains rules and recipes and formalities that must be followed in order to experience the results of their magical techniques. They tried to hold "the knowledge" in books as if it were to be forgotten, but it's because they were only privy to *half the magical equation:* Mother Magic is a Spirit World partnership: the humans make the actions, the Great Mother channels miraculous energy through them. Only the human elements may be forgotten to other humans..but they can always be reclaimed from Spirit through Mediumship. Channeled knowledge remains with the channeler, and what doesn't can be received again form the Spirit World. It's like having a living encyclopedia at the end of a telephone line. Many early cultures, including ones with men, operated orally and spiritually, such as the Druids, and as a result none of that knowledge is written down except for in visual symbolism and statuary used to represent nature's connection to the Spirit World and Universal energy.

Magic itself wasn't banned, but the feminine dispensation of it was attacked; the channeling of the Goddess was no longer seen as benevolent, but a threat to the male rule. They attempted to control this by banning peasant women from using it and instead creating a public forum for prophecy using women, namely the sibyls and pythia, which were female channelers organized in a public was so as to be only accessible by men who used them to divine futures about wars and building cities. Just like the church, only much earlier in history, society was being controlled...the outside was pushing its way inside to separate the individual from natural psychic way of life. So magic remained, in the form of re-organized actions, but the shamanism connection was cut off, new male gods were created and put in the place of the Mother, and magic became about "taking" from someone else, much like the actions of the invaders. Because for Romans, magic was a part of the Emperor's might, and channeling was demoted to a form of divination for war support, and Goddesses were given makeovers to look like "cheerleaders" for their wars. Magic became about "will and might."

In the same was Big Religion has put priests and pastors between people and their gods, male magic placed the High Priest between people and the male gods. There was no longer a direct connection but rather public participation in public temples, or for the initiated in private group rituals.

The people scrambled to use this new truncated male magic to alleviate poverty, to alleviate loneliness. For example, Roman author Paolo Portone shared with me his document "Ossessione erotica e *magia sexualis* nei processi del Sant'Uffizio" (Erotic obsession and sexual spells in the processes of the Holy Office). This paper documents how magic was used during a time period in Italy when the church was forcing "arranged marriages." As a result, people were using spells to attract secret lovers to alleviate unhappiness, or to keep a husband faithful, to win money, etc. The same kind of spells we see today around the world. Lower magic.

They were using actions to physically alleviate a spiritual poverty, after being divided from a more harmonious way of living in accordance with nature. Male temples filled with male gods who became source of all life on the planet. So nature was obscured and perverted..no magic from this viewpoint can be natural, because in nature masculine energy is not the source of life.

As a professional Medium, familiar with a natural protocol of inviting spirit people to communicate with me, I have experienced the "male god" category of Spirit people to be unhelpful, to say the least. While I have male spirit guides in my large Spirit guide team that I regularly work with, the realm traditionally known as "male gods" I found to be disinterested in connecting, teaching, or sharing much of anything except for a glimpse of their energetic form and some support of shows of strength. Yes, the appeared to me. No, they were nothing like their legends, only pale comparisons and pale energy as well. Not engaging at all. They seem more like thought forms rather than conscious beings.

Considering there are parallels between the earthly and Spirit World: (as above, so below…where there's negativity on earth, there is also in the Spirit World), I should comment that the only time I've met Spirits who were unwilling to communicate or even look at me has been in cases of passed-on relatives and friends of people who took their own lives in suicides, people who had mental issues on earth, or other "denial" personalities. In these cases, all these men were not able to or didn't want to look at me and communicate directly. They showed me themselves and their form and perhaps some of their regrets and memories, but mostly they were not forthcoming , they were in denial of something, ashamed. And it has been the same way with male gods, in my experience.

So magic remained, in actions, but the shamanism connection was cut off. New male gods were put in the place of the Mother, and magic became about "stealing " to alleviate poverty, using actions to alleviate a spiritual poverty…division from a more harmonious working with nature. Male temples filled with male Gods who became source of all life on the planet. so nature was obscured and perverted..no magic from this viewpoint can be natural, because in nature masculine energy is not the source of life.

Masculine magic was an eradication of the Great Mother's shamanism. Magic became the tool of men and emperors…and the general population, after people forgot or were forbidden from their natural connection to the Spirit World. The craft of magic, is basically arithmetic and recipes, and this is what remains in the grimoires and spell books found. They look just like magic today. Magic became about "taking (from someone else) controlling for the people in power. For the general population it was a desperate act used to rise up somehow from poverty. In the past, the Spirit World provided the medicine, the means to cure, and more. But under masculine rule, things changed.

We can see this in "milk theft" magic: *"In Valsinni, a mother that is plagued with lack of milk hides a tiny bit of salt in the kid's blanket and ask a friend to go with the kid to visit a luckier mother. Coming back from the magic expedition, the mother without milk will prepare for herself a soup using the salt from the wrapping that she hopes absorbed the milk of the victim. After the rite is done, the milk starts flowing from the breasts of the thief. If the woman that got robbed discovers who is the responsible one, she sends people to call her, and then the two women will have to show each other their breasts, spraying a tiny bit of milk out of it while the one that got robbed says 'I don't want any of yours, and I don't want to give you mine.' This way, the jinx is done."*[268]

Magic is not necessarily used this way in modern times, and in fact many people who practice magic (that is not indigenous to them) do so to come back into harmony with nature and nature's cycles. But in the past, magic was established by the male invaders of harmonious and feminine-dominant societies. So the magical practices that were re-organized were based on male directives and were all about synthetic control of nature and natural forces (and of people, places, and things).

Divine Feminine "magic" was originally given to women from the Spirit World to help them improve life on the planet: it was "something" from "nothing." Mediumship, or receiving communications and assistance from the Spirit World (Spirit partnerships) is abundance. This was the original way: humans had needs, the Spirit World pointed the way to the means…and through the indigenous land around them (what was already available, what they already had, as they were). Spirit gave. No money was needed, no schooling nor classes nor studying: this is why Italy's witchery is from a place of Abundance; the currency of the poor. Mother Magic these days is the same: not having set recipes but receiving an action or a recipe to do something combined with energy from the Goddess in the moment. That action could simply be a change of thought.

SYMPATHETIC MAGIC

Sympathetic magic is something practiced by many naturally Mediumistic Italians. The Italian men I know who practice sympathetic magic don't do so as a "formally trained practice." They didn't learn it in a book or in a class; it's natural, an intuitive ability to finding the personality within a "thing" and making an agreement with it, or listening to its divinatory message. It's not a practice of magic to "get" something or to make a change or go after a "desire" with the will, it's more like a receptive form of communication with the elements of nature (rather than directly with a consciousness).

Channeling is both a natural and a studied practice. Living in nature, naturally, is perhaps the simplest way to find oneself in a receptive state, which opens the doors for connection with the Spirit World and its higher conscious helpers. Nature is a conduit after all.

Magic, which can be found everywhere in Italy, is simply craft-like actions used to get a result which are missing the addition of knowledge and support from the Spirit World... however there are plenty of people, and especially old women who still go to church, are doing something along the lines of Mother Magic. Mostly what can be accomplished or not with magic depends on the abilities of the practitioner. The ability to cure is missing from magic, the true miracle of improving life.

The appeal of the crafty side of magic is understandable: there's more "glory" in craft magic because there are more actions that the human being can or must take...it looks and feels like more of a participation or a control over "doing" and "making" much more of the desired change. It's interactive and empowering in a "physical world" way...with a little bit of energy that is still palpable. And frankly, it's fun. It's like using nature as art supplies, incorporated with prayer and intention AND a decision to change ones self. Magic's effects may occur immediately, it may take a day or a week..or one may never really know.

In Italy however, there are many women who still use their own magic to connect with the Mother. Their magic looks natural, like cooking: folding herbs and prayers into bread, tucking charms into clothing, burying prayers into soil, wearing herb bundles, and more. The objects used for magic are most often not bought in occult stores; the women who make these spells, like the Janara, use simple, daily life supplies or indigenous nature. For a spell they may use sewing needles, stones, coins, thimbles, espresso cups, oil, water, handmade crosses, herbs, bread (like clay), spit, a sung prayer, a playing card, grasses from the outdoors, etc.

This is a very different practice from male ceremonial magic; again a structured, controlled, synthetic experience to recreate something that once happened naturally: using knives (synthetic weapons) and drawing boundaries and commanding spirits and wearing special clothing: ceremonial magic is for those who have money to buy the tools and the clothes and the altar space etc.

Shamanism is for the poor or the average person: it brings something from nothing.

With Mediumship or shamanism, the Spirit people are doing all the "magic" and actions that are far beyond what we can sense. The Spirit guides and healers give humans just a little bit of the work (the prayers, the marks on the body, the preparation of oil and water) and they channel the "miracles" through the simple actions taken. It's much more difficult for an earthly person to say "I did that, I cured that" when they can't exactly be sure of how the miracle that's taking place "in real time" is in fact immediately occurring. And that's the miracle. As ms Domenico said, "It works."

In masculine magic, the magician thinks he is in control of everything, including the spirits. Being in "command" of another consciousness is not likely to be a true command (considering anyone in their energetic spirit form, even a lowly astral ghost, has a bigger perspective that an earthly human does simply because they are using their psychic senses fully; someone on earth can use them partially) , and it is also act against the free will of another, which goes agains the Law of Free Will, which carries a consequence.

With magic, it all depends, It's a crapshoot. can be spotive and negative. can harm, can provide. But the Mediumship, or waiting on the Spirit World of high conscious guides requires surrender; the ability to receive...and what you receive is decided by someone with higher knowledge than you who is looking out for your highest good...so it might not look the way you want it to, but it is for better.

Magic..can attract good, but also can attract the not-so-good. It's vision is limited to what a human can see.

Anytime only the will is used, without a higher perspective, without universal love, there is the potential to attract something lower.

Mediumship in Italy is expressed in many ways and is old here as is the very earth that composes her land.

Chapter 20:
"What's In A name"

VOWEL CODE:
"A" IS PRONOUNCED "about" is the closest...not quite...
"E" is pronounced "ay," like the "a" in "way"
"I" is pronounced "eeee" like the first "e" in "even"
"O" instead of our "ohw" in open is "oh"
"u" is lie "oo" as in "noodle"

amuleti=amulets "Ah moo lay ti"

angeli=angels "ahn jell ee"

l'Anima=soul "ah nee mah"

l'argano=the winch, a torture device used on women during the Inquisition "lar gan oh"

Bagiue=name for witches in Ligurian dialect, also means bitch "bah zhoo ay"

Bajua=derivative of above, in the singular "bah zhoo ah"

Basura=derivative of above, in the singular "ba soor a"

Bazzure=derivative of above, in the plural "ba zoor ay"

la caccia alle streghe=the witch hunts "lah kah tchee ah ahlay stray ghay"

cartomante= Fortune Teller "kahr toh mahn tay"

cataplasmi=poultices "kah tah plah smee"

cattiva="bad" a term of judgement, often used to describe witches as "bad witches" or health "kah ttee vah"

il cavalletto= the tripod, a torture device used on women during the Inquisition "eel kah vah lay toh"

il cerchio=circle "eel kayr chee oh"

chiromanti=palm reader "khee roh mahn tee"

del ciclo naturale delle stagioni=natural cycle of the seasons "dayl chee kloh nah toor ahlay day llay stah gee oh nee"

civette=owl "chee vay ttay"

contadina=peasant "kohn tah deen ah"

coppettazione-=cupping cure" koh pett ah tzee oh nay"

315

croci=crosses " kroh chee"

ctonico-lunari -chthonic-lunar "ktoh nee koh loo nahr ee"

dea=goddess "day ah"

decotti=decoctions" day koh tee"

demoni=demons "day moh nee"

diavolo=devil "dee ah voh loh"

divinatori = diviners "dee vee nah tohr ee"

le donne=women "lay doh nay"

Donna saggia = Wise Woman " doh nah sah jee ah"

erborista=herbalist "air bore eestah "

l'esorcista=the exorcist "laysore seesta"

esorcizzare=to exorcise "aysore chee tzar ray"

fantasmi=ghosts "fantas mee"

le fasi di luna piena= the full moon phases " lay fahsee dee loonah pee ay nah"

Janua=-port/door but a door to Spirit World or hell "yah noo ah"

le fate=the fairies "lay fah tay"

fattuchiera=witch/spell-maker, sorcerer, or negative meaning like "psychic hustling/hustler" "faht too kee air ah

fatture=spells "faht too ray"

fiamelle=flames "fee ah may lay"

filtres= filters "feel trays"

fitoterapia (phytotherapy) =herbal medicine "fee toh tair ah pee ah"

foglie=plant leaves "foh lee ay"

folletti=elve "foh llay ttee"

fortureire=type of witch, in Ligurian dialect "forh too ray eeray"

Fuoco= fire "foo oh koh"

ginestra=a type of broom?? "gee nay strah"

gli scongiuri=incantations "lee skon gee oo ri"

Grande Dea=Great Goddess "grahn day day ah"

Grande Madre=Great Mother "grahn day mah dray"

guaritrici=healers "gooarh ah tree chee"

incantesimi= spells "een cahn tay see mee"

incantanto= spellbound, enchanted "een cahn tahn toh"

infusioni= infusion "een foo see oh nee"

la jettatura="throwing the" evil eye, one who casts the evil eye "lah yet tah too rah"

jettatori=jinxes "yet tah tohr ee"

levatrice=midwives "lay vah tree tchay"

lupo mannaro=werewolf (wolf-man) "loo poh man nahr oh"

maga= female magician "mah gah"

mago=male magician "mag goh"

maghi=wizards, magicians "mah gee"

magie=magic "mah gee ay"

majare=type of witch "mah yahr ay"

mal di testa=headache "mahl dee tay stah"

i malanni=ailments "ee mahl lah nnee"

malattie=diseases "mahl laht tee ay"

malefici=evil, maladies "mah ay fee chee"

medgona=meridian, also type of healer in Emilia Romagna dialect "mayde goh nah"

mezzanotte=midnight "metzah nohttay"

la notte di Natale "lah noh ttay dee Nah tall ay"

il noce= the walnut "eel noh chay"

olio=oil "oh lee oh"

olistici =holistic= "oh lee stee chee"

pagana=pagan "pah gah nah"

paganesimo=paganism "pah gah nay see moh"

piante=plant "pee ahn tay"

pignattin/pignatta=terracotta pot/ pan "peen nya tteen", "peen nyah tah"

pozioni=potion "poh zee oh nee"

pratiche terapeutiche= therapeutic practices, as in healing "prah tee chay tay rah pee oo tee kay"

Preghiera=prayer "pray ghee ay rah"

processo per stregoneria=witchcraft trial "proh chays soh payr stray goh nay ree ah"

radici=roots (plant roots) "rah dee chee"

rito=ritual "ree toh"

riti magici=magical rites "ree tee mah jee chee"

rosso sangue=red blood "roh so sahn gway"

la ruota=the wheel. a torture device used during the Inquisition in Italy "lah roo oh tah"

sabba-Sabbath, witches' sabbath "sah bah"

le sacerdotess=priestesses

del sale=salt "dayhle sah lay"

sangue=blood "sahn gway"

scacciadiavoli= throw out the devils "skah tchee ah dee ah vohl lee"

Scacciaguai=sweeping away the bad troubles "skah tchee ah goo ah ee"

scacciato= to cast out "skah tchee ah toh"

scacciato gli spiriti maligni=throw out the malignant spirits "skah tchee ah toh spee ree tee mah lee knee"

scacciavi-to cast out "skah tchee ah vee"

scambio rituale=ritual exchange between healer and patient "skahm bee oh ree too ahl lay"

scaramantico=superstitious, as in superstitious item like Peperoncino il control malocchio "skar ah mahn tee koh

scongiuri=incantations "skohn gee oo ree"

scongiuro=exorcism "skohn gee oor oh"

scopa=broom "skoh pah"

segnatore=one who marks, as in a type of healing style in Emilia Romagna, invisible marks drawn on body to cure "say nyah tore ay" segnature=signs, as in the secret marks used in lineage curing techniques "say nyah too ray"

serpi-snakes "sayr pee"

spettri=ghosts "spayt tree"

di sortilegi =sorcery/spells "dee sohr tee lay gee"

di specchio=mirror " dee spay kee oh"

Lo Stregale=wizard, (male version of Satanas helper, from Benvento area) "loh stray gahl lay"

stregare=to bewitch "Stray gahr ray"

strege=burden "stray gay"

stregone=sorcerer, wizard, warlock "stray goh nay"

stregoneria=witchcraft (general terms, does not denote female nor male derived) "stray goh nayr ree ah"

stregonesca=witchcraft

stregonesche=witchy "stray goh naysh kay"

strega diabolica=evil witch "stray gah dee ah bohl ee kah"

strix=negative name for "wtich" coming from "night bird" when death became feared and men evil-ized women "streeks"

tre volte= three times, the special number of repetitions used in curing arts "tray vohl tay"

Veggenti=seers "vay jen tee"

il volo notturno=night flying {eel- vohlo nottourno] "eel voh loh noh toor noh"

Be sure to visit the newly re-opened Museo Etnostorico della Stregoneria (The Museum of Ethnographic Witchcraft) in Triora, Italy.

http://www.museotriora.it

Paolo Portone is the Science Director of this museum and has collaborated with others whose idea is to not just show the idea of the witch as the pointed hat and the cauldron, but as the one who is the healer, the one who knows the herbs.

Conclusion: Domina Ludus

How to invite this Italian shamanism into your life?

It's about Mediumship: using tools that are conduits.

Mediumship is for all genders: La Signora del Gioco (and all her Goddess "Agents") help improve life: never anywhere in records has she set in place a set of moral codes intent on controlling peoples' sexuality, nor condemning their natural physiology.

The tools in Italian witchery are "indigenous" to what's around: that could be a teacup, old pot, water, plants outside the house, tree branch, pebbles, spoons cut special way, espresso cup...but primarily your own spirit and body are conduits.

The tools are not the miracle nor the cure; the Spirit Goddess who actually channels the healing energy through the Lineage healer is the Mother Magic. In other magic, the tools are parts of decisions that go into the "recipe" of making magic. Magic is making mental decisions about tools, supplies, actions, prayer, and intention. In Mother Magic, the Spirit Goddess does all the work, so "how " it works remains a mystery.

The Mother's Lineage "magician" remains humble. She recognizes the knowledge and knows how to use it, her eyes recognize who needs it. Other than that, she sinks back into anonymity.

There is nowhere attached to the great Mother Goddess an exclusionary hierarchy and set of "hoops" to jump through, but rather a focus on:

- clean energy
- clear focus
- postiive intention
- a desire to learn
- a desire to be of service

Because the Lineages in Italy are not *created* by earthly people only *passed through* them, I can offer you a way to prepare yourself for the Signora di Gioco and her many Goddess teachers to be able to reach you and communicate with you.

It's up to the Signora di Gioco to decide how your transmission will come and be expressed.

What you can do to prepare yourself as a clear channel, a conduit for the Great Mother Goddess:

1. Dedicate yourself to Something that Spirit can channel through:

Most directly you can learn Mediumship through a Spiritualist Center through the traditional Spirit Circle class. This is a modern version of Signora del Gioco's "Domina Ludus."

In the Spirit Circle, you learn how to cleanly communicate with the Spirit World for a high-quality experience. It is a beautiful, safe way to learn how to be of service as a Medium. From here, the Great Mother Goddess will grow and change your Mediumship.

A Spiritualist community won't want to talk about Goddesses nor angels nor indigenous practices. You will learn the constancy of the Laws of Energy, which is the Abundance magic of the Mother. You will learn a clear, clean organized system for communicating with the Spirit World that allows you to develop a safe and intimate relationship with higher Spirit guides, your personal ones, who help you grow exponentially in ways other modalities can't. This will automatically clean our your "energetic" space if you're someone who has attracted a lot of "ghost traffic."

In the Spirit circle you also have the chance to test your ability of gathering and interpreting information coming from the Spirit World, which is invaluable. It is a scientific testing ground in an environment with people like you.

OR, Learn a healing modality. The ability to channel is often the result of becoming a practicing healer; the channeled information often helps the healing process. The Great Mother Goddess can also channel her healing energy through a willing healer.

2. Bring nature into your meditations.

Simplify your altar, or begin one if you don't have one.

a. Start by using a simple "scopa," or broom to clean the space you sit or kneel in. As you sweep you can make a prayer or invocation for the Great Mother Goddess to clean away things you no longer need in your life, or energies that are keeping you from expanding. The Signora di Gioco, after all, did emphasize keeping a clean house to her "daughters."

b. Your prayer could be: **"Health to you, Lady of the East"/Salute a te, signora Oriente"** as it was a greeting of the daughters in the past.

Your prayer could be: **"Unguento, unguento, mandame ala noce de Benevento, supra acqua et supra ad vento, et supra ad omne maltempo."**

c. Spend a moment holding a black stone. Place it against your heart, and invite the abundance of the Goddess into your life.

d. Fill a small bowl with water and ask the Great Mother Goddess to clarify your psychic vision, your intention, and your mind. Ask her to help you clearly see the truth around you. Dip your hands in and out of the water, imagining your hands becoming purified.

e. Light a candle, asking the Great Mother Goddess to illuminate her teachings within you, and that you may also serve as a light for others. If you are feeling emotional, ask the flame to make clear what you are feeling emotional about. Use the fire to burn away energy or thoughts or limitations that don't belong to you.

Of course, you can and should also spend time in nature doing nothing but listening to the nature.

3. Discipline

Expect the Signora del Gioco to demand a lot of your time. For her, she's been waiting a long tome to reconnect with you, so she wants to really move forward. You can of course say no, slow down, etc. She respects free will. Not everyone can meditate. Truth be told, however, if you're not willing to do the work to train yourself in whatever way works for you and keep it a regular part of your day or week, just accept that and be where you are instead. Because communication with the Spirit World takes practice, and it is a result of development, like learning a new language.

If you're not wiling or able to meditate you can learning to control the frequency of your vibration which sets a clean energetic environment around you and helps your intuitive mind blend with Spirit Guides.

But if you truly want to know her, life may dramatically change around you so that you have nothing standing in the way of this relationship with her. This depends on your soul agreement. It's different for everyone. Your relationship with her will connect you to new people, places, and things.

4. Raise your vibration

Ways to raise your vibration are:

a. Practicing meditation (there are many types: Guided meditations, meditations to heal, etc)

b. listening to music that makes you feel joyful, happy, excited.

c. smelling nature or flower essences

d.   dancing or otherwise moving your body physically

e. using visual cues to "rise up" towards the light

f. using affirmations to declare in-the-moment positivity

g. listening to what your troubling emotions are trying to tell you, then symbolically burning away or washing away their energy

h. spending time doing something that you're passionate about: cooking, making art, music, research, teaching, learning… The Great Mother Goddess loves creativity and will find you and support your creativity despite any limitations you think you might have.

Witchery is the reason society has advanced itself: Mediumship is not limited by how much money you don't have or your education level: the Spirit World of Guides can reach out to assist you right now. You don't need to buy any tools; your body and your conscious spirit are the "medium," you are the the tool, the channel.

The following meditations can be used to raise your vibration and connect to the Spirit World as a clear channel.

BASIC 3 STEP CHANNELING MEDITATION...to prepare yourself to Channel

1. Create a relaxing environment. Play music that feels great to you but does not distract. Sit in a position where your feet are on the floor and hands in your lap, palms facing upwards. Spend time breathing. Imagine breathing into the top of your head, with your breath going all the way down to your feet before you exhale.

2. Imagine rising up high into the Universe's light: You can imagine climbing a small ladder, or using the following imagery I use with my students:

From where you are sitting, imagine the walls and floor dissolving around you. As you breathe in, wiggle your toes and come to find them in the sands of a beach, at night time. You can feel the warmth of your skin against the coolness of the night sands. You feel the cool breeze off the water brush against your cheeks and gently rustle your hair. You feel the wind breeze by your shoulders.

You look forward and you can see the softly lapping waves of the ocean, the dark waters twinkling under the moonlight, as you can also see a small sliver of brilliantly colored light on the horizon, as the sun sets into stripes of hot pink and brilliant orange, against the indigo blue of the night sky.

You feel the breezes wrap around your ankles and feel yourself gently being lifted off the sands as if you are on a magic carpet made of wind. You gently raise off the sands, moving into the beautiful indigo sky, passing by twinkling stars. Your heart swells and opens, colors of emerald green and sensations of joy flow outward and lift you higher. You can imagine the faces of your animal friends and loved ones swelling your heart even more.

3. You float as high as you can imagine, coming to find yourself under the brilliant white light of the moon. This white light represents Universal love, Wisdom, Protection, Higher Learning, and your Highest Good. You allow it to surround you and also fill your body from head to toe.

Once you are filled with white light, allow it to shine out the front of your heart, into the Universe around you. You can also allow it to shine out the back of your heart as well, creating a cross of white light.

You are now ready to invite the Great Mother Goddess or Your Higher Self, or a Spirit Healer into your space.

As you do, accept whatever form She takes. At first, the feeling may be subtle. You may see "nothing." Ask yourself how that "nothing" feels…peaceful? Calm? Do you see color? Do you see a figure?

Just as you would when you meet a new person, begin to ask questions to help you discern what they may look like, what name they would like you to call them, ask them for some encouraging advice, or just a symbolic image.

This is where it starts. It's up to you to develop the process of giving and receiving information through Asking Questions and Receiving Answers.

When you are done, give thanks and gratitude to the Spirit Helpers who appeared.

Take a breath in. Begin to lower yourself from the moon's light, back into the indigo sky, down towards the sacred beach sands, where you become more weighted by gravity, and come to find yourself on the cool sands again.

Breathe yourself into your body, and rub your hands together, run your thighs with your hands, affirm you are back in your body in your room.

Gently open your eyes.

HINT: You can develop this further by asking questions for other people when you are meeting with Spirit.

GOLDEN LIGHT MAGNETISM

When you begin your day, you can invite the Abundance of the Goddess into your life in the following way:

Draw a circle of white light around you, representing: Universal love, Wisdom, Protection, Higher Learning, and your Highest Good.

Then imagine a place high in the Universe, the Source of all energy from which we come. You can imagine it as the Giant Womb of the Great Mother.

Then imagine golden light of Abundance coming from this high place down towards your head. Allow the top of your head to "open" and allow the golden light of Abundance to flow into your body, filling you from head to toe with sparkling, golden light.

Once you are filled and glowing with the golden light of Abundance, allow it to flow out the front of your chest through your heart and

1)   Fill up your room and your house, giving Abundance to whomever else is in the area. You can imagine them looking happy, receiving Abundance in whatever form it is to them.

2) Flow the golden light of Abundance into your neighborhood and entire state, giving Abundance to whomever is in this area. You can imagine them looking happy, receiving Abundance in whatever form it is to them.

3) Flow the golden light of Abundance around the entire planet, giving Abundance to everyone. You can imagine them looking happy, receiving Abundance in whatever form it is to them.

4) Complete the flow of energy by saying "Now I receive."

5) Imagine all the people turning towards you now, sending you golden light of Abundance. Receive it into your body. Be aware of this making you restless and uncomfortable, or emotional, observing any signs of "undeserving," which will fade over time and practice.

As your day continues, and your week as well, you will notice synchronicity happening in your life as the Great Mother Goddess connects you with: people, places, and things that offer your Abundance in some way.

HINT: You can focus this by making a goad with the Goddess. Begin this magnetic meditation with your goal in mind at the start and allow synchronicity to come into play with achieving your goal.

INVITING THE GREAT MOTHER GODDESS into Sexual Repair:

After setting a white circle and using the 3 step Channeling meditation, you can invite in your Goddess Guide(s).

Begin to connect with your physical body by caressing yourself, slowly allowing all the cells in your body to achieve that sense of tingling and openness.

Invite the Goddess into your space as you begin to connect with your place of feminine life force.

You can chant the names of the Signora del Gioco, imagining, with your hand, drawing a spiral into your clitoris: "Aradia, Diana, Iside, Cibele, creating a the rhythm as you work towards orgasm. Don't force any sensations.

When the Goddess joins you in this way, she takes charge of the length, the intensity of the sensations. The experience becomes ecstatic. You simply take actions, but her energy will create the experience.

You may see visions of the Goddess and her many "Agents." You may just feel differently.

Tantra with Goddess is a very long, drawn out process and is largely about the maintenance of energies rather than achieving orgasm.

The first times you try this you may cry, releasing feels of grief. You may feel a joyful realization that you feel safe in your body and you feel free to enjoy this.

DREAMWORK

You can invite the Goddess into your dreams for the purpose of learning while you sleep.

Use the 3 step channeling meditation to raise your vibration.

Use your natural altar to connect with the elements including the moonlight.
Intend to learn through your dreams.

You can, while falling to sleep, create a scene where you find yourself in a learning environment or a sacred place where you prepare to receive instruction.

GUIDES are generally subtle. There are the wonderful moments where they grab out attention, but the purpose of these experiences are to make us seek even more. The reason for subtlety has to do with their energetic vibration being fast and high (not low and slow like ghosts or physical matter).

They honor the Laws of Energy, one being Law of Fee Will, so the won't force their way into your life like a ghost making human-like attempts at grabbing your attention. They will want your attention- so they can teach you and assist you. This is the mark of a Guide- someone who wants to communicate and help you learn, including helping you learn who they are. Guides will get your attention in expansive way: putting together pieces of the puzzle of your life through positive synchronicity: connecting you with a person, place or thing at just the right time.

Side Effects: The more connected you become to Spirit guides (even if aren't yet aware) is that your life will seem to be "doors open" doors closed". Despite shat your wishes are, things will move and flow in your life according to higher plans. When you move in the flow of these plans, doors will open. When you move against these plans, doors will close. It's like being on a quest. For example: your relationship may suddenly end when you thought they would last a long time. You were meant to learn something about yourself and then move on, as painful as this may seem. This often happens when you are still in love with the person or holding on in some way…so things will happen to close that door such as finding your sexuality "shut down."

For feminine identified persons, you are a parallel of the Divine Feminine on earth. As a parallel, you can also look perhaps at your own relationships this way: that you offer a service. That with one partner you can express yourself physically, with another you can't but yet you can connect creatively. As a reflection of Divinely Feminine energy it may become your purpose to illuminate this possibility in others.

The human, smaller part of ourselves may say that we failed all our partners that we're no longer together with. But our more expansive side may say "love is not to hold onto: relationships are mirrors into ourselves so we can learn and grow and then let go. Because no one human can ever know all our aspects as well as we can't know all theirs. But we can find different aspects of ourselves illuminated when in the presence of a variety of people.

What if we accept this is perfection? What might life look like then? The Great Mother Goddess knows us fully and completely, and that is enough. That we have been trying to put a "form" on our relationships of "perfect partnerships that last forever" is maybe something not natural, instead instituted by the church which has never fully worked for people and instead caused suffering. Perhaps that fear of losing a partner is a fear of death and a poverty belief…but a love that is given in the moment, to love just because we can…and to even love the goodbye is a belief in Abundance…that love can't be owned by anyone, just as Mother Magic cannot be either.

And isn't this what the healers, the "streghe" ultimately do when they heal…is to love another human being enough to say here, this is yours, without accepting payment… choosing to believe in love and abundance rather than debt.

REFERENCES:

1. Barbara Ehrenreich, Deirdre English, "Witches, Midwives, and Nurses," http://marxists.org, (first published by The Feminist Press at CUNY, 1973)

2. Antonella Bartolucci, *Le Streghe Buone* (Alberti compagnie editoriale, 2016), 32.

3. Dr. Giovanni Ponti, *L'uomo e la malattia: Il caso delle medicine non Convenzionali* (2003), 18.

4. Ehrenreich, English, http://marxists.org

5. Ehrenreich, English, http://marxists.org

6. Fabio Garuti, *Le Streghe di Benevento-la grande Bugia* (Anguana Edizione, 2014), 58.

7. Garuti, *Le Streghe di Benevento,*(Anguana Edizioni, 2014), 58.

8. Ehrenreich, English, http://marxists.org

9. Ehrenreich, English, http://marxists.org

10. Ehrenreich, English, http://marxists.org

11. Garuti, *Le Streghe di Benevento,*(Anguana Edizioni, 2014), 59.

12. ibid.

13. ibid.

14. Ponti, *L'uomo e la malattia: Il caso delle medicine non Convenzionali*, 19.

15. Ehrenreich, Deirdre, http://marxists.org

16. Marija Gimbutas, *The Goddesses and Gods of Old Europe,* (University of California Press,1974,1982) preface.

17. Marija Gimbutas, *The Language of the Goddess*, (Harper & Row,1989), xix.

18. Erich Neumann, *The Great Mother*, (Princeton University Press,1955,1963), 94.

19. Gimbutas, *The Language of the Goddess*, xvii.

20. Gimbutas, *The Language of the Goddess*, xv.

21. Barbara G. Walker, *The Woman's Encyclopedia of Myths and Secrets* (Harper & Row, 1983), 684.

22. Robert Graves, *The Greek Myths (2 vols), (*New York: Penguin Books Inc., 1955), 1,11

23. Arthur Avalon, *Shakti and Shakta*, (New York : Dover Publications, Inc. 1978), 409.

24. Barbara G. Walker, *The Woman's Encyclopedia of Myths and Secrets* (Harper & Row, 1983), 684.

25. ibid.

26. Gimbutas, *The Goddesses and Gods of Old Europe*, (University of California Press,1974,1982) preface.

27. Walker, *The Woman's Encyclopedia of Myths and Secrets*, 680.

28. Walker, *The Woman's Encyclopedia of Myths and Secrets*, 687.

29. ibid.

30. Walker, *The Woman's Encyclopedia of Myths and Secrets*, 680.

31. ibid.

32. Erich Neumann, *Art and the Creative Unconscious*, (Princeton, N.J.: Princeton University Press, 1959), 11.

33. Walker, *The Woman's Encyclopedia of Myths and Secrets*, 681.

34. ibid., 683.

35. ibid., 683.

36. Georges Dumezil, *Archaic Roman Religion (2 vols)*, (Chicago, Ill.: University of Chicago Press, 1970), 68.

37. Walker, *The Woman's Encyclopedia of Myths and Secrets*, 683.

38. Walker, *The Woman's Encyclopedia of Myths and Secrets*, 681.

39. ibid.

40. ibid.

41. Adolf Erman, *The Literature of the Ancient Egyptians*, (New York: Benjamin Bloom Inc., 1971), 83.

42. Gaston Maspero, *Popular Stories of Ancient Egypt,*(New York: University Books, 1967), 3.

43. Sir E.A.Budge, *Dwellers on the Nile*, (New York: Dover Publications, 1977), 20.

44. Walker, *The Woman's Encyclopedia of Myths and Secrets*, 683.

45. ibid.

46. Robert Briffault *The Mothers (3 vols)*, (New York: Macmillan, 1927), 1, 245, 426.

47. Wolfgang Lederer, *The Fear of Women*, (New York: Harcourt Brace Jovanovich Inc.,1968), 87.

48. ibid.

49. Gimbutas, *The Language of the Goddess*, 110.

50. ibid.

51. Merlin Stone, *When God Was a Woman*, (New York: Dial Press, 1976), 131.

52. *Assyrian and Babylonian Literature, Selected Translations*, (New York: D. & Appleton Co., 1901), 387.

53. Erman,*The Literature of the Ancient Egyptians*, (New York: Benjamin Bloom Inc., 1971), 227-30.

54. Theodor Gaster, *Myth, Legend and Custom in the Old Testament*, (New York: Harper & Rom, 1969), 764.

55. Walker, *The Woman's Encyclopedia of Myths and Secrets*, 685, 686.

56. Dr. Katherine McDonald, "Reitia and the epigraphic habit of Este," http://exeter.ac.uk, (February 8,2017)

57. Walker, *The Woman's Encyclopedia of Myths and Secrets*, 686.

58. *Larousse Encyclopedia of Mythology*, (London: Hamlyn Publishing Group Ltd., 1968), 28.

59. Walker, *The Woman's Encyclopedia of Myths and Secrets*, 683.

60. ibid, 685.

61. ibid.

62. ibid.

63. ibid.

64. ibid.

65. ibid.

66. ibid, 683.

67. J. Oliver Thomson, *History of Ancient Geography*, (New York: Biblio & Tannen, 1965), 244.

68. Walker, *The Woman's Encyclopedia of Myths and Secrets*, 680.

69. Graham Hancock, *Fingerprints of the Gods*, (Three Rivers Press New York, 1995), 135.

70. ibid, 46.

71. ibid.

72. ibid, 47.

73. ibid, 48.

74. ibid, 49.

75. ibid, 135.

76. "Spiritualist Principles", http://www.nsac.org.

77. Michael A. Woodley, Jan te Nijenhuis, Raegan Murphy, "Were the Victorians cleverer than us?" (Elsevier, 2013), https://lesacreduprintemps19.files.wordpress.com

78. ibid.

79. ibid.

80. ibid.

81. Gerald Massey, *Concerning Spiritualism*, (Kessinger Publishing, LLC, (1993), p. 55.

82. "The History and Origin of Reiki," http://www.hallsofreiki.com/reikihistory.html

83. Turville-Petre, E.O.G., *Myth and Religion of the North*, (New York: Holt, Rinehart & Winston, 1964), 261.

84. Walker, *The Woman's Encyclopedia of Myths and Secrets*, 680.

85. Walker, *The Woman's Encyclopedia of Myths and Secrets*, 687.

86. Amaury de Riencourt, *Sex and Power in History*, (New York: Dell Publishing Co., 1974), 20.

87. Walker, *The Woman's Encyclopedia of Myths and Secrets*, 686.

88. Briffault, *The Mothers (3 vols)*, (New York: Macmillan, 1927) 2, 545, 551-52.

89. Margaret Mead, *Male and Female*, (New York: William Morrow & Co.,1949), 94.

90.   Walker, *The Woman's Encyclopedia of Myths and Secrets*, 759.

91. G uy Ragland Phillips, *Brigantia*, (London: Routledge & Kegan Paul, 1976), 94.

92.   Karin Priester, *Geschichte der Langobarden, Gesellschaft-Kultur-Altagsleben*,(Theiss), 16.

93.   Claudio Azzara, *I longobardi*, (Il Mulino), 2915, 8.

94.   Barbara G. Walker, *Man Made God*, (Stellar House Publishing, LLC, 2010), 101.

95.   "Lombards", http://en.wikipedia.org, 2013.

96.   Walter Pohl and Peter Erhart, *Die Langobarden: Herrschaft und Identität*,(Austrian Academy of Sciences; Edition: 1,2005) 449–445.

97.   Gimbutas, *The Language of the Goddess*, (Harper & Row,1989), xiii.

98.   ibid.

99.   ibid.

100. Gimbutas, *The Language of the Goddess*, (Harper & Row,1989), xx.

101. ibid.

102. ibid.

103. "Lombards", http://en.wikipedia.org, 2013.

104. ibid.

105. F.T. Wainwright, *Scandinavian England*, (Sussex, England: Phillmore & Co.,Ltd., 1976) 97.

106. Walker, *The Woman's Encyclopedia of Myths and Secrets*, 687.

107. Francis Huxley, *The Way of the Sacred*, (New York: Doubleday & Co., 1975), 215.

108. Walker, *The Woman's Encyclopedia of Myths and Secrets*, 687.

109. ibid.

110. Mary R. Beard, *Woman as Force in History*, (London: Collier-Macmillan Ltd., 1946, 113.

111. Walker, *The Woman's Encyclopedia of Myths and Secrets*, 687.

112. Mary Daly, *Beyond God the Father*, (Boston: Beacon Press, 1972), 94.

113. Gimbutas, *The Language of the Goddess*, (Harper & Row,1989), xx.

114. ibid.

115. ibid.

116. ibid.

117. ibid, xvii.

118. ibid.

119. Walker, *The Woman's Encyclopedia of Myths and Secrets,* 687.

120. ibid.

121. Gimbutas, *The Language of the Goddess,* (Harper & Row,1989), xx.

122. ibid

123. Robert Graves, *The White Goddess,* The Noonday Press, New York: Farrar, Straus, and Giroux,1948), 10.

124. ibid.

125. ibid.

126. ibid.

127. Paolo Portone, "Ossessione erotica e magia sexualis nei processi del Sant'Ufizio," http://www.paoloportone.it, 2012.

128. Archive for Research in Archetypal Symbolism, *The Book of Symbols,* (Taschen, 2010), Hearth.

129. Noelle Kruslin "Les guerisseurs, au-dela de la science, " http://reportages.corsematin.com (2017) nkruslin@corsematin.com

130. ibid.

131. Pierre-Jean Luccioni,"Les guerisseurs, au-dela de la science, " http://reportages.corsematin.com (2017)

132. Bartolucci, *Le Streghe Buone,* 26.

133. John Randolph Price, "The Law of Abundance", http://www.souldfulliving.com, 1999-2014.

134. Barbara Wren, *Cellular Awakening,* (Hay House, Inc. 2009), 31-33.

135. ibid.

136. Nic Fleming, "Plants talk to each other using an internet of fungus," http://www.bbc.com, 2014.

137. Maria Popova, "The Secret Life of Trees: The Astonishing Science of What Trees Feel and How They Communicate", http://www.brainpickings.org, 2016.

138. ibid.

139. Bartolucci, *Le Streghe Buone,* (Alberti compagnie editoriale, 2016), 34.

140. Sandro Oddo, La Medicine Popolare nell'alta Valle Argentina, (Pro Triora Editore, 1997), 185.

141. ibid, 11.

142. ibid.

143. ibid, 7.

144. ibid, 8.

145. ibid, 11.

146. ibid, 9.

147. Laura dell'Aquila, "L'Iperico e la notte di San Giovanni", http://www.pimpinella.it, 2017.

148. ibid.

149. Oddo, *La Medicine Popolare nell'alta Valle Argentina,* (Pro Triora Editore, 1997), 170.

150. ibid, 181.

151. Bartolucci, *Le Streghe Buone,* (Alberti compagnie editoriale, 2016), 40.

152. ibid, 25.

153. ibid, 35.

154. ibid, 60.

155. ibid, 32.

156. ibid.

157. ibid, 35.

158. ibid, 39.

159. ibid.

160. ibid, 45.

161. ibid, 43.

162. ibid, 51.

163. ibid, 32.

164. 64-66.

165. Enzo Gravina, *Streghe e Magia* (Edizioni B.B.T, Ass. Biblioteche Beniculturali Territorio, 2007), 3.

166. *ATTI-Terzo Convegno sulla Stregoneria* 161, 162.

167. Oddo, *La Medicine Popolare nell'alta Valle Argentina*, (Pro Triora Editore, 1997), 12.

168. Alessandra Scalas, "Il Malocchio: i rimedi popolari sardi per curarlo e prevenirlo", http://www.naturopatiasardegna.blogspot.com, 2014.

169. ibid.

170. ibid.

171. ibid.

172. "Origini E Storia Di Cornetti Per Il Malocchio E Ferro Di Cavallo", http://meiavertigo. over-blog.it, 2012.

173. ibid.

174. ibid.

175. Silvio Falato, *Ce Steva na Vota…Janare-lupi mannari, filastrocche- indovinelli*, 63.

176. Oddo, *La Medicine Popolare nell'alta Valle Argentina*, (Pro Triora Editore, 1997), 183.

177. Gravina, *Streghe e Magia* (Edizioni B.B.T, Ass. Biblioteche Beniculturali Territorio, 2007),

178. *ATTI-Terzo Convegno sulla Stregoneria-LE STREGHE*, (Pro Triora Editore, 2000), 161.

179. Alessandra Scalas, "Il Malocchio: i rimedi popolari sardi per curarlo e prevenirlo", http://www.naturopatiasardegna.blogspot.com, 2014.

180. Ernesto De Martino, Sud e magia, (Universale Economica Feltrinelli, 1959), 89.

181. ibid, 56.

182. ibid, 169.

183. Hutton Webster, *Magic: a Sociological Study* (Stanford University Press, 1948), 151.

184. Spencer e Gillen, *The Aranda*, II, 397.

185 De Martino, *Sud e magia*, (Universale Economica Feltrinelli, 1959), 118.

186. Garuti, *Le Streghe di Benevento*, (Anguana Edizioni, 2014), 92.

187. Thomas F. Mathews, *The Clash of Gods*, (Princeton University Press, 1993), 66.

188. ibid, 67.

189. Ponti, *L'uomo e la malattia: Il caso delle medicine non Convenzionali* (2003), 8.

190. Luisa Muraro, *La Signora del Gioco*, (La Tartaruga edizioni, 2006),12.

191. Ponti, *L'uomo e la malattia: Il caso delle medicine non Convenzionali* (2003), 25.

192. Mathews, *The Clash of Gods*, (Princeton University Press, 1993), 5.

193. ibid, 14.

194. ibid.

195. ibid.

196. ibid.

197. ibid, 11.

198. ibid.

199. ibid, 5-6.

200. ibid, 24.

201. ibid, 72.

202. ibid.

203. ibid, 67.

204. ibid.

205. ibid.

206. Origen *Contra Celsum*, I: 68; cf. Morton Smith, *Jesus the Magician* (San Francisco, 1978), 82-83.

207. Mathews, *The Clash of Gods*, 23.

208. "St. Bernardino of Siena", Religion & Liberty, Vol. 6, Number 2.

209. "Bernardino of Siena", https://en.wikipedia.org, 2017.

210. ibid.

211. R. Moore, *The Formation of a Persecuting Society: Power and Deviance in Western Europe*, (Oxford: Oxford University Press, 1987).

212. Francesa Bezzone, "The Triora Witch Trials", http://www. lifeinitaly.com, 2017/

213. ibid.

214. Gian Maria Panizza, *Triora 1587-1590: bilancio di una ricerca e prospettive per ulteriori indagini*, 1589.

215. Brauner (2001), pp. 33-34.

216. Claudio Coppo, Gian Maria Panizza, *La Pace Impossibile*, (Firenze: leo S. Olschki Editore 1990), 37.

217. ibid, p.42

218. Panizza, *Triora 1587-1590:*, 78.

219. Garuti, *Le Streghe di Benevento,*104.

220. ibid, 86.

221. Muraro, *La Signora del Gioco*, 11.

222. ibid.

223. Ponti, *L'uomo e la malattia: Il caso delle medicine non Convenzionali* ,19.

224. "Wooden Horse (device)" https://en.wikipedia.org

225. Stefano Moriggi, *Le tre Bocche di Cerbero*, (Tascabili Bompiani, 2004/2005), 165.

226. "Triora 1587-1590: bilancio di una ricerca e prospettive per ulteriori indagini"

227. ibid.

228. Falato, Ce Steva na Vota…Janare-lupi mannari, filastrocche- indovinelli, 63.

229. Carlo Napolitano, *Il Triangolo Stregato: Il Mistero del Noce di Benevento*, (CSA Editrice, 2012), 65-66.

230. *Caterina e le altre*, out of print.

231. ibid.

232. James Bonwick, *Irish Druids & Old Irish Religions*, (Barnes & Noble Books, 1986), 211.

233. ibid, 222.

234. ibid.

235. Steven Sora, "Goddess in the Vatican? The Citadels of Christian Culture Often Have Surprising Origins", http://www.atlantisrisingmagazine.com

236. ibid.

237. Gimbutas, *The Language of the Goddess*, 311.

238. ibid.

240. ibid.

241. ibid.

242. "Black Madonnas", https://udayton.edu.

243 Graves, *The White Goddess,* The Noonday Press, New York: Farrar, Straus, and Giroux,1948), 10.

244. ibid, 371.

245. "Culto di Anna Perenna," http:// romanoimpero.com

246. Gimbutas, *The Language of the Goddess*, (Harper & Row,1989), 211.

247. T.C. Lethbridge, Witches, (Seacaucus, N.J.:Citadel Press, 1972) ,71.

248. Walker, *The Woman's Encyclopedia of Myths and Secrets*, 684.

249. Napolitano, *Il Triangolo Stregato,* 40.

250. Muraro, *La Signora del Gioco*, (La Tartaruga edizioni, 2006), 203.

251. Carlo Ginzburg, *Ecstasies,* (New York: Pantheon Book, 1989), 92, 93.

252. *ATTI-Terzo Convegno sulla Stregoneria-LE STREGHE,* (Pro Triora Editore, 2000), 31.

253. Ginzburg, *Ecstasies,* (New York: Pantheon Book, 1989), 91.

254. ibid.

255. ibid.

256. ibid., 37, 38.

257. ibid, 38.

258. ibid, 92.

259. Muraro, *La Signora del Gioco,* (La Tartaruga edizioni, 2006), 63.

260. ibid.

261. ibid, 64.

262. ibid.

263. Lipsey, *Have You Been to Delphi?,* 266.

264. ibid, 268.

265. Terry Pratchett, "The Cunning Man," http://www.wiki.Ispace.org, 2015.

266. Carlo Ginzburg, *The Night Battles,* trans. John and Anne Tedeschi, (Boston: The Johns Hopkins University Press, 1983), 16.

267. De Martino, *Sud e Magia,* 118.

268. ibid, 56.

Made in the USA
San Bernardino, CA
04 November 2018